Successful Real Estate
Sales Agreements

Successful Real Estate Sales Agreements

How to Prepare Contracts for the Sale and Exchange of
Homes, Income Property, and Mobilehomes

Fourth Edition

Erik Jorgensen

AXIOM
Axiom Press, Publishers

This publication is designed to provide accurate and authoritative information in regard to the subject matter covered. It is sold with the understanding that the publisher is not engaged in rendering legal, accounting, or other professional advice. If legal advice or other expert assistance is required, the services of a competent professional person should be sought.

From *Declaration of Principles* jointly adopted by a Committee of the American Bar Association and a Committee of Publishers and Associations

SUCCESSFUL REAL ESTATE SALES AGREEMENTS, Fourth Edition. Copyright © 1976, 1978, 1982, 1983, 1986, 1988 by Erik Jorgensen

Portions of this book were previously copyrighted and published by Executive Reports Corporation and Harper & Row, Publishers.

Printed in the United States of America. All rights reserved.

Fourth update printing: January 1989

Update and New editions

The difference between Axiom Press' update printings and new editions are:

UPDATE PRINTINGS: Every time we print a substantial amount of copies of a current edition, minor but often important changes are made, but not enough for users of the book to discard earlier printings.

NEW EDITIONS: This means one or more major or a number of minor revisions, additions, new clauses and law changes since the previous edition have been made. To stay on top of the latest information, replacing your old edition for the new edition is recommended.

Library of Congress Cataloging in Publication Data

Jorgensen, Erik.
    Successful real estate sales agreements.

    Bibliography: .
    Includes index.
    1. Vendors and purchasers—United States—Forms. I. Title.
KF665.A65J67   1985   346.7304'37   85-28568
                       347.3064'37
ISBN 0-933800-03-7
ISBN 0-933800-04-5

  91 92 15 14 13 12 11

Contents

About the Author

Erik Jorgensen is a San Francisco attorney specializing in real property law. He is also a successful Realtor, has written books and articles, as well as lectured and instructed in real estate subjects at universities and colleges. A great many of the forms used daily in the real estate business in California have been drafted by him. His seminars on effective contract writing for Real Estate Licensees and negotiation are given regularly throughout the state and are eagerly attended.

Mr. Jorgensen has served as a member of the California Association of Realtors (CAR) on its executive committee and as chairman of many of its committees. For more than 25 years he has been involved with the drafting of all CAR's standard forms. He has also served as a member of the Department of Real Estate's Editorial and Curriculum Board, supervising the development of instructors' and students' guides used in real estate instruction at California community colleges. Mr. Jorgensen is an honorary director of CAR for life, and was named Realtor of the Year by the San Francisco Board of Realtors in 1972.

Foreword

Once more unto the breach, dear friends,
once more. . . .

Shakespeare, Henry the Fifth

"The difference between the right word and the almost right word," Mark Twain once observed, "is the difference between lightning and the lightning bug." Twain's concern was literature; ours is real estate sales agreements. But the problem of finding and using the right word remains the same. Another master of expression, Alexander Hamilton, asserted, "The selection of the right word calls for the exercise of man's greatest faculty—that of judgment." Choosing the right word calls for painstaking effort; the "right" word may not come readily to mind. The use of precise, tested clauses for common problems in contract drafting is an obvious advantage. By adopting the habit of employing predrafted wording to express the exact terms of an agreement, the contract writer avoids becoming tongue-tied.

Much contract drafting, particularly by nonlawyers in simple transactions, is repetitive. Thus, accepted, trustworthy clauses can be adapted to each special situation. With rigorous practice this method will create complete, easily understandable contracts. In difficult and unusual transactions the lay contract writer is well advised to seek someone with legal training to draft the contract.

This book is a working tool. It begins where most form books leave off. Practically all of the clauses found in these pages are designed to express "terms and conditions of a factual nature." The substantive law of contracts is not treated. Nor are rights and remedies of parties to real estate transactions covered. Other books deal with these subjects more adequately than the space here allows. This book is intended to be used in practical situations. It evolved on the firing line. Many of its clauses were developed as a result of needs expressed by brokers and property owners. Hopefully, readers will make their needs known to the author so that future revisions will encompass additional material. This fourth edition adds many additional clauses and a chapter on Disclosures all suggested by readers or participants in my seminars and workshops on "Effective Real Estate Contracts." The new 4 page long form which is an expanded version of Model form I is covered in Chapter 12 as Model form II.

Many attorneys and Realtors have given freely of their time and advice in the preparation of this book. I am thankful to them all. Special acknowledgments go to the California Association of Realtors for their gracious permission to reproduce their forms and material. May the readers who use this book to prepare real estate sales agreements end up with only successful ones.

Erik Jorgensen

Chapter 1
The Goal: Well-Prepared Contracts

> *The Realtor shall not engage in activities that constitute the unauthorized practice of law and shall recommend that legal counsel be obtained when the interest of any party to the transaction requires it.*
>
> *Article 17, Code of Ethics*
> *National Association of Realtors*

> *"Practice of law" includes not only the doing or performing services in a court of justice . . . but, in a larger sense, includes legal advice and counsel, and the preparation of legal instruments and contracts by which legal rights are secured. . . .*
>
> *In re Droker, 370 P 2d 242;*
> *and People v. Tipper 61 CA2d 844*

Most real estate transactions are consummated not because of, but in spite of, the contract between buyer and seller. So why improve upon the preparation of standard real estate agreements? Because the contract is indeed important in achieving the client's goal in the transaction and also in building the contract writer's reputation. Though a real estate "Deposit Receipt," or contract, is written to describe the agreement between buyer and seller, it must be designed with a different audience in mind: other brokers and lawyers, title insurers, mortgagors, lenders, escrow officials, and even judges who will be called upon to interpret it if it becomes part of a legal dispute. Most of us who prepare contracts are lucky in that the majority of our efforts will never be questioned. However, one never knows what instrument will be challenged. Therefore, the writer must take pains to say exactly what the parties mean. The contract must be clear, precise, and accurate. No more and no less. Saying exactly what is meant is no easy matter.

Professional Skill and Legal Duty

A lawyer who draws an agreement has a legal duty "to use such skill, prudence, and diligence as lawyers of ordinary skill and capacity, commonly possess and exercise . . .," said the California Supreme Court in a case concerning the drafting of a will.[1] In another case, the same court held that a notary public who drew a will was liable to the intended beneficiaries for his negligence.[2] Consequently, under certain circumstances, a breach of legal duty may make contract writers liable both to their clients and to others affected by their negligence. Because so few cases involving real estate brokers have been decided, however, it is not clear how far their liability for negligently drawn contracts or instruments extends or to what standard of legal competence they will be held.

No doubt the broker's right to commission often depends upon a properly prepared agreement. Brokers' claims for commission have been dismissed in court where the contract was too indefinite to give rise to a binding agreement.[3] Brokers have also been held liable for preparing leases[4] and options not based upon true facts. The defendant brokers were required to "exercise reasonable skill and ordinary diligence and not act negligently." They were expected to have special knowledge with respect to the agency assumed.

The Broker's "Right" to Prepare Contracts

The specific question of what constitutes unauthorized practice of law is involved in the broker's "right" to prepare real estate contracts and other instruments in real estate transactions. Many lay specialists "practice law" in some form or another as a collateral aspect of their main function. In California the filling in of standard forms has become "incidental" to the real estate business. In discussing this incidental function, an authoritative encyclopedia of California law states that

> an established business custom sanctions the activities of real estate and insurance agents in drawing certain agreements in business transactions in which they take part in their respective professional capacities. While these actions are technically within the usual definition of practice of law, they are generally recognized as proper where:
> (1) the instrument is simple or standardized,
> (2) the contract writer or intermediary does not charge any fee for such work other than the regular commission for the transaction, and
> (3) the drafting is incidental to his other activities in the transaction.[5]

This limited exception from the "practice of law" is often misunderstood. Real estate brokers or notary publics may not draft real estate agreements, leases, or deeds of trust when they are not acting as brokers in the underlying transaction. However, if a broker (1) does not select the instrument, (2) and does not make decisions or give advice about its application in the particular instance, but (3) only undertakes to act as a mere scrivener, entering information as stated by the parties themselves on a form selected by the parties, (4) and does no more, such acts would not constitute the practice of law.

The State Bar of California has carefully selected its cases on unauthorized practice of law and prosecuted them with skill. As a result the Bar has obtained several injunctions and consent decrees. Escrow companies, business opportunities brokers, and one of California's largest real estate firms all have consented to limit their activities. Until 1979 treaties with title companies, escrow companies and banks existed as a good-faith guide to what might constitute unauthorized practice of law by such entities.

In 1967, negotiations between the State Bar and the California Association of Realtors led to an agreement by which the two organizations approved CAR's Standard Form "Real Estate Purchase Contract and Receipt for Deposit." The form has since been revised by the two organizations.

In the agreement of implementation, CAR agreed to discourage its members "in every way reasonably possible" from (1) modifying or changing the form of the deposit receipt as written; (2) adding provisions or clauses thereto not required by the printed form; and (3) adding extensive riders, except upon the advice of an attorney representing one of the parties in the particular transaction.[6]

CAR also consented to inform its members that such changes and additions would destroy the purpose sought to be accomplished by joint approval of the form and "may be regarded by the State Bar as subjecting the Broker, agent or salesman responsible therefor to charges of unauthorized practice of law."

As a result of the State Bar of California's revision of its policies about the Unauthorized Practice of Law, the agreement between CAR and the Bar was by mutual agreement cancelled in 1981. The approved form, which is referred to in this book as Model Form I (Modular Edition) has subsequently been published as approved by CAR only. In 1985 CAR developed an alternative form in old fashioned legal sized format. It incorporates the full text of Model Form I and includes the Finance Supplement and some disclosure information condensed from supplements used with the Modular Model Form I. See Comments regarding this form, herein called Model Form II, in Chapter 12. The approved forms are the most widely used deposit receipt forms in California, but a considerable number of other forms abound. This situation has led to expressions of concern from organized real estate. Richard C. Farrer, president of the California Association of Realtors, raised the matter in an article:

No statistics are available to show how many "standard" real estate deposit receipt forms exist in California. A good guess would be in the hundreds. Many local boards of Realtors have adopted their own forms. Quite a few real estate firms have developed special forms. Commercial publishers offer a variety of "boiler plate" contracts. This proliferation of so-called standard forms in itself creates obvious potential dangers to Realtors and their clients.

A few forms, for example, contain clauses or language which the courts have long ago held unenforceable. Others seem to over reach in that the fine print favors the Realtor's position in the transaction, whether it be by directing the closing to a broker-owned escrow, granting the broker unrestricted right to extend the time for performance, or in some other way limiting the free choice of the parties. A few forms defeat their purpose with inclusion of excess "boiler plate" with contingencies to fit every possible situation. This is not conducive to create a contract which the parties fully understand and have, in fact, agreed to. They are veritable traps for the unwary.

Despite warnings, people do not read the fine print. The use of private forms or unfamiliar forms discourages broker cooperation or invites disputes, many times in front of the buyer or seller. Often counteroffers become necessary just to eliminate clauses.[7]

The Fine Print

Buyers and sellers of real property are often cautioned to read the fine print on the contract. Some forms in common use contain minute print that challenges even average eyesight. The minuscule type marches endlessly up and down both sides of the flimsy paper. Such contracts should be viewed with suspicion. Important rights may be surrendered in their dim clauses. Unexpected obligations may arise from obscure paragraphs. The obsolete concept of "buyer beware" may linger in the text. The affirmative duty of "full disclosure" is aborted by typographical concealment. In California, the use of the CAR approved form is only voluntary. But in Utah, Texas and Wisconsin real estate forms are prescribed by statute and approved by state licensing authorities.

In any event, the agreement between the State Bar and CAR, even if now cancelled, may until new abuses occur, have settled the problems of unauthorized law practice in California. As long as brokers use the standard form in simple transactions and do not attempt to draft complex agreements or complicated leases, and do not give legal or tax advice the contracts they draft will be professionally sound. Working within these boundaries, many brokers have developed enviable specialized skills in drafting simple, legally sound deposit receipts. They routinely produce competent contracts. Unfortunately, many new real estate salesperson licensees have little or no experience and training in this area. Their contracts show an alarming lack of competence. The public is forced to suffer new licensee's learn-as-you-go education. Competence is not acquired by trial and error. And competence in this area includes not only drafting ability, but the capacity to determine one's own limits and recognize the need for professional assistance.

A rule of thumb which a real estate licensee about to draw an agreement of sale could apply with some precision emerged in a Minnesota case on unauthorized practice of law.[8] This case was cited with approval in a leading California case involving an accountant denied a fee for unauthorized practice of law.[9]

The court said:

> Generally speaking, whenever, as incidental to another transaction or calling, a layman, as part of his regular course of conduct, resolves legal questions for another at the latter's request and for a consideration—by giving him advice or by taking action for and in his behalf, he is practicing law if difficult or doubtful legal questions are involved which, to safeguard the public, reasonably demand the application of a trained legal mind. What is a difficult or doubtful question of law is not to be measured by the comprehension of a trained legal mind, but by the understanding thereof which is possessed by a reasonably intelligent layman who is reasonably familiar with similar transactions. . . .

Brokers who decline to act beyond their legitimate function will gain respect. They will build a reputation for integrity and attention to detail.

Contract writers may find that they need additional advice at some stage of the transaction. Consultations with escrow agents, title officers, appraisers, surveyors, engineers, architects, hydrologists, building contractors and similar specialized experts may be necessary to successfully complete a transaction. Quite often, such specialized help is invaluable in the actual formation of a deal and in writing the agreement.

The key to successful completion of any real estate transaction is a good sales contract. What is important at the actual closing of the deal must therefore be determined before the contract is drawn. The contract is similar to a blueprint. The parties and their advisors, as well as lenders and escrow holders, if any, look to the contract just as the builder looks to the drawings and specifications. Without a proper contract that incorporates the desires of the parties, problems are bound to arise at the time of closing. Any items which should have been resolved and included but which have been left to later agreement will undoubtedly shake the loose contours of the deal. The more complete the contract, the easier and smoother the road to a satisfactory transaction.

Putting It in Writing

"An oral contract is not worth the paper it is written on," said Samuel Goldwyn. Actually, some verbal agreements are enforceable, but the California

Statute of Frauds requires that real estate contracts be in writing. This statute was enacted to insure stability in legal relations. Specifically, it requires that a contract for the sale, or lease for more than one year, of real property shall be in writing.[10] The statute also requires that in California an agreement authorizing or employing a broker to purchase or sell real estate, or to lease real estate for more than one year, must be in writing.[11]

Even where a writing is not required to form a binding contract, it may be advantageous. An agreement that is put into "black and white" substantially reduces the likelihood of a breach.

Also, when an agreement is written out and signed the basic concept of a contract is clarified and protected. The following elements are necessary to a legal agreement:

1. The parties must be legally capable of contracting.
2. They must give their consent.
3. The object must be lawful.
4. There must be a sufficient cause or consideration.

How the Courts Resolve a Conflict Between Clauses

In the use of printed forms a common rule resolves internal conflicts. Section 1651 of the California Civil Code states:

> Where a contract is partly written and partly printed, or where part of it is written or printed under special direction of the parties, and with a special view to their intention, and the remainder is copied from a form originally prepared without special reference to the particular parties and the particular contract in question, the written parts control the printed parts, and the parts which are purely original control those which are copies from a form. And if the two are absolutely repugnant, the latter must be so far disregarded.

Paragraph 236 (C) of the Restatement of Contracts, is a reminder concerning court interpretation of specific clauses in contracts:

> Where there is an inconsistency between general provisions and specific provisions, the specific provisions ordinarily qualify the meaning of the general provisions.

Real estate licensees using a form contract must be especially careful that they know the form well and understand the import of the the text they insert in the blanks. They should realize that the use of a bad form is not mandatory. They owe it to themselves and their clients to select the best possible printed form and use it judiciously.

The blanks in the printed contract must be filled correctly. What goes into them must express the understanding of the parties concerning the particular circumstances of the transaction. The standard clauses explained in this book will fit most situations. The writer must be certain that each such clause chosen fits the need it is intended to serve. The danger in using such standard "fill-in" clauses is that they may be included without critical analysis of their over-all effect on the contract. Contract writers should not act as mere scriveners. Nor should they paste up contracts consisting of wordy "fill-in" clauses. In using the clauses found in this book, the reader should pay specific attention to the comments regarding their purpose and use.

Ready-made clauses are not a substitute for independent thinking. Do not load up the agreement with unnecessary clauses. Incorporate what is necessary, but strive for simplicity. Never use three words if one will do, but use the *right* word. Avoid "legalese" and be safe. No matter of importance should be left to oral agreement. In the printed form, all blanks should be checked. Printed matter not applicable to the transaction should be X-ed and the deletion or any changes initialed by both parties. The parties should be cognizant of and understand all rights and obligations under the finished contract.

Marshaling of Information

To prepare a properly drawn agreement, all pertinent information must be marshaled. It cannot be assumed that the seller or buyer will volunteer all the necessary information, or that what they do provide will necessarily be correct. The contract writer must learn to interview skillfully, verifying all answers by checking payment-book records or contacting the lender, and checking all relevant legal descriptions, insurance policies, property-tax information, zoning, rental income and expenses related to the property at hand. If the client approves, some facts should be checked with the client's other advisors. If there is more than one owner and the client agrees, all owners should be consulted.

Mere familiarity with legal description, price, loans, and terms of payment is not enough. Unless the broker and the client's counsel understand the motive and business purpose of the transaction as it applies to both buyer and seller, neither can advise correctly.

The agreement should be molded to the purposes of the parties. It is not enough to choose effective provisions; the whole agreement must be proper. Not all transactions fit into a deposit-receipt type of contract. Brokers sometimes succumb to the temptation of fitting the deposit-receipt contract to complex transactions. Doing so is neither to the advantage of the parties nor the broker, and could lead to serious legal consequences.

The broker has a natural inclination to resent "interference" from other advisors in the handling of real estate transactions. When a party to a transaction cautiously insists on obtaining legal or technical advice prior to executing an agreement, the broker often considers such interference as equivalent to the loss of the transaction. Such fears are quite unfounded in fact. The experienced and professional broker has learned to work successfully with the parties' other advisors such as lawyers, bankers, accountants. A broker who candidly and completely explains the transaction to the advisor has nothing to fear from a legal or tax expert. Quite often, the broker will find that a reluctant buyer or seller will readily enter into the proposed transaction when the broker offers to go along on a visit to the client's legal advisor. In exchange transactions particularly, the broker may very well find that advice the client receives from a legal or tax advisor makes the transaction possible and desirable.

Brokers must show the spirit of cooperation and learn the technique necessary to get the most out of a meeting with the client's other advisor. This is not a one-sided affair. Lawyers, too, must realize the limited scope of their role, depending on what clients expect of them. If a lawyer has extensive business and real estate experience, the client may seek basic advice as to the desirability of the transaction. If the lawyer's expertise is limited to advice regarding the various legal questions involved, he or she should only give advice concerning those aspects of the transaction. Starting with the listing, the lawyer may have some reservations concerning the broker's authority as expressed by the broker's listing form. The broker may have to consent to limitations or lose the listing. However, a broker who has the proper understanding of the listing agreement may be able to suggest changes that both will be able to live with. The broker may even suggest an exact wording which may be acceptable to counsel.

A lawyer will not be satisfied with a statement that "no substantial harm" has arisen in the past from the use of the broker's form. That no damage has occurred so far is immaterial to the question of protecting the seller's interest. Neither will a statement that the form is "standard" suffice. The broker should be prepared to make one or two minor changes to gain the lawyer's trust in the agency. Seldom will a fair, properly completed printed form be emasculated in the process.

A preliminary discussion about the seller's legal and tax problems could provide the broker with exceptionally advantageous information. Such a discussion might suggest the type of buyer and the kind of acceptable terms which will lead to a sale and a commission. The attorney's cooperation in drafting the sales agreement should be enlisted at the earliest point of the negotiations. The lawyer may favor specific wordings and insist that they be contained in the offer from the beginning. Ordinarily such requests should be granted without protest. If the buyer will not accept them, they can be renegotiated later.

Generally it is no more difficult to negotiate with the client's attorney or accountant than with the client alone. A broker who obtains the confidence of the client's other advisors may not only smooth the path to the transaction at hand, but also may lay the cornerstone for future transactions with other of the advisor's clients. A lawyer who has a positive attitude and is competent in real estate matters often finds that an initial contact with a real estate broker in connection with a simple contract can lead to increased practice as a "team" member in a large real estate transaction instigated by the broker.

Working with Legal Counsel

A broker with a truly professional approach can expect respectful expeditious treatment from the parties' legal counsel. For example, one leading California Realtor specializing in industrial and commercial leases has compiled a form book which would be the envy of any real estate attorney. Whenever this broker negotiates a lease or a transaction where his client is to build to a tenant's specifications, he makes a tentative draft of an agreement and the particular clauses in the lease. He incorporates therein his understandings of the tentative agreement between his clients. In addition, he draws a memorandum of the safeguards which each party should have inserted in the documents. He then presents the whole package to counsel. More than once, this broker's proposed lease has been adopted by counsel with only minor alterations. Thus, his expertise is recognized, and invaluable time in legal research is saved.

This technique need not be limited to lease transactions. It can lead to well-drawn documents of any sort and to creating a close cooperation between the broker and the real estate attorney. A similar technique has been specifically approved by a California court.[12] The clauses in this book should be helpful in preparing such proposed contracts for examination by the parties' legal advisors.

Using Working Tools

Following this section are a Model Form I—the CAR "Real Estate Purchase Contract and Deposit Receipt"—and a detailed "anatomy" of its contents (Sections I and II below). The advantage of a good printed form is that the form itself serves as a good checklist. Section III reproduces Model Form II, the long form. Section IV contains two fully filled-in Real Estate Purchase Contract and Deposit Receipt forms. These examples demonstrate the recommended schematic approach to the drafting of the various clauses in the form. Alternative clauses to those used in the sample forms are found in the text where the subject matter is treated.

The Model Forms twice warns the broker that it is to be used in *simple* transactions only. The form states: "This standardized document for use in simple transactions has been approved. . . ." And it repeats this warning thus: "It should not be used in complex transactions or with extensive riders or additions."

The transaction for which Example A is included (p. 22) would probably be accepted as a typical "simple" transaction. It covers the sale of a residence, where the buyer is to obtain new financing and is otherwise paying cash. Several riders were added to Model Form I, namely, a structural pest control agreement, a statement of the personal property included, and a provision for prior sale of the buyer's other property.

The transaction for which Example B (p. 26) is included may seem to fly in the face of the warning against using extensive riders with the Model Form.

Several seemingly complex addenda were necessary to express the agreement of the parties. None of these riders, however, was formulated by adding "provisions and clauses not required by the printed form" or required by law. This sample transaction contemplates the sale of a four-unit apartment house partly leased and partly occupied by month-to-month tenants. Considering the type of property and the investment involved, the parties would be well advised to engage counsel to guide them to a clear understanding of the rights and duties created by the contract and the documents they will be asked to sign.

A final note about drafting contracts: Even the best-drawn contract cannot guarantee performance. But a carefully drawn contract will make performance more likely because mistakes and misunderstandings are minimized. To insure such a contract, use the following checklist.

A Checklist for Careful Drafting

1. Obtain all relevant information concerning the property, financing, commitments, and so forth.

2. If you can't type and if you write illegibly learn to print.

3. Study your printed form.

4. Know the legal effect of every part of the printed text.

5. Design insertions in blanks to make an orderly arrangement.

6. Identify each inserted clause with a number such as a subnumber of the paragraph. Example: In "Terms of Payment Clause" use: 1.01, 1.02, etc.

7. Be accurate, concise, and clear.

8. Use well-chosen standard clauses for standard situations.

9. Learn how to adapt standard clauses to unusual situations.

10. Practice writing contracts.

11. Learn to be a good interviewer.

12. Use checklists to obtain all necessary information for listing and sales agreements.

13. Be sure the written contract incorporates the whole agreement between the parties.

14. Leave nothing to oral understanding.

15. Do not make changes in signed documents without written consent of all parties; all parties must initial such changes.

16. Apply the "difficult and doubtful" test, and refer contracts of that nature to competent legal counsel.

The Model Form I (Modular Edition, letter size)

REAL ESTATE PURCHASE CONTRACT AND RECEIPT FOR DEPOSIT

THIS IS MORE THAN A RECEIPT FOR MONEY. IT IS INTENDED TO BE A LEGALLY BINDING CONTRACT. READ IT CAREFULLY.

CALIFORNIA ASSOCIATION OF REALTORS® STANDARD FORM

_____A_____, California. _____, 19_____

Received from ____B_____

herein called Buyer, the sum of ____C_____

_____Dollars $_____

evidenced by cash ☐, cashier's check ☐, or _____ ☐, personal check ☐ payable to _____

_____D_____, to be held uncashed until acceptance of this offer, as deposit on account of purchase price of

_____Dollars $_____

for the purchase of property, situated in _____, County of _____, California,

described as follows: ____E_____

1.   Buyer will deposit in escrow with _____the balance of purchase price as follows:

____F_____

_____

_____

_____

_____

_____

_____

_____

_____

_____

_____

_____

_____

_____

_____

_____

_____

_____

_____

_____

_____

Set forth above any terms and conditions of a factual nature applicable to this sale, such as financing, prior sale of other property, the matter of structural pest control inspection, repairs and personal property to be included in the sale.

2.   Deposit will ☐ will not ☐ be increased by $_____ to $_____ within _____ days of acceptance of this offer.

3.   Buyer does ☐ does not ☐ intend to occupy subject property as his residence.

4.   The following supplements are incorporated as part of this agreement:

Other

☐ Structural Pest Control Certification Agreement   ☐ Occupancy Agreement   ☐ _____

☐ Special Studies Zone Disclosure   ☐ VA Amendment   ☐ _____

☐ Flood Insurance Disclosure   ☐ FHA Amendment   ☐ _____

5.   Buyer and Seller shall deliver signed instructions to the escrow holder within _____ days from Seller's acceptance which shall provide for closing within _____ days from Seller's acceptance. Escrow fees to be paid as follows:

_____

6.   Buyer and Seller acknowledge receipt of a copy of this page, which constitutes Page 1 of _____ Pages.

____F_____   Seller _____

Seller _____

A REAL ESTATE BROKER IS THE PERSON QUALIFIED TO ADVISE ON REAL ESTATE. IF YOU DESIRE LEGAL ADVICE CONSULT YOUR ATTORNEY.

THIS TRANSACTION HAS BEEN APPROVED BY THE CALIFORNIA ASSOCIATION OF REALTORS® IN FORM ONLY.
OF SUPPLEMENTS NOT PUBLISHED BY CAR, THE LEGAL VALIDITY OF ANY PROVISION, OR THE ADEQUACY OF
SECURED IN COMPLEX TRANSACTIONS OR WITH EXTENSIVE RIDERS OR ADDITIONS.

To order, contact—California Association of Realtors®
525 S. Virgil Ave, Los Angeles, California 90020
Copyright California Association of Realtors® (Revised 1978) 1984)   FORM D-11-1

(Form continues on next page)

REAL ESTATE PURCHASE CONTRACT AND RECEIPT FOR DEPOSIT

The following terms and conditions are hereby incorporated in and made a part of Buyer's Offer

7.   Title is to be free of liens, encumbrances, easements, restrictions, rights and conditions of record or known to Seller, other than the following: (a) Current property taxes, (b) covenants, conditions, restrictions, and public utility easements of record, if any, provided the same do not adversely affect the continued use of the property for the purposes for which it is presently being used, unless reasonably disapproved by Buyer in writing within _____days of receipt of a current preliminary title report furnished at _____expense, and (c) _____

Seller shall furnish Buyer at _____expense a standard California Land Title Association policy issued by _____Company, showing title vested in Buyer subject only to the above. If Seller is unwilling or unable to eliminate any title matter disapproved by Buyer as above, Seller may terminate this agreement. If Seller fails to deliver title as above, Buyer may terminate this agreement; in either case, the deposit shall be returned to Buyer.

8.   Property taxes, premiums on insurance acceptable to Buyer, rents, interest, and_____
shall be pro-rated as of (a) the date of recordation of deed; or (b) _____. Any bond or assessment which is a lien shall be ____paid____ by _____. Transfer taxes, if any, shall be paid by_____.
                                assumed

9.   Possession shall be delivered to Buyer (a) on close of escrow, or (b) not later than _____days after close of escrow or (c) _____

10.   Unless otherwise designated in the escrow instructions of Buyer, title shall vest as follows: _____
_____

(The manner of taking title may have significant legal and tax consequences. Therefore, give this matter serious consideration.)

11.   If Broker is a participant of a Board multiple listing service ("MLS"), the Broker is authorized to report the sale, its price, terms, and financing for the information, publication, dissemination, and use of the authorized Board members.

12.   **If Buyer fails to complete said purchase as herein provided by reason of any default of Buyer, Seller shall be released from his obligation to sell the property to Buyer and may proceed against Buyer upon any claim or remedy which he may have in law or equity; provided, however, that by placing their initials here Buyer: (   ) Seller: (   ) agree that Seller shall retain the deposit as his liquidated damages. If the described property is a dwelling with no more than four units, one of which the Buyer intends to occupy as his residence, Seller shall retain as liquidated damages the deposit actually paid, or an amount therefrom, not more than 3% of the purchase price and promptly return any excess to Buyer.**

13.   If the only controversy or claim between the parties arises out of or relates to the disposition of the Buyer's deposit, such controversy or claim shall at the election of the parties be decided by arbitration. Such arbitration shall be determined in accordance with the Rules of the American Arbitration Association, and judgment upon the award rendered by the Arbitrator(s) may be entered in any court having jurisdiction thereof. The provisions of Code of Civil Procedure Section 1283.05 shall be applicable to such arbitration.

14.   In any action or proceeding arising out of this agreement, the prevailing party shall be entitled to reasonable attorney's fees and costs.

15.   Time is of the essence. All modification or extensions shall be in writing signed by the parties.

16.   This constitutes an offer to purchase the described property. Unless acceptance is signed by Seller and the signed copy delivered to Buyer, in person or by mail to the address below, within _____days, this offer shall be deemed revoked and the deposit shall be returned. Buyer acknowledges receipt of a copy hereof.

Real Estate Broker G _____ Buyer H _____

By _____ Buyer _____

Address _____ Address _____

Telephone _____ Telephone _____

I
ACCEPTANCE

The undersigned Seller accepts and agrees to sell the property on the above terms and conditions. Seller has employed _____
_____
as Broker(s) and agrees to pay for services the sum of _____Dollars
($_____), payable as follows: (a) On recordation of the deed or other evidence of title, or (b) if completion of sale is prevented by default of Seller, upon Seller's default or (c) if completion of sale is prevented by default of Buyer, only if and when Seller collects damages from Buyer, by suit or otherwise and then in an amount not less than one-half of the damages recovered, but not to exceed the above fee, after first deducting title and escrow expenses and the expenses of collection, if any. In any action between Broker and Seller arising out of this agreement, the prevailing party shall be entitled to reasonable attorney's fees and costs. The undersigned acknowledges receipt of a copy and authorizes Broker(s) to deliver a signed copy to Buyer.

Dated _____Telephone _____ Seller _____

Address _____ Seller _____

Broker(s) agree to the foregoing. Broker _____ Broker _____

Dated _____By _____ Dated _____By _____

To order, contact—California Association of Realtors®
525 S. Virgil Ave. Los Angeles. California 90020   Page _____ of _____ Pages

The Anatomy of Model Form I

The initial draft of a CAR Real Estate Purchase Contract and Receipt for Deposit (see I above) constitutes only the buyer's offer and a receipt for the deposit. With the seller's acceptance, it becomes a bilateral purchase contract on the terms and conditions of the total agreement. If properly filled out, the acceptance clause also becomes a final employment contract between the seller and the broker, fixing the exact amount due the broker upon "recordation of the deed or other evidence of title."

This form is to be used in simple transactions only. The caveat on the form is explicit: "It should not be used in complex transactions or with extensive riders and additions."

Let's examine the contract point for point. Refer to the indexed form on pages 11 and 12.

A. Insert the name of the city where the buyer actually signs the offer to purchase. In inserting the date, do not abbreviate.
B. The full name(s) of the person(s) receiving the receipt for deposit, which is incorporated in the offer to purchase, should be spelled correctly. Designations such as "husband and wife," "single woman," and so forth may be valuable for identification.
C. The amount of the deposit should first be written out in words, then entered in figures in the appropriate space. If the listing agreement has prescribed a minimum deposit, the broker should, of course, have obtained that amount.
   a. The form contains various boxes to indicate whether the deposit has been paid in cash, by personal check, or by cashier's check. If a promissory note is used for deposit, the boxes should be struck out; in the blank space following "or" insert, for example, "A 30-day note in the amount of $500.00 in favor of sellers."
   b. The check or note should be shown to the seller, who can then decide how to handle it. If the deposit is a postdated check, this fact should be pointed out to the seller. Authorization to hold it until the date indicated should be written into the contract. The form provides that a check may be held uncashed until seller's acceptance.
D. The purchase price offered should be written in both letters and figures in the spaces provided. If a different price is later negotiated, changes should never be made on the face of the contract, but should be made by counter offers.
E. The property should be described with sufficient particularity as to be readily identifiable. For urban property a street address may be adequate. Other parcels may either be identified by a metes and bounds description or by block and lot number.
   a. Where a long legal description is necessary, it is advisable to attach a photocopy of an original instrument rather than to copy it manually.

F. Terms of Sale

1.* This is the nearly all-inclusive, basic "terms of the sale" clause. This paragraph is the place for setting forth "any terms and conditions of a factual nature applicable to this sale, such as financing, prior sale of other property, the matter of structural pest control inspection, repairs and personal property to be included in the sale."

    a. This statement on the form serves as a practical checklist of the items mentioned. Some of these items can be handled by attaching supplements and have them incorporated in the contract by having the buyer initial the appropriate place in paragraph 4. It is always good practice to have such a rider initialed by both parties to insure its authenticity. Extensive riders should, however, be avoided.

    b. The word "financing" in the contract stands for "terms of payment"; the terms must be set forth with certainty. If material elements are left to verbal agreement or future negotiation, no enforceable contract is created.

    c. The following elements are necessary to a clear and concise "terms of payment" clause:

        (1) The amount of increased deposit, if any.

        (2) The amount of total cash down payment.

        (3) When down payment shall be paid.

        (4) The amount of loan or loans expressed in dollars or in percentage of price.

        (5) The length of the loan or loans (unless this can be determined from the amortization rate set out in the contract).

        (6) The rate of interest on each loan. Whether it is a variable or "negotiable" interest.

        (7) The amount of periodic payment and its mode of payment (monthly, quarterly, semi-annually, or annually).

        (8) Whether the periodic payment includes principal, interest, taxes, and insurance.

        (9) Prepayment charges, if any.

        (10) Loan charges, if any, setup charges, assumption fees, and points.

        (11) Specific clauses used in FHA, VA loans.

        (12) Whether or not sale is conditioned upon buyer's ability to obtain a specified loan within a period of time.

        (13) Use of Deed of Trust, Wrap-around Deed of Trust or Installment Land Contract.

    d. If only a few items of personal property are included in the sale price, they can be enumerated in this paragraph. Appliances should

---

*The numbers correspond to the printed numbers of the paragraphs of the 1984 version of the contract.

be described by brand name and as "presently installed and used on the premises" or designated by name and serial number. Don't overlook swimming-pool equipment, where applicable. A separate list can be included in the supplements clause No. 4.

e. Where many items are included in the purchase price, an inventory should be prepared.

2. Deposit increase is registered here. If total deposit to be liquidated damages insert: Buyer and Seller to execute Form RID-11.

3. This is buyers statement that the intent is to occupy the property as a residence. This is important to trigger the liquidated damage clause if the property contains up to four units and the boxes in the liquidated damage clause are filled in.

4. Insert amount of pages in the contract and obtain buyer's initials on supplements to the contract or use checkmarks.

5. Buyer and Seller acknowledge receipt of copy. Both buyer and seller should sign page 1 of the contract and initial paragraph 4.

6. Escrow clause, allows for description of which party to pay fees.

7. At the time of drawing up the buyer's offer, brokers quite often do not have sufficient information about the status of the title to the property. This should, of course, be learned at the time the listing is taken. It may in fact be available to the listing office but not to the selling office.

a. The use of forms that expect a buyer to take title "subject to easements, restrictions, covenants, and conditions of record" is grossly unfair and should be avoided. Any one of these encumbrances may interfere with the buyer's intended use, or be too burdensome. The form gives buyer a right to object to conditions of title unacceptable to the buyer, if buyer is reasonable. In (3) insert unrecorded agreements.

b. In this paragraph, the designation of the purchaser of the title policy and the title company is called for. There are many available endorsements to the so-called "Standard Land Title Associations Policy."

8. This is the proration clause, for income property where other expenses of the property are often prorated. It continues with: "and other expenses of the property." Where security deposits exist, it is better to insert in paragraph 1 of the contract a sentence such as: "Security deposits, advanced rents, or future lease credits shall be credited to buyer."

a. The proration cut-off day should be inserted by using one of the two given alternatives, either the day of recordation or another specific date.

b. The assessment section demands close attention. If the broker has insufficient information about the terms of bonds to be assumed, make the assumption conditioned upon the buyer's consent by inserting: "subject to buyer's approval of terms." If there are no assessments, the whole sentence should be deleted and initialed by all parties.

9. Leaving the date of possession to future negotiations invites trouble. Possession on date of recordation can be inconvenient for the owner. But if the seller is to remain in possession after closing, care should be taken to use an "occupancy agreement after sale." The payment for the stipulated hold-over period can be adjusted in the sales price, in the proration arrangement, or by fixing a per diem rate sufficient to encourage performance. Paragraph 4 provides space for CAR Form RLAS-11.

10. This paragraph includes the timely warning: "The manner of taking title may have significant legal and tax consequences." Though this is perhaps the most important clause, the warning is often over-looked.
   a. Where the buyer is undecided at the time of making the offer or wishes competent legal advice, insert: "Instructions to follow." In any event, check with the buyers before escrow instructions are drawn so that they can decide without being rushed, and direct escrow in their best interests.

11. This clause permits dissemination of MLS information.

12. The text of the liquidated-damage clause in CAR's form is preferable to the clauses found in most other available mass-produced contracts. It gives the parties an option. Leaving the boxes in the clause open abolishes the idea of "liquidation" of damages. Buyers, however, are warned by the terms of the contract that if they default, the seller is released from the obligation to sell the property to the buyer, and "may proceed against buyer upon any claim or remedy which he may have in law or equity. . . ."

13. Optional arbitration is provided for controversies and claims solely pertaining to the disposition of buyer's deposit. Discovery proceedings allowed.

14. Attorney's fees and costs to prevailing party.

15. This is the "time is of the essence" clause. The reason for it is to be certain that performance of any condition takes place by the time indicated, and not at some indefinite later date. It is always advisable to get all parties to agree to any necessary extensions of time.

16. This "mode of acceptance" clause declares that the offer is deemed "revoked" if the buyer does not receive a copy of the contract containing the signed acceptance of the offer by the seller within the prescribed time. This copy must be delivered in person or by mail.
   a. If the seller's absence from the place of negotiation will make strict compliance with the provisions of this clause impossible, the form should be adapted to the prevailing situation.

G. Insert the broker's name and the salesperson's signature, the office address, and telephone number. It may be practical to include a residence telephone number.

H. This is the space for the buyer's final offer and signature. The contract should be signed by all buyers unless the signer has a valid power of attorney. The buyer's home and business addresses and telephone numbers should be inserted to simplify the delivery of the copy of the signed acceptance.

Watch for authority to sign by partnerships and corporations.

I. Seller's Acceptance

1. The balance of the contract contains the acceptance provisions. There is room for inserting the names of cooperating brokers as well as the amount of the commission. If the Deposit Receipt is the instrument which "initially" fixes the commission (where there is no prior listing) insert "as per commission agreement" and have the parties sign CAR. Form CA-11. (Form 6:00 herein.) California's "negotiable commission" law is discussed in connection with this form.

   a. This clause also contains the broker's consent to the terms of the seller's acceptance, creating a bilateral contract for payment of commission and division of forfeited deposits. The consent should be signed by the broker or, in the event of a cooperative sale, by both brokers, unless the brokers have an agreement that the consent of one will bind the other.

Note: CAR has a Finance Supplement Form D-11SF, which can be attached to the contract by reference in the terms of payment clause. In more complicated transactions if properly filled in this supplement may be a true saving.

Caution: Use of such preprinted simple financing terms may discourage sellers and buyers from accepting innovative, creative financing terms. Such preprinted finance terms are also inadequate to spell out terms of ARMS type financing.

CAR has also developed an Investment Property Supplement Form 1P-11S. It includes eight clauses covering such common conditions as: seller warranties regarding official notices, inventory of property, inspections of units and leases, conditions of mechanical features of the property, rental during escrow period, security deposits and agreements with tenants not included in leases.

Model Form II comes in two versions, one with preprinted simple financing terms and one with a blank space sufficient to write a substantial prepayment clause as recommended in this book. If you make mistakes on the front page of either version, pads of the front page can be obtained so you do not have to destroy the whole package. Model Form II is analyzed in Chapter 12.

An investment property form DLIP-14 incorporates the Investment Supplement form with some minor additions, but is otherwise identical with Model Form II. In the sale of residential investment property containing a few units either the supplement or the Investment Property Form may be adequate. They both need careful scrutiny and proper tailoring to the transaction. More comprehensive clauses from this book may be necessary in transactions involving large income property or commercial buildings.

MODEL FORM II

REAL ESTATE PURCHASE CONTRACT AND RECEIPT FOR DEPOSIT
(LONG FORM — WITH FINANCING CLAUSES)
THIS IS MORE THAN A RECEIPT FOR MONEY. IT IS INTENDED TO BE A LEGALLY BINDING CONTRACT. READ IT CAREFULLY.
CALIFORNIA ASSOCIATION OF REALTORS® (CAR) STANDARD FORM

_____, California, _____, 19___

Received from _____
herein called Buyer, the sum of _____ Dollars $ _____
evidenced by ☐ cash, ☐ cashier's check, ☐ personal check or ☐ _____, payable to ___,
_____, to be held uncashed until acceptance of this offer as deposit on account of purchase price of
_____ Dollars $ _____
for the purchase of property, situated in _____, County of _____ California,
described as follows: _____

1. FINANCING: The obtaining of Buyer's financing is a contingency of this agreement.
   A. Deposit upon acceptance, to be deposited into _____ $ _____
   B. INCREASED DEPOSIT within_____ days of Seller's acceptance to be deposited into ___ $ _____
   C. BALANCE OF DOWN PAYMENT to be deposited into _____ on or before _____ $ _____
   D. Buyer to   apply, qualify for and obtain a NEW FIRST LOAN in the amount of............ $ _____
      payable monthly at approximately $_____ including interest at origination not to
      exceed_____%, ☐ fixed rate, ☐ other _____ all due_____ years from date of
      origination. Loan fee not to exceed _____ Seller agrees to pay a maximum of _____
      FHA/VA discount points. Additional terms_____

   E. Buyer ☐ to assume, ☐ to take title subject to an EXISTING FIRST LOAN with an approximate balance of ... $ _____
      in favor of_____
      at_____% ☐ fixed rate, ☐ other _____ payable monthly at $_____ including interest
      Fees not to exceed_____. Disposition of impound account _____
      Additional Terms _____

   F. Buyer to execute a NOTE SECURED BY a ☐ first, ☐ second, ☐ third DEED OF TRUST in the amount of $_____
      IN FAVOR OF SELLER payable monthly at $ _____ ☐ or more, including interest at_____% all due
      _____ years from date of origination, ☐ or upon sale or transfer of subject property. A late charge of_____
      shall be due on any installment not paid within_____ days of the due date. ☐ Deed of Trust to contain a
      request for notice of default or sale for the benefit of Seller. Buyer ☐ will, ☐ will not execute a request for notice of
      delinquency. Additional terms_____

   G. Buyer☐ to assume, ☐ to take title subject to an EXISTING SECOND LOAN with an approximate balance of . $ _____
      in favor of_____ payable monthly at $_____ including interest
      at_____% ☐ fixed rate, ☐ other _____. Buyer fees not to exceed _____
      Additional terms _____

   H. Buyer to apply, qualify for and obtain a NEW SECOND LOAN in the amount of .... $ _____
      payable monthly at approximately $_____ including interest at origination not to exceed
      _____% ☐ fixed rate, ☐ other,
      _____, all due_____ years from date of origination. Buyer's loan fee not to exceed_____.
      Additional Terms _____

   I. In the event Buyer assumes or takes title subject to an existing loan, Seller shall provide Buyer with copies of
      applicable notes and Deeds of Trust. A loan may contain a number of features which affect the loan, such as
      interest rate changes, monthly payment changes, balloon payments, etc. Buyer shall be allowed_____ calendar
      days after receipt of such copies to notify seller in writing of disapproval. FAILURE TO SO NOTIFY SELLER
      SHALL CONCLUSIVELY BE CONSIDERED APPROVAL. Buyer's approval shall not be unreasonably withheld.
      Difference in existing loan balances shall be adjusted in ☐ Cash, ☐ Other_____

   J. Buyer agrees to act diligently and in good faith to obtain all applicable financing. _____

   K. ADDITIONAL FINANCING TERMS:_____

   L. TOTAL PURCHASE PRICE . . . . $ _____

2. OCCUPANCY: Buyer ☐ does, ☐ does not intend to occupy subject property as Buyer's primary residence.

3. SUPPLEMENTS: The ATTACHED supplements are incorporated herein:
   ☐ Interim Occupancy Agreement (CAR FORM IOA-11)   ☐ _____
   ☐ Residential Lease Agreement after Sale (CAR FORM RLAS-11) ☐ _____
   ☐ VA and FHA Amendments (CAR FORM VA/FHA-11)   ☐ _____

Buyer and Seller acknowledge receipt of copy of this page, which constitutes Page 1 of _____ Pages.
Buyer's Initials (_____) (_____)   Seller's Initials (_____) (_____)

To order, contact— California Association of Realtors®
525 S. Virgil Avenue, Los Angeles, California 90020
Copyright©1986, California Association of Realtors®
Revised 12/86

OFFICE USE ONLY
Reviewed by Broker or Designee _____
Date _____

SF-L6-SF

BUYER'S COPY
REAL ESTATE PURCHASE CONTRACT AND RECEIPT FOR DEPOSIT (DLF-14 PAGE 1 OF 4)

Subject Property Address _____

4. ESCROW: Buyer and Seller shall deliver signed instructions to_____ the escrow holder, within _____calendar days from Seller's acceptance which shall provide for closing within_____ calendar days from Seller's acceptance. Escrow fees to be paid as follows: _____

5. TITLE: Title is to be free of liens, encumbrances, easements, restrictions, rights and conditions of record or known to Seller, other than the following: (a) Current property taxes, (b) covenants, conditions, restrictions, and public utility easements of record, if any, provided the same do not adversely affect the continued use of the property for the purposes for which it is presently being used, unless reasonably disapproved by Buyer in writing within _____ calendar days of receipt of a current preliminary report furnished at_____ expense, and (c) _____
Seller shall furnish Buyer at _____ expense a standard California Land Title Association policy issued by _____ Company, showing title vested in Buyer subject only to the above. If Seller is unwilling or unable to eliminate any title matter disapproved by Buyer as above, Buyer may terminate this agreement. If Seller fails to deliver title as above, Buyer may terminate this agreement; in either case, the deposit shall be returned to Buyer.

6. PRORATIONS: Property taxes, payments on bonds and assessments assumed by Buyer, interest, rents, association dues, premiums on insurance acceptable to Buyer, and _____ shall be paid current and prorated as of: ☐ the day of recordation of the deed; or ☐ _____. Bonds or assessments now a lien shall be ☐ paid current by Seller, payments not yet due to be assumed by Buyer; or ☐ paid in full by Seller, including payments not yet due; or ☐ _____ County Transfer tax shall be paid by _____ The _____ transfer tax or transfer fee shall be paid by _____ **PROPERTY WILL BE REASSESSED UPON CHANGE OF OWNERSHIP. THIS WILL AFFECT THE TAXES TO BE PAID.** A Supplemental tax bill will be issued, which shall be paid as follows: (a) for periods after close of escrow, by Buyer (or by final acquiring party if part of an exchange), and (b) for periods prior to close of escrow, by Seller. TAX BILLS ISSUED AFTER CLOSE OF ESCROW SHALL BE HANDLED DIRECTLY BETWEEN BUYER AND SELLER.

7. POSSESSION: Possession and occupancy shall be delivered to Buyer, ☐ on close of escrow, or ☐ not later than _____ days after close of escrow, or ☐ _____

8. VESTING: Unless otherwise designated in the escrow instructions of Buyer, title shall vest as follows: _____

(The manner of taking title may have significant legal and tax consequences. Therefore, give this matter serious consideration.)

9. MULTIPLE LISTING SERVICE: If Broker is a Participant of a Board multiple listing service ("MLS"), the Broker is authorized to report the sale, its price, terms, and financing for the publication, dissemination, information, and use of the authorized Board members, MLS Participants and Subscribers.

10. LIQUIDATED DAMAGES: If Buyer fails to complete said purchase as herein provided by reason of any default of Buyer, Seller shall be released from obligation to sell the property to Buyer and may proceed against Buyer upon any claim or remedy which he/she may have in law or equity; provided, however, that by placing their initials here Buyer: (   ) Seller: (   ) agree that Seller shall retain the deposit as liquidated damages. If the described property is a dwelling with no more than four units, one of which the Buyer intends to occupy as his/her residence, Seller shall retain as liquidated damages the deposit actually paid, or an amount therefrom, not more than 3% of the purchase price and promptly return any excess to Buyer. Buyer and Seller agree to execute a similar liquidated damages provision, such as California Association of Realtors® Receipt for Increased Deposit (RID-11), for any increased deposits. (Funds deposited in trust accounts or in escrow are not released automatically in the event of a dispute. Release of funds requires written agreement of the parties or adjudication.)

11. ARBITRATION: If the only controversy or claim between the parties arises out of or relates to the disposition of the Buyer's deposit, such controversy or claim shall at the election of the parties be decided by arbitration. Such arbitration shall be determined in accordance with the Rules of the American Arbitration Association, and judgment upon the award rendered by the Arbitrator(s) may be entered in any court having jurisdiction thereof. The provisions of Code of Civil Procedure Section 1283.05 shall be applicable to such arbitration.

12. ATTORNEY'S FEES: In any action or proceeding arising out of this agreement, the prevailing party shall be entitled to reasonable attorney's fees and costs.

13. KEYS: Seller shall, when possession is available to Buyer, provide keys and/or means to operate all property locks, and alarms, if any.

14. PERSONAL PROPERTY: The following items of personal property, free of liens and without warranty of condition, are included: ____

15. FIXTURES: All permanently installed fixtures and fittings that are attached to the property or for which special openings have been made are included in the purchase price, including electrical, light, plumbing and heating fixtures, built-in appliances, screens, awnings, shutters, all window coverings, attached floor coverings, T.V. antennas, air cooler or conditioner, garage door openers and controls, attached fireplace equipment, mailbox, trees and shrubs, and _____ except _____

16. SMOKE DETECTOR(S): Approved smoke detector(s) shall be installed as required by law, at the expense of ☐ Buyer, ☐ Seller.

17. TRANSFER DISCLOSURE: Unless exempt, Transferor (Seller), shall comply with Civil Code Sections 1102 et seq., by providing Transferee (Buyer) with a Real Estate Transfer Disclosure Statement: a) ☐ Buyer has received and read a Real Estate Transfer Disclosure Statement; or b) ☐ Seller shall provide Buyer with a Real Estate Transfer Disclosure Statement within _____ calendar days of Seller's acceptance after which Buyer shall have three (3) days after delivery to Buyer, in person, or five (5) days after delivery by deposit in the mail, to terminate this agreement by delivery of a written notice of termination to Seller or Seller's Agent.

18. TAX WITHHOLDING: Under the Foreign Investment in Real Property Tax Act (FIRPTA), IRC 1445, *every* Buyer of U.S. real property *must*, unless an exemption applies, deduct and withhold from Seller's proceeds ten percent (10%) of the gross sales price. The primary exemptions are: No withholding is required if (a) Seller provides Buyer with an affidavit under penalty of perjury, that Seller is not a "foreign person," or (b) Seller provides Buyer with a "qualifying statement" issued by the Internal Revenue Service, or (c) if Buyer purchases real property for use as a residence and the purchase price is $300,000.00 or less and if Buyer or a member of Buyer's family has definite plans to reside at the property for at least 50% of the days it is in use during each of the first two twelve-months periods after transfer. Seller and Buyer agree to execute and deliver as directed, any instrument, affidavit and statement, or to perform any act reasonably necessary to carry out the provisions of FIRPTA and regulations promulgated thereunder.

19. ENTIRE CONTRACT: Time is of the essence. All prior agreements between the parties are incorporated in this agreement which constitutes the entire contract. Its terms are intended by the parties as a final expression of their agreement with respect to such terms as are included herein and may not be contradicted by evidence of any prior agreement or contemporaneous oral agreement. The parties further intend that this agreement constitutes the complete and exclusive statement of its terms and that no extrinsic evidence whatsoever may be introduced in any judicial or arbitration proceeding, if any, involving this agreement.

Buyer and Seller acknowledge receipt of copy of this page, which constitutes Page 2 of_____ Pages.
Buyer's Initials (_____) (_____)   Seller's Initials (_____) (_____)

OFFICE USE ONLY
Reviewed by Broker or Designee _____
BROKER'S COPY   Date _____

EQUAL HOUSING OPPORTUNITY
SF-Aug 87

REAL ESTATE PURCHASE CONTRACT AND RECEIPT FOR DEPOSIT (DL-14 PAGE 2 OF 4)

(Form continues on next page)

Subject Property Address _____

20. CAPTIONS: The captions in this agreement are for convenience of reference only and are not intended as part of this agreement.

21. ADDITIONAL TERMS AND CONDITIONS:
ONLY THE FOLLOWING PARAGRAPHS A THROUGH J *WHEN INITIALED BY BOTH BUYER AND SELLER* ARE INCORPORATED IN THIS AGREEMENT.

Buyer's Initials   Seller's Initials

___/___   ___/___   **A. PHYSICAL INSPECTION:** Within _____ calendar days after Seller's acceptance Buyer shall have the right, at Buyer's expense, to select a licensed contractor(s) or other qualified professional(s), to inspect and investigate the subject property, including but not limited to structural, plumbing, heating, electrical, built-in appliances, roof, soils, foundation, mechanical systems, pool, pool heater, pool filter, air conditioner, if any, possible environmental hazards such as asbestos, formaldehyde, radon gas and other substances / products. Buyer shall keep the subject property free and clear of any liens, indemnify and hold Seller harmless from all liability, claims, demands, damages or costs, and repair all damages to the property arising from the inspections. All claimed defects concerning the condition of the property that adversely affect the continued use of the property for the purposes for which it is presently being used shall be in writing, supported by written reports, if any, and delivered to Seller within_____ calendar days after Seller's acceptance. Buyer shall furnish Seller copies, at no cost, of all reports concerning the property obtained by Buyer. When such reports disclose conditions or information unsatisfactory to the Buyer, which the Seller is unwilling or unable to correct, Buyer may cancel this agreement. Seller shall make the premises available for all inspections. BUYER'S FAILURE TO NOTIFY SELLER SHALL CONCLUSIVELY BE CONSIDERED APPROVAL.

Buyer's Initials   Seller's Initials

___/___   ___/___   **B. GEOLOGICAL INSPECTION:** Within _____ calendar days after Seller's acceptance. Buyer shall have the right at Buyer's expense, to select a qualified professional to make tests, surveys, or other studies of the subject property. Buyer shall keep the subject property free and clear of any liens, indemnify and hold Seller harmless from all liability, claims, demands, damages or costs, and repair all damages to the property arising from the tests, surveys, or studies. All claimed defects concerning the condition of the property that adversely affect the continued use of the property for the purposes for which it is presently being used shall be in writing, supported by written reports, if any, and delivered to Seller within _____ calendar days after Seller's acceptance. Buyer shall furnish Seller copies, at no cost, of all reports concerning the property obtained by Buyer. When such reports disclose conditions or information unsatisfactory to the Buyer, which the Seller is unwilling or unable to correct, Buyer may cancel this agreement. Seller shall make the premises available for all inspections. BUYER'S FAILURE TO NOTIFY SELLER SHALL CONCLUSIVELY BE CONSIDERED APPROVAL.

Buyer's Initials   Seller's Initials

___/___   ___/___   **C. CONDITION OF PROPERTY:** Seller warrants, through the date possession is made available to Buyer: (1) property and improvements thereon, including landscaping, grounds and pool/spa, if any, shall be maintained in the same condition as upon the date of Seller's acceptance; (2) the roof is free of all known leaks and that water, sewer, plumbing, heating, air conditioning, if any, and electrical systems and all built-in appliances are operative, (3) _____

Buyer's Initials   Seller's Initials

___/___   ___/___   **D. SELLER REPRESENTATION:** Seller warrants that Seller has no knowledge of any notice of violations of City, County, State, Federal, Building, Zoning, Fire, Health Codes or ordinances, or other governmental regulation filed or Issued against the property. This warranty shall be effective until the date of close of escrow.

Buyer's Initials   Seller's Initials

___/___   ___/___   **E. PEST CONTROL:** Within _____ calendar days from the date of Seller's acceptance Seller shall furnish Buyer, at the expense of ☐ Buyer, ☐ Seller, a current written report of an inspection by_____ _____ , a licensed Structural Pest Control Operator, of the main building and all structures on the property, except_____

If no infestation or infection by wood destroying pests or organisms is found, the report shall include a written "Certification" as provided in Business and Professions Code 8519(a) that on the date of inspection "no evidence of active infestation or infection was found."

All work recommended in said report to repair damage caused by infestation or infection by wood-destroying pests or organisms found, including leaking shower stalls and replacing of tiles removed for repairs, and all work to correct conditions that cause such infestation or infection shall be done at the expense of Seller.

Funds for work to be performed shall be held in escrow and disbursed upon receipt of written Certification as provided in Business and Professions Code 8519(b) that the property "is now free of evidence of active infestation or infection".

Buyer agrees that any work to correct conditions usually deemed likely to lead to infestation or infection by wood-destroying pests or organisms, but where no evidence of existing infestation or infection is found with respect to such conditions is NOT the responsibility of Seller, and that such work shall be done only if requested by Buyer and then at the expense of Buyer.

If inspection of inaccessible areas is recommended by the report, Buyer has the option of accepting and approving the report or requesting further inspection be made at the Buyer's expense. If further inspection is made and infestation, infection, or damage is found, repair of such damage and all work to correct conditions that caused such infestation or infection and the cost of entry and closing of the inaccessible areas shall be at the expense of Seller. If no infestation, infection, or damage is found, the cost of entry and closing of the inaccessible areas shall be at the expense of Buyer.

Other_____
_____

Buyer's Initials   Seller's Initials

___/___   ___/___   **F. FLOOD HAZARD AREA DISCLOSURE:** Buyer is informed that subject property is situated in a "Special Flood Hazard Area" as set forth on a Federal Emergency Management Agency (FEMA) "Flood Insurance Rate Map (FIRM) or "Flood Hazard Boundary Map" (FHBM). The law provides that, as a condition of obtaining financing on most structures located in a "Special Flood Hazard Area," lenders require flood insurance where the property or its attachments are security for a loan.

The extent of coverage and the cost may vary. For further information consult the lender or insurance carrier. No representation or recommendation is made by the Seller and the Brokers in this transaction as to the legal effect or economic consequences of the National Flood Insurance Program and related legislation.

Buyer and Seller acknowledge receipt of copy of this page, which constitutes Page 3 of_____ Pages.
Buyer's Initials (_____) (_____)   Seller's Initials (_____) (_____)

OFFICE USE ONLY
Reviewed by Broker or Designee
Date _____

BROKER'S COPY

SF Aug 87

REAL ESTATE PURCHASE CONTRACT AND RECEIPT FOR DEPOSIT (DL-14 PAGE 3 OF 4)

Subject Property Address _____
Buyer's Initials   Seller's Initials

_____/_____   _____/_____   **G. SPECIAL STUDIES ZONE DISCLOSURE:** Buyer is informed that subject property is situated in a Special Studies Zone as designated under Sections 2621-2625, inclusive, of the California Public Resources Code; and, as such, the construction or development on this property of any structure for human occupancy may be subject to the findings of a geologic report prepared by a geologist registered in the State of California, unless such a report is waived by the City or County under the terms of that act.

Buyer is allowed _____ calendar days from the date of Seller's acceptance to make further inquiries at appropriate governmental agencies concerning the use of the subject property under the terms of the Special Studies Zone Act and local building, zoning, fire, health and safety codes. When such inquiries disclose conditions or information unsatisfactory to the Buyer, which the Seller is unwilling or unable to correct, Buyer may cancel this agreement. BUYER'S FAILURE TO NOTIFY SELLER SHALL CONCLUSIVELY BE CONSIDERED APPROVAL.
Buyer's Initials   Seller's Initials

_____/_____   _____/_____   **H. ENERGY CONSERVATION RETROFIT:** If local ordinance requires that the property be brought in compliance with minimum energy Conservation Standards as a condition of sale or transfer, ☐ Buyer, ☐ Seller shall comply with and pay for these requirements. Where permitted by law, Seller may, if obligated hereunder, satisfy the obligation by authorizing escrow to credit Buyer with sufficient funds to cover the cost of such retrofit.
Buyer's Initials   Seller's Initials

_____/_____   _____/_____   **I. HOME PROTECTION PLAN:** Buyer and Seller have been informed that Home Protection Plans are available. Such plans may provide additional protection and benefit to a Seller or Buyer. California Association of Realtors® and the Broker(s) in this transaction do not endorse or approve any particular company or program:

a) ☐ A Buyer's coverage Home Protection Plan to be issued by _____
Company, at a cost not to exceed $ _____ , to be paid by ☐ Seller, ☐ Buyer; or

b) ☐ Buyer and Seller elect not to purchase a Home Protection Plan.
Buyer's Initials   Seller's Initials

_____/_____   _____/_____   **J. CONDOMINIUM/P.U.D.:** The subject of this transaction is a condominium/planned unit development (P.U.D.) designated as unit _____ and _____ parking space(s) and an undivided _____ interest in all community areas, and _____ . The current monthly assessment charge by the homeowner's association or other governing body(s) is $ _____ . As soon as practicable, Seller shall provide Buyer with copies of covenants, conditions and restrictions, articles of incorporation, by-laws, current rules and regulations, most current financial statements, and any other documents as required by law. Seller shall disclose in writing any known pending special assessment, claims, or litigation to Buyer. Buyer shall be allowed _____ calendar days from receipt to review these documents. If such documents disclose conditions or information unsatisfactory to Buyer, Buyer may cancel this agreement. BUYER'S FAILURE TO NOTIFY SELLER SHALL CONCLUSIVELY BE CONSIDERED APPROVAL.

22. OTHER TERMS AND CONDITIONS: _____
_____
_____
_____
_____

23. AGENCY CONFIRMATION: The following agency relationship(s) are hereby confirmed for this transaction:

LISTING AGENT: _____ is the agent of (check one):
☐ the Seller exclusively; or   ☐ both the Buyer and Seller

SELLING AGENT: _____ (if not the same as Listing Agent) is the agent of (check one):
☐ the Buyer exclusively; or   ☐ the Seller exclusively; or   ☐ both the Buyer and Seller.

24. AMENDMENTS: This agreement may not be amended, modified, altered or changed in any respect whatsoever except by a further agreement in writing executed by Buyer and Seller.

25. OFFER: This constitutes an offer to purchase the described property. Unless acceptance is signed by Seller and the signed copy delivered in person or by mail to Buyer, or to _____ who is authorized to receive it, in person or by mail at the address below, within _____ calendar days of the date hereof, this offer shall be deemed revoked and the deposit shall be returned. Buyer has read and acknowledges receipt of a copy of this offer.

REAL ESTATE BROKER _____   BUYER _____
By _____   BUYER _____
Address _____   Address _____

Telephone _____   Telephone _____

ACCEPTANCE

The undersigned Seller accepts and agrees to sell the property on the above terms and conditions and agrees to the above confirmation of agency relationships. Seller agrees to pay to Broker(s) _____

compensation for services as follows: _____

Payable: (a) On recordation of the deed or other evidence of title, or (b) if completion of sale is prevented by default of Seller, upon Seller's default, or (c) if completion of sale is prevented by default of Buyer, only if and when Seller collects damages from Buyer, by suit or otherwise, and then in an amount not less than one-half of the damages recovered, but not to exceed the above fee, after first deducting title and escrow expenses and the expenses of collection, if any. Seller shall execute and deliver an escrow instruction irrevocably assigning the compensation for service in an amount equal to the compensation agreed to above. In any action or proceeding between Broker(s) and Seller arising out of this agreement, the prevailing party shall be entitled to reasonable attorneys fees and costs. The undersigned has read and acknowledges receipt of a copy of this agreement and authorizes Broker(s) to deliver a signed copy to Buyer.

Date _____ Telephone _____   SELLER _____
Address _____   _____
_____   SELLER _____
Real Estate Broker(s) agree to the foregoing.

Broker _____   By _____   Date _____

Broker _____   By _____   Date _____

This form is available for use by the entire real estate industry. The use of this form is not intended to identify the user as a REALTOR®. REALTOR® is a registered collective membership mark which may be used only by real estate licensees who are members of the NATIONAL ASSOCIATION OF REALTORS® and who subscribe to its Code of Ethics.

Page 4 of _____ Pages.

┌─ OFFICE USE ONLY ─┐
Reviewed by Broker or Designee _____
Date _____

EQUAL HOUSING OPPORTUNITY
SF-Aug-87

BROKER'S COPY

REAL ESTATE PURCHASE CONTRACT AND RECEIPT FOR DEPOSIT (DL-14 PAGE 4 OF 4)

Sample of Filled-in Forms

A. The Sale of a Residence

REAL ESTATE PURCHASE CONTRACT AND RECEIPT FOR DEPOSIT

CALIFORNIA ASSOCIATION OF REALTORS

THIS IS MORE THAN A RECEIPT FOR MONEY. IT IS INTENDED TO BE A LEGALLY BINDING CONTRACT. READ IT CAREFULLY.

CALIFORNIA ASSOCIATION OF REALTORS® STANDARD FORM

Euphoria California. _December 1_ , 19 _XX_

Received from _RICHARD ROEONE and ELSIE ROEONE, husband and wife_

herein called Buyer, the sum of _FIVE HUNDRED AND NO/100-------------------_ Dollars $ _500.00_

evidenced by cash ☐, cashier's check ☐, or _____ ☐, personal check ☒ payable to _Built-In_
Escrow Co. , to be held uncashed until acceptance of this offer, as deposit on account of purchase price of

FORTY THOUSAND AND NO/100------------------------------------ Dollars $ _40,000.00_

for the purchase of the property, situated in _Euphoria_ , County of _Dreams_ , California,

described as follows: _Lot and improvements commonly known as 1001 Long Lane_

1.   Buyer will deposit in escrow with _Built-In Escrow Co._ the balance of purchase price as follows:

$ 8,000.00   cash including above deposit
     32,000.00   as loan proceeds, conditioned upon Buyer's ability to
                  obtain a new first VIR loan from Gotit S & L Association
                  in that amount, payable at $288.40 monthly, including
                  interest at 9-1/2% at close of escrow. Set up charges
                  not to exeed 1 point.

The principal stockholders of "Old Broker's Company" have an ownership
interest in "Built-In Escrow Co." and "Best Exterminator," which are
providing services herein for which a fee may be charged.

Set forth above any terms and conditions of a factual nature applicable to this sale, such as financing, prior sale of other property, the matter of structural pest control inspection, repairs and personal property to be included in the sale.

2.   Deposit will ☒will not ☐ be increased by $ _700.00_ to $ _1,200.00_ within _five (5)_ days of acceptance of this offer. _Buyer and Seller to sign CAR Form RID-11._

3.   Buyer does ☒ does not ☐ intend to occupy subject property as his residence.

4.   The following supplements are incorporated as part of this agreement:

☐ Structural Pest Control Certification Agreement   ☐ Occupancy Agreement   Other _RKYN_ _Exhibit A_
☐ Special Studies Zone Disclosure   ☐ VA Amendment   ☐ _____
☐ Flood Insurance Disclosure   ☐ FHA Amendment   ☐ _____

5.   Buyer and Seller shall deliver signed instructions to the escrow holder within _15_ days from Seller's acceptance which shall provide for closing within _30_ days from Seller's acceptance. Escrow fees to be paid as follows:
     50/50 Buyer/Seller

6.   Buyer and Seller acknowledge receipt of a copy of this page, which constitutes Page 1 of _2_ Pages.

Buyer _Richard Roeone_   Seller _Hugh Vandon_
Buyer _Elsie Roeone_   Seller _Louise Vandon_

A REAL ESTATE BROKER IS THE PERSON QUALIFIED TO ADVISE ON REAL ESTATE. IF YOU DESIRE LEGAL ADVICE CONSULT YOUR ATTORNEY.

THIS STANDARDIZED DOCUMENT FOR USE IN SIMPLE TRANSACTIONS HAS BEEN APPROVED BY THE CALIFORNIA ASSOCIATION OF REALTORS® IN FORM ONLY. NO REPRESENTATION IS MADE AS TO APPROVAL OF SUPPLEMENTS NOT PUBLISHED BY CAR, THE LEGAL VALIDITY OF ANY PROVISION, OR THE ADEQUACY OF ANY PROVISION IN ANY SPECIFIC TRANSACTION. IT SHOULD NOT BE USED IN COMPLEX TRANSACTIONS OR WITH EXTENSIVE RIDERS OR ADDITIONS.

To order, contact—California Association of Realtors®
525 S. Virgil Ave., Los Angeles, California 90020
Copyright© California Association of Realtors® (Revised 1984)   FORM D-11-1

REAL ESTATE PURCHASE CONTRACT AND RECEIPT FOR DEPOSIT

The following terms and conditions are hereby incorporated in and made a part of Buyer's Offer

7. Title is to be free of liens, encumbrances, easements, restrictions, rights and conditions of record or known to Seller, other than the following: (a) Current property taxes, (b) covenants, conditions, restrictions, and public utility easements of record, if any, provided the same do not adversely affect the continued use of the property for which it is presently being used, unless reasonably disapproved by Buyer in writing within __5__ days of receipt of a current preliminary title report furnished at __Buyer's__ expense, and (c) **
Seller shall furnish Buyer at __Seller's__ expense a standard California Land Title Association policy issued by __Goldedge Title__ Company, showing title vested in Buyer subject only to the above. If Seller is unwilling or unable to eliminate any title matter disapproved by Buyer as above, Seller may terminate this agreement. If Seller fails to deliver title as above, Buyer may terminate this agreement; in either case, the deposit shall be returned to Buyer.

8. Property taxes, premiums on insurance acceptable to Buyer, rents, interest, and __impounds__ shall be pro-rated as of (a) the date of recordation of deed; or (b) ***********************. Any bond or assessment which is a lien shall be __assumed__ by __Buyer__. Transfer taxes, if any, shall be paid by __Seller__.

9. Possession shall be delivered to Buyer (a) on close of escrow, or (b) not later than __Ten (10)__ days after close of escrow or (c) _____

10. Unless otherwise designated in the escrow instructions of Buyer, title shall vest as follows: _____
__Instructions to follow__

(The manner of taking title may have significant legal and tax consequences, therefore, give this matter serious consideration.)

11. If Broker is a participant of a Board multiple listing service ("MLS"), the Broker is authorized to report the sale, its price, terms, and financing for the information, publication, dissemination, and use of the authorized Board members.

12. **If Buyer fails to complete said purchase as herein provided by reason of any default of Buyer, Seller shall be released from his obligation to sell the property to Buyer and may proceed against Buyer upon any claim or remedy which he may have in law or equity; provided, however, that by placing their initials here Buyer: (RRW) Seller: (HV LV) agree that Seller shall retain the deposit as his liquidated damages. If the described property is a dwelling with no more than four units, one of which the Buyer intends to occupy as his residence, Seller shall retain as liquidated damages the deposit actually paid, or an amount therefrom, not more than 3% of the purchase price and promptly return any excess to Buyer.**

13. If the only controversy or claim between the parties arises out of or relates to the disposition of the Buyer's deposit, such controversy or claim shall at the election of the parties be decided by arbitration. Such arbitration shall be determined in accordance with the Rules of the American Arbitration Association, and judgment upon the award rendered by the Arbitrator(s) may be entered in any court having jurisdiction thereof. The provisions of Code of Civil Procedure Section 1283.05 shall be applicable to such arbitration.

14. In any action or proceeding arising out of this agreement, the prevailing party shall be entitled to reasonable attorney's fees and costs.

15. Time is of the essence. All modification or extensions shall be in writing signed by the parties.

16. This constitutes an offer to purchase the described property. Unless acceptance is signed by Seller and the signed copy delivered to Buyer, in person or by mail to the address below, within __-3-__ days, this offer shall be deemed revoked and the deposit shall be returned. Buyer acknowledges receipt of a copy hereof.

Real Estate Broker __OLD BROKER'S COMPANY__   Buyer _Richard Rovine_
By _____   Buyer _Elsie Rovine_
Address __50 Main Street, Euphoria, CA__   Address __50 Grey Cross Ave., Nosuchcity, CA__
Telephone __524-6790__   Res: 342-4788; Bus.297-3259, Ext. 501

ACCEPTANCE

The undersigned Seller accepts and agrees to sell the property on the above terms and conditions. Seller has employed _____
__OLD BROKER'S COMPANY__
as Broker(s) and agrees to pay for services the sum of __6% of sales price__ Dollars ($XXXXXXXXXXXXXXXXXXXXX) payable as follows: (a) On recordation of the deed or other evidence of title, or (b) if completion of sale is prevented by default of Seller, upon Seller's default or (c) if completion of sale is prevented by default of Buyer, only if and when Seller collects damages from Buyer, by suit or otherwise and then in an amount not less than one-half of the damages recovered, but not to exceed the above fee, after first deducting title and escrow expenses and the expenses of collection, if any. In any action between Broker and Seller arising out of this agreement, the prevailing party shall be entitled to reasonable attorney's fees and costs. The undersigned acknowledges receipt of a copy and authorizes Broker(s) to deliver a signed copy to Buyer.

Dated __December 2, 19XX__ Telephone __524-6288__   Seller _Hugh Vendor_
Address __1001 Long Lane, Euphoria, CA__   Seller _Lois Vendor_

Broker(s) agree to the foregoing. Broker _OLD BROKER'S CO._   Broker _____
Dated __December 2, 19XX__ By _Young Newperson_   Dated _____ By _____

To order, contact—California Association of Realtors®
525 S. Virgil Ave., Los Angeles, California 90020
Copyright© California Association of Realtors® (Revised 1984)   FORM D-11-2

Page 2 of 2 Pages

Exhibit "A"

This addendum is part of that certain Real Estate Purchase Contract and Receipt for Deposit dated December 1, 19XX in which Richard Roeone and Elsie Roe-one are named as buyers and Hugh Vendor and Louise Vendor are named as sellers.

Further terms of sale:
1) This agreement is conditioned upon the close of escrow No. H 75 43-11 with West Coast Title Company, Euphoria office, involving sale of buyer's property. Said escrow set to close on November 25, 19XX. Seller shall have the right to continue to offer the herein described property for sale. Should seller receive another offer acceptable to him, buyer shall have 72 hours from the time of receipt of seller's written notice of such offer to remove the above condition. Failure to so waive such contingency shall terminate this agreement and cause the return of buyer's deposit.
2) Included in the purchase price are the following items of personal property to be delivered free of liens and by bill of sale: Mayday Washer and Dryer Models G 1679 and GT 1698; all pool equipment in accordance with inventory to be approved by buyer, all wall-to-wall carpeting and the billiard table in the recreation room.
3) A copy of Structural Pest Control Inspection Report No. 1795 issued by "Best Exterminator" has been exhibited to buyer.

   This offer, however, is conditioned upon Seller furnishing buyer at buyer's expense, an additional Structural Pest Control Inspection Report issued by "Bug-out" Pest Control Company, prepared in conformity with the provisions of "Request for Structural Pest Control Certification Report" CAR Form SPC-2. Seller shall not be obligated to select any other operator than the lowest bidder who will provide a certification "that the property is now free of evidence of active infestation or infection." Buyer may waive performance by seller and accept the amount of the lowest bid as a credit against the purchase price.

RECEIPT FOR INCREASED DEPOSIT AND SUPPLEMENT TO REAL ESTATE PURCHASE CONTRACT

CALIFORNIA ASSOCIATION OF REALTORS® STANDARD FORM

THIS IS INTENDED TO BE A LEGALLY BINDING CONTRACT. READ IT CAREFULLY.

Received from _____ herein

called Buyer, the sum of _____

Dollars ($_____) evidenced by cash ☐, personal check ☐, cashier's check ☐ as

additional deposit payable to _____

for the purchase of the property described in the Real Estate Purchase Contract and Receipt for Deposit dated

_____ executed by _____

as Buyer and accepted by Seller on _____ , 19_____ .

DATE _____

Real Estate Broker_____   By _____

The following is hereby incorporated in and made a part of said Real Estate Purchase Contract and Receipt for

Deposit, which remains in full force and effect:

Buyer hereby increases the total deposit to $_____and Buyer and Seller agree

that should Buyer fail to complete the purchase by reason of any default of Buyer, Seller shall retain the total

deposit as liquidated damages. If the described property is a dwelling with no more than four units, one of which

the Buyer intends to occupy as his residence, Seller shall retain as liquidated damages the deposit actually paid, or

an amount therefrom, not more than 3% of the purchase price, and promptly return any excess to Buyer.

The undersigned agree to the above and acknowledge receipt of a copy hereof.

Date _____   Date _____

Buyer _____   Seller _____

_____   _____

For these forms, address California Association of Realtors®
505 Shatto Place, Los Angeles 90020 (Revised 1978)   FORM RID-11

Sample of Filled-in Forms

B. The Sale of an Income Property Using Model Form I

REAL ESTATE PURCHASE CONTRACT AND RECEIPT FOR DEPOSIT

THIS IS MORE THAN A RECEIPT FOR MONEY. IT IS INTENDED TO BE A LEGALLY BINDING CONTRACT. READ IT CAREFULLY.
CALIFORNIA ASSOCIATION OF REALTORS® STANDARD FORM

_____Nosuchtown_____, California. _____December 1_____, 19 XX

Received from __RICHARD ROEONE and ELSIE ROEONE, husband and wife__
herein called Buyer, the sum of __Seven hundred Fifty and no/100-----------__Dollars $ __750.00__
evidenced by cash ☐, cashier's check ☐, or _____ ☐, personal check ☒ payable to __Goldedge__
__Security Title Company__, to be held uncashed until acceptance of this offer, as deposit on account of purchase price of
__Ninety-two thousand five hundred and no/100----------------__ Dollars $ __92,500.00__
for the purchase of property, situated in __Lotus City__, County of __Aristotle__, California,
described as follows: __Lot and improvements commonly known as 109 Bullfrog Lane__

1.   Buyer will deposit in escrow with __Goldedge Security Title Co.__ the balance of purchase price as follows:
__This agreement consists of this page and Page 2 and Exhibits A, B and C__
__attached hereto. All exhibits to which reference is made herein are__
__deemed incorporated whether or not actually attached.__

Set forth above any terms and conditions of a factual nature applicable to this sale, such as financing, prior sale of other property, the matter of structural pest control inspection, repairs and personal property to be included in the sale.

2.   Deposit will ☒ will not ☐ be increased by $ __SEE EXH. B__ to $ _____ within _____ days of acceptance of this offer.

3.   Buyer does ☐ does not ☒ intend to occupy subject property as his residence.

4.   The following supplements are incorporated as part of this agreement:

☐ Structural Pest Control Certification Agreement   ☐ Occupancy Agreement   Other ☒ __Agreement for entry__
☐ Special Studies Zone Disclosure   ☐ VA Amendment   ☐ __for garbage removal__
☐ Flood Insurance Disclosure   ☐ FHA Amendment   ☐ _____

5.   Buyer and Seller shall deliver signed instructions to the escrow holder within __15__ days from Seller's acceptance which shall provide for closing within __30__ days from Seller's acceptance. Escrow fees to be paid as follows:
__50/50 Buyer/Seller__

6.   Buyer and Seller acknowledge receipt of a copy of this page, which constitutes Page 1 of __2__ Pages.

Richard Roe

Seller _____

Seller _____

A REAL ESTATE BROKER IS THE PERSON QUALIFIED TO ADVISE ON REAL ESTATE. IF YOU DESIRE LEGAL ADVICE CONSULT YOUR ATTORNEY.

THIS STANDARDIZED DOCUMENT HAS BEEN APPROVED BY THE CALIFORNIA ASSOCIATION OF REALTORS® IN FORM ONLY.
NO REPRESENTATION IS MADE AS TO THE LEGAL VALIDITY OF ANY PROVISION OR THE ADEQUACY OF ANY PROVISION IN ANY SPECIFIC TRANSACTION.

To order, contact—California Association of Realtors®
525 S. Virgil Ave, Los Angeles, California 90020
Cop. right© California Association of Realtors® (Revised 1978, 1984)   FORM D-11-1

REAL ESTATE PURCHASE CONTRACT AND RECEIPT FOR DEPOSIT

The following terms and conditions are hereby incorporated in and made a part of Buyer's Offer

7.   Title is to be free of liens, encumbrances, easements, restrictions, rights and conditions of record or known to Seller, other than the following: (a) Current property taxes, (b) covenants, conditions, restrictions, and public utility easements of record, if any, provided the same do not adversely affect the continued use of the property for the purposes for which it is presently being used, unless reasonably disapproved by Buyer in writing within ___5___ days of receipt of a current preliminary title report furnished at __Buyer's__ expense, and (c) __Common garbage entry with 111 Bullfrog Lane property.__

Seller shall furnish Buyer at ___Seller's___ expense a standard California Land Title Association policy issued by Goldedge Security Title Company, showing title vested in Buyer subject only to the above. If Seller is unwilling or unable to eliminate any title matter disapproved by Buyer as above, Seller may terminate this agreement. If Seller fails to deliver title as above, Buyer may terminate this agreement; in either case, the deposit shall be returned to Buyer.

8.   Property taxes, premiums on insurance acceptable to Buyer, rents, interest, and _**************************_ shall be pro-rated as of (a) the date of recordation of deed; or (b) _*****************************_ Any bond or assessment which is a lien shall be ___paid___ by __Seller__. Transfer taxes, if any, shall be paid by __Seller__.

9.   Possession shall be delivered to Buyer (a) on close of escrow, or (b) not later than _***************_ days after close of escrow or (c) _**_ _***_

10.   Unless otherwise designated in the escrow instructions of Buyer, title shall vest as follows: _____
SEE INSTRUCTIONS TO ESCROW

(The manner of taking title may have significant legal and tax consequences. Therefore, give this matter serious consideration.)

11.   If Broker is a participant of a Board multiple listing service ("MLS"), the Broker is authorized to report the sale, its price, terms, and financing for the information, publication, dissemination, and use of the authorized Board members.

12.   **If Buyer fails to complete said purchase as herein provided by reason of any default of Buyer, Seller shall be released from his obligation to sell the property to Buyer and may proceed against Buyer upon any claim or remedy which he may have in law or equity; provided, however, that by placing their initials here Buyer: (   ) Seller: (   ) agree that Seller shall retain the deposit as his liquidated damages. If the described property is a dwelling with no more than four units, one of which the Buyer intends to occupy as his residence, Seller shall retain as liquidated damages the deposit actually paid, or an amount therefrom, not more than 3% of the purchase price and promptly return any excess to Buyer.**

13.   If the only controversy or claim between the parties arises out of or relates to the disposition of the Buyer's deposit, such controversy or claim shall at the election of the parties be decided by arbitration. Such arbitration shall be determined in accordance with the Rules of the American Arbitration Association, and judgment upon the award rendered by the Arbitrator(s) may be entered in any court having jurisdiction thereof. The provisions of Code of Civil Procedure Section 1283.05 shall be applicable to such arbitration.

14.   In any action or proceeding arising out of this agreement, the prevailing party shall be entitled to reasonable attorney's fees and costs.

15.   Time is of the essence. All modification or extensions shall be in writing signed by the parties.

16.   This constitutes an offer to purchase the described property. Unless acceptance is signed by Seller and the signed copy delivered to Buyer, in person or by mail to the address below, within ___-3-___ days, this offer shall be deemed revoked and the deposit shall be returned. Buyer acknowledges receipt of a copy hereof.

Real Estate Broker __OLD BROKER'S COMPANY__   Buyer _Richard Roam_
By _Young Penson_   Buyer _Elsie Roam_
Address __50 Main Street, Euphoria, CA__   Address __5 Nosuch St., Nosuchtown, CA__
Telephone __524-6790__   Telephone __567-8905__

ACCEPTANCE

The undersigned Seller accepts and agrees to sell the property on the above terms and conditions. Seller has employed ___OLD BROKER'S COMPANY___

as Broker(s) and agrees to pay for services the sum of __as per listing agreement dated__ (Dollars $__xxx__ November 18, 19XX), payable as follows: (a) On recordation of the deed or other evidence of title, or (b) if completion of sale is prevented by default of Seller, upon Seller's default or (c) if completion of sale is prevented by default of Buyer, only if and when Seller collects damages from Buyer, by suit or otherwise and then in an amount not less than one-half of the damages recovered, but not to exceed the above fee, after first deducting title and escrow expenses and the expenses of collection, if any. In any action between Broker and Seller arising out of this agreement, the prevailing party shall be entitled to reasonable attorney's fees and costs. The undersigned acknowledges receipt of a copy and authorizes Broker(s) to deliver a signed copy to Buyer.

Dated __December 1, 19XX__ Telephone __209-6432__   Seller _A. Landlord_
Address __109 Bullfrog Lane, Lotus City, CA__   Seller _____

Broker(s) agree to the foregoing. Broker __OLD BROKER'S COMPANY__   Broker _____
Dated __December 1, 19XX__ By _Young Penson_   Dated _____ By _____

To order, contact—California Association of Realtors®
525 S. Virgil Ave., Los Angeles, California 90020   Page __2__ of __2__ Pages

Addendum (Exhibit A)

To Real Estate Purchase Contract and Receipt for Deposit

dated December 1 in which RICHARD ROEONE and ELSIE ROEONE are referred to as Buyer and X. L. LANDLORD is referred to as Seller.

Included in the purchase is all personal property appurtenant to or used in the operation of the premises, the plumbing, heating, lighting fixtures, 7 gas ranges, 7 refrigerators, all shades, screens, blinds, curtain rods and fixtures, drapes, blinds, awnings, wall-to-wall carpets, hall carpets, and all other furniture and furnishings situated herein and belonging to the Seller and not to the tenants, except all furniture and furnishings in Apartment No. 3. A complete inventory shall be delivered to Buyer within 5 days of Seller's acceptance hereof. Seller shall deliver title to the above by Bill of Sale free of all liens and encumbrances.

The purchase price stated herein is allocated as follows: Real property $86,000.00, personal property $6,500.00. The parties agree that this agreement is indivisible even though separate considerations have been stated for the real property and the personal property.

Dated: _____   _____
                                                                Buyer

Dated: _____   _____
                                                                Seller

Addendum (Exhibit B)

To Real Estate Purchase Contract and Receipt for Deposit

dated December 1 in which RICHARD ROEONE and ELSIE ROEONE are referred to as Buyer and X. L. LANDLORD is referred to as Seller.

Buyer will deposit in escrow the balance of purchase price as follows:

$ 5,750.00 within *3 days* of Seller's acceptance hereof as additional deposit. The total deposits hereunder shall be subject to all of the applicable terms and conditions of Paragraph 12 hereof.

$13,500.00, in cash, Buyer's certified check, or cashier's check made payable to the order of escrow holder delivered at least one day before close of escrow in addition to the above deposits.

$61,815.00, conditioned upon Buyer's ability to take title subject to the existing loan of record with George Gotrocks, with a balance in that approximate amount, payable over a remaining term of approximately 18 years at $503.94, monthly, including interest at not to exceed 7% per annum, providing prepayment privilege upon payment of 1% of original principal, and containing no due on sale clause.

$10,685.00 by Buyer executing a note and a Deed of Trust in that amount in favor of Seller secured by subject property payable in equal monthly installments of $000.00, or more, including interest at the rate of 00% per annum, due in full in five years from close of escrow. Said Note and Deed of Trust shall be drawn on the standard forms No. 125 and 137 of Goldedge Security Title Guaranty Company.

Any adjustment in existing balance in loan to be assumed by Buyer including reduction of principal through obligatory payments, shall be made in the principal amount of the second loan to Seller.

Dated: _____   _____
                                                                                    Buyer

Dated: _____   _____
                                                                                    Seller

Addendum (Exhibit C)

To Real Estate Purchase Contract and
Receipt for Deposit

dated December 1 in which RICHARD ROEONE and ELSIE ROEONE are referred to as Buyer and X. L. LANDLORD is referred to as Seller.

Other terms and conditions:

a) Within 3 days from date of Seller's acceptance hereof, seller shall deliver to Buyer an operating statement for the 12 month period ending November 30, 19XX showing the gross rentals received to be no less than $14,400.00 and the total operating expenses to be no more than $4,700.00 and warrant that said statement is true and correct. Said statement is subject to buyer's approval, and Buyer may cancel this agreement if said statement is unsatisfactory to him. If said statement is not disapproved in writing within 3 days of receipt, this condition shall be deemed waived.

b) This offer is subject to Buyer's inspection and approval of all apartments situated on the herein described property within 3 days from date of Seller's acceptance hereof. It is further subject to approval by Buyer within the same time period of a schedule containing a list of the apartments, the names of the tenants occupying each, and the length of such occupancy, the amount of rent, copies of current rental agreements and leases. Said schedule and attachments shall be delivered to Buyer upon Seller's acceptance hereof. Seller warrants that said schedule is a complete list of all rental agreements and leases listed in the schedule. If either the physical inspection or the examination of said schedule and attachments disclose conditions or information unsatisfactory to the Buyer, he may cancel this agreement.

If the apartments or the schedule and attachments or both are not disapproved in writing within 3 days of Seller's acceptance hereof these conditions shall be deemed waived.

c) Security deposits, if any, deposited by tenants according to the terms of the rental agreements or leases, to the extent they have not been applied by the Seller in accordance with such agreements, shall be turned over to the Buyer by the Seller upon close of escrow. The Buyer hereby agrees to indemnify and hold the Seller harmless from liability for the proper application or return of such deposits to the respective tenants in accordance with the terms of the leases and rental agreements.

d) This offer is conditioned upon the close of Escrow No. 5784 with Goldedge Security Title Guaranty Company on or before December 8, 19XX.

e) The Seller agrees that prior to the date set for closing he will at his own cost and expense repair and properly fix the following: 1) The gate leading to the back enclosure including painting same in a matching color. 2) Repair broken shower door in Apartment No. 2.

Dated: _____   _____
                                                                    Buyer

Dated: _____   _____
                                                                    Seller

New Investment Property Form

CAR's Investment Property form (DLIP-14) should make it easier to prepare contracts for the sale of income property. The form will need supplements for specific problems tailored to the particular investment property using clauses found in this book.

Chapter 2
Stating the Deposit and Price, and Describing the Property

If the contract of sale is prepared by the broker for the Seller, ambiguities will be interpreted against the Seller.

Nakatsukasa v. Wade,
128 CA2d 86;274 P2d 918

Most contract forms begin with the place and date of entering into the contract. The right place should be named in full; and the date, of course, should be correct.

The matter of filling in dates does not seem too complicated. Nevertheless, common mistakes are incorrect dates or failure to insert the date of seller's acceptance in the acceptance paragraph or in the counter-offers. The seller's acceptance date is significant because it is used as a reference point in calculating time for performance of any provisions in the contract. When counter-offers go back and forth the final acceptance date becomes particularly important.

Identifying the Parties

In most printed real estate forms the buyer is the first party to be named; this first mention occurs where the receipt for "earnest money" deposit is acknowledged. In the Model Form, the blank calls for the name or names of the buyers. Since the Model Form is a receipt for money as well as a purchase contract, it must acknowledge the receipt of the deposit from the person(s) named. The Model Form is unique in that it contains a separate space for specifying how the buyer wants to take title. This specification permits the taking of a deposit from a person who may not be the ultimate title holder.

The concept of making out a receipt for deposit seems quite simple. However, in a real estate transaction the proper identification of the party who is designated the buyer is crucial. Therefore, in most situations the receipt should be addressed to all the parties who are acquiring an interest in the property. For example, most brokers consider it poor practice to accept a deposit from a married person when the spouse who is to join in taking title does not sign the contract. In the event of a breach of contract, enforcing the contract against only one spouse may be difficult. Similarly, the seller may prefer that anyone who is intended to take title to the property should be included and designated as buyer, so that the subject's rights and duties in the contract are established. (We will discuss the problems of the seller later.) It is also good practice to specify the marital status of the buyers as "John Doe and Jane Doe, his wife," or "John Doe, an unmarried man (not now married)," or "Tom Buyer, a single man (never married)," or "Louise Alone, a widow," and so forth.

When writing in the names of the buyers, be sure to spell them correctly. Do not take it for granted that a man named Smith spells his name that way. Nothing irritates people more than having their names misspelled.

Find out how the client normally takes title to real property or enters into contracts. Often a person uses an abbreviated first name or nickname so freely that he or she has practically forgotten what the real name is. But a deed should not be written to "Bob Smith" if the client is identified on his birth certificate as "Robert John Smith." Similarity in names often occurs in families, and only middle names or initials may differ. Wherever practicable, use the names best identifying the person for the contract and the deed.

Corporate names should be carefully checked. Partnership names should be determined. Some company names are changed after incorporation. It may be necessary in identifying the corporation to state:

X Y Z Corporation (successor to/formerly known as _____)

(or)

ABC Company, Inc., doing business as _____ .

Determining the Capacity of Parties to Enter into Contracts

Correct spelling, though important, is a minor item compared with determining the capacity of the parties to enter into a contract. In general, infants (minors), insane persons, or drunken persons have limited capacities to contract. A real estate contract made by a minor (an unemancipated person under the age of 18) is void. A person who is officially adjudged insane or incompetent and a person for whom a guardian or conservator of his estate is appointed cannot enter into a contract during the period of the guardianship or conservatorship. Any contract such a person might sign is void.

The power of a corporation to buy or sell real estate may be limited by its certificate of incorporation or its bylaws. These instruments may require the consent of specified persons for the execution of any documents. Also, a corporation can be suspended or dissolved; it may thereby lose the necessary powers to convey property unless it is reinstated in good standing. Sometimes approval of the stockholders is necessary. If any such conditions exist, certified copies of appropriate authorizing resolutions must be presented and made part of the transaction.

Powers of attorney are often used in real estate. These should be carefully examined by counsel to ascertain their validity. Counsel should determine that powers of attorney have not been revoked by bankruptcy, death, assignment, or otherwise. The power of attorney should be recorded as part of the transaction. Where either the buyer or seller is a partnership all necessary partners should be included. It is a precaution well taken to have all partners execute papers, even if one partner can legally bind the partnership. Limited-partnership certificates should be examined to ascertain whether or not the general partner's powers are adequate, or if any limited partners must participate in a conveyance or must give approval. Also, questions as to termination of partnership or restrictions against conveyances may be settled by consulting the partnership agreement.

Sometimes contracts must be approved by a court in order to establish the capacity of the party who is making the transfer. Where there are fiduciaries such as trustees, personal representatives, executors, or trustees in bankruptcy, questions should always be raised as to the date of their appointment and their persent authority to act. Certified copy of the letters of appointment should be obtained, and the present condition of the authority ascertained. When a sale has been authorized by a court, a certified copy of the court order must be recorded to pass title.

Fixing the Identity of "Nominees"

It is common practice in real estate transactions to use a nominee, also called a "strawman" or a "dummy," instead of the real party in interest for the purpose of executing various instruments, beginning with the contract of sale. In the absence of fraud or misrepresentation, the use of a nominee is legitimate; even so, as a Missouri court has said, "Real estate transactions made through strawmen and ghosts should always be viewed with suspicion."[1]

The problems inherent in transferring title to a buyer through a nominee are not solved by allowing the buyer to designate the nominee in the contract with the words "John Doe or nominee." Many courts will not allow specific performance by the nominee against the seller because of uncertainty. It has also been held that the word "nominee" is not synonymous with "assignee."[2] Where an assignee or nominee is to execute a purchase-money mortgage in favor of seller, the matter of the buyer's credit is involved. The seller is generally not obligated to accept performance by a third party, but the cases are not uniform. Even prohibition against assignment has been ignored where the assignee tendered full performance.[3] However, a provision which expressly made the contract void if assigned has been upheld.[4] Because legal and tax problems may arise, brokers should be extremely careful in preparing contracts from "buyers or nominee" or "buyers or his assigns" without advising the parties to see legal counsel.

Where legitimate reasons for the use of nominees exist the contract should be specifically drawn by counsel to so provide. The right to assign the contract is involved in the use of the wording "or assignee." (See also Chapter 4 under "Assignment.")

Entering the Deposit and Medium of Payment

The next line in the Model Form reads:

"the sum of _____ Dollars ($_____) evidenced by cash □, cashiers check □, or _____, personal check □ payable to _____ to be held uncashed until acceptance of this offer, as deposit on account of purchase price of _____ Dollars, ($_____). . . .

In this space initial deposit is shown and the medium of payment of the deposit specified by placing an "X" in the appropriate box, or describing in the space provided any other form the deposit has taken. In California brokers are subject to disciplinary action if they fail to show in what manner a deposit has been received.[5] Furthermore, they must also comply with a regulation of the Real Estate Commissioner which demands delivery of the check to the named payee (this includes escrow and title companies), or the principal or agent of the named payee within the next business day following receipt.

California brokers are allowed to hold an uncashed check after the acceptance of an offer when directed to do so by either buyer or seller. The fact that the check is being held in uncashed form should be specifically disclosed to the seller or offeree before the offer is accepted.[6] If the monies or check are not to be deposited in a neutral depositary or into the hands of a principal, brokers in California must maintain a trust account in which all funds entrusted to them must be deposited.[7]

If a buyer's check is postdated or is not to be cashed before a certain date, the broker should exhibit the deposit check to the seller, who must give consent in writing to hold the check uncashed in accordance with the buyer's instructions.

Postdated checks can be shown in the space after the word "or" in the Model Form, but the word "or" should first be deleted and replaced with "postdated, subject to collection." A clause which can be used either in the Model Form or in forms without identification boxes is shown in Form 2:01.

FORM 2:01   POSTDATED CHECKS

$_____ Evidenced by cash □, cashier's check □, or _____, personal check □ payable to _____, _____
                                        subject to collection—check not to be deposited or
_____.
cashed before _____ 19_____

COMMENT ON FORM 2:01: The seller should indicate acceptance of this provision by initialing the notation. The seller should then be informed when the check has been cashed and the funds deposited either in the trust account of the seller's representative or in a neutral escrow.

A personal check can be made payable either to the seller, his agent, or a neutral escrow company or title company. Sophisticated sellers refuse to accept third-party checks from individuals. A cashier's check or treasurer's check should be made out either to the escrow company or to the trust account of the seller's representative. It is always good practice, whenever a personal check is received, to delete the word "or" in the Model Form clause and insert the words "subject to collection." A deposit should never be returned before the original check has cleared the buyer's bank.

Allowing for Notes as Deposits

The "or _____" blank in the Model Form is provided for other types of deposits. Short-term promissory notes made payable to the seller or the seller's agent are very often used. Usually, the note is for not more than thirty days, and the form used is a straight note carrying nominal interest. The description of such a note can be entered as in Form 2:02.

FORM 2:02   **PROMISSORY NOTE AS DEPOSIT**

$_____ evidenced by cash □ cashier's check □ or,

_____ a _____
                                                       days

_____
promissory straight note bearing interest at _____% per annum

_____ .
executed in favor of _____
                                        seller/broker

COMMENT ON FORM 2:02: The note should be exhibited to the seller, and the seller should indicate his or her consent to the holding of the deposit in the form of a note by initialing the above provision. When the note has been paid, the seller should be informed of the disposition of the cash deposit. (For a form of note commonly used, see Form 2:03.)

Some brokers use a special note form as deposit. The note is usually made payable to the broker and is for a limited period of time. A sample note is shown in Form 2:03.

FORM 2:03   **NOTE FOR DEPOSIT**

$_____

                              _____ , California
                              _____ , 19____

(Form continues on next page)

_____ days after date (without grace) I/We promise to pay to the order of _____

_____

_____ Dollars

for value received with interest of _____ %

per annum from _____

until paid. Both principal and interest payable only in lawful money of the United States. I/we understand that by executing this note that I/we are causing said real property described in a separate instrument to be removed from the real estate market. And in case suit is instituted to collect this note or any portion thereof, I/we promise to pay such additional sum as the court may adjudge reasonable as attorney's fees and costs.

Payable at _____ , California.

_____

Due _____ , 19_____

COMMENT ON FORM 2:03: This form includes a statement that the buyer understands that he or she is "causing said real property described in a separate instrument to be removed from the real estate market." No appellate case has been found showing the enforceability of such a note standing alone. It would appear that the note is subject to the contract's provisions pertaining to damages in case of buyer's default.

A buyer's performance of the contract is most often unrelated to the type of deposit given. If the transaction is otherwise acceptable to the buyer, the size, type, or character of the deposit is usually unimportant. However, most sellers require deposits in the belief that the transaction is more likely to be concluded if the buyer has made a reasonable cash deposit as evidence of good faith. Unless a note is exchanged for cash immediately upon the seller's acceptance, its usefulness in this respect is doubtful.

The mere act of taking a promissory note from the buyer does not constitute the receipt of something of value from the buyer, regardless of the wording of the note. It may constitute an act of inexpensive "good faith," but neither the seller nor the broker should delude themselves into believing that the note presents an independently enforceable right against the buyer if buyer defaults.

Providing for Irrevocable Transfer of Escrow Funds

A buyer may wish to use the proceeds from a pending sale as the deposit or part payment of the purchase price on the offer being made. Assuming that such proceeds are held in escrow, an irrevocable transfer order can be incorporated in the purchase contract receipt for deposit, provided the seller understands the arrangement and approves it, as shown in Form 2:04.

**FORM 2:04   IRREVOCABLE TRANSFER OF ESCROW
FUNDS AS DEPOSIT**

$_____ evidenced by cash ☐, cashier's check ☐, or

_____
in form of an irrevocable transfer from escrow #

_____
at _____ ,
escrow holder

which escrow will close on or about _____, 19_____

(optional continue):

Should said escrow not close by _____, 19_____ buyer's obligation
hereunder shall terminate, and any deposit paid or directed to be paid hereunder
shall be refunded or released to buyer.

COMMENT ON FORM 2:04: The seller or the seller's representative should of
course verify that the named escrow is indeed open and that funds are due from
said escrow and available for closing of the new transaction. The optional
clause permits the buyer to hedge on the bet that the first deal will in fact close.
This plan differs from a purchase conditioned upon sale of the buyer's other
property only by the fact that a sale is pending and a closing of that sale is
expected. (For a form to create an irrevocable transfer order to escrow, see
Form 2:05.)

FORM 2:05   IRREVOCABLE TRANSFER ORDER

_____ 19_____

To: _____
(escrow company)

Gentlemen:
    You are hereby instructed and directed to transfer from _____
(all funds

_____ the sum of $_____, due _____ from proceeds of
due me/us)   me/us

escrow # _____ to escrow # _____ with _____
(name of escrow

_____ company on account of purchase price
company or title company acting as escrow)

for the property situated in _____, county of _____ ,
California, described as:

(Form continues on next page)

(Description)

In consideration of the acceptance by sellers of said property of this order as deposit under the Real Estate Purchase Contract and Receipt for Deposit dated _____, 19__, _____ agree that this order is irrevocable by
                                          I/we
_____.
    me/us

Approved and accepted

_____   _____
        (escrow company)
by _____   _____

COMMENT ON FORM 2:05: This form takes the place of a promissory note. It should be issued in duplicate and, when filed with the escrow, a receipt should be obtained.

Writing in the Purchase Price

The clause ". . . as deposit on account of purchase price of _____ _____ Dollars, ($____)" simply requires that the offeror's price be stated in words and figures. One admonition is appropriate here, however. If the seller does not wish to accept the original price, do not change the purchase price by making deletions or corrections on the face of the contract. It is always bad practice to make changes in written documents above the signatures of other persons unless those persons are immediately available to initial the changes. The correct procedure is to have the seller make a counter-offer, which can be written on the reverse side of the contract or on a special printed counter-offer form. The buyer can then accept the seller's counter-offer and complete the contract.

Allocating the purchase price between land and improvements may be desirable for tax purposes. Designating a specific price for personal property included in the sale is also common so that the buyer can take advantage of higher depreciation rates (see Form 6:03).

Providing Property Description

The "description clause" in the Model Form begins this way: "for the purchase of property, situated in _____ , County of _____ (insert state), _____ , described as follows." The property should be described with sufficient particularity as to be readily identifiable. Aside from the use of the street address, which should not be used by itself, urban lots are commonly described by (1) metes and bounds, or (2) block and lot number. Both methods are acceptable so long as they are accurate. In newer tracts, the description is commonly given by reference to a map which is officially recorded. Acreage is sometimes described by government survey or by reference to an attached map. Any such method is acceptable so long as the description is accurate and precise. Makeshift descriptions must be avoided at all costs. Even if a description is sufficient for the contract but inadequate for a deed,[8] the result of misunderstandings or dispute is litigation.

Contract writers have had trouble with descriptions of land for years. It simply does not pay to be careless in this area of the contract. The Statute of Frauds must be satisfied. Parol evidence to identify described land, is admissible but not to supply the description itself. The test used is whether, on the basis of the written agreement and admissible parol evidence, a surveyor could locate the land and establish boundaries.[9] "The next contiguous thirty acres" has been held to be ambiguous and insufficient, because an acre may have any shape.[10]

Another example of a description deemed insufficient was a case in which the property was described as follows: ". . . a portion of Lot 2, Trinidad-Yorba Tract (approximately 12 acres). Buyer to secure survey of property. . . . Seller to approve said description."[11] Even though the parties physically staked out the land, the court held that the description violated the Statute of Frauds because the particular twelve acres could not be located from the writing.

One frequently used method of describing a portion of a lot shown on a recorded map is to refer to a specific fractional portion of the lot, for example, "the north one-half." Such a description is quite acceptable if the lot is completely rectangular. But if the lot is irregular, the reference to a specific fractional portion creates uncertainty as to where the boundary lines in fact are located. The same uncertainty arises in references to a certain quantity of a lot, for example, "the north one hundred feet," or "the south ten acres." Where division of irregular shaped lots or acreage is to be made by a reference to a fractional or quantitative portion of the property, a statement in clear language showing the intention of the parties should accompany the description, or a metes and bounds land description should be used. Even the initial drafting of a purchase agreement involving a fractional portion or quantity of a parcel of land should not be attempted without qualified and competent advice.

The written-description problem is compounded when the acreage measurement is not absolute. Whenever "more or less" clauses are used in the description, the general rule allows only for minor variances. An unreasonable difference in acreage is material and goes to the essence of the contract. The theory is that where the description contains a wording such as "to contain 140 acres, more or less," the sale is "in gross" and not "by the acre." If a deficiency in acreage is challenged in court, the deficiency must be sufficient to "shock the conscience of the court"; otherwise the buyer is understood to have taken a chance upon the quantity in buying the property.

Buyers should take care to determine whether the sale is, in fact, "in gross" or "by the acre." The safest course for buyers is to insist on a survey and bargain for the acreage they expect to purchase. In the absence of a survey, it is better practice in acreage sales with release clauses to establish either natural or artificial monuments for each parcel to be released, and incorporate in the description such monuments to clearly identify the parcel.

Describing the Property Exactly

The broker or attorney should obtain a preliminary title report, and copy the description carefully. It is important, that the description encompass all of what the seller wishes to sell and the buyer expects to buy.

Of course, buyers cannot be sure of actually getting what they inspected. The possibility of being misled was demonstrated in a case in which the broker directed attention to a certain corner of a forty-acre parcel, while the true corner to be sold was in fact a quarter of a mile south and some distance east of the land shown. The buyer did not discover the deception until he had sold off a parcel and was mistakenly improving a part of the land which did not belong to him. The broker was ordered to pay an "out of pocket loss" of $17,000 to compensate for the reduced value of the property that the buyer actually received.[12] A common complaint in rural sales in particular is that brokers and sellers often do not know the actual boundary lines. When fences and survey lines are not the same, the "doctrine of agreed boundary" may apply. The doctrine "requires that there be an uncertainty as to the true boundary line, an agreement between the coterminnous owners fixing the line, and acceptance and acquiescence in the line so fixed for a period equal to the statute of limitations or under such circumstances that substantial loss would be caused by change of its position."[13] It is never safe to guess.

Contracts Subject to Surveys

Where an exact amount of acreage is to be determined by a survey, Form 2:06 can be used.

FORM 2:06   EXACT ACREAGE DETERMINED BY SURVEY

The acreage to be sold shall be determined by a survey to be made by a licensed surveyor selected by a buyer at the expense of _____
                                                    buyer/jointly by buyer and seller/seller
Seller reserves right to have another survey at seller's choice and expense. Any material difference between the two surveys shall be referred to arbitration under the Rules of the American Arbitration Association.

COMMENT ON FORM 2:06: The selection of Arbitration to clear up differences may be advisable. The rules of the American Arbitration Association are available on request from the Association's local offices in major cities.

Because so many owners never have had their property surveyed, they do not know whether neighboring buildings are encroaching or whether their own buildings are encroaching on adjoining land. In large cities where intensive land development is occurring, title lines shown on title searches sometimes vary from the actual physical structure. Such variations may make the title unmarketable or uninsurable. Many sellers' attorneys insist, where there is no survey available, that the buyer take title "subject to any state of facts an accurate survey may show." Or the proposed clause may read, "subject to a survey dated _____, 19____, made by _____ , and to any state of facts the said survey, brought down to date, will show." Both clauses are unacceptable to cautious buyers and their attorneys. To effectively nullify the condition, they may wish to add the words, "provided the same does not render the title unmarketable."

It is not unusual for a seller to present an old survey and request that it be incorporated into the contract. The buyer should accept this request only on condition that any additional facts which may be disclosed by bringing the survey up to date do not make the title unmarketable. This provision may be expressed as in Form 2:07.

FORM 2:07   **UP-DATED SURVEY**

Subject to a survey dated _____ 19_____ made

by _____
                              name of surveyor
and to any state of fact the said survey, brought down to date, will show, provided such additional facts disclosed in such survey by reason of having been brought down to date will not render title _____ .
                                                     unmarketable/uninsurable

COMMENT ON FORM 2:07: If a survey shows any defects which raise doubts as to the marketability of title, the buyers need legal and practical advice which will allow them to determine the extent of the business risk they may be taking by accepting the property with the defect. Buyers can sometimes obtain protection in the form of title insurance for the life of the building.

Providing for a Survey

Where a survey may be desirable in urban areas, the buyer can reserve an option to obtain such survey by inserting a provision in the contract (Form 2:08).

FORM 2:08   **SURVEY OPTION IN BUYER**

The buyer shall have the right to have the property surveyed at _____
his/her
own expense prior to closing date. If the survey shows any encroachments on the
land herein described or that the improvements located on the land herein described encroach on other land, written notice to that effect shall be given to the
seller who shall have _____
days/the same time as the contract allows to cure defects in title
to remove such encroachments.

  If the seller shall fail to remove said encroachments or defects within said
period of time, then, at the option of the buyer the deposit shall be returned to
buyer and this contract shall be terminated, and both parties be released of all
obligations thereunder.

COMMENT ON FORM 2:08: This clause gives the buyer the right to send a
surveyor onto the property at his or her own expense. If the buyer is obtaining
a loan from a mortgagee which demands an American Land Title Association
title insurance policy where available, the survey may not be an added expense,
because a survey is normally required before such policy can be issued. The
buyer, however, should examine the survey. If the encroachments are minor, a
title insuror may still insure the lender.

  The Model Form makes no provision for time allowed to correct title
objections; therefore, in using the above clause a time limitation for the correction of any encroachments should be inserted. Aerial surveys are often used to
supplement ground surveys.

Warranty by Seller

  Sophisticated buyers may place the whole burden upon the seller by demanding a warranty against encroachments. This device is acceptable where the
seller is a responsible person or organization from whom recovery can be had in
the event of breach of warranty. But where the seller could move away and
disappear, such warranty is inadequate. Where there is a possibility of future
dispute over boundary lines, the buyer should insist that the seller provide a
survey and a title insurance policy protecting the buyer specifically against
encroachments. Form 2:09 provides a clause for warranty by the seller.

FORM 2:09   **SELLER'S WARRANTY AGAINST**
                       ENCROACHMENTS

Seller warrants that the improvements on the subject property are within the lines of the subject property, that there are no encroachments on the subject property, and that no person has any right, title or interest in the subject property other than disclosed in the preliminary title report except _____

list exceptions

_____
as rights of tenants in possession under existing rental agreements or leases copies of which have been

_____
exhibited to buyer and approved by buyer.

COMMENT ON FORM 2:09: Before making such representations, the seller should be advised by counsel about the extent of liability under such a warranty. The above clause should be supplemented by a "survival" clause to protect the buyer (see Form 4:46). Where a buyer obtains an extended-coverage title insurance and the parties are willing to pay the additional premium, sticking to the insurance coverage is preferable to warranty. Following this course will necessitate deleting the reference in CAR's form to the Standard California Land Title Association policy and providing for the proper type of title insurance coverage by a special provision in the contract.

Special Agreements

"Party walls" are walls common to two separately owned buildings, and they can create many problems. Sales of property subject to party-wall agreements should be referred to the buyer's attorney. The attorney should examine the agreement and apprise the buyer of rights and obligations thereunder. The property description in the contract should refer to the party-wall agreement. Common driveways, fences, drains, and gutters should also be included in the contract, and the deed may specifically be made subject to any agreement between the seller and the adjoining landowner. Title searches often disclose the existence of such agreements. These should be carefully examined, especially if they appear not to have been drawn by legal counsel. If easements or mining, mineral, or water rights are to be reserved to the seller the contract should so provide, but a broker should not attempt to draw such purely legal provisions.

Alternative Introductions to Legal Descriptions in Contracts

The contract writer has many responsibilities in connection with drafting an accurate description. Some of these cannot be discharged by the writer alone. For example, if the seller wishes to sell only a portion of the property owned and if the land is not divided into described lots, or if an easement is to be granted or reserved in the sale, then the services of a knowledgeable real estate attorney, title expert, and surveyor are called for. Before a sales agreement is prepared the boundaries of the parcel or easement should be determined and described by these experts. A survey and a physical inspection of the property to be described are often necessary. The cost of the survey and inspection should be measured against the possible damages that could result if an incorrect description is created without them.

Forms 2:10 through 2:14 provide clauses for some of the most common ways of handling descriptions in the "Real Estate Purchase Contract and Receipt for Deposit." The clauses all point up the necessity for accuracy.

FORM 2:10   STREET ADDRESS DESCRIPTION

Lot and improvement commonly known and designated as _____

_____, _____,
            number and street name   city
State of _____.

(optional)

Legal description to be furnished by _____.
                                              preliminary report

COMMENT ON FORM 2:10: Some contract writers simply state after the street address, "Legal description to be delivered to escrow." This is unsatisfactory. If the buyer is to approve the legal description, either expressly by agreement or impliedly, it may be a better practice to incorporate a reference to the title report to be delivered under the terms of the contract. The approval of the preliminary report or an abstract of title includes an approval of the description as shown in writing and on any attached map.

FORM 2:11   SAME DESCRIPTION AS IN A DEED

(After description by metes and bounds)

..... being the same premises conveyed to the seller by deed dated _____,
19___, and recorded _____, 19___, in Official Records of the _____,
                                                                          city
County of _____, _____, in _____ No. _____ at _____
                        state   book/reel   page/image
No. _____ as instrument No. _____.

COMMENT ON FORM 2:11: Unless some change of boundaries has been made or the amount of property to be conveyed is different, the same description under which the seller received title is often used in the contract by reference to a certain deed. This method of referral is ordinarily both practical and safe, and eliminates errors in description. Unfortunately, not all sellers have good memories, and sometimes a seller may have forgotten about a transaction in which a corner or an easement has been deeded away. The seller should always be asked if the deed presented is the only deed to the property, since sometimes the original conveyance may have been made through two or more deeds issued either at the same time or on different occasions.

FORM 2:12   **DESCRIPTION CLAUSES**

A: Metes and Bounds:

All that real property and the improvements thereon situated in _____ _____, County of _____, State of _____, being more particularly described as follows:

(insert metes and bounds description)

B: By Reference to a Specific Map:

All that real property and the improvements thereon situated in the _____ _____, County of _____, State of _____, being more particularly described as follows: Lot _____, Block No. _____ _____ tract, recorded 19_____ _____ _____ in _____ County records Map Book No. _____, page _____, also known and designated as _____ Street, _____ ,
                                                                              city

_____ .
         state

COMMENT ON FORM 2:12: Careful contract drafting calls for proper legal descriptions and the avoidance of makeshift descriptions. Where a street-address description is used, reference should be made to the correct legal description, as shown in Form 2:13.

FORM 2:13   **DESCRIPTION**

Lot and improvements commonly known as _____ Street, _____ , _____, more particularly
                    city   state
described in the attached _____
                          deed/title insurance policy # _____
_____ consisting of a _____
preliminary title report # _____   _____story residence/apartment
_____ and _____
house/commercial building/etc.   outbuildings/garage

COMMENT ON FORM 2:13: The description above may be the ideal. However, the original documents mentioned here are not always available. With modern photocopy equipment this problem is easily solved. If the seller has the original, it should be copied and a copy made available to the buyer.

FORM 2:14   COMMUNITY APARTMENT DESCRIPTION

The proprietary lease of Apt. #_____ located in the Community Apartment-house described as _____ together with _____ shares of said corporation allocated to that apartment.

(optional)

Buyer shall have _____ days after seller's acceptance to inspect the current financial statements of the corporation, the condition of its title, to examine and agree to be bound by its articles of incorporation and bylaws, the stockholder's lease and all other documents relevant to the sale. If these documents are not disapproved in writing within _____ days of receipt, this condition shall be deemed waived.

Seller shall have _____ days after seller's acceptance to obtain approval of the sale by the corporate stockholders, its Board of Directors or other proper authority of the corporation empowered to approve sales of leases and shares in the corporation. If within the period stated above such approval has not been obtained this agreement shall terminate and the deposit be returned to buyer.

FORM 2:15   CONDOMINIUM DESCRIPTION

Unit #_____ as shown on that certain Subdivision Map and Condominium Plan entitled "_____" filed for Record in the Office of the Recorder of _____ County, California, on _____ 19_____, in Book _____ of Maps, at page _____ together with _____ percent (_____%) undivided interest in Project Common Area _____ as shown on said Map and Plan together with parking space(s) _____
and subject to the easements, covenants and other reservations as set
_____.
forth in the Grant Deed by which said interest in subject property will be conveyed

(optional [required in California])

Buyer has received as part of this contract copies of the following documents:

(a) Declaration of Covenants and Restrictions, recorded _____, 19_____, in Official Records of the County of _____ in Book _____ at page _____ establishing the Rights and Duties of _____ _____ Association of which buyer upon passing of title shall automatically become a member.

(b) Declaration Establishing a Plan of Condominium Ownership recorded _____, 19_____, in Official Records of _____ County, in Book _____ at page _____.

(Form continues on next page)

  (c) The Articles of Incorporation and Bylaws of _____ Home
Association and its up-to-date statement of the amount of delinquent or
uncollected assessments, penalties, attorneys fees and other charges,
if any, on the unit.

  (d) A copy of the most current financial statements received by seller.

  (e) Sellers or Homeowners Association's statement of any extraordinary or
repair expenses and any pending litigation affecting the condominium
project.

  (f) The Grant Deed by which the above-described interests in property are
to be conveyed.

(If resale of one of two or more units, continue:)

  (g) Condominium public report, amended _____, 19_____.

(Optional)

The above documents are subject to buyer's approval, which shall not be
unreasonably withheld. If not disapproved in writing within _____ days of receipt,
this condition shall be deemed waived.

COMMENT ON FORM 2:15: This clause meets the requirement for a description of an existing unit which should be copied from the deed when possible. It
conforms to California Civil Code § 1360 and other relevant laws.

Many people purchase more than one unit in original project. Offering for
resale or long term lease of one of two or more units automatically cast the
owner and his agent in the role of subdivider. This requires that the buyer *must*
receive a copy of an amended public report and sign a receipt for it before
entering into a contract to purchase or a long term lease.

Access Roads and Easements

Other description problems in contracts arise with regard to the exact
location of access roads to public roads. Where an offer is being made to
purchase a parcel of a larger acreage, the preliminary clause shown in Form
2:15 can be useful. This clause should be inserted when, at the time of writing
the contract, a legal description indicating the exact location of access roads or
easements for ingress and egress is not available.

FORM 2:16   **ACCESS ROAD WARRANTY**

Seller warrants that the title conveyed to buyer includes legal access rights
from the most accessible public road to the building sites on the subject property.
Such access roads shall include, but not be limited to, existing access roads to
building sites in existence, if any, at time of conveyance.

COMMENT ON FORM 2:16: This clause inserted in the offer alerts the seller to his responsibility to provide access rights to a parcel being carved out of a larger plot. The careful seller may counteroffer with a specific representation describing in detail the exact location of access rights which will be included in the deed. Such descriptions should be prepared by a licensed engineer and surveyor and also checked by the title underwriter.

When Long Descriptions Are Necessary

Where a long legal description is necessary, it is advisable to photocopy the description from the original instrument rather than copying it manually. Photocopying insures against mistakes. But if the instrument cannot be incorporated into the contract or if photocopy equipment is not available, a long description can be written either on the back of the contract or on a separate addendum properly incorporated in the agreement. Since there is little room on a printed contract form for an extensive legal description, the space that is allowed can be used for reference clauses such as, "Described as set forth on the reverse side hereof," or "Said description is incorporated herein by reference." If a separate sheet is needed, use this wording: "Described as set forth in Exhibit A, attached hereto and incorporated herein by reference."

In either case, the incorporated description should be initialed by all parties and dated to avoid later claims of alteration.

Regardless of whether the description is long or short, it must be accurate. There really is no excuse for incorporating into the contract an inadequate description of the property to be sold.

A Checklist for Identifying Buyer, the Deposit and Property Description

1. State the correct location and date.
2. Spell the buyer's name correctly and use the style of name which is to be inserted in the instrument of conveyance.
3. Name all buyers if there are more than one.
4. If the buyer is a corporation or partnership, state the correct name. Partnerships should be identified by the names of partners.
5. Always obtain an adequate deposit, and properly identify the medium of payment.
6. The purchase price should be given in words and figures.
7. The description should be adequate to identify the property.
8. Whenever possible use photocopied descriptions taken from the orignal instrument or from title insurance policies.
9. Separately drawn descriptions either on the reverse side of the contract or on an addendum should be incorporated in the text by a reference, and should be dated and initialed by the parties.

Chapter 3
The "Terms of Payment" Clause

The Realtor, for the protection of all parties shall see that financial obligations and commitments regarding real estate transactions are in writing, expressing the exact agreement of the parties. A copy of such agreement shall be furnished to each party upon his signing such agreement.

Article 20, Code of Ethics
National Association of Realtors

The single most important part of the agreement between buyer and seller begins innocently enough in the modular CAR Real Estate Purchase Contract and Receipt for Deposit. "Buyer will deposit in escrow with ____ ____, the balance of the purchase price as follows. . . ." Into the space that follows go all terms and conditions of the sale.

The legal size CAR form contains "precooked" financing clauses. It may suffice with minor amendments in very simple transactions.

Where the terms of the sale are complicated, an addendum can be attached to the contract. All the terms and conditions of the sale can then be written in the addendum. In such situations, insert a reference and delete the boiler plate: "See addendum 'A' attached hereto and made a part hereof by reference."

What Is Escrow?

The CAR forms provides a blank for the designation of an escrow holder with whom moneys and conveyances documents will be deposited. An "escrow holder" is an agent of the parties to an escrow. As defined by the California Financial Code Section 17003, escrow means any transaction wherein one person, for the purpose of effecting the sale, transfer, encumbering, or leasing of real or personal property to another person, delivers any written instrument, money, evidence of title to real or personal property, or other thing of value to a third person to be held by such third person until the happening of a specified event or the performance of a prescribed condition, when it is then to be delivered by such third person to a grantee, grantor, promisee, promisor, obligee, obligor, bailee, bailor, or any agent or employee of any of the latter.

In California, independent or broker-connected escrow companies and title companies handle the escrow in most sales. The blank space in the terms-of-payment clause indicating the escrow holder should, of course, be filled in with either the name of the designated escrow company or the name of the title company. It is careless to insert the words "any licensed escrow company," since the financial worth and stability of the company is important.

Selecting or designating the escrow agent or the title company which is to issue the title insurance policy and other related services is the prerogative of the principals (the seller and buyer). Brokers or lenders of "federally related loans" have no legal right to demand that the services be performed by any particular company. Such action might also be construed as restraint of trade. However, the brokers may recommend a particular company provided they clearly disclose that they have financial interest in such company if this is the case. Where two brokers are involved in the sale, the transaction should not be placed in jeopardy because the brokers do not see eye to eye as to which escrow or title company should handle the matter.

As a practical rule of thumb, many brokers feel that where sellers have no financial reason for selecting the title company—for example, where they are not carrying any loan to be insured—buyers should have the absolute right to select the escrow company and title company. In all other situations the selection should be as the parties agree. Practically speaking, however, most principals are not knowledgeable about the merits of escrow companies and title policies, and have no way of determining whether one company might give better service or charge less than another. Usually, therefore, the selection is left either to the listing broker or the selling broker. In this event the broker's decision must be based on what is best for the principal, not what may be economically advantageous to the agent making the selection.

An Expanded Escrow Clause

In many places, escrow services are usually available from bank and trust companies as well as escrow companies. Attorneys also often act as escrow holders. When escrow is being held by either type of agent, a more comprehensive escrow clause is often used (see Form 3:01).

FORM 3:01   **"ESCROW" CLAUSE**

Within _____ days from the seller's acceptance hereof

_____ shall open an escrow with
                    seller/buyer/both parties/broker

_____
                    name and address of escrow holder

and both parties shall execute instructions providing for closing within
_____ days from seller's acceptance hereof, subject to written extensions
signed by both parties. Failure by any party to execute instructions within the time
prescribed shall be deemed a breach of this agreement. Should both parties fail
to execute instructions, this agreement shall be deemed rescinded, and all
moneys and documents paid or delivered hereunder shall be returned to the party
from whom derived.

COMMENT ON FORM 3:01: This clause sets limits for performance by the
parties, thereby avoiding the law imposing requirements of "reasonable time."
Combined with a time-of-the-essence clause in the contract the time for performance is fixed.

The Importance of Careful Drafting

In describing the terms of payment or the terms of the sale, the price, the
method of payment, and the amount of cash should be stated clearly and pre-
cisely. It must also be specified whether or not the deposit is part of the cash
down payment. If the deposit is to be increased upon the seller's acceptance,
this must be indicated too.

Most buyers who have need of financing to purchase can buy only if they
are successful in obtaining the financing. This complicates setting up the terms
of the transaction since the condition must be clearly stated to avoid defenses of
uncertainty. The minimum amount of the loan, the interest rate, and whether the
loan is of the variable-interest variety should be clearly set out. Also, the maximum amount of the first loan to which a seller is willing to subordinate his or
her junior loan should be given together with maximum interest rate and amortization and term of loan. Set-up charges, prepayment penalties, and the lender's
identity should also appear in the contract as well as loan guarantees from
federal or state governments where appropriate. A time limitation on the
buyer's effort to obtain financing should be incorporated, along with provisions
for termination of the contract if either buyer or seller fails to obtain the necessary financing. "Escalator," "dragnet" (or "omnibus"), and "acceleration"
clauses in either existing or contemplated loans should be carefully examined,
and provisions providing adequate protection should be made part of the agreement.

The buyer will undoubtedly wish to maintain the utmost flexibility in the transaction, while the seller will probably be hesitant to "tie up" the property by an uncommitted buyer. The seller may actively seek to protect against the possibility that the buyer will use the financing clause as an escape hatch. Given these conflicting interests, the contract writer must take particular care with the terms-of-payment clause, perhaps more than at any other point in the drafting process.

Pitfalls of "Terms of Payment" Clauses

It is in the area of terms of payment that the courts have had to cope with the most inadequately drawn contracts. Quite often, the terms are not fully stated or are not determined or even discussed effectively by the parties. Such contracts are unenforceable, because a material element of the contract has been left out. Many Deposit Receipts are in effect only "agreements to agree"; they are often left vague or incomplete because a later contract appears to be intended. A typical example is a contract which gives the buyer a right of first refusal at a price or on terms "to be agreed upon." Or, if a price is mentioned, the contract may fail to state the amount of installments in which the purchase-money deed of trust is to be paid.[1]

Contracts which leave out the interest rate and maturity date are also considered too uncertain and indefinite to be specifically enforced.[2] A court will not make a new contract for the parties. The contract must be enforced according to its terms or not at all. Deferred payments must be specifically expressed in a "purchase money" mortgage both as to interest and maturity. Courts will also refuse to enforce a contract where important details of third-party financing are missing.[3]

It has been held however, that in a sale, which as to the seller is a cash sale a buyer can waive a provision for specific financing, if it is inserted in the contract solely for the buyer's benefit. Thus an otherwise incomplete contract may be saved by a permissible waiver.[4]

The method of securing the deferred payments must also be shown in the contract for it to be enforceable. It was not cured in a California case in which the deferred payments were to be secured in a manner "satisfactory to seller's attorney."[5]

Necessary Information for the "Terms of Payment" Clause

No sales contract can be drawn without a complete terms-of-payment clause. But to draft such a clause the agent needs specific information. Why not make it easy? A broker can get the information—*all* the information—at the time the property is listed. In order to draft the terms-of-payment clause, the contract writer will need the answers to the questions below. The broker taking the listing can incorporate this information as a matter of course.

1. What is the full cash down payment? Does the amount include or exclude the deposit?

2. Is the deposit to be increased?

3. Who holds existing loans? What are the loan numbers?

4. What are the exact balances on the existing loans?

5. When are payments due, in what amount, and at what rate of interest? Is the interest variable or "adjustable"?

6. Can the loans be assumed or taken "subject to"?

7. Are there "acceleration" clauses (due on sale, or early due dates on the loans)?

8. Are there prepayment penalty clauses?

9. What fees will be charged for assumption? Will interest rates be raised, and if so to what rate? Any other changes? Variable-interest or "adjustable" note substitution?

10. Can copies of notes and deeds of trust or mortgages on all existing loans be obtained?

11. Are payment books or loan statements available for checking?

12. What loan commitments are available from conventional lenders?

13. Does the property qualify for a VA or FHA loan or other federal or state insured loan program?

14. To what extent is the seller willing to finance the transaction?

15. What are the seller's terms for such financing?

16. Will the seller sell on an installment-land-contract basis or does he or she wish to pass title immediately and take back a loan?

17. Is outside secondary financing available? What are the terms, points, and prepayment provisions?

Types of Financing

Once the buyer's offering price and the down payment the buyer will or can pay have been established, the terms of financing can be determined. The terms will fall into one of the following categories:

1. All cash to seller, regardless of existing or prospective financing.

2. Cash above existing loan or loans either to be assumed or taken "subject to."

3. Sales financed by FHA, GI loans or other veterans loans.

4. Cash above new conventional loan; no secondary financing.

5. Cash above new conventional loan with secondary financing to be carried by seller or third party.

6. Cash above loan to be carried by seller; problems of tax-installment sale may exist.

7. Seller finances through use of "wrap-around" or "all inclusive trust deed."

8. Seller finances through the use of an installment land contract.

9. Miscellaneous. For example: some cash, unsecured note, transfer of personal property (car, boat, tools, and the like) to seller; assignment of note secured by deed of trust or mortgage on other property plus purchase-money mortgage financing; buyer either assumes existing conventional loan or takes out a new conventional loan with or without secondary financing.
A standard clause for each of these categories is suggested below. The problems involved under each category are discussed separately.

All Cash to Seller

If the buyer says, "I want to offer the seller $50,000 cash," does that mean that the buyer has $50,000 and wants to pay it? Or does it mean the buyer has, for example, $25,000 and is counting on assuming the existing loan of $25,000? Or does it mean the buyer will arrange financing but does not want to make those arrangements a condition of the sale? Before the agreement can be drawn the answers to those questions must be available.

If the buyer has the cash and wants to use it, or if he or she is not concerned about financing as a condition, obviously the answer is "all cash to seller" without reservations of any kind.

A very simplistic way of expressing such a transaction is:

$_____, all cash to seller _____ .
    including/in addition to above deposit

A more useful clause is shown in Form 3:02. The advantage of the latter clause is its adaptability to all transactions wherein a cash down payment is involved.

FORM 3:02   THE CASH DOWN PAYMENT

Buyer will deposit in escrow with _____

the balance of the purchase price as follows:

$_____ cash, _____ above deposit,
             including/in addition to

_____ .

COMMENT ON FORM 3:02: This clause, which could be called the "all cash to seller" clause, is also used as the initial clause in every terms-of-payment clause where the cash is only part of the sales price. In that situation this clause is followed by the amount, type, and terms of financing which, together with the cash down payment, makes up the total sales price.

Form 3:02 only indicates the amount of the cash involved. It does not specify the actual medium of payment or when payment is to be made. Form 3:03 is more specific.

FORM 3:03   **MEDIUM OF PAYMENT**

Buyer will deposit in escrow with _____ the
balance of the purchase price as follows: $_____ in cash, certified check or
cashier's check _____ above

including/in addition to

deposit _____.

on demand of escrow/on delivery of deed

COMMENT ON FORM 3:03: In most standard situations to be handled by
experienced escrow holders such specificity may not be necessary. However,
there are good reasons for specifying the medium and the time of payment
because of the technical complications which can arise at time of closing.

Cash and cashier's or treasurer's checks drawn on substantial banks are
equally good. But the suitability of a certified check depends upon who orders
the certification. If the maker obtains the certification, normal banking practice
allows him or her to stop payment on the check. But if the payee has the
maker's check certified in the maker's bank, the bank cannot honor a stop-
payment notice, since it certified by contract that the money was available to the
payee.

Payment by check at the time of closing gives rise to other problems. If
the checks are drawn on out-of-state banks or on banks not conveniently located, collection will take longer. No seller should allow passing of title where
payment is in doubt. Most escrow holders will protect themselves by waiting
until the check has cleared before delivering the deed for recordation.

The Closing Payment

The closing check should be either a cashier's or treasurer's check drawn
on a substantial bank, or a certified check drawn by the buyer to the direct order
of the seller or escrow. An acceptable alternative may be a cashier's or treasurer's check made payable to the buyer and endorsed to the order of the seller
or escrow. This method is advantageous to the buyer. If there is some delay in
closing, or if problems arise causing the transaction to fail, the buyer can easily
redeposit such a check. However, if the buyer is a corporation and the cashier's
or treasurer's check is made payable to the corporation, obtaining authorization
to endorse may be a problem. In such a case the broker ought to insist that the
check be made payable to the direct order of seller or escrow.

A check drawn by a third party need not be rejected outright. Sellers or
escrow holders can protect themselves by obtaining a letter from a third party
authorizing the use of the funds and treatment of them as the buyer's funds, in

the event of refunds caused by last minute discovery of defective title, condemnation, or rescission of the transaction.

Where large sums of money are transferred, or where delays in closing cannot be tolerated, prescribing the precise medium of payment in the contract may be prudent. It is often too late to control this matter at the time of closing or when the escrow instructions are being drawn.

The clauses in the comprehensive Form 3:04 can easily be adapted to meet the degrees of caution necessary within the specific financial conditions at hand.

FORM 3:04   **COMPREHENSIVE "MEDIUM OF PAYMENT" CLAUSE**

Buyer will deposit in escrow with _____ the balance of the purchase price as follows:

$_____, _____ above deposit _____
      including/in addition to   which shall be
_____ $_____ _____ days of seller's acceptance in cash,
increased to   upon/within
buyer's certified check or cashier's check made payable to the order of _____
                                                                         escrow/
_____ payable _____ . In
seller   on demand of escrow/on delivery of deed/contract of sale
no event shall _____ be obligated to accept an endorsed check.
                 seller/escrow

(Optional—continue):

Check to be drawn on a bank having its principal office in the City of _____
_____, County of _____, State of _____, which is a
member of the _____ Clearing House Association, at the time of closing of _____.
              escrow/title

COMMENT ON FORM 3:04: If escrow instructions do not specify that the "demand of escrow" shall not obligate buyer to deposit payment before a definite time before close of escrow, the use of the phrase "on demand of escrow" may be inadvisable. But some standard escrow instructions in present use provide that the deposit of funds shall take place during business hours and not later than one business day before close of escrow. Where such escrow instructions have been signed, "on demand of escrow" may be adequate. To make the Deposit Receipt conform with such practice when no escrow instructions are signed, the broker is advised to change the above clause by deleting "on demand of escrow" and substituting "by depositing in escrow during business hours at least one business day before close of escrow." (For a discussion of increased deposit, see Chapter 5.)

Security Instruments

The security devices used in real estate transactions are generally mortgages, deeds of trust, and land-sales contracts (also called installment land contracts, agreement of sale, and the like).

Both mortgages and deeds of trust are written instruments executed by a borrower-owner of real property as security for a debt. The main distinction between them is that most mortgages are two-party instruments, whereas deeds of trust are three-party instruments, the parties being the lender, borrower, and trustee. The borrower deeds the property to the trustee who holds it for the benefit of the lender. In addition, a trust agreement is entered into as part of the deed whereby, upon the borrower's default and at the lender's request, the trustee is empowered to sell the property at a public or private sale. Some mortgages also contain such "power of sale."

All Cash to the Seller, Subject to Financing

In the "all cash to seller" situation presented next, the seller of the property eventually receives all cash, but part of the cash comes from financing which the buyer must obtain. The most common version of this situation is that in which the buyer makes the offer contingent upon his or her ability to take over the existing loan or loans. (See comment to Form 3:05.)

FORM 3:05   BUYER TO TAKE OVER EXISTING LOAN

(Conditioned Upon Ability To Take Title
Subject To Or To Assume Loan)

$_____ , conditioned upon buyer's ability to _____
take title subject to/

_____ the existing first _____ loan of record with a balance in that
assume

approximate amount, payable over a remaining term of approximately _____ ,
years

_____ at $_____ , _____ _____
months   amount of periodic payments   "or more"   monthly/

_____ , including interest at _____
quarterly/semiannually/annually   (correct rate)/not to exceed/

% per annum at close of escrow.

(If taxes and insurance are included in payments, continue):

taxes _____ , and insurance

(If note contains "acceleration" or "prepayment" clauses, continue):

Due in full _____ , 19____ , _____
          month   and in the event of sale or transfer of subject

_____ providing prepayment privilege upon payment of _____
property   _____% of original

_____ .
principal/months unearned interest/set out other terms

(Form continues on next page)

(If buyer is to assume VA loan, continue):

Buyer to assume Seller's Potential Indemnity Liability to the U.S. Government for the repayment of the VA loan.

(If buyer is to assume conventional):

Buyer agrees to execute Lender's Assumption Agreement, if any, and pay an assumption fee not to exceed _____.
$_____/_____ points.

(Optional, continue):

Buyer shall _____ seller through escrow any impounds for taxes
reimburse/receive from
and insurance held by lender.

(Where documents have been inspected):

A copy of the note and _____ has been exhibited to and approved
deed of trust
by buyer.

(Where documents are to be inspected and approved by buyer):

Seller shall deliver to _____
buyer/buyer's attorney, name and address
within ___ days after seller's acceptance hereof for buyer's approval true copies of
the note _____ described above together with a beneficiary
and deed of trust
statement showing balance due and last payment date and that no unremedied default exists.

Seller warrants that the note _____ securing it are not in
and deed of trust
default in any respect. If above instruments are not disapproved within 5 days of buyer's receipt thereof, this condition shall be deemed waived.

COMMENT ON FORM 3:05: There is a vast difference between taking title subject to an existing loan and assuming it. In either case, of course, the amount is applied against the purchase price. However, if title is taken subject to the existing loan, the buyer has no personal liability for payment of the loan. If the loan is assumed, the purchaser may become personally liable for the payment of any deficiency should the property be foreclosed upon. This liability of the assuming buyer is subject to the antideficiency statutes adopted in many states. Basically, these laws protect the original borrower and assuming grantee against deficiency judgments on purchase-money mortgages.

The reference to "type" of loan suggests the insertions of the appropriate description such as "fixed interest," "variable interest," "adjustable interest loan," etc. If such a loan is involved, the interest "at close of escrow" should be inserted. See explanation of the different types of loan page 60. If lender has prepared a brochure explaining the loan terms, the broker should provide buyer with a copy and obtain the buyer's acknowledgement of receipt. See Form 9:02.

Acceleration upon Sale

Because of the widespread use of acceleration clauses upon sale of the mortgaged property, it is unwise to draw an agreement whereby buyer is to take title subject to an existing loan if the contract writer has insufficient information about the credit worthiness of the buyer-borrower.

Traditionally, institutional lenders have reserved in their loans an option to accelerate the loan upon a sale so the interest rate could be adjusted to the current market rate, and to exact various fees in rewriting the loan. This right to automatic acceleration was temporarily limited by law in 12 states including California. *Wellenkamp v. Bank of America,* 21 C3d 943, August 25, 1978, held that the due-on-sale clause could not be enforced except to protect "against impairment to lender's security or the risk of default."

Congress, with the much-touted Garn-St. Germain Depository Institutions Act of 1982, solved the lenders' problems, as expected, in the lenders' favor. This act preempted the "due on sale" prohibitions. In a sweeping nullification of state law Congress may unwisely have embarked upon creating a limited federal real estate law.

The Garn Act encompasses institutional as well as private lenders, and covers loans, mortgages, advances and credit sales secured by liens on all types of real property, which is extended to include the stock allocated to a dwelling unit in a cooperative housing corporation and to a residential manufactured home whether real or personal property.

The law provided a 3 year "window" during which the state laws applied. The window closed in California October 15, 1985. Since October 15, 1982, all loans, regardless of type of lender, can contain fully enforceable due on sale provisions.

Under the Garn Act regulations, certain exceptions exist. A lender may not exercise a due on sale clause upon the following events:

a) creation of a junior trust deed, mortgage or other lien on the property, not related to a transfer of the right to occupy the property;

b) a transfer to a joint tenant on the death of another joint tenant;

c) creation of a lease of three years or less which does not contain an option to purchase;

d) transfer to a relative upon the death of a borrower;

e) transfer where the spouse or children of the borrower become an owner of the property;

f) transfer resulting from a dissolution of marriage or legal separation or a property settlement agreement by property;

g) transfer into an inter vivos trust in which the borrower is beneficiary, not relating to a transfer of right of occupancy.

The above exceptions to the enforcement of due on sale clause are restricted to homes (single family dwellings for four or fewer families occupied or to be occupied by the borrower at the time the loan is originated).

Note: Creation of a junior lien, an involuntary transfer such as foreclosure of a junior lien or creation of a lease of any type (unless permitted by the loan documents) would appear to be a "sale or transfer" apparently permitting a senior lienholder to acceleration under a due on sale clause on *all* other types of property.

Of course, if the loan does not contain a due-on-sale provision, it can never be called due because of a transfer. A whole new crop of new mortgage investments are now available to supplement the fixed rate loan.

Fare Well with Arms

Variable rate mortgages (VRMS's) are also appropriately called ARMS since it may seem they could cost the borrower an arm and a leg.

A variable interest rate is a long term loan which increases or decreases with a reference index that reflects changes in the cost of funds to the lender.

ARMS shifts most of the interest risk to the borrower. The lack of uniformity and standardization of the at least 150 variations of ARMS offered make it difficult for the borrower to draw meaningful comparisons. The variations have practically eliminated the use of graduated payment mortgages, GPM's, and graduated payment adjustment mortgages. GPAM's, by incorporation of most of the features of these loans. Many loans have no interest-rate caps, others have negative amortization. The seed of future shocks is planted for borrowers if mortgage payments rise much faster than the borrower's income.

This dramatizes the importance of an independent index. The most stable is the "6 Month Average of Treasury Bills" because the average is figured over 26 months of interest rates. The contract interest rate charged is based upon the index plus a "spread", "margin" or "differential." Lenders use different "spreads" and adjustment intervals vary widely. Interests rate adjustments vary from month to annually with six months being typical. Payments are typically adjusted annually. The APR (annual percentage rate) must be disclosed as required by the "Truth in Lending Act." Many lenders were not disclosing adequately or were miscalculating the APR using only the "teaser" rate instead of the contract rate. As a result Congress asked for revisions of regulations. After October 1, 1988 all federally chartered S&L's, national banks, FHA participating lenders and lenders selling loans to banks and S&L's must provide *identical* disclosures about ARMS used to finance principal residences.

Under the revised disclosure rules, lenders must:

• Make disclosures about the indexes used for adjustments, interest rate and payment features and other terms of specific ARM programs.

• Give borrowers a copy of the "Consumer Handbook on Adjustable-Rate Mortgages," or give the borrowers a "suitable substitute."

• Give borrowers a 15-year historical example of the specific ARM program that illustrates the computation of interest rates and shows how interest rates and payments on a $10,000 loan would be affected. The example must reflect all significant terms of the loan, including rate and payment caps, discounted interest rates, negative amortization and interest carryover.

• Provide an explanation of how consumers can calculate actual monthly payment amounts for a loan amount other than $10,000.

• Disclose the maximum interest rate and payment, calculated on the basis of a hypothetical $10,000 loan originated at the most recent interest rate shown in the historical example. The interest rate would be assumed to increase as rapidly as possible under the restrictions of the specific loan.

Under the standardized disclosure rules, mortgage lenders also must:

• Notify borrowers about payment changes at least 25 days before the new payment is due but no more than 120 days before the due date. If interest rate adjustments do not result in payment adjustments, as may be the case with loans in which the payment is capped but the interest rate is not, lenders will be required to send notice of the interest-rate adjustment once a year.

• Following a payment adjustment, notify the consumer of the adjusted payment amount, interest rate, index rate and loan balance. The lender also will be required to disclose the extent to which any interest rate increase has not been included in the adjustment because of payment or interest rate caps.

• Disclose the amount of payment that would be required to fully amortize the loan, if different from the adjusted payment.

• Disclosure about ARMs with conversion clauses that allow the borrower to convert his adjustable loan to fixed-rate mortgage must be made at the time of application and include all ARM disclosures, including details about the conversion feature.

The FHLBB's amendment regulations also call for information to consumers about lenders rights regarding due-on-sale clauses, explanations of prepayment penalties, expanded disclosure about escrow payments and consumer information about non-amortizing or partially amortizing loans, such as balloon mortgages.

Borrowers should shop for the best possible terms and full assumability. Buyers and Brokers should compare, watch out and remember that all ARMS are not shaped the same or look alike.

Reverse Annuity Mortgage (RAM)

The RAM allows homeowners to draw upon their equity in their home as a source of income. The focus is on elderly homeowners who have significant equities in their property. It allows them to use such equity funds as retirement income or alternatively to pay the unexpected cost of inflation.

There are four basic varieties of RAM:

1. A rising-debt loan involving only a lender and the owner.

2. A fixed-debt loan from a lender. The funds are used to purchase a whole life annuity from an insurance company.

3. A fixed-debt loan from a lender. The funds are used to purchase a life annuity with a refund annuity as a refund feature from an insurance company.

4. A combination of rising-debt loan. The funds are used to purchase a deferred life annuity from an insurance company.

Renegotiable Rate Mortgage (RRM)

The Renegotiable Rate Mortgage (RRM), or rollover loans, a variation of the RRM, have been successfully used in Canada for many years. Renegotiation is a misnomer. The lender tells the borrower what the new rate is. That's the end of "negotiation."

The lender has a choice of offering a loan, which is secured by a long-term mortgage of up to thirty (30) years in duration, for a term of three, four or five years.

At the renewal date, no alterations can be made to the terms of the borrowers' promissory note or deed of trust other than a change in the interest rate resulting in an increased or decreased monthly payment. The interest rate may increase or decrease a maximum of 5% over the life of the mortgage. The borrower has the option of renewing the loan with the initial lender or shopping the loan and finding a better interest rate.

Price Level Adjusted Mortgage (PLAM)

The PLAM is a loan which frees the lender from all inflationary consequences involving the interest rate. The interest rate is calculated based upon a contract rate which is used to compute the monthly payment called for under the term of the loan, and an additional rate which is based upon the recomputation of the mortgage balance in accordance with the cost of living.

The concept of the PLAM calls for the borrower to enter into a loan at a fixed interest rate. Each year, or any other selected period which the borrower and lender agree to, the loan would be revalued in accordance with the inflation index.

In essence, the homebuyer would be making monthly payments based upon a "real" dollar which is tied into the inflation index. The ratio between monthly payment and income would remain relatively constant, assuming for the moment that there is no wage and price controls imposed which would obviate this arrangement.

Flexible Payment Mortgage (FPM)

The FPM includes the benefits of the GPM with the graduated payment for the borrower resulting in level payments for the lender and ultimately provides for conventional underwriting of the loan.

The borrower makes a down payment, which instead of creating cash equity in the real estate, is deposited in a pledged interest bearing savings account with the lender. This interest account serves as cash collateral for the lender and is the source for additional supplement payments for the borrower in the first years of the loan. As a result of the fact that the down payment is deposited into a savings account, the amount of the mortgage will be higher than a conventional 80% loan to value ratio loan. The FPM loan will reduce the borrower's initial monthly payment by as much as 25% in relation to a FRM.

For the past several years developers in California have offered a form of the FPM as a means of financing tract home sales.

Shared Appreciation Mortgage (SAM)

A SAM is a loan which has a fixed interest rate set below the prevailing market rate over the term of the loan and contingent interest based upon a percentage of the appreciation of the property securing the loan at the earlier of maturity or payment in full of the loan or sale or transfer of the property.

SAM's by E.R.I.S.A. pension funds are regulated in California by Civil Code Section 1917.010-1917.075. Other SAM's are regulated by laws of similar nature.

The Alternative Mortgage Instruments are not in themselves the answer to the problem of high interest rates and large monthly payments. At best the AMI's afford the borrower with an alternative; how effective this alternative is will only be answered in time.

When the Buyer Assumes the Loan

The courts have held that an agreement to assume the mortgage debt need not be included as a provision of the deed, but may be included in the contract of sale. It can be a separate agreement written or oral, or it may be implied from the surrounding circumstances. In California, however, the assumption of a mortgage debt must be in writing to be enforceable. This requirement is fulfilled either by a separate written "assumption agreement" or an expressed provision in the deed.

One advantage to the seller when the buyer assumes the loan is that the seller then is only secondarily liable on the indebtedness, while the lender primarily has to look to the assuming buyer for payment. The seller is a "guarantor" unless released by either a new contract or a specific release. It seems somewhat unfair to continue to hold the seller responsible when the lender has obtained various advantages from the assumption. Where a new buyer is a good credit risk, some lending institutions, the Federal Housing Authority, and the Veteran's Administration will release the seller from all future obligations. The standard 203b FHA and VA loans are assumable and can be prepaid without penalty. They can also be taken "subject to" without FHA, VA, or the lender's approval.

The "Statement of Condition"

Where existing financing is to be transferred, the broker should obtain the necessary information and consent from the lending institution and incorporate this information in the agreement between buyer and seller. This information should be gathered before the contract is drawn. To protect the buyer, the information should include: (1) copies of note and deed of trust; (2) the proposed assumption agreement; and (3) the cost of assumption.

It is imperative that the exact terms of an existing assumable loan be ascertained and inserted in the contract. Particular care should be exercised when loans are held by private lenders. If either the broker or buyer should fail to verify the terms, the buyer may unintentionally take title subject to or assuming a loan which is past due or will fall due in full in a few months. It is possible that the note may be due on demand or contain unusual terms which the buyer would not be willing to meet. In addition to verifying the terms of the note and deed of trust or mortgage, the buyer should request that the seller or escrow holder obtain a beneficiary statement or so-called "statement of condition" from the lender stating the balance of the loan.

The seller's advisor should not let the seller inadvertently make any general representations regarding the existing loan. For example, to insert an or more clause in the offer when the contract writer is not sure that the note contains such wording may cause the seller to guarantee a nonexisting provision and expose him or her to liability. The safest way to avoid error is to check the loan documents and have the buyer approve the terms of the instruments. The last optional clause in Form 3:05 covers this approval.

All too often these matters are left to be finalized at the closing. At that point, however, the buyer may discover that the terms of the note are unacceptable, that the assumption fee is very high, or that in the assumption agreement the lender is calling for a variable interest rate which may make the loan more costly than other available financing. Valuable time may have been lost. The seller may not be willing to accept extension of time for performance, or will not—after expecting to close the deal immediately—be willing to make a second loan subject to new, less attractive terms of the first loan. Again, the watchword is "preparation." To avoid spinning wheels, the broker should explore new loan commitments available in addition to offering "assumption" of the existing loan, and be able to enlighten the buyer as to all terms and conditions of available financing. The final choice is, of course, up to the buyer, but the successful broker is the professional who presents all the alternatives.

Assumption of More Than One Loan

In some transactions refinancing is not possible, and the buyer may have to assume or take title subject to existing financing consisting of two loans (see Form 3:06).

FORM 3:06   BUYER TO ASSUME MORE THAN ONE LOAN

(1) $ _____ , conditioned upon buyer's ability to _____
     balance of loan   take title subject to/

_____ the existing first _____ loan of record with an unpaid balance in that
assume   type

approximate amount payable over a remaining term of approximately _____
                                               years/

_____ at $ _____ , _____ _____
months   amount of periodic payment   or more   monthly/quarterly/

_____ including interest at _____ %
  semiannually/annually   (correct interest rate)/not to exceed

per annum, _____
                        at close of escrow

          (If taxes and insurance are included in payment, continue):

and taxes and insurance.

          (If note contains "acceleration" or "prepayment" clause, continue):

Due in full _____ 19_____ _____
         month   and in the event of sale or transfer of subject property

providing prepayment privilege upon payment of _____
                                       _____% of original principal/

_____ .
                 _____ months unearned interest/(set out other terms)

                 (If buyer is to assume, continue):

Buyer agrees to execute lender's assumption agreement, if any, and pay an assumption fee not to exceed _____ .
                             $_____/_____ points

             (Where second loan is involved, continue):

  (2) $_____ , _____ buyer's ability to
       balance of loan   conditioned upon/subject to

_____ the existing second loan of record with an unpaid
   take title subject to/assume

balance in that approximate amount, payable over a remaining term of approximately _____ , _____ , at $ _____ .
              years/months   amount of periodic payment

_____ , _____ including interest at
    monthly/quarterly/semiannually/annually   or more

_____% per annum,

           (If note contains "balloon" clause, continue):

due in full _____ , 19_____ , _____
        month   with a remaining balance payable of

_____ .
           approximately $_____

          (Form continues on next page)

(Optional, continue):

A copy of the _____ and _____ have been exhibited
                    note/notes   first/second deed of trust
to and approved by the buyer.

(Optional, continue):

Buyer shall _____ seller through escrow any impounds for
            reimburse/receive from
taxes and insurance held by lender.

COMMENT ON FORM 3:06: The "correct interest rate" should be the rate which the buyer will have to pay on the assumed loan. Where, for example, a multiple-listing card does not show the necessary information, or the seller's representative is not familiar with the lender's current loan policies, the "not to exceed" provisions can be used. Some private loans contain conditions for providing credit information by an "assuming" buyer.

Where documents are not available for inspection prior to drawing the contract and statements of conditions are not automatically obtained by escrow holder, the use of the optional more extensive approval clause found in Form 3:05 is recommended.

"Prepayment Penalties"

The terms of real estate loans are not uniform. Under normal conditions, lending institutions are competitive on terms. It pays to shop around for terms and compare. Not only are the interest rate and the set-up, or assumption, fees important; sometimes the terms of the "prepayment penalty" can make the difference between loans. The type of prepayment penalty on the existing loan may be of importance to both buyer and seller. Most sellers are not aware of the terms of their loans. It often comes as a surprise to them that a substantial sum can be demanded of them when the loan is paid off in a sale. Since such a payment influences the net amount a seller receives from the sale, the broker should obtain the information at the outset, when the listing is taken. The broker who knows the extent of the prepayment penalty can also help to tailor the buyer's offer in such a manner that substantial savings can be made.

The right of a borrower to pay off the loan or otherwise to perform the condition necessary to discharge the lien is granted by statute. However, this does not necessarily mean that the borrower has an absolute right to prepay the obligation. Obviously, the borrower's rights to prepay are determined by the terms of the obligation. If the note and deed of trust or mortgage contains prepayment provisions, the borrower has the right to prepay upon the conditions set forth. Some lenders, mostly banks and private individuals, use notes which omit reference to prepayment. These notes do not contain the "or more" clause, which is common in most "standard" notes, or a specific clause allow-

ing prepayment privileges. Thus, the terms of prepayment are left up to negotiation at the time of payment. This arrangement can often be unsatisfactory to the
borrower. In effect, the lender may be able to extract a substantial "prepayment
penalty," in that the lender could refuse prepayment or demand the payment of
all the interest that would have been earned had the loan gone to maturity. Some
prepayment-penalty clauses are probably unenforceable. California Civil Code,
Section 2954.9(a) permits restriction on prepayment in the calendar year of
sale. The law specifically permits prepayment penalties without regulating them
except for loans on four family, owner-occupied dwellings. See Comments to
Form 3:20.

Common Prepayment-Penalty Clauses

The most common prepayment-penalty clause provides payment of a certain amount of unearned interest, figured either on the unpaid balance or upon
the original amount of the loan. The difference in cost can be substantial. Other
prepayment schemes are of the "lock-in" type. Here the borrower is precluded
from payment of the loan for a set number of years with graduated penalties.
Another method allows only the prepayment of, say, 20 percent of the original
principal in any twelve successive months noncumulative, and then six months
advance interest on the aggregate amount of all prepayments in excess of the 20
percent. Again, a careful analysis of the cost and the other terms is important.
The borrower must consider whether the loan is temporary and likely to be paid
off at an early stage, or whether its terms will hinder or help a contemplated
future resale.

Because the many variations in terms of loans make uniformity impossible, the contract writer cannot protect the deal by relying on common usage to
add the undisclosed ingredient to the agreement by legal implication. If the
agreement is to be complete it must cover the subject of prepayment.

Whether the loan is an existing loan or a new loan to be obtained by the
buyer, the matter of prepayment privilege should not be left to speculation.
Where copies of the original note and deed of trust or mortgage are available,
it is, of course, a simple matter to exhibit the documents to the buyer for
approval and initialing. But where this expedient is not practical or possible, the
terms of the note and deed of trust should be copied into the agreement or
inserted in an addendum to the agreement. If the prepayment penalty is a simple
payment of a set amount of percentage interest on either the unpaid balance or
the original balance, the clause can be worded as follows:

Prepayment privilege upon payment of _____ percent of

_____.
    unpaid balance/of original principal

(or)

Prepayment privilege upon payment of ＿＿ months unearned interest.

Where unusual conditions for prepayments are contained in the note and deed of trust, the terms thereof should be set forth with particularity in the agreement or copies should be provided to the buyer and his or her legal counsel for scrutiny. The "standard" provision for payment of a set amount and "or more," of course, gives the right to prepay. Unfortunately, some incorrectly drawn notes contain both the "or more" clause *and* a prepayment-penalty clause. In these cases, the notes present problems of legal interpretation.

The extent of prepayment privileges in the drawing of the agreement may be more important where the buyer is contemplating taking title subject to an existing loan. A buyer who plans a resale in the immediate future or the demolition of an existing structure will be vitally interested in what it will cost to pay off the existing loan. Where it has not been possible to learn the exact terms in advance, the buyer may be protected by inserting the following provision in the offer:

Prepayment penalty, if any, not to exceed ＿＿＿＿ months un-
three/six

earned interest.

Then, if the terms of the prepayment penalty differ from this proposal, the seller could either set forth the correct terms of prepayment penalty in the counter-offer and try to get the buyer to approve them, or agree to pay any amount over the buyer's limit. Or, the seller could reduce the purchase price to compensate for the penalty. See comments to Form 3:20.

The "Dragnet" Clause

Another clause found mostly in bank deeds of trust is the so-called "dragnet," or "anaconda" clause an uncommonly descriptive label since anacondas are large snakes who kill their prey by constrictor force. It provides that the lien on the property described in the instrument secures not only the amount of the designated loan which occasioned the instrument and future advances, but also all other obligations, indebtedness, and claims or demands acquired by the bank now and in the future against the borrower, whether secured or unsecured by other property, personal or real. A common dragnet clause reads:

For the Purpose of Securing: (1) Payment of the sum of $ ＿＿＿＿ with interest thereon according to the terms of a promissory note or notes of even date herewith, made by trustor, payable to the order of the beneficiary, and extensions or renewals thereof: (2) Payment of such additional amounts as may be hereafter loaned by beneficiary or its successor to the trustor of any of them, or any successor in interest of the trustor, with interest thereon, and any other indebtedness or obligation of the trustor, or any of them, and any present or future demands of any kind or nature which the beneficiary or its successor may have against the trustor, or any of them, whether created directly, or acquired by assignment, whether absolute or contingent, whether due or not, whether otherwise secured or not, or whether existing at the time of the execution of this instrument, or arising thereafter: (3) Performance of each agreement of trustor herein contained: and (4) Payment of all sums to be made by trustor pursuant to the terms hereof.

The "dragnet clause" is also known as an "other indebtedness clause." It is a form of "cross-collateralization clause." Where the borrower has several loans with the same lender, each containing a dragnet clause, the effect is to make each deed of trust security for all of the loans and conversely to secure each loan with all of the deeds of trust. In addition, any unsecured loans become secured by each deed of trust containing a dragnet clause. "Dragnet" clauses, by their broad and general terms enwrap the unsuspecting debtor in the folds of indebtedness embraced and secured in the mortgage which the debtor did not contemplate.

A defaulting trustor or a junior lien holder wishing to reinstate a first dragnet-clause loan under statutory provisions prevailing in California, where foreclosure by "power of sale" in the deed of trust is available, may be exposed to surprising demands from the bank. For example, the bank may claim, in addition to delinquent payments on the real estate loan, such items as overdrawn balance on the borrower's checking account, defaults on unsecured notes for personal loans, or defaults on automobile or appliance loans. The demands may indeed be so excessive that the bank's "security" exceeds the actual value of the property to the total exclusion of the junior mortgage. The dragnet clause, with its automatic extension of security, can well be attacked on several legal grounds.[6]

Courts have indicated that such grasping clauses are not "highly regarded" and make them subject to strict construction. In an Iowa case the court said: "The use of such a clause is not to be commended, and it naturally arouses suspicion as to the good faith of the mortgagee in the transaction. It might in many cases not require much evidence of concealment, haste or artifice to overturn it."[6] A California court refused to enforce such a clause, where a cotenant was sued to pay a debt owed the bank by the other cotenant.[7] The bank had not disclosed to the defendant that there was a prior debt in existence at the time when the cotenant defendant signed the mortgage to the bank. Most borrowers are totally unaware that their "real estate" loan secures other obligations to the lender.

When presented with a case involving a dragnet clause, the courts will normally attempt to uphold the intentions of the parties rather than enforcing the literal wording of the provision and will place the burden on the proponent of showing that both parties intended the other loan to be included by the dragnet clause. In another California case,[8] the court upheld a dragnet clause as against assuming grantees where the parcels involved were closely related as a single development and were in fact purchased in a single transaction.

Protecting Against a Dragnet Clause

Despite judicial criticisms many lending institutions still use this collection device. However, certain protective measures can be taken against the dragnet clauses. If a seller is to carry a purchase-money mortgage subject to a new first loan to a bank which uses a "dragnet" clause, she or he should be protected by demanding that the buyer obtain a statement from the bank certifying that only the amount shown in the mortgage is in fact the "unpaid balance" which the bank claims secured. Form 3:07 shows a clause requiring such a statement designed for insertion into the Deposit Receipt.

FORM 3:07 **STATEMENT OF CONDITION: NEW LOAN TO BUYER FROM LENDER USING "DRAGNET" CLAUSE**

Buyer shall provide seller with statement from lending institution containing information, as of the time of closing, of the exact amount which said lending institution claims is secured by its _____ . Actual notice by
deed of trust
registered or certified mail, with return receipt, shall be given to lending institution by _____ of the existence of seller's security instrument to
buyer/escrow holder
be recorded junior to lending institution lien. Evidence of such notice shall be delivered to seller upon _____ .
close of escrow

(Optional, continue):

Buyer shall pay cost of preparation and recording of a "Request for Notice of Default and Sale."

COMMENT ON FORM 3:07: This form is intended to be inserted in the Deposit Receipt whenever a buyer proposes to obtain a bank loan from a bank using the dragnet clause and the seller is to carry junior financing. If such a provision is not included in the offer as presented to the seller, the condition should be inserted in the seller's counter-offer. The seller should not agree to assist in junior financing of any transaction in which a bank using a dragnet clause is involved as senior lender unless this condition is agreed to. Dragnet clauses are extensions of "open-end mortgages" and subject to the rules concerning these. (See the discussion in Comment on Form 3:08.)

In California, any person desiring a copy of any notice of default may record a request. After the request is recorded, anyone filing a notice of default must within ten days after recording it mail a copy to the person who filed the request. When a junior lien is recorded, the filing of such notice of request is a protection which should not be overlooked. In addition to this precaution, an actual notice of the junior lien should be served on the first lender. See Form 3:08 for a form giving "actual notice" to a lending institution of the existence of a junior lien.

FORM 3:08   **ACTUAL NOTICE TO LENDER OF
EXISTENCE OF JUNIOR LIEN**

To: _____   LOAN NO. _____

Property Address _____

_____

As the holder of the Note secured by Deed of Trust between _____

_____ , as Trustor,

_____ , as Trustee, and

_____ , as Beneficiary.

Dated _____ , and recorded _____

_____

_____ In Volume _____ Page _____

Official Records of the County of _____, State of California.

YOU ARE HEREBY NOTIFIED THAT

_____ have executed a Note secured by a Deed of Trust

in favor of _____. Said Deed of Trust has been

recorded junior to your Deed of Trust as now appearing in the Official Records of

the City of _____, County of _____ recorded _____

_____ Volume _____ Page _____.

This notice is given you so that you will have actual knowledge of the existence of the Deed of Trust of which _____

is the beneficiary and will therefore make no additional advances wherein your Deed of Trust will in any manner be looked upon by you as additional security for any such sums advanced.

In the event of any delinquency under the terms of your Note and Deed of Trust we ask you to notify _____

_____

at _____ .

Please acknowledge the carbon copy of this notice and return it to the undersigned in the enclosed stamped envelope.

Date _____

_____

_____ Receipt of the above notice is hereby acknowledged

by _____

COMMENT ON FORM 3:08: By statute,[9] California allows "open-end deeds of trust" for future advances establishing priority in advance of actual indebtedness. The "open end" beneficiary's priority depends upon whether the advance is obligatory or optional. If the advance is optional an intervening lien (a junior deed of trust) has priority over a subsequent advance, since the recording of the junior lien is constructive notice to the first lien holder. The commonly used deeds of trust in California also specifically give priority for advances for taxes, assessments, and insurance. Attempts in state legislatures to get statutory priority of all advances on open end mortgages are regularly made by lenders in coporation with title insurers. Current laws should be checked.

However, it is good practice to give *actual* notice to the first lender of the creation of a junior lien. The above form should be sent in duplicate to the lender by registered or certified mail, return receipt requested. At the same time the person who actually mailed the letter should prepare a statement of mailing with a copy of the notice. All the documents should be maintained for the period of the junior loan. Many institutional lenders simply ignore the request for acknowledgment of the actual notice. The burden of proof of its delivery falls on the junior lien holder.

Whenever a junior loan is made by third party or taken back by the seller as junior to an open-end deed of trust such "actual" notice should be given together with a demand for a beneficiary statement (Civil Code Section 2943) showing the amount secured by the first deed of trust at the time the junior lien is about to be made.

Caution: The creation of a junior lien may on certain property "trigger" a due on sale clause in the senior liens. See page 60 and Chapter 9. Form 3:09 is a model beneficiary statement request.

FORM 3:09   STATEMENT OF CONDITION

Date _____

Application No. _____

Escrow Company _____

_____, California _____

Gentlemen:

In reference to that certain Note and Deed of Trust dated _____ ,
19_____, in the original amount of $ _____ , executed by

_____

to _____ ,
secured by property known as _____

_____ ,
the undersigned, beneficiary under said Deed of Trust, do _____ hereby as per your request certify that:

    1. The unpaid principal balance on said loan is $ _____ ;
    2. The interest rate is _____% per annum, payable _____ .
    3. Interest is paid to _____;

(Form continues on next page)

4. Payments are $_____ (or more), per month which amount does (does not) include interest, with a final payment due on or before _____, 19____.
5. Any clause in the Deed of Trust or Note declaring balance due on transfer will (will not) be enforced.

_____

COMMENT ON FORM 3:09: The above form is mailed in duplicate to the lender with the request that it be filled in and returned. The beneficiary statement is useful when a new second loan is placed upon property, or when a first loan is taken subject to.

By Statute (California Civil Code § 2924e.) California lenders of loans secured by one to four residential units upon request must give written notice of all delinquencies over 4 months to a junior loan holder. The borrower must give consent to such request.

The Broker and the Lender's Terms

Prepayment penalties, variable interest rates, and dragnet clauses all represent the lender's efforts to obtain the best possible terms. Brokers should not attempt to interpret the legal effect of these clauses, particularly since the courts have not, for example, fully assessed the validity of dragnet clauses. However, as specialists in real estate sales, brokers must be conversant with the tools of the trade. The types of financing and the terms demanded by lenders are of legitimate concern to brokers if they are to advise their clients correctly. Organized real estate also has a legitimate interest in such matters, since Realtor organizations in themselves constitute the largest organized group of property owners and property-loan borrowers.

The development of standardized mortgage instruments would be a great step forward. Not the least of the advantages would be the standardization of penalty clauses, dragnet clauses, variable-interest-rate clauses, and so on, making the wording of these conditions identical regardless of where the loan was obtained. Consumers would know what they were signing and the facts about loans could be readily obtained.

New Financing as a Condition

Contracts for the sale of real estate which call for the buyer to obtain new financing should also make the financing a *condition* of the sale. Thus, the party for whose sole benefit the condition is included is not bound to perform unless or until performance of the condition. By itself the phrase "subject to" indicates that the promise is conditional,[10] but this interpretation is rendered certain by the use of the word "condition," as in the phrase "subject to the following conditions." In order to clarify and simplify, the use of the unequivocal phrase "conditioned upon" is recommended. In the forms which follow this usage has been adopted.

Generally, a contract does not lack mutuality because it contains a condition precedent as, for example, "conditioned upon buyer's ability to obtain certain financing."

In contracts that are "conditioned upon buyer's ability to obtain financing," it is good practice to insert this sentence: "Buyer shall diligently apply for said loan." As an additional precaution, it may be wise to allow the buyer a certain amount of time to obtain such a loan and also to provide for the agent's or seller's right to assist the buyer in obtaining the proper financing. In some situations, the seller may wish to limit the buyer's time to obtain a satisfactory loan, offering to return the deposit if the loan is not available within the prescribed period. These and other problems of buyer financing are treated in the following sections. A clause demanding the buyer's "due diligence" in obtaining financing is found in Model Form II and in Form 3:10.

FORM 3:10   DILIGENCE IN OBTAINING LOAN

_____ shall diligently apply for such loan.
        the buyer/the seller

(Optional for Other Party's Benefit, continue):

If the _____ shall be unable to obtain a commitment for such loan with-
        buyer/seller

in a period of _____ days after the date of seller's acceptance hereof, then the _____ shall have a period of _____ days after notice of _____
    buyer/seller   buyer's/seller's
inability to satisfy this condition or after the expiration without notice of said period in which to secure a commitment for such a loan for and on behalf of _____

_____. The _____ shall execute and furnish documents and supply all
buyer/seller   buyer/seller
information reasonably requested by the lending institutions in connection with his applications. If neither buyer nor seller shall obtain a commitment for such loan then this agreement shall be terminated and all funds paid hereunder shall be refunded to buyer except_____ .
                        cost of title examination and termite report as provided for below

COMMENT ON FORM 3:10: The clause above can be adapted to a loan commitment from either party. In the event that the buyer is to obtain the loan commitment, the seller should be allowed equal time to obtain the loan on behalf of the buyer, if the buyer fails. (See also Forms 3:13 and 3:14.)

FHA and VA Loans

In inflationary times most sales are made with new financing. Foremost in this respect are the various types of government-insured loans. Specific provisions are required for FHA and VA loans. Forms 3:11, 3:12, and 3:13 cover FHA and VA loans, respectively.

FORM 3:11   BUYER TO OBTAIN FHA LOAN

$_____, conditioned upon buyer's
                (amount of new loan)
ability to obtain an FHA loan secured by the property in that amount, for _____ years, payable at approximately $_____ per month, including interest at _____% per annum, FHA mortgage insurance, taxes, and hazard insurance. Seller to pay a loan fee not to exceed _____%, necessary to obtain FHA financing.

(Continue):

It is expressly agreed that notwithstanding any other provision of this contract, the buyer shall not be obligated to complete the purchase of the premises and shall not incur any penalty or loss of his deposit money or otherwise unless the seller has delivered to the buyer a written statement issued by the Federal Housing Commissioner setting forth the appraised value of the property for mortgage insurance purposes of not less than $_____, which statement the seller shall deliver to the buyer promptly after such appraised value statement is made available to the seller.

The buyer shall, however, have the privilege and option of proceeding with the consummation of this contract without regard to the amount of the appraised valuation made by the Federal Housing Commissioner. The appraised valuation is arrived at to determine the maximum mortgage the Department of Housing and Urban Development will insure. HUD does not warrant the value or the condition of the property. The purchaser should satisfy himself/herself that the price and condition of the property are acceptable.

(Optional, continue)

Seller shall not be obligated to complete the sale, if FHA requirements for repairs including any recommended structural pest control work exceeds _____
_____ or if FHA
the sum of $_____/_____% of sales price
appraisal is less than contract price.

COMMENT ON FORM 3:11: The underlined provision in this clause is mandatory. The broker should carefully explain to both parties the relevant policies of the FHA, including the going rate, costs, points, and so on. CAR prints an FHA amendment, which does not include the optional limitation on seller's obligation to repair or to accept a low appraisal.

FORM 3:12   BUYER TO OBTAIN VA LOAN

$_____, conditioned upon buyer's ability to obtain a VA
(Amount of new loan)
loan secured by the property in that amount for _____ years, payable at approximately $_____ per month including interest at _____% per annum, taxes
and hazard insurance. Seller to pay the loan fee necessary to obtain VA financing
not to exceed _____%.

Seller to pay escrow fees and structural pest control inspection fee.

It is expressly agreed that, notwithstanding any other provisions of this contract, the purchaser shall not incur any penalty by forfeiture of earnest money or
otherwise or be obligated to complete the purchase of the property described
herein, if the contract purchase price or cost exceeds the reasonable value of the
property established by the Veterans Administration. The purchaser shall, however, have the privilege and option of proceeding with the consummation of this
contract without regard to the amount of the reasonable value established by the
Veterans Administration.

COMMENT ON FORM 3:12: The last provision is mandatory. The policies and
practices of the Veterans Administration are constantly changing. The nearest
office of the Veterans Administration will provide sellers and purchasers or
their agents with the rules for eligibility, maximum loan amounts, forms, etc.

Cal-Vet Loans

California has a unique financing arrangement for California veterans.
The program is self-supporting, and its benefits come from proceeds of bonds
sold by the State of California. It is administered by the Department of Veterans' Affairs of the State of California only to veterans who were California
residents at the time of their enlistment or induction into the armed forces. The
financing is for homes and farms, and special distress areas. Cal. Guard loans
are also available. Form 3:13 is a deposit-receipt clause covering Cal-Vet financing.

FORM 3:13   CAL-VET FINANCING CLAUSE

$_____, as loans proceeds, conditioned upon buyer's
Amount of Cal-Vet loan
ability to obtain a new first loan in that amount from the Department of Veterans'
Affairs of the State of California evidenced by an agreement of sale for the subject
property with repayment terms at current legal rates and amortization.

COMMENT ON FORM 3:13: Of course, where the broker knows the exact
terms, these can be inserted in the usual manner. Some brokers also make the
offer conditional upon approval of the qualifications of buyer and property.
These conditions are actually included in the general ''ability to obtain'' condi-

tion. When a Cal-Vet loan is contemplated, the clause indicating how buyer wants to take title should read: "The Department of Veterans' Affairs of the State of California."

Cash Above New Conventional Loans

In cases where the buyer and broker have already discussed the existing loan commitments on the property and where the buyer has made a choice, there is usually little difficulty in writing the contract. Uncertainty and ambiguity arise when the buyer in the offer wants room to shop around for a loan, and when the seller's representative wants to be sure that the seller is adequately protected. The clause in Form 3:14 covers cash above a new first loan, where the terms of the loan are known.

FORM 3:14   **CASH ABOVE NEW FIRST LOAN**
                       (TERMS KNOWN)

$_____ , as loan proceeds conditioned upon buyer's ability
    amount of new loan

to obtain from _____ or other source acceptable
                   an institutional lender/name of lender

to buyer a first _____ loan in that amount secured by the property payable at
             type

$_____ , _____ , including interest at
               monthly/quarterly/semiannually/annually

rate of _____% per annum _____ with a
                    at close of escrow and taxes and fire insurance

prepayment penalty not to exceed _____
                              _____% of original principal/_____ months

_____ . Buyer to pay set-up charges not to exceed _____ .
unearned interest $_____/_____ points

(Optional clauses):

A. Buyer shall have _____ days from date of seller's acceptance within which to obtain such loan, or this provision shall be deemed waived.

(or):

B. In the event buyer is unable to obtain such loan within _____ days from date hereof, buyer may, at his option, declare this contract terminated. The deposit and other sums paid hereunder shall then be returned to buyer and buyer shall have no further liability hereunder except for the cost of title examination and _____ as agreed below.
        termite inspection

(Form continues on next page)

(or):

C. Should a loan on the above terms be unobtainable by buyer, seller or agent within _____ days from _____ this
date of seller's acceptance/opening of escrow
agreement shall become null and void and upon refunding the money deposited hereunder without interest both parties shall be released from any liability hereunder except for cost of title examination and _____
termite
_____ as agreed below.
inspection

COMMENT ON FORM 3:14: The clause above should be used only where the exact terms of the new loan are known based upon a prior commitment. "Institutional" or "conventional" lender may not include a pension fund or a Small Business Corporation, etc.

Optional clause "A" is least advantageous to the buyer. Optional clause "B" favors buyers allowing those who cannot obtain financing an out. Optional clause "C" permits the seller or agent to attempt to find financing if the buyer is unable. (For a compromise optional provision, which demands "diligence" on the part of the buyer but permits seller to assist in finding financing, see Form 3:10.)

When Exact Terms Are Not Known

When the exact terms of a new loan are not known but the contract writer has a general idea of what financing is available, a satisfactory agreement can still be drawn. A valid clause can also be drawn when the buyer expresses a desire to improve on the terms of the available commitment but is willing to settle for the known terms if no better terms can be found (see Form 3:15).

FORM 3:15   **CASH ABOVE NEW FIRST LOAN
(EXACT TERMS NOT KNOWN)**

$_____ as proceeds conditioned upon buyer's ability to obtain
amount of new loan
from _____ or other source acceptable to buyer
an institutional lender/name of lender
a new first _____ loan in not less than that amount secured by the property
type
payable at no more than $_____, _____
monthly/quarterly/semiannually/
_____ , including interest not to exceed _____% per annum _____
annually at close of
_____ and _____ , to be amortized over not less than
escrow taxes and fire insurance
_____ years, with a prepayment penalty not to exceed _____
_____% of original
_____ . Buyer to pay set-up charges not to
principal/_____ months unearned interest
exceed _____ .
$_____/_____ points

COMMENT ON FORM 3:15: Where the balance of the purchase price is to be paid in cash, the clause above containing only a statement of the minimum loan amount may be acceptable to seller. This clause can be used with the optional provisions of Forms 3:10 and 3:14.

　　Where the above clause is to be used in connection with secondary financing, the seller may wish to indicate a maximum first loan to which he or she is willing to make the second loan subject. (See also Form 3:26.)

Loan as Percentage of Price

　　In drafting the finance terms the outside limit of desirable financing is often described by indicating a percentage of the purchase price. This practice stems from the provisions of the state and federal laws governing the loan limits of savings and loan associations, expressed as up to 80 percent of value or 90 percent of "market value." Where "market value" is equivalent to sales price, this may be a satisfactory way of writing the offer (see Form 3:16).

FORM 3:16　　　　　**CASH ABOVE NEW FIRST LOAN
(Percentage of Purchase Price)**

$_____ as loan proceeds, conditioned upon buyer's ability to obtain a
　　amount of new loan

new first _____ loan from _____
　　　　　　　type　　　　　　　　　　an institutional lender/name of lender

or other source acceptable to buyer, secured by the property in not less than
_____ payable at no more than
that amount/an amount equal to _____% of salesprice

$_____, _____, including
　　　　　　　　　　monthly/quarterly/semiannually/annually or more

interest not to exceed _____% per annum _____.
　　　　　　　　　　　　　　　　　at close of escrow

　　　(If taxes and insurance to be included in payments, continue):

and taxes and insurance.

　　　　　　　(Continue in all cases):

to be amortized over not less than _____ years, with a prepayment penalty not to
exceed _____. Buyer
　　　　_____% of original principal/_____ months unearned interest

to pay set-up charges not to exceed _____ .
　　　　　　　　　　　　　　　$_____/_____ points

COMMENT ON FORM 3:16: The clause above is best used where the contract writer knows that the purchase price offered is acceptable to seller and has a very good idea that the proposed loan is obtainable. The amount of the new loan should be figured by applying the percentage to the purchase price. Where it is known that a lender will allow secondary financing, the clause above may be used in combination with a clause covering the seller's second loan. Form 3:27 is such a combination form.

The clause above can be used in connection with the optional provisions of Forms 3:10 and 3:14.

Limits and the Purchase Price

The disadvantage in using a percentage of the purchase price becomes evident when the seller makes a counteroffer. The seller's idea of value may very well exceed the lender's estimate. Where loan ratio is too closely tied to purchase price, the contract writer's task is more difficult. An amazing amount of misinformation is floating around concerning loan limitations of various lending institutions. Uninformed persons often add to the confusion by making such statements as, "I can get you financing at 80 percent of sales price." Obviously, this is true only where sales price is equal to appraised value and the lender is willing to lend this percentage on its appraisal. The seller/broker should therefore advise the buyer to agree to outside limits which the broker knows from experience are available on the market.

When the Seller Furnishes Financing

As brokers with experience in handling home sales know, the seller is often the best source of financing for the deal—especially the seller who is anxious to sell, owns marginal property, or simply feels that first mortgages are "good enough."

The seller will usually give better terms than lending institutions, but a private lender will rarely allow as long amortization time as an institution. Being mortal, the seller cannot wait for twenty-five or thirty years for the loan to be paid off. However, exceptionally good financing may be worked out by applying an amortization rate based upon a 25-to-30-year term but inserting an acceleration date at the 10- or 15-year stage.

In California, where a seller participates in financing through an "arranger," which includes the selling broker, in-depth disclosures of the terms must be given both seller and buyer. CAR Form SFD-11 complies with Civil Code Sections 2956-2967.

When the Seller Carries a "Purchase Money" Mortgage

If the seller is to carry a "purchase money" mortgage, the contract should so specify. It is important that the contract spell out in detail the amount of payments, the rate of interest, the amortization time, and all other specifics of the financial terms of the sale. Form 3:17 is designed to arrange for equal periodic payments of principal and interest. An optional clause for reducing the time for payoff is incorporated. For additional "wrinkles" in seller assisted financing, see Chapter 9.

FORM 3:17   **SELLER TO CARRY**
"PURCHASE MONEY" MORTGAGE
AMORTIZED NOTE, INSTALLMENTS
INCLUDING INTEREST

$_____ by buyer executing a note and _____
   amount seller to carry   mortgage/deed of trust

in that amount in favor of the seller secured by the property payable in equal _____ installments of $_____,
              monthly/quarterly/semiannual/annual

_____, _____ interest at the rate of _____% per annum from
 or more   plus/including

date of closing.

(Where limited installments and payoff within specified time, continue):
due in full _____ from date of closing
            _____ months/_____ years

(If "acceleration" clause upon sale at holder's option, continue):
and at holder's option in the event of sale or transfer of title to subject property.

(Optional):

Said note _____ shall be
            and due on sale clause and Deed of Trust

drawn on the standard form _____ of _____ .
                form no.   name of issuing company

Buyer shall within 7 days after seller acceptance supply credit information as customarily required by institutional lenders. At buyer's expense seller may order and obtain a credit report from a credit-reporting agency. If seller does not disapprove in writing the credit information within 7 days of receipt, the buyer's credit worthiness shall be declared established.

COMMENT ON FORM 3:17: In California, a mortgage or deed of trust taken back by the seller is by definition always a "purchase money" mortgage or deed of trust and subject to the antideficiency statutes. However, California CCP 580b also defines as a "purchase money" mortgage subject to no deficiency judgment "a deed of trust, or mortgage, on a dwelling for not more than four families given to a lender to secure the repayment of a loan which was in fact used to pay all or part of the purchase price of such dwelling, occupied, entirely or in part by purchaser." Non-recourse loans are sometimes available for commercial property loans. See Chapter 9, Creative Financing.

A seller not in the business of making real estate loans may require a buyer to meet credit standards "customarily applied by other similarly situated lenders or sellers in the geographical market within which the transaction occurs," for similar loans and property.

The use of the phrase "or more" has been held to permit "prepayment." Some situations call for more specifics regarding prepayment. See Form 3:20.

"Balloon Payments"

Especially in purchase-money mortgages, the buyer's installment payments are sometimes cut to an amount lower than that which would amortize the loan fully over a given length of time. Under these terms, the final installment may in fact represent nearly the total principal, since the monthly installments had been set so low, they were practically all interest. This final "balloon payment," then, is inflated to the hilt. Unfortunately, the buyer is often not sufficiently made aware of this situation and is not prepared for the "balloon" when the time arrives for payoff. Balloon-payment notes do serve a valid purpose, and quite often make a deal possible.

Form 3:18 is a full-disclosure balloon-payment clause. When the seller of a residential property up to four units takes back the loan and is selling the loan immediately, therefore acting only as a conduit, then a truth-in-lending statement *must* be given to the buyer.

FORM 3:18   SELLER TO CARRY LOAN WITH "BALLOON" PAYMENT

$_____ by buyer executing a note and _____
   amount seller to carry   mortgage/deed of trust
in that amount in favor of seller secured by the property payable in _____ equal
_____ installments of $_____, _____,
   monthly/quarterly/semiannual/annual   or more
_____ interest at the rate of _____% per annum from date of closing and
   plus/including
one final installment of approximately $_____ on the _____th anniversary of the date of closing together with accrued interest.

(Form continues on next page)

(Optional):

Said note and _____ shall at holder's option be due and pay-
                mortgage/deed of trust
able in full in the event of sale or transfer of title to subject property.

COMMENT ON FORM 3:18: The above clause is designed to show the approximate balloon payment due after a certain amount of periodic payments have
been made. Such a balance can easily be calculated on a pocket computer. An
approximation can be obtained by using a table with equal periodic payments.
As an example, take a five-year second loan with an amount of $2,000 payable
at $20 monthly including interest at 7 percent. First find the total amortization
period for a loan at $2,000 at $20 per month by following the table across until
you reach the nearest figure of $20, namely $20.57. That amount is found in the
amortization period of twelve years. After five years of sixty monthly payments
of $20, seven years of the loan will remain. Take the seven-year column and
follow it downwards to a monthly payment again closest to $20, or $19.63.
Follow this figure to the left on the same line and the amount found is $1,300,
the approximate balance to be paid on the sixty-first payment. California's statute, Civil Code Section 2966 *et seq,* requires full disclosures and at least 60
days and not more than 150 days notice before a balloon-payment note can be
enforced.

If the seller is to carry purchase-money mortgage, where the amortized
note will have the installments of principal and interest separately stated, see
Form 3:19.

FORM 3:19   **SELLER TO CARRY**
                  "PURCHASE MONEY" MORTGAGE
             Amortized Note, Installments of Principal
              and Interest Separate. Specific Prepayment
                 Privilege With or Without Penalty.

$_____ by buyer executing a note and _____
   amount seller to carry   mortgage/deed of trust
in that amount in favor of seller secured by the property payable as follows:
interest at the rate of _____% per annum from date of closing, payable on a date
_____ months after said date and _____
                              monthly/quarterly/semiannually/annually
thereafter. Principal payable on a date _____ month(s) from date of closing in the
sum of $_____, and _____
                          a like sum/$_____ monthly/quarterly/
_____ until _____ years from date of closing, when the
semiannually/annually
balance of _____ shall become due and payable.
            approximately $_____
                    amount of balloon

(Form continues on next page)

(Optional):

(If "acceleration" clause at option of holder on resale)

Said note and _____ shall at holder's option be due and
mortgage/deed of trust
payable in full in the event of sale or transfer of title to subject property.

(Optional—if no "prepayment penalty"):

The entire balance of principal may be prepaid at any time prior to maturity, on
_____ days prior written notice, with interest to the date of such payment only.

(Optional—if "prepayment penalty" clause):

The entire balance of principal may be prepaid at any time prior to maturity on
_____ days prior written notice and upon payment of _____ months unearned
interest in addition to interest to date of such payment except that in calendar
year of sale only obligatory installment payments may be made.

COMMENT ON FORM 3:19: Of course, any combination of acceleration
clauses and prepayment clauses can be drafted. The optional prepayment clause
cannot be used in California on loans on one- to four-family, owner-occupied
dwellings. See comments on Form 3:20. If prepayment penalty is desired the
note must specify. If contract is silent about prepayment penalty, no penalty can
be imposed without a new agreement with borrower. The exception above is for
tax deferred installment sales. A California seller who takes back not more than
four purchase-money mortgages in a calendar year may prohibit prepayment in
such calendar year. Advantages thereof is now limited. See page 88 "Tax
Installment Sales."

FORM 3:20   **PREPAYMENT CLAUSE**

In any 12 month period within the first five years of the loan _____
except in the
_____ the buyer may prepay up to 20% of original loan amount
first calendar year
without penalty; any excess prepayment is subject to a six month advanced interest charge.

COMMENT ON FORM 3:20: The extent of prepayment penalties on four-
family owner-occupied dwelling loans are now prescribed by statutes.[11] The
clause above spells out the California prepayment penalty for one- to four-
family owner-occupied dwellings under Civil Code Section 2954.9(b). Mortgage Loan Broker loans are regulated by Business and Professions Code Section
10242.6. Current local law should always be checked before drafting notes with
prepayment penalties involved.

Form of Mortgage

One of the most common provisions found in real estate contracts is that "any purchase money mortgage shall be in the usual or customary form." The use of such a phrase is not recommended, unless "common or customary forms" have been established by court decision or by statute. If a seller wishes to use a certain printed form commonly in use in the community or available from the title company which is to issue its title insurance, the form should be identified in the contract by title or number. Form 3:21 is designed to cover this problem.

FORM 3:21   **THE TYPE OF MORTGAGE**
                           FORM TO BE USED

Said note and _____ shall be drawn on the
                        mortgage/deed of trust

standard form of _____
                              name of issuing company

Forms No. _____ and _____.

COMMENT ON FORM 3:21: Even better, the terms of the proposed documents can be filled in on the desired forms. What is not to be incorporated therein can be deleted and the parties can initial the forms. The filled-in forms then can be attached to the agreement as exhibits and incorporated in the agreement by reference. This reference can read "Said note and _____
                                                    mortgage/deed of trust

shall be drawn as shown in Exhibits A and B attached hereto and incorporated herein by reference." See also Form 9:01.

Late Charges

If a provision for late charges on the note to be taken back by the seller is contemplated, this must not be left to decision in escrow. The contract should spell out the exact terms of the late charges. A popular form for a late-charge payment clause is shown in Form 3:22.

FORM 3:22   **LATE CHARGE**

The said note shall provide for a late charge of _____
                                                $5.00/6% of the installment due

_____ if any installment is not paid or tendered
of principal and interest

in full on or before its due date, or within 10 days thereafter.

COMMENT ON FORM 3:22: Late charges are regulated by statute in certain loans in California.[12] The above clause contains the permissible late charges for loans on single family, owner-occupied dwellings. The $5.00 late charge applies to all installments up to $83.33; above this figure the permissible charge is 6% of the installment of principal and interest. Local current law should always be checked before notes be drawn containing late charge provisions.

Be Prepared to Explain

Combination phraseology combining provisions for prepayment charges and late charges can be used, but the contract writer must then be able to accurately explain what the law is. In the real estate agreement, but not in note, the following wording can then be inserted: "The note shall provide for statutory charges for prepayment and late payment."

"Acceleration" Clauses

Most standard-form mortgages and deeds of trust contain "acceleration" clauses upon resale. If the seller wishes only to lend a helping financial hand to the present buyer, a proper acceleration clause must be found in the instruments. The due-on-sale clause shown in previous forms takes care of the condition only so far as the purchase agreement is concerned.

The role of the seller as lender is often misunderstood. I recall an elderly gentleman who felt he had been cheated when he found out that the buyer, after having made payments for two years on the note, wanted to pay the balance off. "I wanted monthly income for my older days," said this fine gentleman, who at that time was eighty-six. "Now I find that I have to be bothered with banks or stocks." Of course, the seller had not made any condition on the note for prepayment penalty. He just thought that because the note obligated the buyer to make monthly payments for fifteen years, he was entitled to receive the money in that manner and not before.

The contract writer is often caught in the middle on this issue. The buyer prefers the easiest possible terms, and expects a transferable loan and the right to prepay at any time. The seller may want higher payments than a conventional lender, but does not ask for points or penalties. At the time of sale, the seller may be very flexible and accept any deal which sounds reasonable. But when the payments start coming in small monthly dribbles, he or she may have a change of heart. Many people are not emotionally suited to invest their money in mortgages. After a while, they wish to sell the loan. Trouble brews when they find out that the size of the discount is influenced by the terms of the note. If the note lacks a reasonable maturity date, if the amortization is too low, if there are no provisions for prepayment penalty or late charges, or if the note or mortgage does not contain an enforceable acceleration clause, the mortgage is less valuable on the market. On the other hand, the broker who tries to protect the seller by making the buyer's note subject to most or all of these conditions, especially in a low-down-payment deal, is criticized later by the buyer. The buyer who wants to resell finds him- or herself in a "locked-in" position.

For a sample of a more comprehensive acceleration clause, see Form 3:23. See also Chapter 9, Creative Financing.

FORM 3:23   COMPREHENSIVE "ACCELERATION" CLAUSE

The said note shall contain the following provisions:

The payment of the entire unpaid balance of principal may be accelerated by the holder at holder's option except as expressly limited by law if the maker or his successor without the holder's prior written consent does any of the following:

(1) Fails to make any payment of principal or interest when due or defaults in any of the covenants and conditions contained in the _____ _____ securing this note or any prior encumbrances.
     mortgage/deed of trust

(2) Causes or permits or accepts any advance under or modification or extension of any prior encumbrance if any.

(3) Sells, conveys, contracts to sell, alienates or further encumbers all or any part of the property.

(4) Leases all or any part of the property for a term, together with all exercisable options, of 5 years or more.

(5) Suffers the title or any interest in the secured property to be divested, whether voluntarily or involuntarily.

(6) Changes or permits to be changed the character or use of the property.

(7) Is a partnership and any of the general partners' interests are transferred or assigned, whether voluntarily or involuntarily.

(8) Is a corporation with fewer than 100 stockholders at the date of execution of this Deed of Trust and more than 10% of its capital stock is sold, transferred or assigned during a 12-month period.

COMMENT ON FORM 3:23: Ordinary forms of mortgage contain limited acceleration clauses which usually cover only defaults in installment payments. If more comprehensive acceleration provisions are desired they should be inserted both in the note and the security instrument. A complete copy of the note with all of its provisions can be attached to the agreement as an exhibit.

Tax Installment Sales

Connected with these problems are the tax-deferment "installment sale" provisions of the Internal Revenue Code.[13] An "installment sale" is a disposition of real property or a disposition of personal property where at least one payment is to be received after the close of the taxable year in which the disposition occurs. The method permits the spreading of gain and the income tax on that gain over the period in which the payments of the sales price is actually received.

The Tax Reform Act of 1986, touted as "simplification" of the Tax Code, created a nightmarish monster called the *"proportional disallowance rule",* which limited use of the installment method for dealer sales and for sales of real property used in the taxpayer's trade or business, or held for the production of rental income where the selling price of such real property was greater than $150.000.

Under the proportionate disallowance rule, a pro rata portion of the taxpayer's indebtedness is allocated to, and is treated as a payment on, the installment obligations of the taxpayer.

In the Revenue Act of 1987 (H.R.3545) signed by President Reagan on December 22, 1987, Congress reversed itself, reducing the impact of the "proportional disallowance rule." In the process, it made things more difficult for "dealers" in real estate. Here are the changes:

1. "Dealers," defined as taxpayers who holds real property for sale to customers in the ordinary course of the taxpayer's trade or business, cannot use the installment sale method for dispositions after December 31 1987. All payments to be received by such a taxpayer are treated as received in the year of the disposition.

2. Non-dealer installment sales transactions are defined as dispositions of real property that is used in a taxpayer's trade or business, or that is held for the production of rental income, where the sales price of the real property is greater than $150.000. The proportionate disallowance rule is repealed for installment obligations arising out of the disposition of such real property. An interest charge is imposed on the tax that is deferred under the installment method to the extent the amount of the deferred payments arising from all dispositions of such real property during any eyar exceeds $5 million. If a non-dealer installment obligation is hypothecated, the net proceeds of the secured indebtedness are treated as a payment on such installment obligation as of the later of the date that the indebtedness is secured, or the date that the net proceeds are received by the taxpayer. Gain is recognized in an amount equal to the product of the net loan proceeds received and the gross profit ratio applicable to the installment obligation. The repeal of the proportionate disallowance rule covers dispositions occurring in taxable years beginning after December 31 1987. "Non-dealer real property installment obligations" arising out of dispositions occurring after August 16, 1986, in taxable years beginning before January 1 1988, are subject to the proportionate disallowance rule in any later taxable year for which the taxpayer has allocable installment indebtedness.

3. The term "non-dealer real property installment obligation" does not include any installment obligation that arises out of the disposition by an individual of personal use property or the disposition of any property that is used or produced in the trade or business of farming. Additionally, such term does not include any installment obligation which arises out of a disposition of a residential lot or "timeshare" if the taxpayer elects to pay interest on the amount of the deferred tax attributable to the use of the installment method.

These rules means in effect that the installment sales method is alive again with some restrictions. "Non-dealers" can still take advantage of the method, but pledging or hypothecating the installment obligation triggers tax liability. For personal use property, such as owner occupied residences, personally used second homes, the installment method will still be part of creative financing. An installment obligation arising out of such seller financing can be pledged or hypothecated without tax consequences.

In the disposition of "non-dealer" property, the seller must be warned about the "net proceeds" rule upon pledging or hypothecating the installment obligation. For the purpose of this rule, the law provides, that an indebtedness is secured by an installment obligation to the extent that the payment of principal or interest on the indebtedness is *directly* secured (either under the terms of the indebtedness or any other arrangement) by an interest in the installment obligation. A sophisticated tax adviser should be able to devise a method whereby the installment obligation can be used to obtain credit without an assignment or direct pledge of the instrument or the payments thereunder.

The Tax Reform Act of 1986 and the Revenue Act of 1987 did not change the *minimum* rate that must be charged on seller financing. It is the *lower* of 9% or the "applicable federal rate" (AFR) for federal tax purposes.

Installment Sale and an Exchange

No gain or loss is recognized if property held for productive use in trade or business or for investment is exchanged solely for property of a like kind. Where property is transferred in exchange for like kind property plus other types of property of money, the gain, if any, to the recipient is recognized, but in an amount not in excess of the sum of the money received and the fair market value of the other property (Code Section 1031(b)).

Where the like kind property is received along with cash and other property in an installment sale, the like kind property can qualify for the nonrecognition treatment described above.

The basis of the like kind property received is determined as if the obligation had been satisfied at its face amount. Thus, if a taxpayer transfers property in exchange for like kind property, other property, and an inst⁻'' ment obligation, the taxpayer's basis in the property transferred would first to be allocated to the like kind property received (but not in excess of its fair market value), and any remaining basis is used to determine the gross profit ratio. (Code Sec. 1031(d)). For more on Exchanges see Chapter 8.

In structuring an installment sale in California the limitations on seller's right to limit the buyer's payments must be considered. There is no right to prepay a loan unless allowed by the lending instruments. However by statute, part prepayment is permitted at any time of a loan on residential property of four units or less secured by a lien on such real property. A seller who takes back a security interest can restrict payments in the *calendar* year of sale, provided the seller does not take back four or more such security interests in the same calendar year (see Form 3:20). The California restrictions can defeat a seller's plans for spreading the income over a number of years.

Prepayment penalties on commercial property or residential property in excess of four units are not regulated. The only limitations are that a prepayment penalty cannot be unconscionable or exorbitant. The prepayment penalty can be calculated to be equal or close to the additional tax liability caused by the premature payment. In *Williams v Fassler* 110 CA 3d 7 a penalty of 505 of any prepayment was upheld upon evidence that the additional tax caused by the prepayment amounted to 41 % of the prepayment.

FORM 3:24   **TAX INSTALLMENT SALE**
                          (Seller to Carry First Loan)

$_____ by buyer executing a note and _____
    amount seller to carry   mortgage/deed of trust
in that amount in favor of the seller secured by the property, payable in equal
installments of $ _____ ,
                               monthly/quarterly/semiannual/annual
_____ interest at the rate of ____% per annum from date of closing.
   plus/including

(Optional):
(If no prepayment penalty)

Said note shall provide for interest payments only in year of sale and prepayment
without penalty at any time after _____ 19____.

COMMENT ON FORM 3:24: This clause can be supplemented with the prepayment clauses shown on Forms 3:19 and 3:20. Because complete agreement
concerning the provisions of an installment sale is crucial, some contract writers
prefer to attach the exact form of the note as an exhibit to the agreement. (For
tax installment sale where buyer assumes existing loan and seller carries second
loan, see Form 3:26.)

    In some situations prepayment of interest is desirable (see Form 3:25).

FORM 3:25   **PREPAID INTEREST**

2) $_____ additional cash, which constitutes the prepayment of interest at
the rate of ____% per annum on the note secured by deed of trust described in
(3) of this paragraph for a period of ____ months from the date of closing.
3) $_____ by buyer executing a note and a _____
    amount seller to carry   mortgage/
_____ in that amount in favor of seller secured
purchase money mortgage/deed of trust
by the property, payable in _____ installments
                             monthly/quarterly/semiannual/annual
of $_____, including interest at the rate of ____% per annum, beginning
_____.
  date

(Optional):

Said note shall provide for prepayment without penalty at any time after _____
_____, 19____.

COMMENT ON FORM 3:25: All cash method taxpayers are required to deduct
prepaid interest for personal, business or investment purposes over the period of

the loan to the extent the interest represents the cost of using the borrowed funds during each taxable year in the period. Taxpayers on the accrual method of accounting accrue interest ratably over the loan period and must deduct it ratably over this period, regardless of whether the interest is prepaid.

When the Seller Carries Junior Financing

In one very common type of financing the seller participates by carrying the secondary financing. We have already covered the situation where the second loan is junior to an existing first loan. An additional problem arises here if there is prolonged time for closing and the seller is expected to make additional payments on the first loan. This problem calls for a special provision. Either the buyer should agree to increase the cash down payment by the amount of the reduction in the first loan's principal balance, or the second loan principal should be increased in the same amount. The two optional clauses in Form 3:26 are designed to give a choice in drafting, depending upon the intent of the parties.

FORM 3:26   **SELLER TO TAKE BACK SECOND LOAN—BUYER TO ASSUME FIRST LOAN**

(Precede with Form 3:05 [Taking Over of First Loan] and Continue):

$_____ , by buyer executing a note and _____
           amount seller to carry   mortgage/

_____ in that amount in favor of seller(s) secured by the property, pay-
deed of trust

able in equal _____ installments of $_____,
                              monthly/quarterly/semiannual/annual

_____, _____ interest at the rate of _____% per annum.
or more   plus/including

(Optional):

due in full _____
       _____ months/_____ years from close of escrow _____, 19_____

and _____ .
                   in the event of sale or transfer of subject property

(Select one of the following clauses):

a) Any adjustment in existing balances by obligatory payment will be made in cash.
b) Any adjustment in existing balances including reduction of principal through obligatory payments is to be made in the principal amount of the second loan to seller.

(Form continues on next page)

(Optional):
(If installment sale after assumption of first loan, continue):

No additional payments on principal on the note executed to seller shall be made in year of sale ending _____ , 19_____. Only obligatory payments of
date

principal and interest due under the note and _____ assumed
mortgage/deed of trust

by buyer shall be made in the year of sale, ending _____ , 19_____.
date

COMMENT ON FORM 3:26: Installment sales are automatic if a single payment is made after the close of the year of sale regardless of the size of the initial payment. The proper structuring of an installment sale is important. Sellers who have in mind to sell or borrow against an installment note should be aware that such disposition may have tax consequences resulting in immediate recognition of gain. Hypothecating a note in an amount equal to the face amount at maturity may be held to be a disposition triggering recognition of gain. Installment tax problems should always be discussed with seller's tax counsel before the agreement is drafted. See page 88 for 1987 law changes.

Seller to Carry Second Loan

In taking back a second loan behind an existing loan the seller as well as the buyer is concerned with the first lender's attitude as to assumption and advances, whether under open-end mortgages or dragnet clauses. If the seller is to carry secondary financing behind a new first loan, this financing must be carefully integrated with the buyer's plan for institutional financing. All the terms of the new first loan are important to the seller. He or she may be requested to subordinate the second loan to a new loan which may be either a replacement of the first or a construction or improvement loan. The buyer may want to include clauses releasing certain parts of the land after payment of stated sums. The seller, who can never exclude the possibility of having to foreclose the lien and take over the property again, has a vital interest in the terms and conditions of any loan to which the mortgage or deed of trust is subordinate. The time to start the protection is in the drawing of the terms-of-payment clause.

Again, we start with the loan commitments. If all of the commitments are known and are satisfactory to the buyer and acceptable to the seller, there is no difficulty in drawing the offer. When the amount of the down payment, the amount of the first loan, and the amount of the secondary financing are all known, the terms-of-payment clause can be drafted to fit these specifics (see Form 3:27). For more sophistication see Chapter 9.

FORM 3:27   **NEW FIRST LOAN—TERMS KNOWN
SELLER TO CARRY SECOND LOAN**

(Precede with Form 3:14)

$_____ , by buyer executing a note and _____
    amount seller to carry   mortgage/

_____ in that amount in favor of seller secured by the property, payable
deed of trust

in equal _____ installments of $_____,
          monthly/quarterly/semiannual/annual

_____, _____ interest at the rate of ____% per annum.
or more   plus/including

(Optional)

due in full _____
      _____ months/_____ years from close of escrow _____ , 19____

and _____.
     in the event of sale or transfer of the property

COMMENT ON FORM 3:27: This clause can of course be supplemented by adding the appropriate prepayment or late charge clauses.

Ideally, all transactions should be clearcut but in practice all sorts of problems arise. We have already discussed the great variety in terms by first lenders. Buyers are beginning to be sophisticated. They may reject out of hand a suggestion that the loan commitment the broker suggests is the best obtainable. They want to tie up the property while they shop around for the best loan. Sellers, of course, are not sympathetic to this strategy unless the buyer is apparently bound to perform. Again, the recourse must be to a "loose" contract, which may be unenforceable. Sellers who consider this risk acceptable can protect themselves by inserting a time limitation for the buyer's "shopping" so that the property is not unduly tied up.

It is a fact that very often contracts are drawn at the time of the buyer's offer, and are based upon insufficient information or wishful thinking concerning obtainable financing. Subsequent to the seller's acceptance, actual loan commitments may show a higher amount available, with perhaps corresponding higher interest rates. The seller may desire to obtain as much cash as possible, and may be willing to make a second loan subject to the higher first despite its more onerous terms. The buyer may believe that in the long run he or she would rather have a transferable lower first loan with lower or variable interest rates and have the seller carry the maximum second loan, preferably transferable too.

The result of such conflicting priorities is often an oral agreement in which the broker is the only party who knows the exact terms. Not until the final escrow instructions are drawn is the agreement set down on paper. The original Deposit Receipt is, in effect, replaced by a novation. Most brokers will recognize this pattern of negotiations. Some will recall situations in which the loan arrangements were changed several times verbally as new loan commitments came in. Practically speaking, this adjustment period probably cannot be avoided. However, the broker should realize that until the agreement is drafted and signed, no binding, enforceable contract between the parties exists. Relying on a set of escrow instructions may be hazardous to the broker's commission. The commission is not earned before the transaction is, in fact, consummated upon the terms to which all parties finally agree.

Where the parties are concerned with maximum flexibility and are reluctant to begin the transaction without it, form 3:28 may be a solution. It is a departure from all the other clauses in this chapter in that the clause for secondary financing does not contain a specifically stated dollar amount for the second loan. Thus the purchase price cannot be totalled up in the left-hand column of the terms-of-payment clause.

FORM 3:28   BUYER TO OBTAIN NEW FIRST LOAN
SELLER TO CARRY SECOND LOAN
(No Exact Amount, but Limitations)

$_____, as loan proceeds, conditioned upon buyer's ability
  amount of new loan

to obtain a new first _____ loan secured by the property from a conventional
                        type

lender or other source acceptable to buyer, in an amount not less than _____% of

purchase price, payable at no more than $_____, _____
                                                                    monthly/quarterly/

_____, including interest not to exceed _____% per annum
semiannually/annually

_____   _____.

at _____   and taxes and fire insurance
       date of escrow

To be amortized over not less than _____ years, with a prepayment penalty

not to exceed _____ .
                        _____% of original principal/_____ months unearned interest

Buyer to pay set-up charges not to exceed _____ .
                                                            $_____/_____ points

(Secondary financing by seller, Continue):

Buyer to execute a note and _____ in
                                            mortgage/deed of trust

favor of seller, secured by the property in an amount equal to the difference

between the sum of $_____ plus the principal amount of the new
                          cash down payment

first loan and the total sales price, payable in _____
                                                                monthly/quarterly/semiannual/annual

installments of _____ ,
                        _____% of principal amount of note/no more than $_____

_____, _____ interest at _____% per annum from date of
or more   plus/including

closing.

(Where limited installments and payoff within specific time, Continue):

due in full _____ from date of closing.
                         _____ months/_____ years

(If "acceleration" clause upon sale at holder's option Continue):

and at holder's option in the event of the sale or transfer of title to the property.

COMMENT ON FORM 3:28: In order to use the combination form above, the broker should have a pretty good idea of the possible first-loan financing and the amount of second-loan financing the seller would be willing to carry. This form allows flexibility in that the buyer may obtain a larger first loan on acceptable terms through careful "shopping," thereby reducing the seller's obligation to carry the full amount of secondary financing.

The broker should exercise caution in estimating the payments on the second loan so that they will be adequate to amortize this loan in a reasonable time. By using the optional acceleration clause, a balloon-payment clause is possible (see page 82).

If a second loan can be obtained from a mortgage company, Form 3:28 can be adjusted by inserting after the words "in favor of seller" the phrase "or any other source acceptable to buyer." An appropriate clause for liability for payment of loan fees, if any, should then be inserted.

Additional Security

In some situations, the seller feels that the property is not sufficient security for a secondary note. This may be especially true when the first loan is being refinanced, and the seller's second loan is not repaid in full. Circumstances may have changed, property deteriorated, and so forth. In such a case, the seller may wish to protect his or her interests by obtaining additional security on other property owned by the buyer-borrower. This situation can be accommodated by inserting in the agreement a clause providing for such additional security (see Form 3:29). Of course, the other property should be inspected and the loan information verified in the normal manner, and the note, mortgage, or deed of trust should be drawn properly. The problems involved in case of foreclosure are very technical. Before the seller makes arrangements for such additional security, therefore, counsel should review the seller's legal position. If the property which is to be used as additional security is located in a county different from that in which the main property is located, additional problems concerning recording arise, increasing the need for legal advice.

FORM 3:29 **ADDITIONAL SECURITY ON OTHER
PROPERTY OWNED BY BUYER**

The above _____ shall be additionally secured by the property
_{deed of trust}
owned by the buyer and described as follows _____ ,
which property is presently encumbered _____ with a first _____ loan in
_{only} _{type}
the approximate amount of not more than $_____ , payable in _____
_{monthly/}
_____ installments of $_____ , _____ ,
_{quarterly/semiannual/annual} _{or more}
including interest at the rate of _____% _____ in favor of
_{at close of escrow}
_____ .
_{lender}

(Optional):

Buyer shall, at buyer's expense, provide seller with a policy of title insurance insuring seller's mortgagee interest in said property and obtain a certificate
of the hazards insurance on said property with mortgagee's endorsement in favor
of seller.

Refinancing Problems

Sometimes the property is sold either "subject to" an existing loan or
buyer is to assume existing loans which have a limited time to run. Both parties
to the transaction may therefore contemplate the necessity for refinancing. The
seller who is to take back secondary financing has an immediate interest in such
refinancing because he or she may have agreed to subordinate the existing
secondary loan to a new loan. Several possible situations could arise. Where,
for example, both buyer and seller contemplate refinancing with a new first loan
in an amount in excess of the first and second loan, the seller may retain an
interest in the proceeds of such refinancing as part of the purchase price for the
property. The seller's interest may be limited to getting his or her secondary
financing paid off in a given time. This can be accomplished through (1) including an acceleration clause, (if enforceable) in the contract and mortgage; or (2)
incorporating an agreement to refinance the property at a given time or upon
notice by either party. The problem of the seller retaining a mortgage interest in
the property after such refinancing is discussed below under the heading Subordination Agreements. (For a form permitting replacement plus consideration,
see Form 3:30 and also Chapter 9.)

FORM 3:30 **ADDITIONAL CONSIDERATION FROM
REFINANCING LOANS**

(Precede with clauses for Assumption or Taken
subject to Existing Loans—See Form 3:05)

In addition to the above purchase price, it is further agreed, that such purchase price is to be increased by the additional payment as follows:

_____ of the net proceeds from refinancing of existing loans in one
   percentage

transaction. The net proceeds to be figured as follows:

a) The principal balance then remaining unpaid on first loan.

b) The principal balance then remaining unpaid on second loan.

c) All prepayment penalty charges, reconveyance fees, recording fees and brokerage fees in connection with such refinancing, together with such refinancing.

d) Such refinancing shall take place no later than _____, 19___ ___, or upon _____ days' written notice by either party by certified or registered mail. Upon such notice the seller shall designate two brokers to obtain such refinancing without obligation for paying such broker's fee, which shall be payable out of the proceeds of the accepted new loan.

e) The terms of the new loan shall be as follows:

f) Seller shall obtain any necessary consent from lessees of the property which may be required by the new lender.

g) This agreement shall survive the closing of title and shall be binding on the heirs, personal representatives, successors and assigns of the parties.

COMMENT ON FORM 3:30: This type of agreement should never be prepared without the advice of both seller's and buyer's counsel.

Subordination Agreements

Is is common practice for sellers of land for development, in addition to releasing parts of the land from the security of the purchase money mortgage or deed of trust, to subordinate their mortgage or deed of trust to further loans obtained by the buyer for financing subdivision improvements or constructing buildings. This situation even occurs in simple transactions in crowded cities when the owner of a small, obsolete house on a lot whose zoning has been changed is induced to subordinate to a construction loan. In most cases, subordination is advantageous to both parties: The seller can command a better price, and the buyer can buy with limited capital. But dangers are inherent in the practice of subordination as well. The seller needs not only a competently drawn contract and mortgage provision, but also an adequate guarantee as to the reliability and financial security of the builder-developer. Many a small home-owner with an extra lot has had a subordinated loan wiped out when the builder, in the middle of construction, collapsed and the construction lender had to take over. A conscientious broker will not leave the parties to their own devices in such a sale, but will, before any contract is executed, suggest legal advice.

Subordination agreements are in the nature of "joint ventures." The seller provides the land, the financing institution, the construction loan, the buyer-builder-developer, the "know-how." The seller's original senior purchase-money mortgage or deed of trust is subordinated, by agreement, to the loan from which the funds are coming to pay the joint venturers. The moment the construction loan is taken out, the property is, of course, overencumbered. Not until the project is completed is there sufficient security for the seller or the lender. The problem in drawing the original agreement, as well as the clause in the purchase-money mortgage for subordination, is that the seller obviously wants to be guaranteed that all the funds from the construction loan to which he or she subordinates are indeed used to improve the property. Exceptions may be made for loan charges, points, and so on.

If they desire, the parties can mutually agree to disbursements of necessities other than improvements and loan costs, but this is most unusual. Typically, the loan proceeds are to be used for purposes which would enhance the seller's equity in case of default, or provide funds from which the seller will be paid or derive sufficient money to complete the project.

Such subordination agreements are strictly construed. Provisions, for subordination in initial contracts must be spelled out with particular certainty. The maximum amount of loan, its length, interest rate, terms of prepayment, the disbursement of funds for other than direct construction must be specified. Ambiguity which could prevent specific performance could also warrant denial of damages for breach.

In practice, the subordination clauses found in the so-called Deposit Receipt, or the initial contract, are often fatally defective. Defects are sometimes cured by insertion of more specific subordination agreements in the purchase-money mortgage or deed of trust itself. Attempts to make such subordination clauses automatic without further agreements often fail because of uncertainty or unfairness in the provisions, or because a title company, in examining the notes of the construction loan, finds that it contains "hidden terms"—for example, increase in interest rates upon default in payment which exceed the maximum interest allowed by the agreement. In such a case, if the seller then agrees to execute a new, separate agreement specifically subordinating his/her loan to the specific loan the buyer has obtained, the seller thereby waives all objections and the title company can insure. If title insurance of "automatic subordination" clauses is anticipated, all agreements and instruments should be presented to the insurer before execution. Some title associations have adopted special subordination agreements for use by their member firms. It is often a condition for issuance of insurance policies that such forms are used in the transaction.

Because of the complexity of subordination agreements, no standard clause is suggested for simple sales agreements other than a contract clause for subordination of seller's loan on an improved lot or building site (see Form 3:31).

FORM 3:31   **"SUBORDINATION" CLAUSE**
               (Improved Lot or Building Site)

The _____ in favor of seller shall contain a
          mortgage/deed of trust

subordination clause providing that said _____ may within
                                    mortgage/deed of trust

_____ months from date of note and provided that _____
                                              the payments due under said

_____
mortgage/deed of trust and taxes are not then in default/no unrescinded Notice of Default

_____ , be made subject to and subordinated
under its terms then appears of record

to a new _____ _____ to be executed by buyer(s) in favor
          type   mortgage deed of trust

of any banking institution, federal or state savings and loan association, insurance
company, or pension fund made primarily for the purpose of construction
improvements on the property described herein and to secure a note with an

          (where terms of construction loan known)

amount not to exceed $_____, payable at no more than $_____ per

_____ (including interest not to exceed)
     month/quarter/semiannually/annually

_____% per annum _____ and _____. To be
                     at close of escrow   taxes and insurance

amortized over not less than _____ years or more than _____ years with a
prepayment penalty not to exceed _____

_____
          _____% of original principal/_____ months advanced interest

such other terms as may be required by the lender thereof.

                    Or:
     (where terms of construction loan unknown)

amount not to exceed _____
                              $_____/_____% of appraised value by FHA/VA/

_____ bearing interest not to exceed _____% per annum _____
lender   at close of escrow

_____ payable at times and on terms required by lender but to be amortized over
not less than _____ years or more than _____ years.

               (Optional, continue):

The loan shall be used for _____ of a
                              (specify, e.g.) construction on the described land

_____. The proceeds of
     dwelling, etc./an apartment house consisting of _____ room units

the loan shall be disbursed for, or portions thereof be applied in payment of, costs
including but not limited to, one or any more of the following:

          (Form continues on next page)

Offsite improvements on the land described in such _____ ,
mortgage/deed of trust
on site improvements, architectural fees, engineering fees, termite and inspection
fees, escrow charges, premiums for hazard insurance, title insurance, loan costs,
including discounts, interests, commissions, overhead charges and costs, advertising expenses of sales and other costs, incurred in connection with such contemplated improvements, with any remainder of such loan, after all payments
have been made to the buyer.

COMMENT ON FORM 3:31: In examining the cases concerning subordination
clauses, one must distinguish between cases based upon the clause in an executory contract and those decided after title has passed. The courts seem to have
taken the attitude that enforceability of the executory marketing contract depends upon whether the contract indicates "an agreement to agree" or a "second look" by the seller as to the type of mortgage to which he or she
subordinates the purchase money mortgage. The contract writer is often frustrat-
ed because the type of building contemplated, the cost, and the terms of construction money are unknown at the time of drafting the contract. Most court
decisions on this matter seem to make it a prerequisite that the contract be
specific concerning these points, and will not enforce contracts which do not
meet the minimum requirements of amount, terms, interest rate, points, prepayment penalties, etc. Perhaps the solution is to accept the inevitable. Where most
or all of these terms are speculative, it may be better to accept a vague subordination clause and negotiate specific terms later. If the seller is anxious to make
the deal, the buyer runs little risk. Even a well-drafted subordination clause may
be defective in some respect, and may be too uncertain and lacking in fairness
for specific performance. The seller's breach may only result in nominal damages, so in either event, the parties would gain more by negotiating a satisfactory subordination when all the facts are in, rather than being precipitous.
"Simple" solutions to drafting this type of contractual provision do not exist.

The first optional clause in Form 3:31 is designed to acquaint the seller in
advance with the buyer's contemplated use of the loan proceeds. Often, uninformed sellers have been unaware of the fact that up to 25 percent of a "construction" loan would not be used to actually improve the property. Most
"boiler-plate" subordination clauses fail to alert the seller to this fact. To protect against misinterpretation, use of funds for certain items could be prohibited,
and percentage figures for the size of construction loan to FHA and GI apprais-
als could be included. Control of loan funds by voucher systems as increased
restraints upon disbursement procedures could be worked into the contract.
Often the construction loan becomes the permanent loan. However, if the construction loan is a temporary loan which must be paid in full on completion,
subordination to a "take out" permanent loan may become necessary. To minimize a subsequent misunderstanding, specific, rather than general, terms for
such additional subordination should be drafted by competent counsel.

Down Payment in Other Than Cash

Sometimes the buyer is not able to pay all of the down payment in cash, desiring to use instead a mortgage or deed of trust on other property, as part or all of the down payment. Or, the buyer may wish to apply a boat, trailer, or personal automobile as part of the down payment. The following forms are designed to meet the most common situations. In transactions where the buyer wishes to use a parcel of real property, improved or unimproved, as part or all of the down payment, the use of a printed exchange contract is recommended. The exchange should be carefully analyzed for possible tax savings, and the property inspected by the proposed recipient.

Where a buyer wishes to transfer a note secured by mortgage on other real property, the clauses in Form 3:32 may be appropriate.

FORM 3:32   TRANSFER OF NOTE AND DEED OF TRUST AS PART PAYMENT

$_____ (credit allowed) by buyer's transferring and assigning _____ (with/without) recourse to seller, a note dated _____ , 19___. with an unpaid balance _____ (in that amount/of $__) with interest at the rate of ___% per annum paid to _____, 19___. Said note is payable _____ (monthly/quarterly/semiannually/annually) in installments _____ (including/plus) interest of $___, or more.

(Where limited installments and payoff within specific time):

and is due in full _____ (___ months/ ___ years) from date of note

(If acceleration upon resale or transfer):

and contains an acceleration clause at the option of holder in the event of sale or transfer of the property described in the _____ (mortgage/deed of trust) .

(In all cases, continue):

Said note is secured by a _____ (deed of trust) on the real property described as:

(insert description)
(If the note offered is a second loan):

subject only to the following encumbrances:

A ___ (first) _____ (type) loan with an approximate balance not in excess of $_____ payable at $___ _____ (monthly/quarterly/semiannually/annually), _____ (or more) including interest at ___% per annum _____ (at close) _____ (of escrow) in favor of _____ (lender) .

(Form continues on next page)

(If the note offered is a third loan):

and subject further to a _____ loan with an approximate balance not in
                         second

excess of $_____, payable at $ _____
                                                              monthly/quarterly/

_____ , _____, including interest at the rate of _____%
semiannually/annually   or more

per annum, due in full _____, 19_____.
                            date

(Optional, continue):

A true copy of said note and _____ are attached hereto as Exhibits
                              deed of trust

_____ and incorporated herein by reference. Buyer agrees to execute
   "A" and "B"

proper recorded assignment and deliver original note and _____ and
                                                           deed of trust

_____ and warrants the accuracy of the balance
endorsed title and fire insurance policies

due and that there are no defenses or set-offs due payor of said note. All transfer
costs including title insurance to be at expense of buyer.

COMMENT ON FORM 3:32: The seller's acceptance of a mortgage on other
property constitutes a risk. The seller should be totally satisfied that the property
is adequate security for the loan before agreeing. If the assigned note and mortgage are to be resold by seller, a determination of the exact value on the market
should be made, so that the seller is fully informed of the actual sales price he
or she is receiving for the property being sold. The sales price may be reduced
with the discount and brokerage expenses of a second transfer. In accepting the
mortgage as part of the down payment, the seller should obtain from the transferor, and if possible from the payor under the note, a statement that there are
no set-offs or defenses to the loan and that the unpaid balance as stated is
correct. Obtaining an endorsement of the holder's title insurance policy is recommended.

Whether the seller should take the note with or without recourse is a legal
problem. If a bare transfer is intended, the words "without recourse" are not
used. The adding of "without recourse" creates a qualifying endorsement.
Qualified endorsement transfers title to the instrument, but the endorser is not
liable for its payment.

For income tax purposes, the acceptance by seller of a mortgage on other
property is equivalent to receipt of cash to the extent of the market value of the
mortgage at the time of sale.

Personal Property as Part Payment

In addition to cash, other mortgages, and so forth, personal property can
be used as part of the down payment (see Form 3:33).

FORM 3:33   TRANSFER OF BOAT, CAR, TRAILER, TOOLS, AS PART OF DOWN PAYMENT

$_____ by buyer assigning, transferring by bill of sale all
credit allowed

his right, title and interest in the following personal property warranted to be ____

_____, to wit:
owned by him/of which buyer is registered owner

a _____ , _____ , _____ ,
(describe) boat/automobile/trailer/mobile home   type   model

_____, together with all _____
year   equipment/furniture according to inventory attached

and all warranties, guarantees of manufacturers or suppliers presently in force.

(If seller is to assume financing):

subject to seller's ability to _____ existing financing in the
take title subject to/assume

amount of $_____, payable at $_____, _____
monthly/quarterly/

_____ installments in accordance with the _____
semiannual/annual   conditional sales

_____ dated _____, 19____,
contract/security agreement/chattel mortgage

executed by buyer to _____, a copy of which is attached hereto
lender/seller

and made part hereof.

COMMENT ON FORM 3:33: The seller should ascertain whether buyer's title to the personal property is good. Financing documents should be carefully examined, and confirmation of the right to transfer or conditions for transfer should be obtained from lender. Official records should be checked to assure that the buyer has not given additional security interest in the personalty to anyone other than the original lender or seller (see Form 9:13). All necessary documents of title, registration, and insurance should be examined and transferred to seller at cost of buyer. Sometimes contracts contain credit insurance with prepaid premiums. Considerations should be given to cancellation of existing financing and new financing obtained from the seller's own lender on terms perhaps more advantageous than the existing financing. (Note: Real estate brokers need a special license to handle transactions involving boats.)

Proper Scheduling of Payments

Lending institutions are quite capable of protecting their own interests. Nevertheless, they find from time to time that the routine handling of mortgage lending does not properly protect them against the "milking" of the property by the buyer in possession during the time of default and before dispossession through foreclosure. Whoever arranges for the seller to provide financing of the property should be alert to these problems and advise the seller of the necessity for precautions. Where income property is involved, for example, an examination of the terms of the various liens on the property should be made. The payment dates on the encumbrances may have been scheduled in such a manner that the buyer is in the position to "milk" the property and collect rents or operate the apartment house, motel, or resort, for a number of months until defaulting on the mortgage. If the payments are timed incorrectly, the seller may find that when he or she forecloses, interest payments and taxes for at least six months are due. If the payments are scheduled correctly this problem can be avoided.

Another common situation is the cancellation by an owner planning default of an onerous lease for a cash payment by the tenant. If seller-mortgagee has relied upon the continuance of the lease as security for the loan, cancellation will substantially impair that security. But an alert broker can spot such at the time of sale. The contract and mortgage documents can then be drawn in a way which will protect the seller-lender. For example, the mortgage can provide that the owner may not change the terms of the lease without the written consent of the mortgagee, or the leases can be specifically assigned to the mortgagee with copies of such assignments delivered to each lessee.

Modification of Terms

It is also well to remember that an institutional or private first lender may waive amortization or modify the terms of the existing encumbrance (see Form 3:34). The holder of a secondary financing, of course, must adjust the payments in accordance with the buyer's ability to pay on both loans. The buyer naturally would like to keep the payments as low as possible to have a larger cash flow, while the holder of secondary financing would prefer the principal payments to be as high as possible so his or her junior position would steadily improve. If the buyer is able to have the senior loan reduced, modify its payment schedule, or waive some obligatory payments, the seller holding the second loan may suffer. This possibility is particularly relevant in the sale of apartment houses, motels, resorts, and the like, where the first lender may be a previous owner or construction loan lender.

Where desirable, the contract can, of course, provide for a prohibition against any changes in prior liens (see Form 3:35).

FORM 3:34   WAIVED OR DECREASED AMORTIZATION ON PRIOR ENCUMBRANCE TO BE APPLIED TO JUNIOR LOAN

The above described _____
                                            mortgage/deed of trust
in favor of seller shall contain a provision that if in any calendar year the amount paid in reduction of the first mortgage is less than the reduction indicated by applying the regular payments according to the schedule of amortization attached hereto and made a part hereof, then the difference between the sum of the

scheduled regular principal payments in such calendar year and the sum actually paid shall be paid and applied in reduction of the principal sum of the _____
_____ in favor of seller in addition to the payments provided for
mortgage/deed of trust

in said _____
note

on or before _____
January 31st of the year next ensuing/and shall be due and payable on the

_____.
succeeding January 1st

COMMENT ON FORM 3:34: The purpose of this provision is to keep the annual amount payable on the loan constant until the loans are paid off. The holder of the secondary financing is thereby protected against any waiver of amortization or modification of the senior encumbrance which will affect his or her security. This form does not preclude a modification of the terms of senior loan, but only forces the mortgagee to apply any "saving" to the junior encumbrance.

Amortization schedules are available at nominal cost from various publishers. They are tailor-made to each individual loan and can, of course, be obtained on existing notes as well. The information necessary is the monthly payment, the amount of interest, length of loan and amount.

FORM 3:35   NO CHANGE IN PRIOR LIENS

The second deed of trust shall require the trustor to keep all prior liens and encumbrances in good standing and preclude the trustor from accepting modifications of, or future advances under, a prior deed of trust.

COMMENT ON FORM 3:35: Special clauses should not be inserted in security instruments without advice of counsel.

Other problems that can affect the lender's security are tenants' rights in certain fixtures and conditional sales contracts having priority over the intended mortgage. Where a leasehold interest is particularly important to the seller-lender, a direct assignment of the lease to the lender may be considered. Because of the many different factual situations and legal considerations, no attempt has been made to suggest clauses covering these situations. Any competent real estate attorney can draw such clauses to protect the interest of the seller-lender.

"Release" Clauses

As the result of the population explosion and the corresponding hectic development of land for residential and commercial purposes, the sellers of raw acreage commonly are forced to participate in the financing of the property. The subordination of the seller's purchase money, deed of trust, or mortgage to construction loans and partial releases of the seller's lien as the developer-buyer moves ahead have become a way of life. In fact, the seller may now become a joint venturer with the developer. However, if the seller cannot devise a satisfactory cooperation-type of financing on the property, he or she may not be able to sell it at all.

In some instances, subordination and releases overlap, and the seller must decide whether or not to cooperate in both activities. This is a business judgment, which ultimately depends upon the buyer's integrity and credit standing. The release provisions are tailored to the needs of the buyer. The seller is often quite willing to accommodate the buyer provided that a release is backed by adequate consideration and that the seller is not left with inadequate security for the balance of the mortgage.

Sometimes the biggest problem lies in finding a formula for releasing choice parcels so that the seller's security does not end up consisting of scattered or "landlocked" parcels. Quite often, the buyer is more sophisticated than the seller and will attempt to dictate terms that are so "flexible" that, if unscrupulously used, they will leave the seller "holding the bag." Competent legal advice will be needed so that the interest of both parties can be protected.

The "release plan" is a necessary part of the initial purchase agreement, and is often subject to considerable bargaining between the parties. This particular clause, as well as the subordination clause, ultimately ends up in the security instrument and is affected by rules of certainty and specific performance similar to those discussed earlier in this chapter.

The most common problem arises when the buyer wishes to obtain full credit for the down payment and releases of each lot by dividing the amount of units into the balance of the purchase money mortgage. The seller wants to protect his or her security, and will not give credit for the down payment or, sometimes, the amortized payments either. The buyer wants unlimited right to pick and choose the land to be released. The seller wants protection against unrestricted selection to guard against the most desirable portions being released first, leaving the balance of the purchase-money mortgage secured by undesirable parcels, since this could lead to the buyer's abandonment of the remaining project. If the property to be sold is currently undivided, partial releases will probably constitute division of the property requiring compliance with the Subdivision Map Act (Gov C Sections 66410-66499,58). Releases should be subject to compliance with the Act.

Factual situations differ so much that it is not possible here to suggest clauses to cover them all. The clauses in Forms 3:36 through 3:39 are therefore examples only of possible solutions to simple problems. They are strictly for use in the initial contract only, and must, of course, be supplemented by the proper clause in the security instruments.

FORM 3:36   **RELEASE CLAUSE IN PURCHASE**
AGREEMENT
(Subdivided Lots)

The _____ in favor of seller shall contain a release clause
_____mortgage/deed of trust_____
providing that _____ of the _____ will release
_____holder/trustee_____ _____mortgage/deed of trust_____
not less than _____ contiguous lots at one time at the rate of $____ per lot
to be applied to the principal amount due provided that _____
_____the payments due under_____

_____
said mortgage/and taxes are not then in default/no unrescinded notice of default under

_____. Buyer to pay cost not to exceed $_____
its terms then appears of record
of drawing and recording each release.

COMMENT ON FORM 3:36: The language stating that payments be current is
important. If such a provision is absent in the security instrument, partial satisfaction and reconveyance can be compelled notwithstanding that the mortgage
is in default. If the lots are of unequal value, it may be advisable to modify the
clause by adopting a schedule for release with designated amounts for each lot
which can be attached to the agreement and also to the security instrument.

FORM 3:37   **"RELEASE" CLAUSE IN PURCHASE**
AGREEMENT (ACREAGE)

The _____ in favor of seller shall contain
_____mortgage/deed of trust_____
a release clause providing that the holder of the _____ will re-
_____mortgaged/deed of trust_____
lease any one or more acres at the rate of $_____ for each acre or fraction
thereof, to be applied upon the principal amount due provided that _____
_____the payments_____

_____
due under said mortgage and taxes are not then in default/no unrescinded Notice of

_____ .
Default under its terms then appears of record.

Buyer to pay cost not to exceed $_____ of drawing and recording
each such release and to obtain compliance with the Subdivision Map Act.

COMMENT ON FORM 3:37: Aside from demanding that all payments and
taxes be current, the only condition in this clause is that the release be for one
or more acres. This clause can be expanded to include the provisions for specific selection of certain acres of parcels, or in accordance with a specific schedule.

FORM 3:38   "RELEASE" CLAUSE, LAND TO BE
SUBDIVIDED OR SOLD AS ACREAGE

The _____ in favor of seller shall contain a release clause
mortgage/deed of trust
providing that the holder of the _____ will release not less than
mortgage/deed of trust
_____ contiguous lots into which the land which is the subject of this contract may
be subdivided, upon the payment of an amount, to be applied to the principal
amount due, for each such lot to be determined by dividing the total original
amount of the note by the total number of lots _____ as shown by a
less one
subdivision map filed of record covering the said land.

Prior to subdividing of the land which is the subject of this contract, the
holder will release any one or more of the acres at the rate of $_____ for
each acre or fraction thereof, provided however that the first acre to be so
released must be contiguous to acreage previously released.

Provided further that _____
the payments due under said mortgage and taxes are not

_____ .
then in default/no unrescinded Notice of Default under its terms then appears of record
Buyer to pay cost not to exceed $_____ of drawing and recording each
such release.

COMMENT ON FORM 3:38: See Comment on Form 3:36.

FORM 3:39   RELEASE OF PART OF PARCEL
WHEN CERTAIN SUM HAS BEEN PAID

The _____ in favor of seller shall contain a release clause
mortgage/deed of trust
provided that the holder of the _____ will release 1/3 of the
mortgage/deed of trust
property upon payment of the sum of $_____, provided that _____
the payments

_____
due under said mortgage and taxes are not then in default/no unrescinded Notice of Default under

_____ .
its terms then appears of record
Buyer to pay cost not to exceed $_____ of drawing and recording of
said release. For this purpose, the property shall be divided in 3 parcels as shown
on the map attached hereto and made a part hereof by reference. The buyer shall
have the option to select the first such parcel to be released provided that the first
parcel to be released shall be either parcel A or C. In the event either parcel A or
C has been released, the next parcel to be released shall be parcel B in accordance with the terms of this paragraph.

COMMENT ON FORM 3:39: In drawing a release clause as above, the contract
writer must often use the expert skill of other professionals such as engineers,
surveyors, and title company personnel. It is especially important that the de-

scriptions in the ultimate documents to be recorded are checked and doubled-checked. A parcel map must be obtained for subdivisions of less than five parcels or exempted under California Gov C Section 66426.

Using Installment Land Sales Contracts

In several types of real estate transactions the seller technically retains title. These types are closely related; they are the installment land contract, and a long-term escrow. A cousin to these is the lease-with-option-to-buy provision.

Where a "thin" security device is necessary, many "sales" are handled by giving the buyer a lease with an option to buy. Problems arise if the lessee-buyer defaults, especially if part of the rental payment is credited towards the purchase price. To regain possession of the property, the seller must bring action to quiet title, which is often expensive and time-consuming.

Whether the transaction is to be "secured" by a land contract or by a long-term escrow, the usual transaction begins with a standard Deposit Receipt. The final contract is usually drawn by the seller's counsel or by counsel for the title company. For a clause in the Deposit Receipts when a security installment land contract is contemplated, see Form 3:40.

**FORM 3:40   SALE ON SECURITY (INSTALLMENT)
                    LAND CONTRACT**

$_____ cash down payment including deposit.

$_____ by buyer and seller executing a Long Form Security (Installment) Land Contract with Power of Sale with _____
name of title company

as Trustee providing for buyer taking subject to and paying through seller the balance of $ _____

of the existing loan with _____
name of lender

of record, payable at $_____ per month including interest at _____% per annum _____
including impound for taxes/and insurance

and

$_____ by buyer paying seller in monthly installments of $_____ including interest at _____% per annum. Any balance due seller may be prepaid at any time _____
after the calendar year in which the security land

_____ .
contract was recorded

(Optional, but recommended clauses):

This offer is subject to buyer's and seller's attorneys' approval within 10 days of opening of escrow. Unless written notice of disapproval is delivered to escrow within that time the agreement shall be deemed approved.

(Form continues on next page)

(continue):

Buyer shall provide information for credit report and financial statement through escrow within _____ days after opening of escrow. Unless written notice of disapproval is delivered within five days of receipt, buyer's financial statement and credit report shall be deemed approved.

COMMENT ON FORM 3:40: This clause is inserted in the deposit receipt contract. Because of erosion of seller's rights through judicial decisions, installment land contracts have become obsolete. Their use is not recommended.

FORM 3:41   **DISCLOSURE STATEMENT**

The undersigned hereby acknowledge that they have been advised by __ _____ Realtors, as follows:

1. The real property located at _____ which is the subject of this sale under a "Real Estate Purchase Contract and Receipt for Deposit" dated _____ is subject to trust deed(s).
2. The trust deed(s) contain(s) a provision providing for acceleration of the loan upon sale of the property and the lender may attempt to accelerate and declare the entire balance now due and payable as a result of this transaction.
3. The parties to this transaction should have all documents which they are required to execute reviewed by their attorney since this transaction may create or change existing legal rights of the parties.

The undersigned hereby agree to hold _____ Realtors, its employees, agents and representatives harmless from any loss, including attorneys' fees, which either party may suffer as a result of an acceleration of the trust deed(s).

Seller: _____   Buyer: _____

Dated: _____   Dated: _____

COMMENT ON FORM 3:41: This disclosure statement warns about the problems involved in land sales contracts. In California it does not substitute for the seller financing disclosures required by law. See Page 80.

Lease with an Option to Purchase

Rather than preparing elaborate option agreements which will have to be tailored to the specific case, a purchase-option provision can be inserted in a lease and a fully prepared sales agreement attached to the lease. The terms of the sale are set forth in the Real Estate Purchase Contract and Receipt for Deposit as in an ordinary real estate transaction. In addition to stating the actual terms of sale the contract will incorporate the option through the clause in Form 3:42.

FORM 3:42   EFFECTIVENESS OF SALES AGREEMENT

This agreement is effective only upon exercise of the option contained in the attached lease, which is incorporated herein by reference, and shall be deemed to have been executed upon the date of the exercise of the option.

COMMENT ON FORM 3:42: The sales agreement should be prepared as carefully as any real estate contract. However, one should take into account that loan balances will be reduced as a result of payments made during the lease period. Provisions for the payment of taxes and insurance should be incorporated.

FORM 3:43   OPTION TO PURCHASE

The lessee shall have the option to purchase the leased premises at any time prior to _____ , provided the lessee has complied with all of the
date
terms of the lease and the rent is current. The option is to be exercised by giving written notice to the lessor not less than 30 days prior to said date. Exercise of the option shall be upon the terms and conditions contained in that certain "Real Estate Purchase Contract and Receipt for Deposit" attached hereto and made a part hereof by reference. Said agreement shall be deemed to have been executed by both parties on the date of exercise of the option.

(Optional):

_____ of the rent paid hereunder shall be applied on the
$_____/_____%
purchase price.

(Optional):

The lessor agrees to pay _____ a selling commission of _____
broker $_____/
_____ in the event lessee purchases the property described
_____% of selling price
herein during the term of the option or any extension thereof.

COMMENT ON FORM 3:43: By fixing an exact date for termination of the option, misunderstanding regarding the "rights" of lessee during "extensions" or "hold over" periods are avoided. A memorandum of the lease and option can be recorded to give notice of the lessee's interest. Such recordation creates, however a 'cloud' on the title, which may be difficult to remove if lessee is uncooperative upon termination or abandonment of the lease (see Form 9:12).

Cost of Financing

The cost of obtaining financing is usually borne by the buyer; however, the parties can agree to the seller's paying all or part of the cost. Cost includes the set-up of loan charge of the lender, the brokerage fee to a mortgage loan broker, points on government-insured loans, fees for drawing papers, and recording fees for transfer taxes. A distinction should be made between set-up charges and the cost of paying off and reconveying existing encumbrances. Some contract writers merely write, "Buyer to pay usual closing costs." Such unspecific treatment invariably leads to disputes at the time of closing as to the appropriateness of the various charges. It is safer to itemize the charges or refer to a set of rules adopted by the local board of Realtors.

Clauses cited in this chapter make provisions for the payment of set-up charges on conventional and government-insured loans. Where the seller is to bear all costs including the additional cost of brokerage, the contract could contain the provision in Form 3:44. When the buyer is to pay all financing costs, the clause in Form 3:45 is recommended.

FORM 3:44   SELLER TO PAY COST OF FINANCING

Any charges or fees for brokerage, procurement or placement of said loan including lender's charge for set-up fees, appraisal, drawing of documents, tax-service fee as shown on lender's closing statement, shall be at seller's sole expense, except that buyer shall bear cost of recordation of documents.

FORM 3:45   BUYER TO PAY COST OF FINANCING

Any charges or fees for _____ , procurement or placement of
                                brokerage
_____ including lender's charge for set-up fees, appraisal,
said loan/new first loan
drawing of documents, tax service fee as shown on lender's closing statement and cost of recordation of documents shall be at buyer's sole expense _____
                                                                              but shall

_____.
not exceed the sum of $_____/_____ points

COMMENT ON FORMS 3:44 and 3:45: The above comprehensive loan-charge clauses are an improvement over the usual provisions found in Deposit Receipts. Some brokers are unwilling to specify loan charges, but attempt to include them in the term "closing costs." This method usually backfires, since at closing all the charges and costs have to be accounted for. (See Chapter 5.)

The proration of taxes, insurance, rents, and so forth, often mistakenly considered closing costs by buyers, are discussed in Chapter 5.

The Truth-in-Lending Act

The federal Truth-in-Lending Act was enacted to help consumers learn what their credit actually costs by requiring creditors to disclose, among other things, credit charges in a dollar-and-cents amount and also as the annual percentage rate called the finance charge. Almost everyone extending consumer credit is subject to the disclosure requirements of the law and the regulations prescribed by the Federal Reserve Board. The law has an impact in various degrees upon the activities of lenders on and sellers of real estate as well as real estate brokers. It, therefore, affects contracts for sale or financing of real estate in all states.

The essence of the Truth-in-Lending Act—Title I of the Federal Consumer Credit Protection Act (P.L. 90-321, 82 Stat. 146, 15 USC 1601) is consumer protection. Every person granting consumer credit must disclose required data. The law applies to any person who in the ordinary course of business (1) Regularly extends, whether in connection with loans, sales of property or services, or otherwise, consumer credit which is payable by agreement in more than four installments or for which the payment of a finance charge is or may be required, and (2) is the person to whom the debt arising from the consumer credit transaction is initially payable on the face of the evidence of indebtedness or, if there is no such evidence of indebtedness, by agreement. Credit extensions for business or commercial purposes other than agricultural, or for organizations, governments, or governmental instrumentalities are not within the scope of the act. "Organizations" here include corporations, trusts, estates, partnerships, co-ops, and associations. Sales and loans to such organizations are therefore not affected by the provisions of the law.

First mortgage lenders are subject to all but two of the same disclosure requirements placed on all other creditors. The total finance charge in dollars and cents over the life of the mortgage need not be disclosed in connection with a first mortgage made to finance the purchase of a dwelling. First mortgages— whether created, retained, or assumed to finance the acquisition of a dwelling in which the debtor resides or expects to reside—are exempted from the requirement that the creditor grant the customer a three-day right of rescission where a lien is placed on the customer's residence. A "dwelling" under the Act is a residential-type structure containing at least one or more family housing units. It must be real property. It may be a residential condominium.

In real estate transactions, certain charges such as most ordinary closing costs need not be included in "finance charge." Points and discounts, however, must be included in the finance charge. The finance charge is therefore more comprehensive, and the lender's disclosure statement of the annual percentage rate (APR) may be higher than the real estate sales contracts' rate of interest.

Handling the Finance Charge

The question arises as to how the contract writer should handle the finance charge in the ordinary real estate transaction. If an ordinary seller, other than for example a developer or builder, takes back a mortgage, he or she is not subject to the law at all. Loans on commercial and business property other than agricultural do not fall within the law. In these situations, a sales contract can be drawn without reference to the Act.

Because the sales contract is between the buyer and seller, it need not include any disclosures demanded by the Act. If the loan itself falls under the Act, the creditor will be subject to the Act and the lender-creditor must give a disclosure statement before the loan transaction closes. In most transactions, the use of the clauses included in this chapter are applicable without reference to the Act. The buyer of a dwelling, for example, needs to know what the annual finance charge will be in order to compare rates when they are quoted as a "finance-charge" rather than as annual interest. However, buyers are also vitally interested in knowing what the points and set-up charges are individually, and not as calculated into the finance charge, because they must adjust their own available cash funds accordingly. To avoid confusion between finance charge and interest alone, brokers may find it advisable, in all transactions in which the Act is applicable, to insert the following clause in the sales contract after all the standard terms of a first loan are set forth: The annual percentage rate _____ % per annum.

to be/not to exceed

If a second loan at the time of sale of a dwelling is placed by a lender who in the "ordinary course of business extends consumer credit," a creditor's disclosure statement must be given to the buyer. This statement will include the finance charge as an annual percentage and as a total cash amount. If the property is a residence in which the buyer intends to reside, the lender in addition must give notice to the buyer's three-day right to rescission of the transaction.

Selective "Terms of Payment" Clauses

Some contract writers who have become accustomed to using greatly abbreviated versions of terms-of-payment clauses or to using forms where part of the payment terms are printed in the form may find the proposed clauses in this chapter unnecessarily wordy. Clarity, however, is achieved by specific rather than vague language. Sadly, far too many real estate contracts are defective in the terms-of-payment clause. Sometimes the excuse is that there is not sufficient space on the form to "get it all in." The solution is, of course, either to redesign the form or to add an addendum to the form on a separate sheet of paper and incorporate it into the contract. The typical hastily scribbled contract replete with interlineations, corrections, and imprecise language is a disgrace. The use of the clauses set forth in this chapter should hasten the demise of such unprofessional work. For additional seller financing clauses see Chapter 9.

A Checklist for "Terms of Payment" Clause

An adequate "Terms of Payment" clause should specify the following:

1. The amount of increased deposit, if any.
2. The amount of total cash down payment, including or excluding the deposit and its medium of payment (cash, type of check acceptable).
3. When the down payment shall be paid and to whom.
4. The amount of loan or loans expressed in dollars or in percentage of price.
5. The length of the loan or loans (unless it can be determined from amortization tables based on the information set out in the contract).
6. The rate of interest on each loan and whether it is variable, renegotiable or can otherwise be adjusted.
7. The amount of periodic payment and its mode of payment (monthly, quarterly, semiannually, or annually).
8. Whether the periodic payment includes principal, interest, taxes, and insurance.
9. Prepayment charges, if any.
10. Loan charges, if any.
11. Set-up charges, loan and appraisal fees or assumption fees to be paid by buyer. Points to be paid by seller.
12. If the transaction is an installment tax sale: Limitations on payments in year of sale and other provisions inserted for tax reasons.
13. Where secondary financing is taken back by seller, provisions against modification of terms of prior loan, acceleration clauses, late charges, and so on.
14. A provision allowing the return of deposit if required loan is unavailable within stated period. Possible waiver.
15. A provision allowing seller or broker or both to obtain loan commitment, if buyer is unable to arrange financing.
16. The type of note and security instrument used in purchase money loans.
17. Specific clauses used in FHA and GI loans.

Chapter 4
Factual Contract Terms and Conditions

No representation is made as to the legal validity of any provision or the adequacy of any provision in any specific transaction.

Caveat in California Association of Realtors' Real Estate Purchase Contract and Receipt for Deposit.

In most well-designed printed forms for Deposit Receipts, a provision is made or a blank is left for insertion of the words, "Other terms or conditions." This space is the catch-all, designed to incorporate any terms and conditions not covered in the printed provisions or in other blanks of the form. But quite often the space provided for such "other terms and conditions" is much too small to allow even the most Spartan recital. It is therefore impossible to draw an adequate contract without attaching an extra sheet to the printed form and incorporating the addendum by referring to it in the text.

In the original Model Form, the other-terms-and-conditions clause is part of the terms-of-payment clause and bears these instructions: "Set forth any terms and conditions of a factual nature applicable to this sale, such as financing, prior sale of other property, the matter of structural pest control inspection, repairs and personal property to be included in the sale."

Once price and financing terms are settled, the negotiations usually turn to other items, which involve warranties, covenants and conditions designed to protect the interests of each party. The range of possibilities is limited only by the contract writer's imagination and the parties' anticipation of problems. Most problems involve legal implications which may make the transaction undesirable to one of the parties. The majority of conditions are requested by buyers. They usually limit the buyer's obligation in some way. Others, such as warranties and covenants, may extend the seller's area of responsibility. Few contracts contain all the protective equipment which experienced contract writers have devised. Fewer contracts still are without warranties, conditions, and covenants altogether. Every situation is different, and even so-called "simple" transactions have troublesome areas.

Conditions are usually instigated by buyers who want to protect themselves while they check out the property. They affect the buyer's performance with respect to the happening or nonhappening of an event, or the existence or nonexistence of a fact. They may create a condition requiring someone's approval of an element of a transaction. They may also be used as an out if, after more searching investigation, the property does not measure up to the buyer's initial expectations. Nevertheless, conditions are useful to commit the buyer, although conditionally, while binding the seller to perform when the conditions have been met.

Conditions may affect the usual requirement of mutuality of bilateral contracts. While the tendency of the courts is to find a contract rather than to destroy what appears to be an agreement, conditions often lead to litigation.

Contracts which make one party's duty to perform conditional on his or her "satisfaction" fall into two primary categories: (1) those where the condition calls for satisfaction as to commercial value or quality and/or operative fitness or mechanical utility; and (2) those involving fancy, taste, or judgment. In the first category, dissatisfaction cannot be claimed arbitrarily, unreasonably, or capriciously; the standard of a reasonable person is used in determining whether "satisfaction" has been received. In the second category, the promisor's determination that he or she is not satisfied, when made in good faith, is a defense to an action on the contract. See Form 4:27.

To avoid some of the inherent risk in conditions, it is usually preferable to incorporate provisions which obligate the buyer or seller to perform certain acts in trying to meet the demand of the conditions. Where the conditions can be defeated by unsuccessful attempts by one party to perform, the other party may wish to retain the right to obtain the performance of the conditions. This is particularly true in financing situations.

Providing for Waiver of Conditions

The party for whose sole benefit a condition exists may waive it. Where a condition is benefiting more than one party, such other parties must also waive to make the waiver effective. Waiver rests on intent, since it is "the intentional relinquishment of a known right after knowledge of the facts." It assumes the existence of an opportunity for the choice between relinquishment and the enforcement of the right. A waiver requires a clear showing of intent, and doubtful cases will be decided against waiver by the courts. Waiver can be automatic or elective if the agreement so provides. Or the agreement may give one of the parties an obligation or election to cure the defect. To be complete, the contract should provide for what will happen if a condition cannot be performed. If the contract is to be terminated, it should provide that the deposit be restored to the buyer.

Sometimes it is not possible to impose or negotiate a condition, and the buyer may elect to extract a covenant (specific agreement) or a warranty from the seller that the property meets certain criteria. The buyer's remedies upon a breach of covenant or warranty are damages or rescission. The disadvantage with such covenants and conditions is that they may not survive the delivery of the deed. (See "Survival of Deed" in this chapter for a more complete discussion.)

Performance by one party may be conditioned upon several items. The most practical way of expressing this situation is to set forth a list of conditions as follows:

FORM 4:00   **MULTIPLE CONDITIONS AND
                        WARRANTIES**

Buyer's obligation to perform this agreement is subject to the following terms and conditions:

    (1) _____.

    (2) _____.

If these conditions are not satisfied, Buyer may, at Buyers election waive the conditions or terminate this agreement. If Buyer gives no notice of disapproval to Seller within _____ from seller's acceptance or _____, the con-

               days   set forth above

dition shall be deemed waived.

(Optional, continue):

When above conditions have been satisfied Buyer shall forthwith increase the Deposit to $_____, _____ .

                                   and execute Form RID-11.

(Optional, continue):

Seller warrants and represents the following:

    (1) _____.

    (2) _____.

The above warranties and representations shall survive delivery of Deed.

The seller's warranties or representations can be handled in a similar manner: *COMMENT ON FORM 4:00:* Some buyers will not increase the deposit before they have removed all contingencies pertaining to inspection of the premises, leases or records. See liquidated damages. For "survival of deed," see comment on Form 4:46.

Using Addenda

Whenever insufficient space makes it impossible to incorporate all of the terms of the contract in the space allowed for each item, or where a printed clause must be deleted and a new clause substituted, it may be necessary to affix a rider to the agreement. A physical attachment may not be legally important, but including it is, of course, better practice." Even in "simple" transactions, however, it may be necessary to attach to the form as exhibits such documents as structural pest control agreements, inspection reports, required disclosure statements, inventories, rent statements, preliminary title reports, and so forth. The Model Forms have space for the inclusion of such supplements. Riders setting forth additional terms should be referred to in the contract itself (see Form 4.01), and a crossreference to the contract should appear on each addendum (see Form 4:02). Both referrals and addenda should be initialed by all parties.

FORM 4:01   **ADDENDUM**

The attached addendum consisting of _____ pages is part of this agreement and is incorporated herein by reference.

COMMENT ON FORM 4:01: Insert in Deposit Receipt.

FORM 4:02   **ADDENDUM**
                    (Heading—At Top of Addendum:)

Addendum to _____ , dated _____, 19_____,
                    title of contract
in which _____ is referred to as Buyer and _____
            name of buyer   name of seller
is referred to as Seller.

(Continue with terms of Addendum):

COMMENT ON FORM 4:02: This heading will refer the addendum to the specific contract even if it may not be attached thereto physically. Where only a few lines are necessary, the addendum may be written on the reverse side of the contract. Again the addendum should be incorporated in the contract by using appropriate referrals, such as "continued on the reverse hereof," or attached hereto as Exhibit "_____." and incorporated herein and by having both addenda and referrals initialed by the parties.

Noting an Allocation of Purchase Price

In sales of furnished apartment houses, motels, and hotels, the total purchase price may include personal property as well as real estate. Both the seller and the buyer may desire, for tax reasons, to allocate a particular amount to the various items. The interests of the buyer and the seller in assigning values to certain assets may conflict. Before the contract is drawn, these allocations should be discussed with tax counsel for each of the parties to avoid distorted values. A simple wording of the allocation in the contract will suffice (see Form 4:03).

FORM 4:03   ALLOCATION OF PURCHASE PRICE

The above stated purchase price is allocated as follows:
Real property $_____. Personal property $_____. The parties agree
that this agreement is indivisible even though separate considerations have been
stated for the real property and the personal property.

COMMENT ON FORM 4:03: The allocation of purchase price is usually significant in the sale of income property, particularly to establish the cost of
depreciable property. Seller should get tax advice because of risk of recapture of
depreciation.

Incorporating Oral Agreements

Unfortunately, many small matters arise during the period between the
seller's acceptance and the day of performance. Loan commitments may cause
a change in terms, or overlooked items and second thoughts by the buyer may
lead to new conditions agreed to orally by the seller. These agreements may be
incorporated in the final closing agreements or escrow instructions, but they are
often left to verbal understanding, causing later problems of interpretation. A
contract for the sale of real property can under certain circumstances be altered
by oral agreement (see Form 4:04).

The broker should be careful when incorporating such side agreements
into the contract or as addenda to the contract. Items such as the designation of
who is to perform pest control inspection, roof and plumbing inspection, and
the like should not be left to oral agreement or determined by the broker.
Written instructions should be used in every transaction as a matter of course.
The selection of contractors should be the responsibility of the parties.

FORM 4:04   AMENDMENTS TO BE IN WRITING

This agreement may not be amended, modified, altered or changed in any
respect whatsoever except by a further agreement in writing duly executed by the
parties hereto.

COMMENT ON FORM 4:04: While a written agreement may not generally be
altered or changed by an oral agreement, nevertheless the law does recognize
exceptions to this rule. CAL Civil Code section 1698 provides that a written
contract may be modified by an oral agreement to the extent it is "executed by
the parties," or "unless the contract expressly provides" if supported by consideration and the statute of frauds is satisfied. In addition, the doctrines of
recission, waiver, novation and substitution, estoppel and independent or collateral agreements are other theories under which a written contract can be modi-

fied by an oral agreement. The CAR Model form expressly states: "All modifications or extensions shall be in writing signed by the parties." See also Form 4:08.

Sales made by minors or incompetents, and by executors, administrators, and other trustees are subject to court approval. The offer should so provide, as in Form 4:05.

FORM 4:05   **APPROVAL OF COURT**

It is understood that seller is acting in the capacity of _____
                                                        executor/
_____ , and that this sale is subject to the approval of the
administrator/trustee
_____ Court of the County of _____ , State of _____ .

COMMENT ON FORM 4:05: Where a sale is to be confirmed by a probate court, the attorney for the personal representative of the estate will usually prepare a contract and the petition for submission to the court. A broker quite often will use the regular Deposit Receipt as the initial contract to accept buyer's deposit. If this is done, the above clause should be inserted in the Deposit Receipt, and the deposit should conform to the legally sufficient deposit in the manner prescribed by law.

"As Is" Clauses

Frequently, sales are made of real property "as is," that is, no representation is made by the seller as to the condition of the property. Only rarely, however, is the seller completely free of responsibility. Even an "as is" clause combined with a general "disclaimer" clause will not protect against the consequences of fraud perpetrated by a seller.

In a good example of misuse of the "as is" clause, one court held the clause to mean that buyers take the property in the condition visible to or observable by them.[1] When a seller or broker actively misrepresents the true condition of the property, or fails to disclose true facts of its condition which are unknown to the buyer, the "as is" clause will not protect them against their active or negative fraud. In the case mentioned above the broker knew that the Health Department had condemned an outside stairway, but did not disclose this information to the buyer. The broker was held liable for fraud. As the court said, "An 'as is' provision may therefore be effective as to a dilapidated stairway, but not as to a missing structural member, a subterranean creek in the back yard, or an unexploded bomb buried in the basement, all being known to the seller."

In situations where the buyer consciously wishes to waive all conditions, for example because he or she intends to demolish the building, the "as is" clause in Form 4:06 can be used.

FORM 4:06   ALL-INCLUSIVE "AS IS" CLAUSE

The buyer represents that he has made a complete investigation and has inspected the building, furnishings and equipment of the premises, and is fully aware of their condition, and agrees to accept the improvements "as is" subject to all existing building, health and safety regulations, and to waive _____

any residential

_____ .
requirement report/any structural pest control inspection report

COMMENT ON FORM 4:06: This clause includes the so-called 3-R report, which by ordinance must be delivered by the seller to a buyer in certain cities before close of the transaction unless waived upon a special form. This clause should be used with caution. If any specific illegality is present in the building and the buyer is willing to accept the building with such defect, an express statement to that effect is preferable (see Form 4:22).

In another case,[2] the Deposit Receipt provided that "buyer agrees to waive termite clearance and to absolve the seller of any warranty, accepting house as is." But the termites must have kept the house standing by holding hands, so heavily infested and decayed were the premises. The court found liability against the seller despite the fact that the transaction was handled exclusively by a broker. Again, the "as is" provision was held to protect the seller only in regard to a defective condition visible to or observable by the buyer.

"As is" clauses should be used with caution, they will not protect against fraud by seller or agent. For a discussion in depth about disclosures, see Chapter 11.

Making Disclosures in Writing

A seller acting upon the duty of disclosure should do so in a manner which would make proof of disclosure easy if dispute should arise. Just telling the broker to tell the buyer of a situation that should be disclosed in writing is obviously insufficient. Nothing less than a clearly worded disclosure inserted in the sales contract will do. If the disclosure does not appear in the original version of the Deposit Receipt, it should be made by an addendum to the agreement delivered to and initialed by the buyer. If overlooked at the time of delivery, the buyer should be apprised of the situation before the close of escrow or delivery of deed so that he or she may elect to rescind or close the transaction despite the disclosure of the defect. The most common defects which arise in fraudulent situations concern misrepresentation in investment property, number or legality of multiple units, illegal work on the premises, the existence of termites and dry rot, nonvisible conditions of soil (for example, filled land or subterranean creeks), quality of land and misdescription of geography of land including boundaries and undisclosed easements or encroachment agreements. The buyer can be protected by the insertion in the sales agreement of appropriate representations. Preferably, these representations by the seller should be in the form of warranties. This chapter contains clauses designed to provide such warranties. See also Chapter 11 Disclosures.

Combining "As Is" and "Disclaimer" Clauses

"As is" and "disclaimer" clauses are often used together. In "boilerplate contracts," disclaimers are often part of the printed matter. Their validity is doubtful and they will not provide immunity against fraud. But a disclaimer such as that in Form 4:07 in combination with an "as is" clause consciously entered into by both parties is of higher purity.

A distinction between general and specific disclaimers may exist. A buyer who claims, subsequent to closing, that the very subject of a specific disclaimer was orally misrepresented, may have some trouble convincing the court of the truth of such assertion. Nevertheless, it is universally true that a perpetrator of fraud cannot, by the very instrument which is part of the fraud, escape from the consequences by inserting an immunity clause.

Forms 4:07 through 4:10 are examples of several types of disclaimer clauses.

FORM 4:07   **"DISCLAIMER" CLAUSE AND
"ENTIRE CONTRACT" CLAUSE**

This agreement constitutes the entire contract between the parties hereto, and the seller is not liable or bound in any manner by expressed or implied warranties guarantees, promises, statements or representations pertaining to said premises, the conditions thereof, the rentals, or any other matter whatsoever, made or furnished by any real estate broker, agent, employee, servant or other person representing or purporting to represent the seller, unless such warranties, guarantees, promises, statements or representations are expressly and specifically set forth herein.

COMMENT ON FORM 4:07: This is a final, exculpatory clause often sought and inserted by sellers' attorneys. It can be used in combination with Form 4:06. Such a general disclaimer clause will not give the seller immunity against an action based upon fraud.[3]

Whenever a seller's attorney wishes to have such a general disclaimer clause inserted in the agreement, the buyer's attorney should inquire of the buyer whether any statements have been made by the seller or the seller's agent and whether the buyer has relied on such statement in entering into the contract. If the inquiry discloses such statements, the seller should be required to make express representation about such matters in the contract. A broker who receives a counter-offer from a seller which includes such a disclaimer clause should refer the matter to the attorney for the buyer, or recommend that the buyer obtain legal counsel.

FORM 4:08   **ENTIRE AGREEMENT**

All prior agreements between the parties are incorporated in this agreement which constitutes the entire contract. Its terms are intended by the parties as a final expression of their agreement with respect to such terms as are included herein and may not be contradicted by evidence of any prior or contemporaneous agreement. The parties further intend that this agreement constitutes the complete and exclusive statement of its terms and that no extrinsic evidence whatsoever may be introduced in any judicial or arbitration proceeding, if any, involving this agreement.

COMMENT ON FORM 4:08: The purpose of this provision is to establish that the written agreement does in fact incorporate all prior agreements between the parties. It will not exclude the introduction of evidence to show the invalidity of the contract on the grounds of fraud, mistake, or lack of considerations. A court must satisfy itself that the parties clearly intended the writing to contain the entirety of their agreement. Form 4:08, which utilizes the specific statutory language, can be inserted in the contract. A similar clause is part of the "boiler-plate" of Model Form II.

FORM 4:09   NOTICE TO SELLER OF BROKER'S AGENCY

_____ is acting in this transaction as the agent and broker
            name of broker
for the buyer.

In _____ seller agrees, that the broker has
        accepting the buyer's offer
made no representations or warranties to induce seller to enter into the transaction except the representations and warranties made on buyer's behalf in writing signed by buyer. Seller relies solely on provisions contained in writings signed by buyer.

COMMENT ON FORM 4:09: Where the purchase price is "net" to seller and the seller is not paying the commission, or where the broker is acting as agent for the buyer, this provision may be helpful. It limits the buyer's responsibility for the acts of agent. Such a disclaimer clause will not, however, protect a party against the consequences of any fraud he or she might have perpetrated.

FORM 4:10   BROKER "DISCLAIMER" CLAUSE

Responsibility of Purchaser: It is expressly understood by the purchaser that the agent has not made any investigation or determination other than specifically expressed herein with respect to: the legality of the present, contemplated, or future use or uses of the property; or violations of any federal, state, county, or municipal ordinances, statutes, zoning, tract restrictions and set back ordinances; planned or proposed acquisition of the property or any portion thereof by the federal, state, county, or municipal governments, or any other governmental agency for public or private use; the presence or absence of fungi or wood destroying organisms; the correctness of income and expense information, existence and text of leases, options, or party wall agreements, if any, and the purchaser agrees that such investigation and determination has been his sole responsibility and the agent shall not be held responsible therefor.

COMMENT ON FORM 4:10: This clause is being used by a leading California broker. His Deposit Receipt contains this provision in bold print and the following legend: "This is not a standard agreement of sale and deposit receipt. Please read this contract carefully." This clause is reproduced here only as an illustration. This "hands off" attitude expressed by the broker raises moral and ethical questions of what functions the broker has undertaken in the transaction other than collecting the commission. The use of a similar disclaimer clause as part of the "boiler plate" in any printed form should not be undertaken without legal advice.

Assigning the Contract

Buyers may desire to assign the purchase contract for several reasons (see Form 4:11 for a right-to-assign clause). They may wish to resell the property to a buyer for a profit prior to actually exercising the contract. Or they may wish to assign the contract to a wholly controlled corporation, to be formed, perhaps, to avoid personal liability on mortgage obligations. Tax considerations may also be involved. (See Form 4:13, below.)

A contract for the sale of real property not involving personal services to be performed is assignable by the buyer. An option to purchase real property is also assignable. This general right to assign is conditioned upon the parties' intent. If, by its terms, the contract is intended to be reassignable, or if performance by another would deprive the seller of his or her bargain or impair performance, assignment will not be permitted.[4] The seller may not wish to allow the assignment, and can make consent of seller to such assignment a condition precedent to the validity of the assignment. A provision expressly voiding the contract if assigned without the seller's consent is enforceable (see Form 4:12). For a discussion of "nominee" versus "assignee" see page 33.

FORM 4:11   **RIGHT TO ASSIGN**

Buyer shall have the right to assign this agreement and all rights thereunder, provided the assignee assumes all obligations of buyer and seller approves assignee's financial responsibility within _____ days after receipt of notice of assignment.

Seller shall not disapprove unreasonably. If assignment is not disapproved in writing within said time, this condition shall be deemed waived.

(Optional, continue):

Seller's approval of the assignment shall not relieve buyer of liability hereunder.

COMMENT ON FORM 4:11: An assignment does not normally relieve the buyer of liability unless the agreement between seller and buyer so provides. In most situations the seller may wish to hold the buyer to the original agreement. It is usually a good idea to make assignment conditioned upon seller's approval of the assignee's financial responsibility.

FORM 4:12   **PROHIBITION AGAINST ASSIGNMENT
OF CONTRACT**

Buyer expressly agrees neither to assign this agreement nor to transfer in any manner any right, title or interest herein without first procuring the written consent of seller. Any assignment or transfer of this agreement shall terminate it and release seller of all obligations hereunder.

COMMENT ON FORM 4:12: Whenever the question of the buyer's intended assignment of the contract is raised, the broker should advise the seller to retain legal counsel. The legal questions regarding assignment of contracts and the enforcement thereof, in particular where purchase-money obligations are involved, are complex. If an assignment is contemplated, the contract should expressly permit it. (See Form 4:11.)

The Limited Right to Assign

Sometimes a buyer wishes to have permission to assign the contract to a controlled corporation which has not yet been formed. Such limited right to assign involves important legal questions, not the least of which are tax considerations. Generally speaking, it is preferable to complete the formation of the corporation before title passes. Form 4:13 is an example of a limited right to assign.

FORM 4:13   **ASSIGNMENT TO A**
                    CONTROLLED CORPORATION

Buyer shall not assign this contract or any right or interest hereunder without the prior written consent and approval of seller, except that buyer shall have the right without first obtaining the consent and approval of seller to assign buyer's entire rights under this agreement to a _____
                                                    state
corporation in which buyer owns at least 50% of the voting stock, provided however that buyer shall remain liable hereunder, notwithstanding such assignment.

COMMENT ON FORM 4:13: Frequently a buyer wishes to purchase realty in the name of a not-yet-incorporated corporation. The controlling stockholder can enter into a contract which provides, as in the clause above, for a transfer thereto. It is practical to provide for a notice to seller of such assignment before closing so that all documents can be drawn properly with the assignee corporation's name. Important tax problems are encountered when not-yet-formed entities are involved in real estate transactions. (See IRC 167, IRC 1551.)

It is commonly provided that a contract survives the death of the parties and is binding upon the heirs, personal representatives, and any other successor in interest. Where such is not the case, form 4:14 can be used.

FORM 4:14   **"BINDING CLAUSE"**

This contract shall extend to and be binding upon the heirs, administrators, executors, successors, and assignees of the parties hereto.

Transfering Blueprints

Many owners have in their possession the original blueprints and architectural renderings and specifications for the premises being sold. These documents are valuable to the buyer, particularly if repairs should be needed, for locating wirings, studs, and so forth. The contract should provide for delivery of these items or they may be overlooked and subsequently destroyed (see Form 4:15).

FORM 4:15   **BLUEPRINTS**

Seller agrees to deliver to buyer all blueprints, architect's drawings; landscape architect designs; and all building and landscaping specifications, surveys and maps describing the property, presently in the seller's possession.

COMMENT ON FORM 4:15: Condition for survey is specifically dealt with later in this chapter.

Distributing Crops

The question of who is entitled to the crops upon the sale of land under cultivation is always a matter requiring negotiation, and decided with respect to readiness for harvesting. Forms 4:16 through 4:20 are sample clauses of various methods used to resolve this matter.

FORM 4:16   **CROPS**
(after description):

... together with the crops growing thereon.

COMMENT ON FORMS 4:16 through 4:19: Where buyer is to have all crops as part of purchase price, the short form above can be used. Forms 4:17, 4:18 and 4:19 are used to place restrictions on the distribution and use of crops.

FORM 4:17   **RESERVATION OF CERTAIN CROPS**

The buyer recognizes that the seller has planted _____ _____ on the premises, and is entitled to harvest the same during the year 19_____.

FORM 4:18   **DIVISION OF CROPS**

It is understood and agreed between the parties hereto that the hay and grain produced on the property during the year 19_____ shall be equally divided between the seller and the buyer immediately on and following the close of

_____ .
escrow/this transaction

FORM 4:19   **EXCLUSION OF ALL CROPS**

It is understood and agreed between the parties hereto, that the seller shall retain all crops, rentals of land and profits collected by or due prior to _____ _____ 19_____.

FORM 4:20   **BUYER TO TAKE POSSESSION**
BEFORE CLOSING

It is understood and agreed between the parties hereto that the buyer may enter into and take possession of said land and premises on the _____ ___ 19_____, and from that day on shall take and be entitled to all rents, issues and profits thereof and to _____ for buyer's own use and
all growing crops thereon

benefit, _____.
except (state exception)

COMMENT ON FORM 4:20: Where possession is given prior to closing, the date of proration should be the date of possession, and seller should provide in the agreement that buyer take out liability and fire and other casualty insurance. See Form 5:21.

Using Exhibits

The various documents referred to in a contract may be attached to it as exhibits. As with addenda, the exhibits should be incorporated in the contract by reference in the text. Exhibits should be labeled "A," "B," and so forth, and initialed by the parties. Photocopies should be made of the marked exhibits to insure authenticity and attached to all copies of the contract. Form 4:21 indicates the manner of incorporation of exhibits.

FORM 4:21   **EXHIBITS**

_____ is attached hereto as
Exhibit _____ and incorporated herein by reference.

(or where there are several exhibits separately stated in various parts of the contract):

All exhibits to which reference is made are deemed incorporated, whether or not actually attached.

COMMENT ON FORM 4:21: The second provision avoids repetitive incorporation by reference each time an exhibit is mentioned. It is recommended that in the original of the contract all exhibits be labeled with the identifying letter and the word "attached."

Disclosing Illegalities

Where a specific unit, whether in a residence or apartment house, does not comply with regulations or codes, the buyer is entitled to full disclosure. In order to protect the seller and his or her representative against later claims of nondisclosure, such information should be incorporated in the agreement, even at the risk of losing the sale.

FORM 4:22   **"AS IS" KNOWN ZONING AND**
BUILDING CODE VIOLATIONS

Buyer represents that _____ has been informed that property is zoned
                        he/she

_____ and that _____ does not meet
                        apt.number/basement apartment

local zoning requirements. Buyer agrees to accept building "as is," subject to all existing building, health, safety, zoning ordinances and regulations issued by any governmental authority.

(Or):

Buyer represents that _____ has been informed that _____
                        he/she   apt. number,

_____ _____ meet building Code or Health Code requirements.
  social room, etc.   do/do not

Buyer agrees to accept building "as is," subject to all existing building, health and safety, zoning ordinances or regulations issued by any governmental authority.

COMMENT ON FORM 4:22: Use these clauses with caution. Where known violations exist and the buyer nevertheless wishes to purchase the property, these clauses can be adapted to any particular situation. Where a suspected violation can be corrected, the buyer can make the offer "conditioned upon issuance of legal permit for use of _____ ,"
                                        apt. number/basement apartment

or conditioned upon compliance with building and health codes. For a "no violation" clause used in certain communities, see the section headed "Violations of Codes and Ordinances" in this chapter. The use of wording such as "may or may not conform," where the seller or the seller's representative know that a violation exists, is deceptive. See also Form 4:71.

Broker Statements

The so-called "set-up," or broker's statement describing income property, is often more fantasy than fact, though usually through no fault of the broker. Rentals are represented by sellers to be "scheduled rents," but these are not in fact always the actual rents received. The seller has sometimes given tenants concessions in the form of several weeks free rent, "transfer" of small appliances, gifts, and the like, which do not appear on the statements. The statements seldom show any vacancy factor, and actual expenses of management are not disclosed. Tax and utility figures are frequently only estimates, especially in brand new buildings. Insurance is nearly always understated.

It is quite incredible but true that a large proportion of the sales of income-producing real estate is made haphazardly. Therefore, knowledgeable buyers should, as a matter of course, discount brokers' statements and make their own estimates. Unfortunately, inexperienced buyers are at the mercy of the unscrupulous sellers, who may themselves have acted in the dark when they bought. Only when a transaction is handled by a conscientious broker or supervised by a knowledgeable attorney can buyers expect to get what they bargained for.

In a leading California case the court emphasized that the law imposes on real estate brokers the same obligation of undivided service and loyalty that it imposes on trustees in favor of beneficiaries.[5] With regard to broker statements, the court said: "As brokers, they knew that the primary purpose of the broker's statement was to provide a basic description and information to the buyer, and that the information was incomplete and had to be supplemented, and that some aspects, such as vacancy figures, were based upon 100 percent occupancy and were simply 'puffing.' "

Careful buyers insist on seeing the seller's books, or demand an operating statement which the seller must warrant to be correct. Minimum requirement is a rental statement showing the true rents and terms. The buyer should also check taxes and insurance costs, and examine all utility and other bills. The minimum information that a buyer should demand is called for in Form 4:23. Form 4:24 contains a clause making the buyer's approval of the seller's books a condition of the agreement, and Form 4:25 provides a clause stating that the books have been examined by the buyer and warranted by the seller. The clause in Form 4:26 is a warranty of the seller's estimate of income and costs at the time the deposit is taken.

FORM 4:23   **INCOME STATEMENT SUBJECT TO**
                          BUYER'S APPROVAL

Within _____ days from date of seller's acceptance hereof, seller shall deposit with _____ an operating statement for the 12-month period
                escrow/buyer
ending _____ 19_____ showing the gross rentals received to be no less than $_____, and total operating expenses to be no more than $_____, and warrant that said statement is true and correct. Said statement is subject to buyer's approval, and buyer may cancel this agreement if said statement is unsatisfactory to _____.
                                            him/her

If said statement is not disapproved in writing within _____ days of receipt, these conditions shall be deemed waived.

COMMENT ON FORM 4:23: This clause gives the buyer the right to approve or disapprove the statement of operating costs. In this form, as in the warranty in Form 4:26, contemplated operating costs include everything the seller has received and expended upon the property during the twelve-month period preceding the date shown. If the seller wishes to limit the information provided to certain recurring expenses, he or she can so indicate in a counter-offer. The buyer can, of course, limit the inquiry to actual rents received and standard expenses, not including decorating, improvements, and repairs.

FORM 4:24   **EXAMINATION OF BOOKS AND**
                         RECORDS AS CONDITION

Within _____ days from date of seller's acceptance hereof, seller shall deliver to buyer, or buyer's duly designated agent for buyer's approval, originals or conformed copies of _____.
                     books and records/books, records, and tax returns
Seller warrants and represents that the books and records are those kept and maintained by seller in the ordinary and normal course of business _____
                                                                      and used
_____.
by the seller in the computation of his/her federal income tax returns
If the examination of the books and records discloses conditions or information unsatisfactory to the buyer, _____ may cancel this agreement. If not
                                         he/she
disapproved in writing within _____ days of receipt of the books and records, this condition shall be deemed waived.

COMMENT ON FORM 4:24: The above condition for approval of the actual books and records can be inserted in the buyer's offer if the books and records have not been examined before the offer is made.

In the case mentioned in the text (*Ford v. Cournale*), the court understood that the books and records of the previous owners were available for inspection, but that "in fact, Mr. Cournale believed that it was not necessary to verify the information provided by the former owner.'' The amount of net income was a material fact in this case (as it is in most income-property transactions). All real estate licensees have an affirmative duty not to misrepresent the material facts of the amount of income and a duty to disclose all material facts.

FORM 4:25   EXAMINATION OF SELLER'S BOOKS

Buyer acknowledges that he has examined seller's books and records, and that buyer is relying on such examination and not upon any representation made by seller or seller's agents concerning the income or expenses of said property.

Seller warrants and represents that the books and records examined by buyer are those kept and maintained by seller in the ordinary and normal course of business and used in the computation of the seller's federal income tax returns.

COMMENT ON FORM 4:25: In any sale of income-producing property, whenever the buyer has actually examined the seller's books, the above clause should be inserted in the contract. If inspection of books is not included in the offer as a condition, the seller may wish to incorporate the above clause in the counteroffer or the final agreement so that the buyer admits to relying exclusively upon the state of facts found in the books and records in buying the property.

FORM 4:26   SELLER'S WARRANTY OF
INCOME AND EXPENSES

The seller represents that the operating statement for the 12-month period ending _____, 19_____ showing gross rentals received of $_____ ___ and total operating expenses of $_____ is true and correct and agrees that said statement as attached hereto is a part of this agreement, and understands that the buyers in purchasing the property is relying on said statement.

COMMENT ON FORM 4:26: If the broker does not have a true operating statement available at the time of the taking of the deposit but only the owner's estimated figures, the above clause should be amended. Provision for delivery of an operating statement by the seller to the buyer can be made a condition of the sale (see Form 4:23).

For their own protection, buyers should always inspect the complete property, though this may not always be possible at the time the Deposit Receipt is drafted. Therefore, it is especially important that provisions be inserted to protect the buyer's right to complete inspection before being obligated to consummate the transaction.

Several types of inspection may be called for. First, of course, the buyer may wish to inspect all units of an apartment house, motel, or hotel. Second, he or she may wish to have the property inspected by a variety of experts for specific purposes. Third, if extensive remodeling is contemplated, architects, engineers, contractors, and rental specialists may be called in to examine the premises. In the meantime, of course, the buyer would like to have the owner tied up on a contract which is conditioned upon these inspections. The seller, however, will be reluctant to become immobilized by a contract which may be unenforceable. Again, the matter calls for great skill in negotiation and some compromise of the two viewpoints.

**FORM 4:27   INSPECTION BY BUYER'S SPOUSE OR
DESIGNATED PERSON**

This offer is subject to inspection and approval by _____
_____ of the herein described property within
buyer's spouse/named person
_____ days of date of seller's acceptance. If not disapproved in writing within said date and time, the condition shall be deemed waived.

COMMENT ON FORM 4:27: The buyer's silence is equal to approval. The buyer must make a definite effort to cancel the agreement; otherwise he or she is bound. A statement reading, "Inspected and approved _____,"
date and hour

should be signed by the buyer after the inspection and attached to the agreement. See Form 4:33.

FORM 4:28   TECHNICAL INSPECTIONS

This offer is subject to inspection by buyer or _____ authorized
his/hers
agents of the roof, plumbing, heating and wiring, or other physical conditions of the property. If such inspections disclose conditions unsatisfactory to the buyer, he/she may cancel this agreement. If notice of such disapproval has not been delivered in person or in writing to the seller within _____ days of date of seller's acceptance, this condition shall be deemed waived. A copy of all written inspection reports, if any, shall be immediately delivered to seller.

COMMENT ON FORM 4:28: Careful buyers will insist on a clause allowing them to arrange for technical inspections of the premises in addition to a structural pest control inspection. In order to protect the seller against unreasonable delay, however, such provisions should contain a time limit. Otherwise, the buyer could wait until shortly before closing to cancel.

Whenever possible, of course, such inspections should be made prior to entering into the contract so that the contract can be drawn free of any contingencies. Since this is not always possible, the parties must be prepared to include an "inspection contingency" clause in the Deposit Receipt. Such a clause can be adapted to encompass only one or two of the items mentioned.

The contract should also provide for the seller's delivery of keys to the premises. This provision is especially important in income property. Care should be taken to insure that all sets of keys under the seller's control or in his or her possession are delivered.

FORM 4:29   **KEYS**

It is understood and agreed between the parties hereto, that the seller will deliver to buyer at time of closing _____ to the premises.
all keys/the following keys

COMMENT ON FORM 4:29: Vaults and combination safes should be checked, and seller should explain their use and provide keys or combinations and any existing instruction books. Model Form II includes a key clause.

Leases

Except where the buyer is purchasing a residence occupied by the seller or a vacant property, most income property is occupied by tenants. From the seller's standpoint, the ideal transaction regarding rentals is one in which the buyer takes subject to leases and tenancies as they may exist at the time of closing. But a cautious buyer will not accept such a provision sight unseen. In fact, the buyer should not enter into any contract without first examining all existing leases and having the seller warrant that the leases are currently in effect and that no credits or concessions have been given. Ideally, the leases should be scrutinized by the buyer's attorney, particularly as to the wording of options and renewals. Provisions for repair by the lessor should be followed up with written assurance from both the tenant and the seller that the work has been performed. Estoppel letters from tenants are extra precautions (see Form 4:34).

Unusual provisions in leases are usually found in the form of renewal options, cancellation privileges, rent concessions, parking privileges, and employment arrangements such as part-time management of buildings. Whenever inquiry or inspection of leases disclose that concessions in rent payment have been made, the buyer should proceed with caution. Such concessions may indicate that the property is overpriced, or that the stated rent is, in fact, unobtainable. Concessions could also mean that the financial condition of the tenant is unsound. The more important the continued existence of a certain lease or leases is to the buyer, the more careful this investigation must be.

An option to cancel the lease upon sale of the building if often found in leases. If the option is to be exercised by the seller, the contract should so provide; and the responsibility for the timely vacating of the tenant should be placed upon the seller where possible. In California a statute requires that tenants be given notice within a few days after closing concerning the disposition of security deposits. Some leases provide that the lessor-seller may even turn over the security deposit to buyer-lessor and be relieved of all liability for it. Regardless of statute, it is good practice to obtain a release of liability from the tenant, and a "hold harmless" agreement from the buyer. See Form 4:51.

Percentage leases raise questions concerning adjustment of rent; these can be resolved either through proration in favor of the seller or through a possible refund to the buyer of previously paid rent. Adequate provisions for such contingencies should be drawn by counsel for the parties. Similar problems are involved in tax clauses providing for tenants' participation in tax increases, labor costs, or other expenses.

Some leases provide for renewal commissions to brokers who negotiated the lease, or for commissions to be paid in the event of sale of the property to the lessee. The seller may wish to have the buyer directly assume the obligation for such commissions. The buyer should carefully examine the provisions to ascertain the extent of these obligations.

Unfortunately, very few sellers are willing to place actual leases in the hands of the broker before he or she presents an offer. However, the broker should have no problem in obtaining photocopies of all leases at the time of listing. But, because so many commercial buildings and apartment houses are offered on the market without exclusive listings, the broker often has only limited information about the terms of the leases when the property is presented to the buyer.

If a buyer is eager to make an offer before actually examining leases or rental agreements, the offer can provide for approval of the leases. It is unwise to set forth a capsule description of any lease in the contract itself; this could lead to disputes about the total wording. The safer method is to provide the buyer with a copy of the lease or refer to a schedule of leases and exhibit each copy to the buyer for approval and initialing. Forms 4:30 through 4:33 cover possible situations involving leases.

FORM 4:30   LEASES

Subject to leases in schedule "A" attached hereto. Copies of said leases have been exhibited to and initialled by buyer. Seller warrants that schedule "A" is a complete list of all leases under which seller has any benefit or obligation. Seller represents that no tenant is entitled to any rebate, concession, or other benefit except as set forth in the leases listed in schedule "A."

COMMENT ON FORM 4:30: This clause can be inserted in paragraph 1 of the Model Form whenever the leases have, in fact, been exhibited to the buyer. The buyer thereby agrees to take the property subject to the existing leases. The seller's warranties are protective of the buyer's interests.

FORM 4:31   **MIXTURE OF LEASES AND
MONTH-TO-MONTH TENANCIES TO BE
APPROVED BY BUYER**

This offer is subject to the approval by buyer on or before _____ at _____ p.m. of a schedule containing a list of units, names of tenants, amounts of rent for each unit, with length of occupancy, copies of current rental agreements and leases. Seller warrants that said schedule is a complete list of all rental agreements and leases under which seller has any benefit or obligation. Seller represents that no tenant is entitled to any rebate, concession or other benefit except as set forth in such rental agreements and leases listed in the schedule. Said schedule shall be delivered to buyer (with attachments) upon seller's acceptance of this offer. If the information contained therein is unsatisfactory to buyer, _____ may cancel this agreement.

he/she

If the seller's statement, the attached leases, and rental statements are not disapproved in writing within said date and time, this condition shall be deemed waived.

COMMENT ON FORM 4:31: It is always best to provide a definite deadline for the accomplishment of any specified act. In an initial offer it is practical to define the date of seller's acceptance as the focal point, thus: "within _____ days from date of seller's acceptance. . . ."

This clause may be used either separately or in conjunction with an inspection clause. (See Form 4:27. For a combination form, see Form 4:33.)

FORM 4:32   LEASES SUBJECT TO BUYER'S APPROVAL

Existing leases as shown on schedule to be provided buyer by seller upon acceptance hereof. This offer is subject to buyer's examination and approval of such leases on or before _____ at _____ p.m. If such examination discloses terms and conditions unsatisfactory to the buyer, _____ may cancel this agreement. If the schedule and attached leases are not disapproved in writing within said date and time, this condition shall be deemed waived.

COMMENT ON FORM 4:32: This clause can be inserted in paragraph 1 of the Model Form. The buyer's silence is equal to approval. The prudent seller or the seller's representative obtains the buyer's signature on each lease with the wording: "Examined and approved _____."

The seller often handles the matter of approval by providing for such condition in the counter-offer. For example, a buyer who approves other terms than those offered may then be asked to waive such contingencies as further inspections, examination of leases, etc.

FORM 4:33   INSPECTION OF UNITS AND LEASES SUBJECT TO APPROVAL BY BUYER

This offer is subject to buyer's inspection and approval of all _____
units/
_____ situated in the herein described property on or before
apartments/rooms
_____ at _____ p.m.

It is further subject to approval by the buyer on or before _____
at _____ p.m. of a schedule containing a list of _____ ,
units/apartments/rooms
the names of tenants occupying each, and the length of such occupancy, the amount of rent, copies of current rental agreements and leases. Said schedule and attachments shall be delivered to buyer upon seller's acceptance hereof. Seller warrants that said schedule is a complete list of all rental agreements and leases under which seller has any benefit or obligation. Seller represents that no tenant is entitled to any rebate, concession or other benefit except as set forth in such rental agreements and leases listed in the schedule. If either the physical inspection or the examination of said schedule and attachments disclose conditions or information unsatisfactory to the buyer, _____ may cancel this
he/she
agreement.

If the _____ or the schedule and attachments,
units/apartments/rooms
or both, are not disapproved in writing within said date and time, these conditions shall be deemed waived.

COMMENT ON FORM 4:33: The above is a combination clause used in the sale of apartment houses and smaller motels operated on a weekly or month-to-month basis. It is designed for use in an offer where the buyer has not been able to inspect all units or examine a complete rental schedule or the owner's books.

Upon termination of inspection and examination of the schedule and rental agreements, good practice dictates that the buyer waive these conditions in writing rather than relying on the silent approval contained in the clause.

Estoppel Certificates

If property is to be bought subject to existing tenancies, it is always a good precaution for the buyer to ascertain the status of the tenants. All the information necessary will not be found on the leases or rental agreements.

Interviews with the tenants may be necessary. Landlords have often been known to make promises of repairs or improvements and then decide to sell before such promises are fulfilled. The warranties contained in Form 4:30 provide useful protection. In addition, the buyer may wish to obtain a certificate of estoppel from each tenant as an extra precaution (see Form 4:34).

FORM 4:34   LESSEE'S ESTOPPEL CERTIFICATE

To _____

The undersigned declares:

1) I am the tenant in possession of _____ under a
   description of premises
   _____ a conformed copy of which is attached hereto and
   lease/rental agreement
   made a part hereof.

2) The _____ is in full force and effect.
   lease/rental agreement

3) As of the date of this certificate no breach exists on my part as tenant under the _____.
   lease/rental agreement

4) As of the date of this certificate no breach exists on the part of the landlord, so far as known to me.

5) No rent has been paid in advance except _____
   the current month's rent/and the
   _____ and I have no claim against the landlord for
   last month's rent under the lease
   any deposits _____ and no defenses or offsets under the
   other than _____
   specify
   _____.
   lease/rental agreement

(Optional):

6) That I have no option to renew said _____ for any further period of
   lease
   time or to purchase or rent all or any part of the premises.

Dated _____, 19_____.

_____
Signature of Tenant

COMMENT ON FORM 434: This certificate can be adapted to set forth the general terms of the rental agreement or lease if attaching copies is undesirable. Signatures can, of course, be acknowledged before a notary public.

Possession Free of Tenancy

If the proration clause in the original Model Form, paragraph 8, is filled in, the buyer implicitly agrees to buy the property subject to the rights of tenants in possession.

If either the whole property or a unit thereof is presently occupied by tenants, but the seller is to deliver the property free of occupancy or lease, the agreement should so provide (see Form 4:35). A buyer who has only placed a deposit on the property has, of course, little bargaining power to demand that a seller evict a tenant in order to deliver the premises free of tenancy. Sellers are reluctant to lose the rent or risk a prospective loss of rent if the deal should fall through. But the buyer who wishes to guarantee tenant-free possession can agree to compensate the seller for such rental loss; otherwise the buyer may have to give the seller a reasonable amount of time after the closing of the transaction to provide for the vacancy. Even leases which are to be terminated should be examined by the buyer, and estoppel certificates should be obtained from the tenants.

FORM 4:35   DELIVERY FREE OF TENANCY

Seller warrants that _____, the tenant occupying
_____ is a month-to-month tenant and that seller within _____ days
<u>unit/apartment no.</u>

of seller's acceptance/of buyer's deposit of the additional deposit provided for in paragraph _____
will give said tenant a ____ days' written notice to quit and vacate as required
30/7

by _____.
<u>the law of this state/the rental agreement</u>

If at the end of the time specified in said notice the tenant or any other person remains in possession or assert a right to possession, buyer shall be entitled to all rents accruing therefrom, and to all costs and attorney's fees actually paid or incurred by buyer for dispossessing the tenant.

(Optional, continue):

If the tenant under said notice is to vacate after the close of _____
<u>the transaction/</u>
_____ the sum of $_____ shall be withheld from monies otherwise due seller
<u>escrow</u>
as security for the performance of this agreement.

COMMENT ON FORM 4:35: The optional clause affords the best protection for the buyer.

Net Rental Leases

Where the real property being sold is leased under a net rental lease, the contract should set forth a description of the lease and a warranty that the lease is in full force and effect. An estoppel letter obtained by the tenant confirming the lease is an extra precaution (see Form 4:34).

The most common net-lease transaction is the sale of an apartment house leased to an operator, or a commercial building leased to one tenant on a net lease. Form 4:36 can be adapted to such situations. It is recommended the buyer's legal counsel review the lease and explain the tax consequences concerning rights to depreciation deduction, and the like.

FORM 4:36   **WHOLLY LEASED PROPERTY**

Buyer represents that _____ has examined and approved a copy of
he/she
the lease dated _____, 19_____, entered into by the seller, as lessor and _____ as lessee, pursuant to which the entire premises to be conveyed hereunder, have been leased to said lessee for a term beginning _____, 19_____ and expiring _____, 19_____ at a net monthly rental of $_____ payable in advance on the _____ day of each month.

Seller represents and warrants that said lease is presently in full force and effect and unmodified, that neither party is in default in the performance of any obligations thereunder, and that this state of fact will be true as of date of closing.

Seller agrees to deliver on day of closing an affidavit or letter from said lessee certifying that the lease is then in full force and effect, has not been modified, and that the lessor is not in default in any obligations thereunder.

COMMENT ON FORM 4:36: This clause presupposes that the buyer had had the opportunity to examine the lease prior to the drawing of the contract. (For estoppel affidavit, see Form 4:34.)

Maintenance and Vacancies

Where a relatively long period elapses between the acceptance of the offer and the day set for closing, an agreement concerning maintenance of the premises is important. Closely related to this problem is the handling of vacancies in rental property during the same period. Buyers and sellers have a common interest in these matters even if their motives may be different. The seller does not want to lose rent before closing, and wants to maintain full occupancy in the event of buyer's default. The buyer desires to take over a fully rented building, except, perhaps, for the unit he or she wishes to occupy.

Allowing the seller to rent any vacant space freely during this time period may not be in the buyer's interest. The buyer may authorize the seller to renew leases, rent month-to-month to new tenants, or decorate or paint such units, but only within certain specified limits. Where a lease is to be modified during the period before closing, the buyer's consent should be obtained. The seller is well-advised not to rely on verbal agreements, but to insist that the buyer issue the authorization in writing.

These situations call for skill in negotiation. They invariably involve some compromise. Sellers may not wish to subject their actions regarding rental arrangements to approval by the buyer. Tenants may be scarce, and there may not be time to obtain the buyer's approval. Nevertheless, all suitable arrangements made during the period before closing should be incorporated in the contract. See Forms 4:37 through 4:39 for clauses relating to renting and maintenance.

FORM 4:37   RENTING OF VACANCY DURING ESCROW PERIOD

It is understood by and between the parties hereto, that should any apartment become vacant between the execution of this contract and the date set for giving possession, the seller may relet such apartment for a term of _____
month-to-
_____ at a rental to be not less than $_____ per month payable on
month/one year
the _____ day of each month. If rented for a period of one year, the seller shall collect a security deposit of $_____. The _____
month-to-month rental agreement/lease
shall be on the standard form issued by _____. No expenditure for painting or decorating, cleaning, etc., in excess of $_____ shall be made by the seller to obtain such new tenancy without the buyer's written approval having first been obtained. The cost of such painting, decorating, cleaning, etc., together with any brokerage commission or rental fee shall be prorated as of date of closing.

COMMENT ON FORM 4:37: This clause gives the seller some freedom in renting during the escrow period.

FORM 4:38   GARDEN MAINTENANCE

Seller agrees to maintain the trees, shrubs, plants and lawn in good condition and keep them watered during escrow period and to date of delivery of possession.

COMMENT ON FORM 4:38: In some situations, it may be better for the buyer to obtain permission to enter the premises for the purpose of maintaining plants and lawn. There seller is still in possession, provisions as indicated in this clause should be made in the contract for the interim maintenance.

Rent Control Disclosures

Rent Control is in effect in many communities. Special disclosures may be necessary or required by local law.

FORM 4:39   MAINTENANCE OF SWIMMING POOL

Seller agrees to maintain the swimming pool, hot tub, jacuzzi, spa, if any, and heating and filter equipment in good condition during the period from the date of execution of this agreement and the date set for closing.

COMMENT ON FORM 4:39: This clause encourages the seller to continue swimming-pool services during the interim period. This provision is quite important. Many a buyer has had to pay substantial amounts of money for cleaning a neglected pool. Swimming pools and hot tubs must be cared for properly even during the winter months, so this clause is important regardless of the season.

Establishing a Policy for Notices

Whenever a contract provides that notice is to be given by any party, provisions for the type of notice and method of delivery should also be included. A simple clause is found in Form 4:40.

FORM 4:40   NOTICES IN WRITING

Notices, requests, or demand by either party shall be in writing or shall be given personally or by Registered or Certified Mail, postage prepaid, addressed to seller and buyer at the addresses set forth herein. Notice shall be deemed given, when mailed.

Handling a Lessee's Option to Buy

Leases frequently give the lessee a conditional option to purchase or a right of first refusal in the event the seller wishes to sell the property. To give fair protectzon to the broker and clarify the condition to the buyer, the buyer's offer should include a provision indicating such right of first refusal (see Form 4:41). Obviously, a broker is entitled to the protection of an exclusive-listing agreement or an agreement by the seller to pay the broker's commission if the "optionee" elects to exercise the option.

FORM 4:41   **PRIOR OPTION TO PURCHASE**
                       IN TENANT

The buyer has been informed that the seller is required to give notice to
_____, of the terms of this agreement, and if, within a period of _____
   lessee

days after the giving of such notice, _____ shall elect to purchase the
                                          lessee

premises upon the same terms as are stated in this agreement, the sellers will be

obliged to convey the premises to _____ . Accordingly, it is expressly agreed
                                      lessee

that if _____ shall so elect and shall purchase the premises, this agreement
          lessee

shall be deemed cancelled; and the sellers shall return to the buyer all sums

which shall have been paid on account of the purchase price, and the sellers shall

pay to _____ the same commission that the broker would have earned if
       name of broker

title had been conveyed to the buyer named herein pursuant to this agreement.

COMMENT ON FORM 4:41: Brokers who do not actively protect their right to
commission may find, should the tenant buy, that they have caused a sale for
which they are not entitled to a commission. Any listing agreements where
tenants have prior option should specify further rights to commission in the
event the tenant exercises the option.[6]

Personal Property Included in the Sale

Ordinarily, in the sale of a residence only a few items of personal property
are included in the purchase price. Such items should be listed specifically and
described accurately. Appliances should be identified with the name of the
manufacturer and serial number where possible. Otherwise these items could
conceivably be replaced with older models.

If no identifying number is available, it may suffice to insert a provision
stating that included in the purchase price are certain items described generical-
ly and with this legend: "presently situated in or affixed to the premises." One
popular clause is of the catch-all variety, designed so that nonapplicable items
can be deleted. This clause also provides a space for the insertion of specific
items not included in the printed clause. Versions of this clause for residential
property and income property are found in Forms 4:42 and 4:43.

A wide variety of items should be specifically included in this clause: fire
irons, fire screens, mirrors, disposal units, built-in bar and stools, built-in hi-fi
sets and stereo equipment, intercom systems, kitchen appliances such as built-in
food centers with accessories, space heaters, window air-conditioners, swimming-pool equipment. Always remember that where a list is included in the

contract, a court may well find that, since an attempt was made to include certain items, those not included were excluded by implication.

Adding to any of the clauses the words "and all other fixtures" may defeat the original purpose. It is in just such situations that the rule of construction called *Ejusdem Generis* raises its ugly head. This rule says that where general words follow an enumeration of persons and things in words of a particular and specific meaning, such general words are not to be construed in their widest extent, but are to be held as applying only to persons or things of the same general kind or class as those specifically mentioned.[7]

Where furnished apartments or hotel or motel property is being sold, an up-to-date inventory should always be prepared and initialed by both parties. Sometimes, for tax-depreciation purposes, a portion of the purchase price is specified in the contract as applying to the personal property. A better practice is to state in the contract that a bill of sale will be delivered to the buyer. If the bill of sale is subject to a chattel mortgage (under Uniform Commercial Code security agreement or financing statement), the contract should so state. Any personal property bought under a conditional sales contract should be included, and the buyer must ascertain whether the financing can be transferred or whether new financing is necessary.

Some mortgages contain wording which indicates that the holder has a lien interest in the personal property used in the operation of the property.

The original Model Form does not contain a "personal property" clause; therefore, the contract writer in each instance must insert such a clause. Probably the easiest procedure is to adopt a standard clause (see Form 4:42) and simply stamp this clause in the space provided and make whatever changes are necessary to fit each factual situation. If a stamp is not desirable, a mimeographed rider can be made up containing a standard text adapted to the most common items found in homes in the Broker's area. The rider can then be attached to the purchase agreement and incorporated therein by a simple statement in the Model Form: "The personal property agreement attached hereto as 'Exhibit A' is incorporated herein by reference." Model from paragraph 4 can also be used by inserting: Personal Property Agreement. A precaution where substantial personal property is included in the sale is to conduct a property title search, also called: "Uniform Commercial Code Financing Statement search" (see Form 9:13). The contract should contain the following wording if seller is taking back a loan, which is partially secured by personal property: "As additional security buyer shall execute a UCC-1 financing statement to be filed with the Secretary of State on any personal property included in the purchase price."

A sample personal-property agreement is found in Form 4:42. Personal property in income property is covered by Form 4:43 and the comment to that form.

FORM 4:42   PERSONAL PROPERTY AND FIXTURES

All fixtures and articles of personal property attached or appurtenant to, or used in connection with, said premises are represented to be owned by the seller, free from all liens and encumbrances except as herein stated, and are included in the purchase price. Without limiting the generality of the foregoing, such fixtures are articles of personal property and include plumbing, heating, lighting and cooking fixtures, air-conditioning fixtures and units, ranges, refrigerators, radio and television aerials, bathroom and kitchen cabinets, mantels, door mirrors, venetian blinds, shades, screens, awnings, storm windows, window boxes, storm doors, mailboxes, weather vanes, flagpoles, pumps, shrubbery, outdoor statuary, and the following items: _____
List of items

_____

COMMENT ON FORM 4:42: Deletions or additions should be initialed by all parties. Do not overlook swimming-pool fixtures such as heater, skimmer, filter, and the like where appropriate. In income-property sales it is better practice to use an inventory of the personal property rather than a predrafted personal property clause (see Comment on Form 4:43).

FORM 4:43   PERSONAL PROPERTY IN
INCOME PROPERTY

Included in the purchase is all the personal property appurtenant to or used in the operation of said premises, the plumbing, heating, lighting fixtures, _____ _____, gas/electric ranges, _____, refrigerators, shades, screens, blinds, curtain rods and fixtures, drapes, awnings, wall-to-wall carpets, hall carpets, and all other furniture and furnishings situated herein and belonging to the seller and not to the tenants _____
except (for example, furniture and furnishings in
_____ . A complete inventory shall be delivered to buyer within 5
seller's apartment)
days of seller's acceptance hereof. Seller shall deliver title to the above by Bill of Sale free of all liens and encumberances except _____ .
description of instrument

COMMENT ON FORM 4:43: An inventory of the personal property should be made at the time the property is put on the market so that a copy will be ready for buyer's signature. When an inventory is used the clause above is not necessary. Instead, attach the inventory and incorporate it as follows. ''The purchase price shall include all personal property, furniture, furnishings and fixtures listed on the inventory attached hereto as 'Exhibit A,' which has been examined and approved by buyer. Seller shall deliver title to said items by Bill of Sale free of all liens and encumbrances.'' See also Form 9:13.

If no inventory is available, use the clause in this form. If there is a blanket encumbrance on the personal property, the contract should include the following conditions: "Subject to the lien or encumbrance of _____ in _____ .
security agreement and financing statement filed as follows: _____

**FORM 4:44   PERSONAL PROPERTY AGREEMENT
(PRIVATE RESIDENCE)**

Exhibit _____ to Real Estate Purchase Contract and Receipt for Deposit by and between _____ and dated _____ _____, 19____, and included therein by reference.

Included in the purchase price are such of the following items as may be on the premises, which will be delivered by bill of sale free and clear of any encumbrances except as herein set forth: all garden bulbs, plants, shrubs and trees, screen doors and windows; electric lighting fixtures; window shades, curtain rods and venetian blinds; bathroom accessory fixtures, central heating units and attached equipment; water heaters, water softeners; linoleum cemented floors; carpeting in living room, dining room, hallway and stairs; awnings; exterior attached antennas and _____ .

The personal property listed above is subject to the following lien and encumbrances _____ .

The following items are not to be included in this sale: _____ _____ .

Dated _____, 19____

Buyer _____   Seller _____

Buyer _____   Seller _____

COMMENT ON FORM 4:44: This form contains a sample personal-property agreement. Brokers seeking to create a standard form for their own use should adapt the list in this clause to include those items most often found locally. (See Comment on Form 4:42.) This type of agreement is not usually used in sales of income property; in such sales a complete inventory should be used instead.

Personal Property Substitutions

It often happens that the seller wishes to retain a special item of personal property or a fixture, replacing it with a substitute. Chandeliers, mirrors, rare bushes or shrubbery are items sellers often desire to retain. The agreement should so provide, since the removal of any items without prior consent of the buyer clearly leads to misunderstandings.

FORM 4:45   **SUBSTITUTION OF CERTAIN PERSONAL PROPERTY**

It is understood and agreed between the parties hereto, that the _____
                                                                          description
_____ is not to be included in this sale. The seller will
of item and location
replace said _____ with another now stored in the
                                item
_____ of the building and which was the one originally installed.
   garage/basement

COMMENT ON FORM 4:45: This form can be adapted to most items where the substitute is in existence on the premises. In replacing plants, the seller may be better advised to compensate the buyer by reducing the purchase price rather than providing an actual substitution, since the seller may be involved in a dispute if the replacement plant fails to grow.

The "Survival of Deed" Clause

A concept more legalistic than practical is the effect of merging the contract into the deed upon the delivery to the buyer. In the absence of fraud, mistake, or intent, the merger discharges the seller's obligation. Collateral matters sometimes can give rise to separate actions for damages. Buyers are not generally concerned with niceties of the law. They want assurance that all the seller's representation, warranties, and covenants will survive the deed. To give the buyer such protection, a "survival of deed" clause (Form 4:46) is usually inserted in the contract.

FORM 4:46   **SURVIVAL OF DEED**

All warranties, covenants and other obligations contained herein shall survive delivery of the deed.

COMMENT ON FORM 4:46: Generally speaking, all prior negotiations and agreements are merged into the deed upon the buyer's acceptance thereof. Collateral agreements may not merge, but survive the deed independently. The merger will discharge seller's obligation. To avoid the effect of merger, most attorneys for buyers insist on a provision calling for survival of the obligations beyond the delivery of the deed.

From the seller's point of view, a blanket survival clause, such as the one in this form, is not particularly desirable, especially if the seller carries financing in the form of a purchase-money mortgage. The seller may desire that the buyer make a thorough investigation of the property before the consummation of the sale and raise all possible objections then, so that the seller is not bound to further performance after the deed has passed. As a compromise to the blanket survival clause, the seller may agree that specific covenants rather than all covenants survive the delivery of the deed.

Providing for Repairs

An inspection of the premises may reveal the necessity for certain immediate repairs. The most obvious of these are leaks that are visible or show telltale signs. Waterproofing may be needed, the roof may leak, the elevator may operate poorly, or faucets and toilets may operate incorrectly.

Before the buyer signs any contract agreeing not to rely on any representation by seller or agent, every nook and cranny of the premises should be inspected. If considered necessary, a provision for proper inspection by experienced advisors, such as plumbers, contractors, engineers, and so forth should be provided (see Form 4:28). Where the seller agrees to repair or finish repairing or painting certain items or parts of the premises, the contract should so specify. A provision can also be made, where enforceable, for the deduction of a reasonable sum from the purchase price if the seller does not perform the agreed-upon repairs (see Form 4:47). If the work is not completed before closing, a hold-back of seller's funds in escrow is recommended. For a provision for repairs conditioned on buyer's notice, see Form 4:48. (For a "warranty" clause concerning various equipment and the roof, see Form 4:69).

FORM 4:47   **REPAIRS**

The seller agrees that prior to the date set for closing _____ will at own
                                                        he/she
cost and expense repair and properly fix the following:

(itemize)

In the event the repair is not made by the date set for closing, the seller hereby agrees to reduce the cash down payment of the purchase price by the sum of $_____, and no further claim, right or obligation and regard hereto shall exist or be enforceable by either party.

COMMENT ON FORM 4:47: This provision is enforceable if the reduction is reasonable. It is probably subject to the rules for interpretation of "liquidated damage" clauses.

FORM 4:48   **REPAIR OF EQUIPMENT UPON**
                          BUYER'S NOTICE

Prior to closing or possession, whichever occurs first, upon written notice from buyer, seller shall make such repairs to the plumbing, heating, air-conditioning and electrical equipment on the premises as are reasonably required to make them operable.

COMMENT ON FORM 4:48: See also Form 4:69.

Sale of Other Property

Often a buyer wishes to make his offer conditioned upon the sale of his or her own residence. Such a sale can be handled in many ways. The simplest method is, of course, to make the buyer's offer conditioned upon the prior sale of the buyer's residence. The consequence of this arrangement is that the seller's property is tied up until the buyer finds a buyer. Where one broker has both listings, the problem may not be too involved, and the broker will have the incentive of two commissions to encourage his or her best efforts. However, sellers agreeing to the buyer's condition may wish to protect themselves with a "contingency release" clause allowing them to cancel the conditional offer upon notice. See Form 4:49 for a clause describing the condition of sale plus optional buyers' and sellers' release clauses.

FORM 4:49   **OFFER SUBJECT TO SALE OF OTHER**
                  PROPERTY AT A CERTAIN PRICE

This agreement is conditioned upon the sale by buyer for not less than $_____, of the buyer's real property situated at _____ _____ within _____ days from date of seller's acceptance hereof, and receipt by buyer within such time, of not less than $_____ as proceeds of such sale.

Optional
("Buyer's release" clause)

If the condition is not satisfied, buyer may, at _____ election, waive
                                                his/her
the condition or cancel this agreement. Buyer shall notify seller in writing of such waiver or cancellation. If no notice is given within _____ days of date set for close of _____, this condition shall be deemed waived.
      escrow/transaction

Optional
("Seller's release" clause)

Seller shall have the right to continue to offer the herein described property for sale. Should seller receive another offer in writing acceptable to seller, buyer shall have _____ days from receipt of written notice to remove this condition. Failure to waive this condition in writing within the time stated in seller's notice to buyer shall terminate this agreement and cause the return of buyer's deposit.

COMMENT ON FORM 4:49: If the other property is already in a pending transaction the above clause can be amended to read: "This agreement is conditioned upon the close of _____ under an agreement
escrow/a transaction

with _____ dated _____, 19____ on or before the date set for closing of _____
escrow herein/this transaction

See also Form 2:05 for an irrevocable transfer order.

Developers often insist on a "seller's release" clause as shown in the second optional section. Usually the time limit on the buyer is not more than 72 hours.

FORM 4:50   STANDARD CONTINGENCY ESCAPE CLAUSE

Should seller receive a bona fide written offer from a third party, which offer is deemed more desirable by seller, seller may notify buyer or buyer's agent by written notice personally delivered or mailed, addressed to buyer at _____

of the receipt of such an offer. In the event of written notice personally delivered, the buyer shall have 72 hours from the time of receipt of said notice, or in the event of mail, buyer shall have until 6:00 o'clock p.m. of the third day following the date of mailing such notice, to deliver to seller or seller's agent buyer's agreement in writing to removal of the contingency herein set forth. In the event buyer shall fail so to agree to the removal of such contingency, this contract shall be of no further force or effect and the parties shall stand relieved of all further obligation.

Buyer's Initials _____   Seller's initials _____

COMMENT ON FORM 4:50: The above standard contingency escape clause can be included in the Deposit Receipt. CAR also publishes a Contingency Release form, a notice to buyer to remove contingency and a Contingency Removal form.

Tenant's Security Deposits

Security deposits paid by tenants to the seller represent a problem. The amount and the terms of deposits' return or application should be carefully examined. The buyer or buyer's representative should always inquire as to whether such deposits have been paid. Often they are not mentioned in rental agreements, but the lessor may have given separate receipts for them. The buyer may be responsible for returning such deposits without having, in fact, received them at transfer of title. Both parties may therefore wish to have the deposit situation clarified in the agreement, as in Form 4:51. Under CAL Civil Code Sections 1950.5 and 1950.7 tenants must be notified about transfer of deposit to buyer and acknowledge receipt of such notice.

FORM 4:51   SECURITY DEPOSITS

Security deposits, if any, deposited by tenants according to the terms of leases or rental agreements, to the extent they have not been applied by the seller in accordance with such agreements, shall be turned over to the buyer by seller upon close of _____.
                                                escrow

The buyer hereby agrees to indemnify and hold the seller harmless from liability for the proper application or return of such deposits to the respective tenants in accordance with the terms of the leases or rental agreements.

Sewer Connections

Form 4:52 provides a clause where sewer hook-up is in question.

FORM 4:52   SEWER CONNECTIONS

If property is required to be hooked up to a sewer, seller agrees to pay all expenses for sewer connections and/or any sewer bonds or fees, which may be a lien not yet payable, recorded or unrecorded.

COMMENT ON FORM 4:52: In some situations the property sewer connections may not have been completed at the time of sale. Where seller agrees to pay for sewer hook-up, a clause such as this one should be inserted in the contract. This clause can be readily adapted where the parties may agree to share the cost.

FORM 4:53 REAL ESTATE LICENSEE BUYING AS PRINCIPAL

Seller acknowledges that Buyer is a real estate licensee buying the property for _____ own account for occupancy, investment or possible resale.

his/her

COMMENT ON FORM 4:53: A Seller is entitled to know that the Buyer is a real estate licensee when the licensee buys directly from the Seller. It would seem that if a licensee is acting as a principal in the "arms length" transaction through another broker not connected with the licensee, that such disclosure is not called for. The licensee should not extract a commission in a sale in which the licensee is acting as principal, since the licensee thereby may assume all usual fiduciary duties to the seller.

Structural Pest Control Reports

A real estate broker may not have the affirmative legal duty for alerting the buyer during negotiations to the availability or advisability of a structural pest control inspection. Nevertheless, the matter is raised directly in CAR's Real Estate Purchase Contract and Receipt for Deposit by an instruction in bold-face type which reads: "Set forth any terms and conditions of a factual nature applicable to this sale, such as financing, prior sale of other property, *the matter of structural pest control inspection,* repairs and personal property to be included in the sale" (emphasis added).

The existence of this notice and the possibility of a subsequent claim of collusion to conceal defects not discoverable by a simple observation suggests that the broker may be subject to liability as well as fail to represent the seller's best interests, where the broker fails to mention to the buyer at least the availability of inspection. If the broker acquires knowledge of infestation or infection by wood-destroying organisms or any structural defect caused by wood-destroying organisms on the subject property the broker must disclose to any prospective sellers or parties to an exchange such knowledge "as soon as practical." This duty is subject to disciplinary action. A violation of such disclosure may be basis for civil fraud liability as well.

A Business Decision

Whether in the individual case, the broker decides to bring the availability of inspection to the buyer's attention is basically a business decision, keeping in mind the risks inherent if the broker refrains from giving such information. Similarly, a business decision is involved in recommending that the seller obtain an inspection report prior to a contemplated sale.

Once a buyer has been informed of the availability of a structural pest control inspection, the buyer can, of course, waive such an inspection (see Form 4:54).

FORM 4:54   **WAIVER OF PEST CONTROL**
                       INSPECTION REPORT

_____ have satisfied _____ about the condition
   I/We   myself/ourselves
of the property and its improvements and agree to purchase the property in its present condition without requiring a structural pest control inspection. Broker has made no representation to induce the execution of this waiver. Neither broker nor seller shall be liable for any condition or to repair any condition which might have been disclosed by an inspection report by a licensed Structural Pest Control Operator.

COMMENT ON FORM 4:54: In a situation where the facts are as described, this waiver can be included in the Real Estate Purchase Contract and Receipt for Deposit. It should be used with caution.

Except in situations where the buyer's intended use of the property precludes the necessity for a structural pest control report, or where recent certification exists, the safest course is a new inspection.

The California Certification Program

As a result of changes in the Structural Pest Control Act, effective July 1, 1975, a reorientation of the "termite problem" in real estate sales has taken place. Certain mislabeled concepts are disappearing from the licensees' language. Expressions such as "completion certificate," "corrective or preventive work," and "termite clearance" are no longer, if ever they were, useful or correct.

The law is detailed in a brochure titled "Structural Pest Control Handbook for Real Estate Licensees." The law makes the obtaining of a pest control report *voluntary*. However, once a structural pest control inspection report is made a condition of the contract affecting the transfer of real estate or imposed as a condition for financing such transfer, it triggers a *mandatory* provision of the Civil Code. Then the seller "transferor, fee owner, or his agent *as soon as practical and before* transfer of title or execution of a real property sales contract as defined in Civil Code Section 2985" (an installment land sales contract) must deliver a copy of the inspection report to the buyer. Belated delivery by an agent designated to make such delivery may lead to disciplinary action. Licensees are required to keep a record of their actions in such respect for a period of three years from close of the transaction.

In cooperative transactions, the broker-licensee who obtains the buyer's offer is the agent who must deliver the inspection report to the buyer if such a report is required in the transaction,[8] unless the seller has given written authorization to another broker acting as agent in the transaction to effect delivery.

Certification by Request

Another aspect of the new law is the Certification Program. The structural pest control operator now *must if requested* issue a certification attesting to the absence or presence of wood-destroying pests and organisms and to the operator's recommendations for repair of damage, if any, which appear on the report. The certification must also set forth the recommendations, if any, which have not been completed at the time of the certification.

Requests for the issuance of certification should always be in writing. The structural pest control operator should also clearly identify the findings in the following categories:

(a) Work recommended to repair damage caused by *existing* infestation or infection of wood-destroying pests or organisms and all work recommended to correct conditions that caused such infestation or infections.

(b) Work recommended to correct conditions *usually deemed likely* to lead to infestation or infection of wood-destroying pests or organisms, but where *no evidence of active infestation or infection* is found with respect to such conditions. (Emphasis added.)

A separate request form is available from CAR. The form serves a dual purpose: (1) Requesting certification in writing; (2) Designating the report's identification of the two concepts mentioned in the text.

It is only logical that parties to a real estate transaction should agree as to the extent of each party's obligation to pay for recommended structural pest control work. In doing so it is natural that a distinction be made between (1) the obligation to repair damage caused by *existing* infestation or infection and to correct the conditions that caused it; and (2) the obligation to correct conditions usually deemed likely to lead to infestation or infection, where no evidence of existing infestation or infection is found.

The seller would be responsible only for the first obligation, with such modification as the buyer may accept, while the buyer would have the right to elect to have the *second* type of work done at his or her own expense. Most importantly, of course, full disclosure concerning the condition of the property would be provided. See Form 4:55 for a copy of the CAR standard Pest Control Certification Agreement.

FORM 4:55   **STRUCTURAL PEST CONTROL**
CERTIFICATION AGREEMENT

BROKERS COPY

STRUCTURAL PEST CONTROL CERTIFICATION AGREEMENT

California Association of Realtors ® Standard Form

This agreement is part of and is hereby incorporated in that "Real Estate Purchase Contract and Receipt for Deposit" between the parties hereof dated _____ 19 _____ pertaining to the property described as follows: _____

1 _____

_____ Seller/Buyer _____ agrees at his expense to furnish

_____ Buyer/Seller _____ within _____ days from date

of SELLER'S approval of this agreement with a current written report of an inspection by a licensed Structural Pest Control Operator of the main building and all attached structures

(specify any additions or exceptions)

2. If no infestation or infection of wood destroying pests or organisms is found, the report shall include either in the form of an endorsement or as a separate written statement by the inspecting licensed Structural Pest Control Operator a CERTIFICATION to provide in accordance with B & P Code 8519(a): "This is to certify that the above property was inspected on _____ (date) in accordance with the Structural Pest Control Act and rules and regulations adopted pursuant thereto, and that no evidence of active infestation or infection was found".

3. All work recommended in said report to repair damage caused by infestation or infection of wood-destroying pests or organisms found and all work to correct conditions that caused such infestation or infection shall be done at the expense of SELLER.

(specify any additions or exceptions)

Funds for work to be performed shall be held in escrow and disbursed upon receipt of a CERTIFICATION on the "Notice of Work Completed" to provide, in accordance with B & P Code 8519(b): "This is to certify that the property described herein is now free of evidence of active infestation or infection".

4. With the additions or exceptions, if any, noted below, BUYER agrees that any work to correct conditions usually deemed likely to lead to infestation or infection of wood-destroying pests or organisms, but where no evidence of existing infestation or infection is found with respect to such conditions, is NOT the responsibility of the SELLER, and that such work shall be done only if requested by BUYER and then at the expense of BUYER.

(specify any additions or exceptions)

5. If inspection of inaccessible areas is recommended in the report, BUYER has the option of accepting and approving the report or requesting further inspection to be made at the BUYER's expense. If further inspection is made and infestation, infection, or damage is found, repair of such damage and all work to correct conditions that caused such infestation or infection and the cost of entry and closing of the inaccessible areas shall be at the expense of SELLER. If no infestation, infection, or damage is found, the cost of entry and closing of the inaccessible areas shall be at the expense of BUYER.

6. _____ Seller/Buyer _____ hereby selects the following named licensed Structural Pest Control Operator: _____
SELLER consents to such inspection.

COPY OF REPORT TO BUYER

SELLER acknowledges his responsibility under Civil Code Section 1099 to deliver to BUYER as soon as practical before transfer of title or the execution of a real property sales contract as defined in Civil Code Section 2985 a copy of the inspection report, a "NOTICE OF WORK COMPLETED" OR A "CERTIFICATION pursuant to B & P Code 8519" as may be required.

SELLER directs _____
_____ name of Broker
to deliver such copies of the above documents as may be required.

BUYER AND SELLER ACKNOWLEDGES RECEIPT OF A COPY OF THIS AGREEMENT WHICH INCORPORATES THE EXCERPTS FROM THE BUSINESS AND PROFESSIONS CODE AND THE CIVIL CODE PRINTED ON THE REVERSE HEREOF.

APPROVED AND ACCEPTED: APPROVED AND ACCEPTED:

Dated _____ 19 _____   Dated: _____, 19 _____

Buyer _____   Seller _____

NO REPRESENTATION IS MADE AS TO THE LEGAL VALIDITY OF ANY PROVISION OR THE ADEQUACY OF ANY PRO-VISION IN ANY SPECIFIC TRANSACTION. A REAL ESTATE BROKER IS THE PERSON QUALIFIED TO ADVISE ON REAL ESTATE. IF YOU DESIRE LEGAL ADVICE CONSULT YOUR ATTORNEY.

To order, contact CALIFORNIA ASSOCIATION OF REALTORS®
525 South Virgil Avenue, Los Angeles, California 90020

(Revised 1980)   SPC-1

WHAT IS A STRUCTURAL PEST CONTROL CERTIFICATION?

California Business and Professions Code Section 8519 reads:

Certification as used in this section means a written statement by the licensee attesting to the statement contained therein relating to the absence or presence of wood-destroying pests or organisms and, listing such recommendations, if any, which appear on an inspection report prepared pursuant to Section 8516, and which relate to (1) infestation or infection of wood-destroying pests or organisms found, or (2) repair of structurally weakened members caused by such infestation or infection, and which recommendations have not been completed at the time of certification.

Any licensee who makes an inspection report pursuant to Section 8516, shall, if requested by the person ordering such inspection report, prepare and deliver to such person or his designated agent, a certification, to provide:

(a) When the inspection report prepared pursuant to Section 8516 has disclosed no infestation or infection: "This is to certify that the above property was inspected on_____(date) in accordance with the Structural Pest Control Act and rules and regulations adopted pursuant thereto, and that no evidence of active infestation or infection was found".

(b) When the inspection report prepared pursuant to Section 8516 discloses infestation or infection and the notice of work completed prepared pursuant to Section 8518 indicates that all recommendations to remove that infestation or infection and to repair damage caused by that infestation or infection have been completed: "This is to certify that the property described herein is now free of evidence of active infestation or infection".

(c) When the inspection report prepared pursuant to Section 8516 discloses infestation or infection and the notice of work completed prepared pursuant to Section 8518 indicates that the licensee has not completed all recommendations to remove that infestation or infection or to repair damage caused by it: "This is to certify that the property described herein is now free of evidence of active infestation or infection except as follows: ___   ___ (describing infestations, infections, damage or evidence thereof, excepted)".

Such certificate shall be accompanied by a copy of the inspection report prepared pursuant to Section 8516, and by a copy of the notice of work completed prepared pursuant to Section 8518, if any such notice has been prepared at the time of the certification, or such certification may be endorsed on and made a part of that inspection report or notice of work completed.

California Civil Code Section 1099 reads:

(a) As soon as practical before transfer of title of any real property or the execution of a real property sales contract as defined in Section 2985, the transferor, fee owner, or his agent, shall deliver to the transferee a copy of a structural pest control inspection report prepared pursuant to Section 8516 of the Business and Professions Code upon which any certification in accordance with Section 8519 of the Business and Professions Code may be made, provided that certification or preparation of a report is a condition of the contract effecting that transfer, or is a requirement imposed as a condition of financing such transfer.

(b) If a notice of work completed as contemplated by Section 8518 of the Business and Professions Code indicating action by a structural pest control licensee in response to an inspection report delivered or to be delivered under provisions of subdivision (a), or a certification pursuant to Section 8519 of the Business and Professions Code, has been received by a transferor or his agent before transfer of title or execution of a real property sales contract as defined in Section 2985, it shall be furnished to the transferee as soon as practical before transfer of title or the execution of such real property sales contract.

(c) Delivery to a transferee as used in this section means delivery in person or by mail to the transferee himself or any person authorized to act for him in the transaction or to such additional transferees who have requested such delivery from the transferor or his agent in writing. For the purposes of this section, delivery to either husband or wife shall be deemed delivery to a transferee, unless the contract effecting the transfer states otherwise.

(d) No transfer of title of real property shall be invalidated solely because of the failure of any person to comply with the provisions of this section unless such failure is an act or omission which would be a valid ground for rescission of such transfer in the absence of this section.

COMMENT ON FORM 4:55: This form advises the buyer as to what certification is and what it encompasses. The use of this form in any individual transaction should be carefully analyzed. Where a preexisting structural pest control certification report is available, the use of the form may be unnecessary. The buyer should examine the report before making the offer. The report may have the certification attached or endorsed on the report itself. In such situations, the buyer can acknowledge receipt of a copy and approval of the report itself directly on a copy of the report. Many brokers have stamps for such approvals. The Real Estate Purchase Contract and Receipt for Deposit may also carry reference to such approval.

Preexisting Report

Brokers specializing in older homes often find that the ideal situation is to obtain a structural pest control report at the time of listing the property. If the report is available when the offer is prepared the hurdle of an unfavorable report is easier to overcome. The seller may at that time give prior commitment as to the extent of his or her contribution to repair or correct conditions if the asking price is met. A report available with the listing also makes the buyer's decision to purchase more realistic and avoids tying up of the property while the parties consider their positions. Form 4:56 is an approval of a preexisting report.

FORM 4:56   **PEST CONTROL REPORT EXHIBITED**
                          TO BUYER

A copy of Structural Pest Control Report No. _____ , issued by _____ , dated _____ 19_____ has been exhibited to and
<u>name of operator</u>
initialed by buyer and is hereby incorporated herein. Buyer agrees to buy the property subject to the conditions and recommendations as shown in said report _____ . Upon seller's acceptance of this
<u>and to accept the certification shown on the report</u>
offer, seller shall deliver to buyer a copy of said report.

COMMENT ON FORM 4:56: Where a preexisting report is available at the time the buyer is making an offer, this statement can be included in the Real Estate Purchase Contract and Receipt for Deposit. This clause is also designed for use where no active infestation is disclosed in the report, and where there are no recommendations concerning conditions usually likely to lead to infestations or infections.

If the report contains recommendations for corrections or work to be performed, the buyer has several options:

(1) The buyer can accept the property subject to the conditions and recommendations of the report and waiving any liability on behalf of the seller.

(2) The buyer can accept a sum of money or a deduction from the purchase price in lieu of having the recommended work performed. She or he should also execute a waiver of future liability on behalf of the seller in this case.

(3) The buyer can demand that the seller pay for all or part of the recommended work and possibly contract with the operator for that part of the recommended work to be performed at the buyer's own expense.

Form 4:56 above and Forms 4:57 through 4:61 are designed to cover these various options.

**FORM 4:57   PEST CONTROL REPORT EXHIBITED
TO BUYER; BUYER ACCEPTS CASH
IN LIEU OF WORK**

A copy of Structural Pest Control Report No. _____ ,
issued by _____ , dated _____ , 19____,
name of operator
has been exhibited to and initialed by the buyer and is hereby incorporated herein. Buyer elects to accept credit toward the purchase price in the sum of $_____ in lieu of having recommended work performed. Buyer acknowledges receipt and acceptance of said report, and hereby releases seller and broker(s) from all liability for any Structural Pest Control work as recommended in the above named report or which may in the future be recommended by any licensed Structural Pest Control Operator with respect to the subject property.

COMMENT ON FORM 4:57: This clause can be inserted in the offer when the buyer has examined the report and chooses not to have the seller arrange for recommended work to be performed, but to accept cash in lieu thereof. It is particularly important to the seller and broker that the waiver provision be included.

**FORM 4:58   PEST CONTROL REPORT DELIVERED
TO BUYER BEFORE SALE,
SELLER TO PAY FOR WORK**

A copy of Structural Pest Control Report No. _____ ,
issued by _____ , dated _____ , 19____,
name of operator
has been exhibited to and initialed by the buyer and is hereby incorporated herein. Seller agrees that the sum of $_____ shall be withheld in escrow and may be disbursed when the operator delivers to escrow a "Notice of Work Completed" with a Certification that the property "is now free of evidence of active infestation or infection." Upon acceptance of this offer, seller shall deliver to buyer a copy of the said inspection report.

(Form continues on next page)

(continue where applicable):

Buyer agrees that seller shall have no liability for correction or repair of items ___ _____ in the report and agrees to purchase the property subject to said conditions and recommendations.

(alternate where applicable)

Buyer agrees that seller shall have no liability for correction or repair of items _____ in the report, but may separately contract with Operator to have these items corrected or repaired without any liability on the part of seller therefor.

COMMENT ON FORM 4:58: Where a preexisting inspection report discloses that conditions exist which must be corrected, this statement can be incorporated in the Real Estate Purchase Contract and Receipt for Deposit. The first additional clause makes it possible to specify the items of "conditions usually likely to lead to infestation or infection," which the seller is not obligated to pay for. The last clause is used as an alternative addition if the buyer wants to have this work performed and will contract directly with the operator to pay for it.

FORM 4:59   SELLER TO DELIVER CERTIFICATION

Buyer shall at _____ expense obtain within ____
                        his/her
days from date of Seller's acceptance, a current written report from a licensed structural pest control operator of the main building and all attached structures. All work recommended in the report to repair damage caused by infestation or infection of wood-destroying pests or organisms found and all work to correct conditions that caused such infestation or infection shall be done at the expense of Seller. However, any work to correct conditions usually deemed likely to lead to infestation or infection of wood-destroying pests or organisms, but where no evidence of existing infestation or infection is found with respect to such conditions, is not the responsibility of the Seller. Structural pest control operator shall deliver to Buyer a certification that the property is at the day of the report or of the Notice of Work Completed free of active infestation or infection of wood-destroying pests or organisms.

COMMENT ON FORM 4:59: Incorporating this simple statement in an offer may well be the most desirable solution from the buyer's point of view, even if it leaves the seller free from liability for recommendations to correct conditions which usually are deemed to lead to infestation or infection where no active infestation or infection is found.

However, when the property has not been inspected recently, the seller may be reluctant to accept an offer containing this clause. The seller may either counter with a dollar limitation on his or her liability or obtain a report before entering into a binding contract.

The broker who wishes to simplify the whole process can insist at the time of accepting the listing that the seller authorize an inspection to be made, so that any offers can be shaped in accordance with the information in the report. To assure that the report is made in the most informative way, the broker may request that the seller sign the order on Form 4:54, "Request for Structural Pest Control Certification Report," which calls for identification and separation of the various findings of the report and of the bid.

**FORM 4:60   BUYER'S WAIVER OF SPECIFIC
CONDITIONS OR RECOMMENDATIONS**

Buyer agrees to purchase said property subject to _____
Items _____ as set forth in _____
said report/

_____ issued by _____
Report number   operator
without further repair or correction to be performed by seller thereon, provided seller furnishes Certification on Notice of Work Completed by the operator, covering repair and correction of Items Nos. _____ as set forth therein.

COMMENT ON FORM 4:60: This paragraph can be used where an existing pest control report is presented to the buyer before the offer is drawn. It can also be used where negotiations lead to counter-proposals limiting the work to be paid for by the seller and leaving some recommended work unperformed. Accuracy in designating the items determines the usefulness of this type of agreement.

FORM 4:61　　　**BUYER ACCEPTING CREDIT IN LIEU**
OF HAVING WORK PERFORMED

Escrow No. _____
Escrow Holder _____

Buyer _____ to accept a credit toward the purchase price of the
　　　　　elects/has elected

sum of $_____ in lieu of seller's obligation to pay for Structural Pest Control
work recommended in Inspection Report No. _____, dated _____
___ 19____, issued by _____ on the property located
　　　　　　　　　　　　　name of operator

at _____. Buyer acknowledges receipt and accep-
tance of said report. Buyer hereby releases seller and broker(s) from all liability
for any Structural Pest Control work which now or in the future may be recommended by any licensed Structural Pest Control Operator with respect to the
subject property.

Dated: _____

_____
Buyer

_____
Buyer

COMMENT ON FORM 4:61: After the original sales agreement and the pest
control agreement have been entered into, buyers often decide to accept a credit
toward the purchase price rather than arranging for funds to be withheld in
escrow and disbursed when the work has been performed. This form constitutes
a new agreement between the parties. The seller's escrow instructions should
include a demand for the buyer's signature to the above release of liability for
any unperformed work.

Certain provisions limiting dollar costs or allowing for the sharing of costs
are helpful in counter-offer situations or in specific clauses of the buyer's offer
(see Forms 4:62 and 4:63. Other eventualities regarding pest control inspection
are covered in Forms 4:64 through 4:68.

FORM 4:62　　　　　　　**DOLLAR LIMITATION**

Regardless of the amount quoted by the Pest Control Operator for the work
set forth above and more particularly as described in the inspection report, seller's
liability for such work shall not exceed the sum of $_____ .

COMMENT ON FORM 4:62: This statement can be inserted in Form 4:55, paragraph 3, at the time the offer is drafted if the broker knows the seller's dollar limitation. It can also be inserted as a counter-proposal by the seller upon acceptance. It can then be approved by the buyer, who should initial the change.

FORM 4:63   DIVISION OF COST

Paragraph 3 is hereby amended to provide that seller's liability shall not exceed _____ of the amount quoted by the

designate proportion
Pest Control Operator for the work described herein and more particularly in the report, and in no event shall exceed the sum of $_____.

COMMENT ON FORM 4:63: This clause can be used in Form 4:55 where the buyer and seller are to divide the cost of the recommended work.

FORM 4:64   ADDITIONAL WORK TO BE
PAID BY SELLER

"If the inspection report discloses excessive cellulose debris, earth-wood contacts and plumbing leaks affecting wood members, the seller shall pay the cost for the removal, correction or repair thereof as recommended in the report."

COMMENT ON FORM 4:64: A buyer may wish to state in the offer that all or some of the above items be corrected or repaired at the expense of the seller.

FORM 4:65   PLUMBING LEAKS

If the inspection report discloses plumbing leaks affecting wood members, the seller shall pay for the repair thereof as recommended in the report.

COMMENT ON FORM 4:65: Stall showers often create leaks which may affect wood members of the structure, even if at the time of inspection no evidence of fungus infection is apparent. The inspection report may disclose such a leak. To provide for necessary correction at seller's expense, the above clause can be inserted in the agreement.

FORM 4:66   INACCESSIBLE AREAS

To be used in lieu of §5 in Form 4:55 or to be inserted
as a counteroffer after buyer has requested inspection of
inaccessible areas:

Seller consents to buyer's requiring inspection of inaccessible areas, but if infestation or damage is found, seller reserves right to refuse to correct the conditions. Upon seller's refusal, buyer may elect a) To accept the property without
abatement in the purchase price; or b) To cancel this agreement. Such cancellation shall not relieve buyer of the obligation to repair damages caused by entry to
the inaccessible areas.

Buyer has deposited the sum of $_____ with
_____ to guarantee payment
                name of Pest Control Operator

of repairs of damages caused by entry to "inaccessible" areas. These funds are
to be refunded to buyer if seller assumes responsibility to pay such costs and to
repair any damage found and to correct conditions causing such damage.

COMMENT ON FORM 4:66: Substantial repairs may be necessary after inaccessible areas have been opened up. Many sellers refuse to sign a blank check
for such recommended work. This clause permits a buyer and seller to compromise by sharing the cost after further negotiations.

FORM 4:67   LIMITATION ON SELLER'S LIABILITY

To be inserted as a separate counter-offer after buyer has
requested inspection of inaccessible areas:

Seller consents to buyer requiring inspection of inaccessible areas, but if
infestation, infection or damage is found, the seller's responsibility, regardless of
the amount quoted by the Pest Control Operator to perform the recommended
work, shall not exceed the sum of $_____.

COMMENT ON FORM 4:67: This consent to further inspection limits the seller's liability to a specified dollar amount.

FORM 4:68   MULTIPLE INSPECTION REPORTS

This _____ is conditional upon delivery by _____
      offer/counter offer   seller/buyer
at _____ expense to _____ of an additional Structural Pest
   seller's/buyer's   seller/buyer
Control Inspection Report by _____ prepared in conformity with
                              name of operator
the provisions of the "Request for Structural Pest Control Certification Report,"
dated _____, attached hereto as Exhibit _____ and incorporated
herein.

Regardless of the amount quoted by the above operator, seller shall not be obligated to select any other operator than the lowest bidder who will provide the certification required. Buyer, however, may waive performance by seller and accept the amount of the lowest bid as credit against the purchase price.

COMMENT ON FORM 4:68: Bids of varying amounts by different operators can lead to much discord. It may be practical to preempt such problems by establishing the limit of seller's liability at the amount submitted by the lowest bidder. However, this solution presupposes that the findings of the reports are identical. Even when this is not the case, using the lowest bid as the dollar limitation may make negotiations easier. A release as contained in Form 4:57 should always be signed in escrow where the buyer accepts cash in lieu of having work performed.

The California certification program and the mandatory delivery of structural pest control reports, if any are involved in the transaction, has lead to more clarity and protection for real estate buyers.

Warranties

Form 4:69 provides for the seller's warranty of mechanical equipment included in the sale.

FORM 4:69   **WARRANTIES**

Seller warrants that the roof is free of leaks and that water, sewer, plumbing, heating and electrical systems and all built-in appliances are in normal working order and will be on the date of delivery of possession.

(Optional):

Buyer shall inspect property 24 hours prior to close of escrow and file written waiver of this condition with the escrow holder.

COMMENT ON FORM 4:69: Many buyers insist on the seller's warranting that the mechanical equipment in the building they are about to purchase is in working order. The salutary effect of this type of provision is interesting. A seller who is asked to sign a warranty is more careful in pointing out minor defects, and will not withhold information of insufficient repairs.

FORM 4:70   HOME PROTECTION PROGRAMS

Buyer and Seller acknowledge that _____ Realtor has advised them that certain home protection programs are available and that _____ Realtor has not made any representations or warranties concerning such programs, their effectiveness or extent of protection. Buyer and Seller shall make their own investigations concerning such programs.

(Optional):

Buyer and Seller agree:

1. _____ Home Warranty Program shall be purchased by _____ effective at close of escrow. Funds to purchase program shall be _____ by program purchaser.
authorized paid by escrow/deposited in escrow

COMMENT ON FORM 4:70: Recent years have seen the emergence of Home Protection Plans (sometimes called ''warranty programs'') which purport to protect the Buyer against defects in major systems (electrical, heating, plumbing) and against malfunction of built-in appliances. These service plans often start 15 days after the beginning of a listing, protecting the Seller, and then picks up Buyer protection at close of escrow.

Disclosing to the parties of the availability of such plans, without singling out any particular plan, may be good practice to avoid vicarious liability. A broker should not recommend a specific company unless he acts as authorized agent for it, or is held harmless by the company in the event it defaults on the contract. Model Form II contains a Home Protection Disclosure form.

Violations of Codes and Ordinances

A prudent buyer will ascertain whether a building conforms with existing building codes and its construction complies with all legal requirements. This is, of course, a tall order. For the benefits of buyers, some cities have enacted ordinances which prescribe that a buyer receive a ''Report of Residential Building Reports,'' popularly called a 3-R Report, on the building under consideration. These reports purport to contain information concerning zoning classification, occupancy classification, date of original construction and original occupancy and use, all construction and alterations permits issued, and whether a certificate of occupancy or other city licenses have been issued.

In California, failure to inform the buyer of building violations known to the seller is sufficient fraud to allow the buyer to rescind the contract.[9] When the seller knows of no violation on the subject property, the clause in Form 4:71 may be used.

FORM 4:71   **NO NOTICES OF VIOLATIONS**

Seller warrants that _____ has no knowledge of the existence of any
                        he/she
notices of violations of city, county or state building, fire and health code or ordinances filed or issued against the property described herein. Such warranty shall be effective at the date of closing _____.
                                            escrow

COMMENT ON FORM 4:71: Where sellers are sure that no notices of violations have been issued or served upon them or their agents, the above clause is of limited risk. This clause is recommended instead of the provisions often used in exchanges, where "each party warrants that he or she has no personal knowledge of the existence of any violations on his or her property. . . ."

Earthquake Disclosures

It is no secret that California is earthquake country, even if the state's inhabitants do not worry about the geological condition of their property daily. The state of California and local government units have taken several steps to minimize the effects of this geological phenomenon. These include control of land use and specific requirements for construction incorporating greater earthquake-resistant design in areas designated as earthquake-prone.

California Public Resources Code Section 2621-2625, also called the Alquist-Priolo Special Studies Zones Act, identifies specified areas as "Special Studies Zones"; included are all "potentially and recently active" faults in the State.

Within these Special Studies Zones, all applications for new projects as defined in the law, which include real estate developments for structures for human occupancy, must be accompanied by a geological report unless waived by the city or county because "no undue hazards exist." Single-family wood-frame dwellings not exceeding two stories are exempt from the report requirement. Twenty of California's fifty-eight counties are affected. Within the twenty counties only portions are in these zones. The areas involved can be identified from an index map showing all the involved zones contained in a brochure issued by the State Division of Mines and Geology, Post Office Box 2980, Sacramento, California 95814.

Most local Real Estate Boards in affected areas have state and local maps more specifically identifying the affected areas. These maps should be consulted. Many cities and counties but unfortunately not all have translated these state maps into local assessor's maps, so that individual parcels may be identified in relationship to the special zones.

Owners and potential buyers of property improved or unimproved face additional responsibilities before they can use land in the Special Studies Zones, which may be severely restricted. The broker dealing in such property has the responsibility to make full disclosure of the fact that the property is located within a Special Studies Zone. The broker cannot be expected to predict whether an earthquake is imminent, and no broker should give advice about the type of construction allowed within the zone. Also, if a broker does not have clear, unequivocal information that the property is within a Special Studies Zone but suspects it, he or she should obtain advice *in writing* from the appropriate city or county official. Such a statement should then be attached to the contract as an addendum and incorporated in the contract by reference thereto. Any "guessing" by either the seller or broker in this matter can lead to lawsuits and, so far as the broker is concerned, to possible disciplinary action.

Full disclosure should be made to a buyer where the broker knows or suspects that the property (improved or unimproved) subject to the offer or sale may be in a Special Studies Zone. Form 4:72 is such disclosure; it can be attached to the Deposit Receipt and appropriately incorporated in the contract. This wording is also included in Model Form II. For alternative supplementary clauses, see Forms 4:73 and 4:74.

FORM 4:72   SPECIAL STUDIES ZONE ACT

The property which is the subject of the contract is situated in a Special Study Zone as designated under Sections 2621–2625, inclusive, of the California Public Resources Code; and, as such, the construction or development on this property of any structure for human occupancy may be subject to the findings of a geologic report prepared by a geologist registered in the State of California, unless such report is waived by the city or county under the terms of that act. No representations on the subject are made by Seller or Agent, and the Buyer should make his/her own inquiry or investigation.

Note: California Public Resources Code #2621.5 excludes structures in existence prior to May 4, 1975;

California Public Resources Code #2621.6 excludes wood frame dwellings not exceeding two (2) stories in height and mobilhomes over eight (8) feet in width;

California Public Resources Code #2621.7 excludes conversion of existing apartment houses into condominiums;

California Public Resources Code #2621.8 excludes alterations and additions under 50% of value of structure from the Special Studies Zone Act.

COMMENTS ON FORM 4:72: Sellers, lessors, and brokers dealing in improved or unimproved property located or suspected to be located within the Special Studies Zones and described in the Alquist-Priolo Special Studies. Zone Act, must disclose such material fact to potential buyers and lessees, since it directly affects the use of or construction of improvements on such property. This CAR form, available as a printed standard form titled "Addendum Special Studies Zone Act" (Form SS D-FHD-11), is a combination disclaimer and warning, designed to satisfy the requirement for disclosure. The legal protection it offers may, however, become illusory if its salutary effect is tranquilized by accompanying verbal intonations of "don't worry" or similar statements discouraging or inhibiting the buyer's "own inquiry or investigation." Sufficient time ought to be allowed for the buyer or lessee to make inquiries. For a clause designed to further protect the buyer of a parcel of property located within a Special Studies Zone, see Form 4:73.

FORM 4:73   SPECIAL STUDIES ZONES INQUIRY

The buyer is allowed _____ days from date of seller's acceptance hereof, for his inquiries concerning the use of the subject property under the terms of the Alquist-Priolo Special Studies Zone Act and local building, zoning, fire, health and safety codes. If such inquiry discloses conditions or information unsatisfactory to the buyer, _____ may cancel this agreement. If notice in writing
                    he/she
thereof has not been delivered within such time, this condition shall be deemed waived.

COMMENT ON FORM 4:73: This clause can be inserted in a Real Estate Purchase Contract and Receipt for Deposit whenever a Special Studies Zone Disclosure is used and the buyer wishes that a time period be specified in which the recommended investigation can be made. The wording is included in CAR's Special Studies Zone Disclosure Form and in Model Form II.

FORM 4:74   PROPERTY LOCATED IN A
SPECIAL STUDIES ZONE

Buyer represents that he has been informed that the subject property is located within a Special Studies Zone as designated under the Alquist-Priolo Special Studies Zone Act, Sections 2621–2625 inclusive, of the California Public Resources Code, and as such construction or development on this property of any structure for human occupancy may be subject to the findings of a geologic report prepared by a geologist registered in the State of California.

(Form continues on next page)

(Optional for improved property):

In addition, the property may be required by local building, health and safety codes to incorporate features of greater earthquake-resistant design.

(Optional where building inspection report is available):

Attached hereto as Addendum _____ and incorporated herein by reference is an inspection report dated _____ issued by
_____ pertaining to the requirements
                City Building Inspection Department
for bringing the improvements of the subject property in compliance with applicable codes.

(Continue):

Buyer agrees to accept building "as is," subject to all existing building, health and safety and zoning ordinances or regulations by any governmental authority.

COMMENT ON FORM 4:74: This clause can be used where the broker or seller has *actual* notice or knowledge that the property is located within a Special Studies Zone. It eliminates the necessity for the use of Form 4:72, since it affirmatively states that the buyer has been informed. The two optional clauses are self-explanatory. The first one is recommended where the seller or broker does not *know* that the building will need certain improvements to comply with construction in a Special Studies Zone. Where the seller has not made the necessary alterations, but has a building report requiring them, the second optional clause can be used. The last clause is the buyer's waiver and agreement to purchase "as is." This type of clause should be used with caution, as indicated in the discussion under the heading "As is" Clauses earlier in this chapter. If the buyer requires time to study the problem, the wording from Form 4.73 can be incorporated herein.

Environmental Control

Since most local governing bodies have amended their zoning ordinances to give the California Environmental Quality Act substantive effect, more problems have arisen concerning disclosure by sellers and brokers. Almost every land use will eventually be controlled, directly or indirectly, by findings in the Environmental Impact Report. Subdivisions, for example, must conform to the Special Plan enacted pursuant to the State Special Planning Act.

Most brokers dealing in land in Special Studies Zones are aware of the duty of disclosure raised by the Alquist-Priolo Special Studies Zone Act. The question is, Will this disclosure requirement establish a bothersome precedent with regard to other land-use and environmental regulations?

The various regulations on land use are subjectively applied by the authorities to a final plan proposed by the owner or developer of the land. A seller or a broker negotiating the sale of unimproved land can probably not safely refrain from reference to zoning laws, environmental impact reports, county regulations, and the like, but should certainly avoid making any representations about their impact in connection with the buyer's intended use of the property. A disclaimer clause for insertion in all contracts involving unimproved land is found in Form 4:75.

Sophisticated buyers will probably insist that the agreement allow the longest possible time for investigating all aspects of land use before they are obligated to purchase. A contract to purchase land for future development should not be drafted on a printed Real Estate Purchase Contract. Such contracts are better left to individual tailoring by legal counsel.

FORM 4:75   **LAND USE AND ENVIRONMENTAL CONTROL WARNING**

Due to the uncertain effect of land use and environmental regulations which may apply to the subject property, and which may depend upon aspects of buyer's plan for use, buyer should make _____ own inquiry or investigation
                                                                                his/her
concerning permissible uses, and seller and agent make no warranty or representations.

COMMENT ON FORM 4:75: Whenever unimproved property is subject to negotiation or sale, this clause can be used as a general disclaimer regarding land use and regulations for environmental control. A careful buyer thus alerted may desire to make the agreement contingent upon investigation of such problems or upon obtaining necessary permits. Usually a time limitation is advisable. The wording in Forms 4:73 can be incorporated in Form 4:74.

Zoning

The real estate expert must be knowledgeable concerning the classifications of zoning and the uses permitted under such classifications. Zoning designations vary from one community to another. A cautious buyer will examine the zoning ordinance and confer with the zoning authorities concerning the available use. Future changes in zoning should be anticipated.

Form 4:76 is a clause warranting that the piece of land under consideration is zoned in a certain manner. Clauses for "re-zoning" or "variants" are not shown, since these definitions create technical difficulties and legal problems. Such clauses should be drawn by counsel to correspond with necessary applications to the zoning authority.

FORM 4:76   **ZONING WARRANTY**

Seller warrants and represents that at this time and as of _____
                                                                                close of escrow/
_____ the property is and will be zoned _____
delivery of deed   designation
under the laws and ordinances of _____
                                                    city/county

COMMENT ON FORM 4:76: Where a certain zoning classification is important to the buyer, a warranty by the seller is necessary stating that the property is in fact zoned as represented. It is preferable that the seller simply warrants the correct zoning designation and refrains from making any warranty as to specific use. This clause places the risk of change in zoning before closing upon the seller.

Organic Gardening

The following condition was inspired by the movement subscribing to the healthfulness of organic foods. Form 4:77 contains a warranty on the property with respect to chemical treatment of the property and vegetation thereon.

FORM 4:77   **ORGANIC GARDENING WARRANTY**

Seller warrants that for a period of _____, no poisonous sprays, insecticides, pesticides or herbicides, or chemical fertilizers have been used in any way on the subject property, or applied to the vegetation thereon.

COMMENT ON FORM 4:77: Sellers who represent themselves as organic gardeners or farmers should not object to the warranty expressed in this clause. If they are recent converts to the organic-foods persuasion, however, they will probably wish to limit the scope of such a warranty.

Special Flood Hazards

Where special flood hazards exist and the buyer is to obtain a loan from a lender who is federally regulated or the loan is to be federally insured a special disclosure of the necessity for flood insurance must be made to the buyer. Form 4:78 is designed to make such disclosure.

FORM 4:78   **DISCLOSURE STATEMENT**
                       SPECIAL FLOOD HAZARDS

Flood Hazard Zone Disclosure: The subject property is situated in a "Special Flood Hazard Area" as set forth on a Federal Emergency Management Agency (FEMA) "Flood Insurance Rate Map" (FIRM) or "Flood Hazard Boundary Map" (FHBM). The law provides that, as a condition of obtaining financing on most structures located in a "Special Flood Hazard Area", lenders require flood insurance where the property or its attachments are security for a loan.

COMMENT ON FORM 4:78: C.A.R. has a Combined Special Studies Zone and Flood Hazards Disclosure form SSD-FHD-11. This form alerts the buyer that flood hazard insurance must be carried if property is located within a "Flood Zone." The two clauses are incorporated in Model Form II.

Water Tests

Most land is valueless without water. A source of water should be found and tested for reliability and quality. When municipal or local water systems water is not available, the property owner must rely on wells, springs, creeks, ponds, deeded water and water easements for use of the neighbors water. Deeded water is specified in the deed and measured by the inch. Distribution is supervised by a water master, an employee of the California Department of Water Resources. Water easements should be examined by an experienced attorney. In buying country land the sale should be conditioned upon the results of tests and investigation regarding the water source. See Form 4:79.

FORM 4:79   **WATER TESTING**

This offer is conditioned upon inspection by experts of buyers choice of the condition of the well, pump and water. If such inspections disclose conditions unsatisfactory to the buyer, the buyer may terminate this agreement. If notice of such disapproval has not been delivered in person or by mail to seller within _____ days of date of seller's acceptance, this condition shall be deemed waived.

COMMENT ON FORM 4:79: If an existing well is on the property it should be inspected and checked for recovery of water and for the physical condition of the equipment, and a well report issued. Most counties require 5–10 gallons per minute to qualify for a building permit. A large garden may call for at least 10 gallons per minute, large scale irrigations at least 50 gallons.

Septic Tank

A permit is needed to install a septic tank. In order to install one the land must pass a percolation ("perk") test. The test should be done before the contract becomes binding. Existing septic tanks should be examined by an expert. The wording in Form 4:80 can be amended by adding and "of the condition of the septic tank and the plumbing system" and otherwise contain the same right to cancel if disapproved. For a "perk" test condition see Form 4:80.

FORM 4:80   **PERK TEST**

This offer is conditioned upon a percolation test report by a tester approved by the health department of _____ County. If such report discloses conditions unsatisfactory to the buyer, the buyer may terminate this agreement. If notice of such disapproval has not been delivered in person or by mail to seller within _____ days of date of seller's acceptance, this condition shall be deemed waived.

COMMENT ON FORM 4:80: The perk test should be done before escrow closes. Sometimes sellers will have a perk test available, but buyer should inquire if it is still approved by the health authorities.

Parcel Maps

The California Attorney General in his Opinion No. 80-407 states that:

A person may not offer to sell or lease a parcel of real property for which a final map is required under the Subdivision Map Act, where such map has not been filed, even though the offer is expressly conditioned upon the map being approved and filed.

Such final map is required for all subdivisions creating five or more parcels. A lot split involving four or less parcels do not require a *final* map, but does require a *parcel* map. The law further provides (Government Code Section 64499.30(b) as follows:

No person shall sell, lease or finance any parcel or parcels of real property . . . for which a *parcel* map is required by this division or local ordinance, until such map . . . has been filed for record by the recorder of the county in which any portion of the subdivision is located.

It is therefore legal to enter into a contract subject to delivery of a parcel map, but illegal if the map required is a tentative or *final* map. Form 4:82 contains such a condition for a parcel map. However under B&P Code Section

11018.2 no parcel for which a *public report* is required can be offered until the report is issued.

Lot Split Warranty

In several areas of California illegal lot splits have taken place. Where a buyer or broker has suspicion that an illegal lot split may have taken place, a thorough investigation should be undertaken. It is also important to obtain a representation by the Seller that an illegal lot split is not involved. Form 4:81 covers such warranty.

FORM 4:81   WARRANTY AGAINST ILLEGAL LOT SPLIT

The Seller warrants that the property described herein has not been subject to an illegal lot split.

(Optional continue):

Seller further warrants that in subdividing the land of which the herein described parcel _____
previously was/is
a part he/she has complied with all provisions of the Subdivision Map Act and all other applicable laws and regulations.

COMMENT ON FORM 4:81: Many properties have been "subdivided" by the process of "four-by-fouring" circumventing the law by making transfer to four straw grantees and again dividing the parcels into four parcels. The provisions of the Subdivided Lands Law are designed to provide prospective Buyers with a full disclosure of the risk involved in buying land. See also Form 4:82.

FORM 4:82   SALE SUBJECT TO PARCEL MAP

This offer is conditioned upon Seller delivering to Buyer within _____ days approval from respective local and state governmental entities of a parcel map including the property described in this agreement.

COMMENT ON FORM 4:82: A Seller and the Seller's agent should familiarize themselves with the requirements for obtaining a parcel map. The regulations of sale of subdivided land is complex and contains pitfalls which can lead to costly litigation.

Insulation Disclosure Rules for New Construction

The Federal Rules issued by the Federal Trade Commission as they appear in the Federal Register, Section 460.1 through 460.24 impose an affirmative obligation on a builder to include in every sales contract after November 30, 1979, the following information, (a) the type of insulation in the home, (b) the thickness of the insulation, (c) the resulting R-value of the insulation.

The Rules also provide that if the insulation varies from one part of the home to another part the above information must be provided for each type used and the areas where each type is installed must be specified. If a broker lists and markets new homes the broker is required under the law to include the information in sales contracts the broker is negotiating. F.T.C. Thermal Insulation Disclosures form is a C.A.R. Supplement Form.

Disclosures of Waste Deposit Sites

Sellers, Lessors and Brokers owe an affirmative duty to disclose to a buyer or lessee whether a parcel of land is in a hazardous waste or border zone. California Health and Safety Code 25220–25240 sets forth the provisions for use of land on which a significant disposal of hazardous waste has occurred or is within Two Thousand (2000) feet of such a significant disposal site. Form 4:84 provides minimum disclosure information for Hazardous Waste disclosure, which must accompany all lease or rental agreements, but can also be used in the sales agreement.

FORM 4:84   HAZARDOUS WASTE DISCLOSURE

The land described herein contains hazardous waste or is within 2,000 feet of land that contains hazardous waste. Such condition renders the land and the owner, lessee, or other possessor of the land subject to requirements, restrictions, provisions, and liabilities contained in Chapter 6.5 (commencing with Section 25100) of Division 20 of the Health and Safety Code. This statement is not a declaration that a hazard exists. (H & S Code 25230(b).

COMMENT ON FORM 4:84: An active hazardous waste disposal site is automatically classified as hazardous waste property. Hearings by the California Department of Health Sciences are held when an owner, lessee or governmental agency has probable cause to believe that a land is hazardous waste property. When it is determined that the land must be so designated serious restrictions on its use is promulgated. Substantial penalties are provided in the law for its violation.

"Granny" Apartments

The California Legislature decided in its 1981–82 session that steps should be taken to encourage the creation of more residential units for persons over the age of sixty (60) since there was a serious shortage of housing for such persons. The Legislature found that there was an important need to maintain senior citizens in independent living situations and also to encourage housing arrangements which would prevent isolation of elderly persons and reunite families. Government Code Section 65852.1 therefore permits any city, including a charter city, or county, or city and county to issue a zoning variance or a special use permit, or a conditional use permit for a dwelling unit to be constructed, or attached to, a primary residence on a parcel zoned for a single family residence if the dwelling unit is intended solely for the occupancy of one adult or two adult persons who are sixty (60) years of age or over, and the area or floor space of the dwelling unit does not exceed 640 square feet. Form 4:85 is designed to obtain from a seller of such specially described apartment evidence that the apartment has been built under one of the enumerated variances.

FORM 4:85   SENIOR CITIZEN APARTMENT VARIANCE

Seller warrants that the apartment in the subject property was constructed under a valid _____

zoning variance/special use permit/conditional use permit
and will provide buyer with a copy of the zoning variance ordinance or the permit under which the unit was constructed and warrants that the apartment _____

has been/is
occupied in accordance with the terms of the variance or permit.

COMMENT ON FORM 4:85: The so-called "Granny" apartments constructed with such variance or permit is legal. A real estate licensee should ascertain if an existing apartment in a single family residence was built under such permit and obtain a copy of the permit since there may be future limitations on the permitted use. For apartments built without permit see Form 4:22.

Chapter 5
Title, Possession, Risk of Loss, and Damages for Breach

The Realtor shall avoid exaggeration, misrepresentation, or concealment of pertinent facts. He has an affirmative obligation to discover adverse factors that a reasonable, competent, and diligent investigation would disclose.

Article 9, Code of Ethics
National Association of Realtors

"Covenants, Conditions, Restrictions, and Easements"

At the time of preparing the buyer's proposed offer, the contract writer is not always in possession of special knowledge concerning covenants, conditions, restrictions, or easements affecting the property. Printed contract forms, therefore, usually contain clauses expressly designed to cover this problem. Quite often, these standard contracts obligate the buyer to take title subject to "covenants, conditions, restrictions or easements of record." Some forms presume acceptance of title subject to "current taxes not yet due and payable, zoning regulations, recorded tract restrictions, set-back lines and utilities easements set forth on recorded maps or in recorded tract restrictions." In either case, such clauses may be tricky and unfair to the buyer. Any one of the enumerated items may interfere with the buyer's intended use of the property.

The excuse for these "boiler plate" clauses is, of course, that in the ordinary sale of a residence, buyers impliedly understand that they are buying the property subject to "usual" tract restrictions, set-backs and utility easements, and that in thereby accepting the residential type of zoning they cannot be hurt. This may be true, but unfortunately the forms are used for many transactions other than sales of homes in fully developed areas or known housing tracts.

Difficulties for the Broker

The title clause in the Model Forms attempts to avoid forcing buyers to make a blanket endorsement of restrictions on the title which they have no opportunity to examine. Should the seller be unable to produce the title in compliance with the buyer's requirements, the deal will be off unless the parties agree to extend or amend.

Obviously, this procedure creates problems for the broker. The clause in the form itself requires the broker to obtain perhaps as early as at the time of listing the property, a preliminary title report. Later, at the request of the buyer, the broker may have to procure copies of covenants and conditions described therein. The broker or an attorney for the buyer must then explain utility easements, tract restrictions, and so on. Thus, in the attempt to protect the buyer against blanket acceptance of unwanted restrictions or conditions, the form may have become an invitation to further problems, rather than a solution to problems more imaginary than real.

It is practically impossible for the broker to have available when taking the offer from a prospective buyer copies of all title company reports, tract restrictions, easements, and so on, for exhibit to the buyer before he or she signs on the dotted line. And multiple-listing cards cannot contain such information in detail so that it will be available to all cooperating brokers.

**FORM 5:01   ACCEPTANCE OF COVENANTS NOT
              INTERFERING WITH PRESENT USE**

Title is to be free of liens, encumbrances, easements, restrictions, rights and conditions of record, known to seller, other than the following:
Current property taxes, and covenants, conditions, restrictions, and public utility easements of record, if any, provided the same do not adversely affect the present structure on the premises and the continued use thereof for the purposes for which it is presently being used, unless reasonably disapproved by buyer in writing within _____ days of receipt of current preliminary title report furnished at _____ expense, and (3) _____

COMMENT ON FORM 5:01: The first half of this clause which is found in the Model Forms represents a frequently used compromise. It is not prejudicial to the buyer, where he or she is not contemplating or foreseeing any use of the property different from the present, and where the improvements are permanent. This clause is not advisable where, for example, a single-family residence is situated on a large lot zoned for multistory or commercial use. In such a case, the buyer should examine all easements, covenants, and conditions carefully prior to signing the offer, since someday he or she may wish to sell the property for a higher and better use.

The second half of the clause presupposes that the buyer immediately receives a preliminary title report within a certain time period to be designated. Obviously it would be most practical to do this right away, so buyer can waive this condition promptly. The inclusion of this clause in the new Model Form is a return to the earlier forms wherein buyers had the right to object to conditions of title, and the sellers were given a period of time in which they were to cure any "cloud" on the title. This period was 90 days in some contracts creating possible tax problems. Here both parties can rescind. It also will assure that buyers not agree inadvertently to conditions of title which will adversely affect their future plans for the property. Careful broker's will obtain written waivers of this condition of the contract by having the buyer specifically approve the title company report. The space designated by (3) can be used to include unrecorded agreements.

The above form is also usable in subdivisions or tracts where the broker has made a collection of the existing tract restrictions in each subdivision, and is aware of the utility easements. Whenever an easement for utilities crosses land on which buildings, even of a nonpermanent nature, are presently situated, the buyer's attention should be alerted. Of course, other types of easements should be specifically examined by counsel as to legal effect.

Residential sales in well-known tracts are often made with only scant reference to covenants and conditions, restrictions and easements. That this casual attitude can be dangerous is demonstrated in a case where the property in question contained a thirty-foot-wide waterpipe and utilities easement.[1] When the buyers inquired about the easement, they were told "not to worry." The court held the real estate salesmen liable for the decrease in value caused by the easement, and stated: "The defendant . . . is a real estate agent, and as such is supposed to possess ordinary professional knowledge concerning the title and natural characteristics of the property he is selling." This case points up the necessity for carefully examining any unusual features of property offered for sale, and full disclosure thereof.

In many printed deposit-receipts forms a clause is incorporated by which the property is sold subject to recorded encumbrances, easements, and so on, "common to the neighborhood." The above case illustrates the danger inherent in such blanket, unrestricted approval.

Our Model Forms requires that the title be free of any "liens, encumbrances, easements, restrictions, rights and conditions" *known* to the seller. Thus, the form places upon the contract drafter the additional burden of inquiring of the seller whether any "licenses" to pass over land have been given to neighbors, any oral or written agreement made with neighbors or tenants creating some "rights" in the property, and so on.

When such unrecorded easement, license, or agreement is known to the contract writer at the time the offer is drafted, reference should be made to it following any of the clauses set forth in Forms 5:01 and 5:03. If the contract writer does not have knowledge of any unrecorded agreement, he or she should alert the seller to the contract provision and protect the buyer by inserting a warranty such as that found in Form 5:02.

**FORM 5:02   WARRANTY AGAINST EASEMENTS
                        NOT OF RECORD**

Seller warrants to buyer that the title delivered to buyer will not be encumbered by any easements, licenses, or other rights not disclosed by the public records other than _____ .
list

This warranty shall survive the delivery of deed.

COMMENT ON FORM 5:02: The Model Forms specifically mentions easements and rights *recorded* as well as those *known to seller*. A careful inspection of the property may reveal visible signs of implied easements, including pipelines for irrigation purposes. To be safe and to raise the question concerning such "rights" known to seller, the above clause should be inserted. In Model Form 11 the insertion is most practicable under paragraph 1. It may be possible to dispense with this warranty if extended coverage title insurance is available to buyer. Our model Deposit Receipt, however, only contemplates the issuance of a standard owner's policy of title insurance which excepts "any state of facts which a personal inspection of the premises might disclose." Therefore, a warranty is necessary. This warranty should survive the merger of the contract into the deed. If there are other warranties and conditions intended to survive, a blanket clause as shown in Form 4:46 can be substituted for the last sentence in the above form.

Inspection of the Title Company Report

Various provisions can be designed which will clear title exceptions on the basis of a title company report. While in most situations this lengthy procedure is unnecessary, situations do arise where the contract writer may wish to incorporate a provision allowing the buyer an inspection of the covenants and conditions shown in the title report.

In some situations, the seller's representative can make copies of a preliminary title company and the documents referred to therein available to the buyer for examination and approval before the offer is executed. This ideal situation may call for the inclusion of a provision indicating approval of the report and the documents referred to therein. Form 5:03 approves the report only.

**FORM 5:03   TITLE COMPANY REPORT DELIVERED TO
                    BUYER BEFORE OFFER**

Title is to be free of liens, encumbrances, easements, restrictions, rights and conditions of record, known to seller, other than the following:

Exceptions No. _____ and _____ only, as shown in preliminary report issued by _____ Company, dated _____, 19_____ bearing order number _____.

(Form continues on next page)

(If new loans are to be recorded, continue):

and such other exception which may be included in the policy of title insurance caused by recording of the deed(s) of trust referred to herein.

COMMENT ON FORM 5:03: This form can be used when title company report is available when the buyer makes the offer. If the report contains exceptions that are to be eliminated, the exceptions acceptable to the buyer should be identified clearly by number. The wording will also protect against any late-recorded lien or other defects, since it specifies the only acceptable exceptions.

Careful brokers and lawyers obtain, before closing, acknowledgments from the buyer that he or she has examined the report and agreed to the exemptions shown therein. If the title report is available for examination before the offer is executed the buyer's acknowledgment can, of course, be incorporated in the contract itself. Most likely, acknowledgment that the title report has been examined must be obtained later. The seller's representative should be particularly careful in obtaining a written agreement to accept title which differs from the wording contained in the Deposit Receipt. Form 5:04 can be mimeographed and used in such situations. (Of course, the directions given in parentheses should not be incorporated in the document.)

In one instance, a court has held a broker liable for his negligent failure to advise his principal to have a title search before he purchased the property.[2]

FORM 5:04   EXAMINATION OF TITLE COMPANY REPORT

Buyer acknowledges that he has examined a preliminary report issued by _____ Company, dated _____, 19____, bearing order number ____ regarding the property described _____.
          herein/therein

Provided that the Standard California Land Title Association Policy will not show any other exceptions not shown in such preliminary report,

(If any new loans are set forth in the "terms of payment" part of contract, continue):

except such other exceptions caused by the recording of the deeds of trust (and _____) if any referred to in
          financing statements/chattel mortgages

this agreement/in the Real Estate Purchase Contract and Receipt for Deposit dated _____

(If certain items such as attachments, judgments, homesteads, actions, etc., are to be removed, continue):

and will further not show exceptions number _____ of said report, _____ through _____ inclusive,

(In all situations, continue):

then buyer expressly approves such title company report and agrees to accept title subject to the exceptions stated above.

COMMENT ON FORM 5:04: This clause is an acceptance of the title report for use either in the original offer or as a separate memorandum after the buyer has inspected the preliminary report. Great care should be taken in comparing the exceptions named in the report with those named in this clause. This form can also be used as an addendum to the Model Form. If used as a separate memorandum, it should be dated and signed by the buyer acknowledging the receipt of a copy thereof.

If the buyer knows of recent remodeling or construction done on the premises and is obtaining title insurance, a mechanic lien endorsement is available. If no title insurance is contemplated, the seller should either warrant the property to be free of any mechanic liens, or obtain lien waivers from all contractors, laborers, and suppliers.

Conditions of Title

The second half of the title paragraph of our Model Forms reads as follows: "Seller shall furnish Buyer at _____ expense a standard California Land Title Association policy issued by _____ Company, showing title vested in Buyer subject only to the above. If Seller (1) is unwilling or unable to eliminate any title matter disapproved by Buyer as above, Seller may terminate this agreement, or (2) fails to deliver title as above, Buyer may terminate this agreement; in either case, the deposit shall be returned to Buyer."

In the absence of the provision used in the Model Form, the seller would be obligated to convey "good and marketable title." It has been held that title insurance is a "reasonable method" of determining marketability.[3] Marketability and insurability are, however, not necessarily synonymous.

The variety of matters to which marketability is related staggers the imagination.[4] A policy of title insurance operates, however, as a readily identifiable means of title evidence. Since all title insurance companies are not alike in size, reserves, claims policy, and so forth, the title clause in the form obligating the buyer to accept title insurance as evidence of good title should contain a selection of a *specific* title insurer, not just a reference to "any title company."

The California Insurance Code provides that a preliminary report does not describe the status of the title, only the terms and conditions on which the title company will issue a policy of title insurance.

Standard-Policy Coverage

The CAR forms are unique in that, by referring in the officially approved form to a third organization, the California Land Title Association, a third party is indirectly made part of the contract. California Association of Realtors has no major influence upon what the California Land Title Association may wish to include or exclude from coverage under its standard form. Nevertheless, the form assumes that a standard-form coverage is all the average buyer of California real estate is normally entitled to.

With the growing practice of developing and selling participation in loans, most institutional lenders are not satisfied with the standard-form coverage, which apparently is good enough for owners only, but insist that the buyer pay for the American Land Title Association lender's form coverage. The latter includes such risks as unrecorded liens or easements, rights of parties in possession, and rights or claims which a survey or physical inspection of the property will show. It is possible in some instances for private owners and mortgagors to obtain similar coverage under special endorsements to the standard policy.

Title insurance standard-form coverage designated in the Model Form is minimum coverage. Over a hundred special endorsements may be added to the standard policy by request. Even if not all companies will issue all of these endorsements, the coverage is generally available if the party is aware that he or she needs the coverage and is willing to pay the price.

The difficulty with standard-policy coverage usually lies in the policy buyer's failure to fully appreciate what is covered in the policy. In addition to needing title insurance, buyers are badly in need of ready access to unbiased, realistic, and comprehensive explanation and assistance in evaluating what is covered under the standard policy. The title insurer's counsel represents the insurer and is concerned with its risk. Many brokers are inadequately equipped for advising in this area, and since they often represent the seller only, they may not be unbiased agents for the buyer in any event. Only independent counsel can guide the buyer in this matter. Title companies are now making available an American Land Title Association (ALTA) Residential Policy covering one-to-four family residences. This policy is also called the ALTA *plain language* policy. That's a real misnomer, for it contains convoluted sentences six lines long! The policy nevertheless, is a substantial improvement over standard coverage. Several lender protective endorsements are obtainable.

In CAR's 1988 revisions of the model forms it is expected that the ALTA residential policy will replace the present choice. In CAR's Investment Property form, the reference will be to the revised ALTA regular owner's policy.

Customs of payment for title insurance often vary from county to county within a state. Our Model Form, therefore, provides that the party who is to be responsible be specified. In some counties it will be necessary to insert, "one-half buyer's and one-half seller's," in order to express the local custom.

The CAR forms states: "If Seller fails to deliver title as above Buyer may terminate this agreement . . ." This clause does not clarify whether "termination" precludes the right to damages for breach. Nor does it fully answer the question as to whether the buyer, by accepting such title as seller can deliver, is entitled to an abatement in the price commensurate with the cost of removing the defect in the title. Furthermore, this clause does not indicate whether the seller, upon notice of the buyer's objection to the title, is allowed a reasonable amount of time within which to cure the defect. These very real issues remain to be decided by the parties. In earlier editions of CAR's Deposit Receipt, these problems were handled by allowing the seller time to cure the defect and by giving the buyer the right to withdraw if the seller refused to cure the defect upon refund of all other sums paid by the buyer under the contract, including fees for preliminary title reports, termite reports, surveys, or other types of title examination and so forth, to which obviously the buyer would be entitled. Form 5:05 provides a clause for handling a defect in the title.

FORM 5:05   **DEFECT IN TITLE**

If the seller shall be unable to deliver title as herein provided, the deposit and all other sums paid by buyer shall be refunded and this agreement shall be of no further effect, except that the seller upon written notice to buyer shall be entitled to an extension of time for closing of escrow of not more than 60 days to permit him to remove any outstanding interest or question of title not expressly agreed to by buyer. The buyer shall have the option to accept such title as seller can deliver without reduction of the purchase price or any credit against same, and without liability on the part of the seller.

COMMENT ON FORM 5:05: This clause specifically allows the buyer a refund of all sums paid under the contract. It also gives the buyer an option to accept title in the condition the seller can convey. The clause also gives the seller sixty days to cure any default.

Because of the ramifications concerning defects in title and seller's liability for them, it is recommended that any clause concerning this matter should be drawn by counsel.

The "Proration" Clause

Paragraph 8 of the Model Form is the customary "proration" clause. The language here is more precise than in such clauses in most forms. Paragraph reads:

Property taxes, premiums on insurance acceptable to buyer, rents, interest, homeowners dues, and _____ shall be prorated as of (a) the date of recordation of deed or (b) _____. Any bond or assessment which is a lien shall be ___paid___ by _____. _____ shall pay cost
                                   assumed
of transfer taxes, if any.

The subject of prorations deserves more attention than it is usually given. It may be very important at the time of closing, since proper timing may make a difference in the buyer's actual cash outlay. When there is a small down payment, and the seller is to carry financing, it may be advantageous for the seller to insist on the inclusion of a provision that any apportionment of items to which the buyer is entitled to credit shall not be paid in cash, but by a comparable reduction in the mortgage. See Form 5:06 for such a provision.

FORM 5:06   PRORATION CREDITS BY REDUCTION IN "PURCHASE MONEY" MORTGAGE

The principal amount of the _____ and _____
                              note   deed of trust
in favor of seller shall be reduced by an amount equal to the prorated credits due buyer, if any.

COMMENT ON FORM 5:06: Many sellers do not wish to have the buyer's cash down payment reduced by prorations of items which result in a credit to buyer. Where the seller is to carry either all or part of the financing, cash payment of the credit due the buyer can be avoided by allowing for a reduction in the mortgage. This clause can be inserted in the Model Form's terms-of-payment clause, but if this is done the broker must remember to insert in the proration clause such a reference as "and loan trust funds," or "impound funds," if these funds are to be included in the calculation.

A common problem in proration is how to handle rents which are unpaid to the seller at the time of closing. This matter is, of course, subject to negotiation. If rents are delinquent and are being prorated, the seller has paid for rents not received and may have difficulty in collecting from the tenant when title has passed. If rents are not prorated, the buyer starts with a delinquent tenant. Forms 5:07 and 5:08 may be used as alternative methods of dealing with unpaid rents.

FORM 5:07   UNPAID RENT TO BE PRORATED

Rents remaining unpaid during the period of closing shall be prorated and the buyer assigns to the seller all _____ interest in the unpaid rent for the
his/her
prorated period.

COMMENT ON FORM 5:07: This clause can be used when the rents are to be prorated.

FORM 5:08   UNPAID RENT NOT TO BE PRORATED

Rents remaining unpaid during the period of closing shall not be prorated, and seller assigns to buyer all _____ interest in the unpaid rent for that
his/her
period.

COMMENT ON FORM 5:08: This clause is to be used when rents are not to be prorated. Some contract writers using the Model Form simply insert in the blank space either "including unpaid rents at time of closing," or "not including unpaid rent at time of closing." This solution may be an oversimplification.

In some situations the buyer agrees to collect the rent and forward the seller's share after receipt. Form 5:09 is an example of such an agreement.

**FORM 5:09   UNPAID RENT TO BE COLLECTED BY
              BUYER ON BEHALF OF SELLER**

If at the time of _____ there are
delivery of deed/close of escrow
past-due rents owed from tenants for periods not exceeding one month, and seller is entitled to all or part of the same, buyer agrees that the first moneys received from said tenants will be received in trust for seller on account of such delinquent rentals, and paid over to seller upon receipt unless said tenants claim to have made prior payments thereof to seller.

COMMENT ON FORM 5:09: This clause can be inserted in any space provided for "other terms and conditions." Of course, the exact amounts due should be determined at close of escrow. Some buyers refuse to act as a collection agency for the seller.

With high loan ratio to value it is necessary for institutional lenders to protect their loans against delinquences caused by failure to pay taxes or insurance. The method most often used is the trust impound, or escrow account, whereby monthly additions are made to a fund sufficient to pay taxes and insurance premiums when due. When a sale takes place sellers are entitled to a refund of the fund, or they can agree to assign it to the buyer.

In connection with the assumption of an existing loan, one can visualize three factual situations: (a) the buyer pays for escrow account; (b) the seller assigns escrow account; and (c) the seller assigns escrow account and paid unearned insurance premium. All three possibilities are based on the proposition that the escrow account be current at the time of closing. Where the seller assigns escrow account only, it is in lieu of proration of taxes and interest. The buyer then has the option either of paying the seller the unearned premium on insurance or taking out new insurance. Where the assignment is of both the escrow and the insurance policy, the consideration is in lieu of proration taxes, insurance, and interest. Whether or not an assignment of the escrow account with or without unearned insurance premiums in lieu of other prorations is favorable to the buyer depends on the particular situation. Few people probably give this problem much thought when entering into an offer. It seems better to arrange for proration of all items and give the buyer an option either to prorate the old insurance or take out another policy.

Since taxes and assessments, and possibly insurance premiums, have been prorated under the proration clause of the Model Forms, the seller is entitled to be credited with the prepayment for these items. Form 5:10 provides for such credit.

FORM 5:10   IMPOUND FUND CREDIT TO SELLER

Buyer shall be charged and seller credited with any impound funds on loan remaining on record at close of escrow.

COMMENT ON FORM 5:10: This clause is usable if the buyer assumes the existing loan, but only if the items covered by the impound—that is, taxes, insurance premiums, and assessments—are being prorated.

Many Boards of Realtors have adopted "customs of title closing," spelling out the rules for proration based upon 360 days in a year, 30 days in a month, and so on.

Proration of Taxes

The proration of taxes is becoming more and more important with increased assessments and rising tax rates. The incorporation of personal property taxes as a lien on the real property, which is a trend encouraged by tax assessors, raises other problems. Unless the written part of the contract properly provides for handling these matters, or a custom and practice clause is incorporated in the form, the contract is defective. Often the tax rate has not been fixed at the time of the contract. Most lawyer-prepared contracts provide for a readjustment when the rate is fixed by including a clause to that effect, as shown in Form 5:11.

The Model Forms give the buyer an option to reject existing casualty insurance policies. This option is fair to the buyer, but undesirable to the seller, who will suffer the loss inherent in short-term cancellations. However, the option does protect the buyer against being saddled with long-term excessive-coverage insurance policies, and may therefore be a practical provision.

Supplemental Assessments

California law requires that property which *changes ownership* or is *newly constructed* be revalued at the time the transfer occurs or the construction is completed.

Supplemental assessments represent the difference between the base year value and that determined by the Assessor upon transfer or completed construction. Supplemental assessments will result in a supplemental tax bill provided the new valuation is greater than the base year value. If the new value is less, a refund will occur.

If the change in ownership or new construction is completed between March 1 and May 31, there will be two supplemental assessments. The first for the fiscal year ending June 30, and the second for the next fiscal year. Property taxes calculated on supplemental assessments are prorated from the date of change for the remaining months in the fiscal year (July 1 through June 30). This information should be given to the buyer.

FORM 5:11 **TAX RATE NOT FIXED AT TIME OF CONTRACTING**

If the closing of title shall occur before the tax rate is fixed, the proration of taxes shall be upon the basis of tax rate for the next preceding year, applied to the latest assessed valuation.

(Optional continue):

Upon subsequent ascertainment of the new tax rate, any difference in such proration which would result from applying the new tax rate shall be paid by seller to buyer or vice versa, as the case may be.

COMMENT ON FORM 5:11: This is a standard clause, to be used where reference to a customary rule of closing prorations is not found or where such a closing rule does not provide for later readjustment. If desired by either party or their counsel, this clause can be inserted in the Model Form.

If there are no items to be prorated other than the ones enumerated in the printed text of the Model Forms (property taxes, premiums on insurance policies, rents, and interest), the blank space should be crossed out by dashes or asterisks, or a line should be drawn through it. The use of the word "none" makes the sentence rather meaningless. If words are desired, the wording "no other items" will make the sentence read correctly.

Items to Be Prorated

The most common items to be prorated are:

1. Property taxes. Personal property taxes are prorated only where the buyer takes over the personal property.
2. Rent, when and if collected.
3. Interest on loans.
4. Mortgage bonus or premiums.
5. Mortgage impounds, escrow funds for taxes and insurance.
6. Insurance premiums.
7. Water rents.
8. Heating and electricity service, unless closing bills are issued.
9. Garbage removal or incinerator service.
10. Elevator service.
11. Sewer charge.
12. Building employees' vacation pay, pursuant to collective bargaining agreement.
13. Broker's commissions for renting apartments before closing.
14. Expenses for painting and decorating vacant apartments, janitor or superintendent maintenance.
15. Homeowner Association dues.
16. Other service contracts, such as pool service, linen contracts, and so on. The Real Estate Purchase Contract should call for assignment of such service contracts.

No specific wording is necessary for most of these items, since the mentioning of each is proper identification.

The "Assessment" Clause

The "proration" clause in our Model Forms makes it possible to insert a date for proration other than the closing date. Remember to strike the alternative. The "assessment" part of the clause, too, provides for alternatives. Of course, if there are no bonds or assessments, the whole line can be deleted and initialed by the parties. Some contract writers insert the words "not applicable" in the assessment clause, which is probably as clearly understandable as a complete deletion.

Spaces for inserting of city and county transfer taxes are also found in the proration clause. The assessment language has been changed to read: Bonds or assessments now a lien shall be [   ] paid current by Seller, payments not yet due to be assumed by Buyer; or [   ] paid in full by Seller, including payments not yet due; or [   ] _____.

This new wording is an improvement, but the real problem is determining what the terms of such bonds and assessments are, and when they constitute a "lien." Does the contract mean that the buyer only agrees to assume the assessments if they are a lien at the time of closing? Ordinarily in California assessments are a lien from the start, but they may not be shown as a lien on a title search before bonds are issued.

In any event, if the buyer is to pay bonds and the broker has insufficient information, the blank should read as in Form 5:12.

FORM 5:12   BUYER TO APPROVE TERMS OF BONDS

The amount of any bond or assessment which is a lien shall be assumed by buyer subject to buyer's approval of terms. If not disapproved within 5 days of buyer's receipt of title report, this condition shall be deemed waived.

COMMENT ON FORM 5:12: This clause may be important, since the terms may be unacceptable to buyer. Sometimes a treasurer's sale has been held, and a special time for redemption is allowed by statute. If the redemption time has lapsed, only payment in full may be possible. In the latter case, the bonds cannot in fact be assumed, and the buyer is entitled to a rescission.

Good practice requires that the contract writer examine the seller's last property tax bill to ascertain terms of assessments and bonds.

Bonds as Part of the Purchase Price

Another important aspect of the problem involving the assessment clause was pointed up by a case[5] in which a contract requiring the buyer to "assume" existing assessments was held too ambiguous because it could not be determined whether the buyer could deduct their amount from the purchase price. The contract read, "Buyer agrees to assume existing loans and assessments and pay the balance in cash." To avoid such ambiguity, which can easily slip into the Model Forms when the word "paid" is struck out, it is recommended that the contract writer spell out the assumption of the assessments in the terms-of-payment clause if the assessments are to be included in the purchase price.

Use the appropriate terms-of-payment clause and add the assessment clause shown in Form 5:13.

FORM 5:13   **ASSESSMENTS AS PART OF PURCHASE PRICE**
Insert in "terms of payment" clause as part of the purchase price.)

$_____ conditioned upon buyer's ability to assume existing _____ in that approximate amount,
bonds/assessments

(If terms are unknown, continue):

subject to buyer's approval of terms. If not disapproved within 5 days of buyer's receipt of title report, this condition shall be deemed waived.

COMMENT ON FORM 5:13 The terms of bonds and assessments are usually not fully set forth in title reports, but the buyer can ascertain whether any irregularities are shown in the report. In addition, of course, the tax bill should be examined, and if necessary, the bondholder should be contacted.

Approximation of Closing Costs

Prepaid expenses, insurance proceeds, tax prorations, reserves, and impounds are part of the closing costs of a sale, but may not be "true" closing expenses, although they are usually the largest expenditures made at that time. Buyers may erroneously feel that these expenditures are additional charges by lenders. Unfortunately, because of the various charges for points, tax agency fees, appraisal fees, fees for drawing of instruments, assumption fees, prepaid interest prorations, recording fees, notary fees, escrow and title fees, and attorneys' fees, anticipating the actual closing cost in any given transaction at the time when the offer is drafted is quite difficult.

Many brokers try to calculate an anticipated amount of closing cost and insert in the agreement the words "buyer to pay usual closing cost." Another customary statement is, "Pay-offs of existing loans shall be at seller's expense, and any new loans obtained by buyer shall be at buyer's expense, except where federal regulations provide otherwise." Neither solution is totally satisfactory. The best practice is, of course, to specify in the terms-of-payment clause more accurate estimates of the closing cost.

As our Model Forms are designed, closing costs are spread over several paragraphs. Some closing costs are found in the title clause, which designates who pays the policy of title insurance; some are in the proration clause; and some, such as the cost of termite inspection and the like, would be included in the terms and conditions of a factual nature of the terms-of-payment clause. Under the Real Estate Settlement Procedures Act (RESPA) lenders are required to give the borrower a written estimate of charges the borrower is likely to incur. RESPA, however does not apply to various types of loans, such as mortgaged property over 25 acres and certain construction loans, home improvement loans and loans on property where the primary purpose is resale.

Premature Possession

The typical "marketing contract" does not contemplate transfer of possession before delivery of the deed. Contrary to the land contract, which is a security device more akin to mortgages and deeds of trust, the marketing contract provides that the buyer wait for possession until the close of the transaction. In some situations, the buyer is anxious to move in, and the property is available because the seller has already vacated. The broker must have strong nerves to deny the buyer the right to take possession. However, the careful broker and the prudent seller will resist the buyer's overtures. The potential difficulties are just not worth it!

Because the remedies open to the seller in case of default by the buyer in possession are often cumbersome and expensive, the buyer should not be placed in possession under a marketing contract before the title passes.

Realtors should actively initiate and support legislation similar to the New York statute which permits summary proceedings against a buyer in possession who has defaulted under a contract which was to be completed within 90 days after its execution.

In addition to the problem of recovery of possession, the seller is exposed to possible mechanic liens which may take priority over any purchase-money mortgage. A buyer who *is* allowed to take possession should not be permitted to make any repairs, redecorations, or alterations, before the contract has been completed. Otherwise the seller may wind up paying the bills for these improvements ordered by the "buyer."

Should the seller concede to let the buyer take possession as a tenant and make improvements, the seller-lessor may file notice of nonresponsibility. In addition, the seller must consider the issue of insurance and risk of loss of the property by destruction or damage during the buyer's occupancy.

Neither party should rely on the seller's insurance. The insurer should always be informed of the contract of sale of the realty, and appropriate endorsements of the policy should be obtained. To assure maximum protection for the seller, the seller should insist that the buyer take out insurance with protective endorsement in favor of the seller. Similar considerations should be given on liability insurance policies (see Form 5:21).

If the broker is unable to discourage the parties from agreeing to the buyer taking possession before closing, the clause in Form 5:14 may be used in the Possession Clause of the Deposit Receipt.

FORM 5:14   **BUYER TO TAKE POSSESSION**
BEFORE TITLE PASSES

Possession shall be delivered to buyer:
  (a) on close of escrow, or
  (b) not later than _____ days after closing escrow, or
  (c) immediately upon payment of the deposit required hereunder and any rental deposit required under the Rental Agreement between the parties hereto dated _____, 19_____ and by reference made a part hereof.

COMMENT ON FORM 5:14: The recommendation against allowing a buyer under a Deposit Receipt to take possession before title has passed bears repeating. If this situation is unavoidable, however, the above clause and a rental agreement similar to Real Estate Purchaser's Rental Agreement found in Form 5:15 can be used.

Seller Remaining in Possession After the Sale

A similar series of questions arises when the seller remains in possession after title has passed. Generally speaking, the seller does not become a tenant by holding over. A landlord-tenant relationship can be created by the contract, where the seller wishes to maintain possession for a limited time after title has passed. Another method is to provide that a substantial sum of the purchase price be withheld by escrow as a guaranty of prompt removal. A high per diem rate for any days the seller "stays over" the designated time can also encourage performance.

By statute in California,[6] sellers who hold over and continue in possession may be served with a three-day notice to quit where the property has been duly sold and the title under the sale has been duly perfected. This statute makes possible the summary action of unlawful detainer.

The "possession" clause in the Model Forms, reads:

Possession shall be delivered to Buyer:
(a) on close of escrow, or _____
(b) not later than _____ days after closing escrow, or _____
(c) _____ .

The first two possibilities are self-explanatory. However, the warnings regarding hold-over mentioned above are applicable to point (b). Except where the property is vacant or the seller is being transferred and is therefore anxious to move, making possession and close of escrow concurrent is impractical.

The better practice, therefore, is to establish a date certain for possession, thereby ignoring, in effect, both clauses (a) and (b), and inserting the day as agreed upon between the parties, in the blank labeled (c). The seller may have indicated at the time of listing how much time he or she needs. At the time the offer is drawn, the careful contract writer will set the date for possession in accordance with the seller's desire. This precaution will insure against creating a conflict on this matter which could necessitate a counter-offer. Clause (c) could then read: "on or before noon, _____ day of _____ , 19_____."

Some sellers insist on 30 days free rent after the buyer has taken title. This condition, in effect, is part of the consideration for the sale. Buyers may not consider it as such, and at least in rental situations often feel that they should be entitled to collect rent, since they have all the risk and all the expense of the property.

To guarantee performance by the seller and removal on the day designated, preventive law prescribes the use of an agreement charging a daily rental for any day the seller remains in possession, or making a holding over seller subject to the provisions of the "Unlawful Detainer" statutes. This precaution can most easily be included by inserting the following in the blank labeled (c): "Seller shall pay $_____ per day from date of recordation to date of possession. The sum of $_____ shall be held in escrow and disbursed to the persons entitled thereto."

Covering the Buyer as Tenant

When a buyer takes possession before closing, a specially drafted buyer's rental agreement is frequently used. This situation arises most often in sales of vacant GI or FHA property, where obtaining loan insurance generally takes a long time. A form for a rental agreement commonly used by brokers specializing in such sales appears in Form 5:15.

FORM 5:15   REAL ESTATE PURCHASER'S RENTAL AGREEMENT

This purchaser's rental agreement made this _____ day of _____ , 19_____ by and between _____ , herein called Landlord, and

seller's name

_____, herein called Tenant.

buyer's name

Tenant has agreed to purchase the property described as _____ _____ as evidenced by Real Estate Purchase Contract and Receipt of Deposit executed by the parties hereto, dated _____, 19_____.

Tenant has made application for a loan on said property to _____ ___ in accordance with the terms of said contract and wishes to take possession prior to closing of the sales transaction and before title has passed to tenant as buyer. Tenant hereby agrees that in entering possession of the premises prior to close or title, that he enters as a week-to-week tenant and agrees to pay landlord the sum of $_____ per week as rent until close of escrow as follows: _____ _____. Receipt of the sum of $_____ for the period _____ _____, 19_____ to _____, 19_____ $_____ as security has been deposited. Landlord may use therefrom such amounts as are reasonably necessary to remedy tenant defaults in the payment of rent, to repair damages caused by tenant, or to clean the premises if necessary upon the termination of tenancy. If used toward rent or damages during the term of this agreement, tenant agrees to reinstate said total security deposit upon 5 days written notice delivered to tenant in person or by mail. The balance of the security deposit, if any, shall be mailed to tenant's last known address within 14 days of surrender of premises. Alternatively, and upon completion of sale, said security deposit shall be mailed to tenant at the subject premises within 10 days of close of escrow.

Tenant agrees to give peaceful possession of said premises within ten (10) days after the final _____ report has been given if it is unfavorable, or

VA/FHA loan

if loan application is not acceptable to lending institution, upon 7 days written notice by certified mail of termination.

The prevailing party in any action or proceeding between the parties shall be entitled to reasonable attorney's fees in addition to all other relief to which he or she may be entitled.

Tenant acknowledges receipt of a copy thereof.

Dated _____ , 19_____.

_____	_____
Tenant	Landlord
_____	_____
Tenant	Landlord

COMMENT ON FORM 5:15: The rental agreement contained herein has been used successfully in California for years. The use of a ''standard'' landlord-tenant rental agreement is not recommended. CAR has also a printed general buyer-tenant form available, Form 10A-11.

When the Seller "Holds Over"

To protect the buyer from the seller's unreasonable use of the premises in ''holding over'' after the close of escrow, or where by agreement the seller is allowed a period of ''free rent,'' a possession agreement such as the one in Form 5:16 is often used. Usually such a clause provides for a reasonable rental, but requires a deposit as a guaranty of performance in excess of the total amount of rental payment.

FORM 5:16   **"POSSESSION" CLAUSE (SELLER
TO PAY PER DIEM RENT)
(Insert in Model Form, paragraph 4):**

Possession shall be delivered to buyer. . . .:
(c) as per agreement attached hereto as Exhibit "A" and made part hereof by reference.

(Attach following Agreement):

Possession Agreement
Addendum to the Real Estate Purchase Contract and Receipt for Deposit dated _____, 19____ of which it forms a part and which by reference is incorporated herein.

Seller may after close of escrow occupy the property for a period ending _____ day of _____, 19____ for the sum of $_____ per day. If seller has not removed from the property at time of close of escrow, there shall be withheld from monies otherwise due seller under the Purchase Agreement:
(1) the daily rental for the entire period, and
(2) the sum of $_____ as a security deposit.

If the seller vacates the property on or before _____, 19____ without legal action and without waste or damage, reasonable wear and tear excepted, seller shall receive the whole sum withheld, less the daily rental for the period of the occupancy. Otherwise, the buyer shall receive the whole sum withheld.

(Form continues on next page)

Of the security deposit buyer may use therefrom such amounts as are reasonably necessary to remedy defaults in the payment of rent, to repair damages caused by seller, or clean the premises if necessary upon the termination of tenancy. If used toward rent or damages during the term of this agreement, seller agrees to reinstate said total security deposit upon 5 days written notice delivered to seller in person or by mail. The balance of the security deposit, if any, shall be mailed to seller's last known address within 14 days of surrender of the premises.

Seller shall obtain and maintain during the term of this lease, public liability insurance naming both seller and buyer as co-insureds in the amount of not less than $_____ for injury to one person; $_____ for any injury to a group; and $_____ for property damage. If permitted, seller agrees to retain existing fire insurance on the premises in a sum of not less than designated as the sales price of the subject property.

The property shall be delivered in broom-clean condition without debris or rubbish of any kind remaining. In the event legal action is instituted to enforce this agreement, the prevailing party shall be entitled to reasonable attorneys' fees and costs as fixed by the court.

(optional):

Any holding over beyond the date indicated above shall be subject to provisions of Section 1161-a of the California Code of Civil Procedure providing for summary action.

(continue):

The parties hereto acknowledge the receipt of a copy hereof.

_____ Dated _____, 19_____
Buyer _____   Seller _____
Buyer _____   Seller _____

COMMENT ON FORM 5:16: The withheld amount should be sufficiently large to cover the rent for the estimated period of seller's holding over plus any possible further holding over during which summary action may be instigated. CAR has a similar form, RLAS-11.

The "Escrow Instruction" Clause

The "escrow instruction" clause in the Model Form reads:

Buyer and Seller should deliver signed instructions to the escrow holder within _____ days from Seller's acceptance and shall provide for closing within _____ days from Seller's acceptance. Escrow fees to be paid as follows:

The closing date should be calculated from the date of seller's acceptance, which is a date certain.

Most escrow companies prefer to have just one set of buyer's and seller's instructions. Precautions should be taken against premature or incomplete instructions which call for supplementary instructions or which change the terms of the transaction.

The Model Forms specifies that modifications or extensions shall be in writing signed by the parties. This eliminates the common provision that the broker may extend the time for closing where he or she "deems the extension advisable." This type of clause, which gives brokers the right to interfere with performance under a contract to which they are not party, has been severely criticized. That such powers are not conferred upon the broker should not create any real hardship, since cautious brokers would not extend time for performance without the principals' consent anyway.

The clause in the Model Forms, however, requires that extensions of time be handled by written agreements. Normally, escrow instructions provide for some leeway. Where handled by independent escrow, the principal's representative(s) should supervise the drawing of these instructions to be sure that they incorporate the understanding of the parties, both as to terms and time for performance. Whenever any extensions become necessary as a result of closing problems with financing or otherwise, the appropriate extensions of time should be inserted in the escrow instructions, stating that the new closing agreement supersedes the agreement found in the original contract.

"Vesting of Title"

The "vesting title clause" of the Model Form reads:

Unless otherwise designated in the escrow instructions of Buyer, title shall vest as follows: _____ .
[The manner of taking title may have significant legal and tax consequences. Therefore, give this matter serious consideration.]

As a general rule, a broker should not advise the buyer on how to take title. The broker who gives advice in this respect is actually giving legal advice. Brokers may believe that the escrow instructions which they draft or "joint tenancy" deeds and other instruments conveying title which they direct will accomplish their purposes. However, if no meaningful advice is given concerning the matter of taking title and its consequences in the event of death, divorce, or for tax purposes, brokers who assume the role of attorneys in attempting to give advice should realize that they also assume the responsibility and possible liability therefore.

If buyers know what they wish to insert in this paragraph, brokers drawing the contract may act as scriveners by filling in the blank as requested with the appropriate wording. Should a buyer ask for advice regarding the proper way of taking title to the property, the broker ought to suggest that the buyer obtain legal and tax advice, and insert in the blank the phrase, "instructions to follow in escrow." Or, if more specific wording is desired, the broker may write: "Manner of taking title shall be designated in buyer's escrow instructions."

Nevertheless, brokers should be familiar with the manners of taking title.

Who Runs the "Risk of Loss"?

A few states, including California,[7] have adopted the Uniform Vendor and Purchaser Risk Act, which is deemed incorporated in any contract for sale of real property unless the parties expressly provide otherwise. This act makes the risk turn upon possession. If the buyer is in possession, he or she bears the risk of loss; if the buyer is not in possession, the seller bears the burden prior to title passing. But when the buyer is in possession, or when title is passed, the buyer is not relieved from the duty to pay the purchase price if all or any part of the premises are destroyed or taken by condemnation. Nor is the buyer entitled to refund of any down payment in such an event. If the seller is in possession of the property, or title has not passed, and "all or a material part thereof is destroyed without fault of the purchaser or is taken by eminent domain," the seller cannot enforce the contract, and the buyer is entitled to recover the down payment.

"Risk of Loss"—An Open-Ended Issue

Although the seller cannot enforce the contract against the buyer if a material part is destroyed, it does appear that the buyer can enforce the contract against the seller. But whether or not the buyer is entitled to an abatement in price is not clear. The question of what is material and what is immaterial is also left open to judicial construction. The law, therefore, leaves important problems unsolved.

The "risk of loss" clause in the Model Form was an arbitrary partial departure from the Uniform Vendor and Purchaser Risk Act. The clause made the risk turn upon title passing only, not possession *or* title passing as the law does. In the 1978 version the "Risk of Loss" clause has been eliminated and the Uniform Vendors and Purchaser Risk Act applies.

The Model Forms can be changed by specifically incorporating the previous provision and incorporating the remaining provisions of the Uniform Act (see Form 5:17). To avoid litigation regarding what constitutes material loss, a definition could be included (see Form 5:18).

FORM 5:17   UNIFORM ACT TO GOVERN EXCEPT
AS EXPRESSLY AGREED

If the improvements on the property are destroyed or materially damaged prior to close of escrow, then, on demand by Buyer, any deposit made by Buyer shall be returned to him and this contract thereupon shall terminate.

Except as expressly provided above, this contract shall be governed by the provisions of _____.

(title and section of code)

COMMENT ON FORM 5:17: The insertion of this clause makes the Uniform Vendor and Purchaser Risk Act applicable to the extent that it is not in conflict with the printed text. Used in connection with the Model Form, it reincorporates in the contract the provisions of the Act concerning condemnation.

FORM 5:18   DEFINITION OF MATERIAL LOSS

A destruction shall be considered material if the cost of repair or replacement without deduction for depreciation exceeds 10% of the purchase price. Any work exceeding the repair or replacement of actual damage caused by the enforcement of applicable building codes, laws or regulations shall be deemed included in the cost. A taking by eminent domain is material if the diminution of market value exceeds the percentage stated above.

COMMENT ON FORM 5:18: Some contract writers prefer to state the amount of damage which shall constitute a material loss in a dollar amount. For use in printed forms, however, a percentage clause is probably more effective in preventing errors.

A Comprehensive "Risk of Loss" Form

Much dissatisfaction has arisen with respect both to case law concerning risk of loss and the Uniform Act. Therefore, in most contracts drawn by lawyers, as opposed to printed broker's forms, more precise provisions are encountered. Such comprehensive risk-of-loss clauses can vary considerably. The most common of these clauses are as follows:

1. The clause can allow the seller an option to restore the premises, and if the seller fails to do so, it can allow the buyer an election between (a) terminating the contract and getting the down payment back, or (b) accepting the premises as is and obtaining the proceeds of the fire or other insurance less any reasonable cost of collection and assignment of seller's right in the policies.

2. The clause can establish a percentage of purchase price—for example, 10 percent—and state that the buyer is obligated to complete the contract if damage is less than 10 percent, but that if damage is more than 10 percent the buyer may have an option either to terminate or accept. If the buyer elects to complete the contract, she or he can collect an abatement in the price in the amount of the damage.

3. The buyer can be obligated to complete purchase without abatement in price, but will receive proceeds of insurance and assignment of policies. The seller may wish to insert a provision giving him or her an option to cancel the contract if the insurance proceeds exceed a certain sum.

4. If the damage does not exceed a stated sum in dollars, the buyer can be obligated to accept the property in its damaged condition, while maintaining the right to insurance proceeds and assignment of the policies. Should the damage exceed the stated sum, the buyer can have an option either to terminate the contract or accept on the same conditions as set forth in 2. above.

5. In most comprehensive clauses, either "material damage" is defined as a certain specified percentage of purchase price or a dollar amount, or the problem is referred to arbitration or to an architect or contractor appointed by the parties whose decision is final.

6. With regard to condemnation, the clauses also vary. Some allow either party to cancel. If the parties agree to leave the contract in effect, the seller agrees to assign to the buyer all awards for the taking. If an immaterial part has been condemned, neither party is allowed to cancel, but the buyer is entitled to an abatement in price to the extent of the taking.

Suggested Solutions to "Risk of Loss" Problems

The clauses in Forms 5:19 through 5:21 are examples of some solutions to the risk-of-loss problem. Because the factual situations differ, only a competent attorney should decide how to incorporate one or more of the above provisions in the contract where desired.

FORM 5:19   **WAIVER OF LAW AND EQUAL CANCELLATION RIGHTS**

The parties hereto waive the provisions of _____
                                        code section describing Uniform

_____.
Vendor and Purchaser Risk Act

If prior to close of escrow:

(a) all or any material part of the main building on the premises is destroyed or damaged by fire, the elements or by any cause beyond either party's control; or

(b) all or a material part of the premises is taken by eminent domain, either party may, by written notice to the other, cancel this agreement prior to close of escrow.

In the event of such election, then this agreement shall become null and void; and upon refunding of the moneys deposited hereunder without interest, both parties hereto shall be released from any liability hereunder except for cost of _____ and _____ as agreed below.
          title examination   termite report

COMMENT ON FORM 5:19: This clause gives both parties an option to cancel if the main building is destroyed or materially damaged. It also covers condemnation. In addition, the form specifically waives the Uniform Vendor and Purchaser Risk Act. (Calif. Civil Code Section 1662)

However, this clause leaves open to dispute the determination of materiality of damage. If desired, the clause in Form 5:18 or the arbitration section in

Form 5:20 can be adapted as part of this clause, but this procedure is not recommended without legal counsel.

**FORM 5:20   WAIVER OF LAW, EQUAL CANCELLATION
RIGHTS, PAYMENT OF INSURANCE
CONDEMNATION PROCEEDS, DETERMINATION
OF DISPUTES BY ARBITRATION
(Begin with Form 5:19, continue with
Form 5:18, and continue):**

Should the parties elect not to so cancel this agreement, it shall remain in full force and effect. Upon close of escrow and receipt by seller of the purchase price, the seller shall pay to the buyer any sums received by the seller under any policies of insurance or renewals thereof _____
                                            copies of which are attached hereto/

_____ .
        listed in Exhibit "A"attached hereto and made part hereof
insuring against the loss sustained, after deduction of any amounts the seller shall have agreed to be obligated to pay under the terms of the policy for any repairs. The seller shall further assign and transfer all right, title and interest in said policies, and any sums due or payable thereunder. In the event any part or all of the premises have been taken by eminent domain, the seller shall assign all right, title and interest in the condemnation award payable for such taking.

If prior to close of escrow (a) an immaterial part of the main building on the premises is destroyed or damaged by fire, the elements, or by any cause beyond either party's control; or (b) an immaterial part of the premises is taken by eminent domain, neither party shall be entitled to cancel this agreement, but the buyer shall be entitled to an abatement on the purchase price to the extent of the destruction, damage, or taking.

Any controversy or claim arising out of, or relating to, this part of this agreement shall be settled by arbitration in accordance with the rules of the American Arbitration Association, and judgment upon the award rendered by the Arbitrator(s) may be entered in any court having jurisdiction thereof.

COMMENT ON FORM 5:20: This clause leaves very little to chance. It also provides the machinery for determining any dispute concerning the materiality of destruction or taking. If arbitration is not desired, the parties could, of course, agree to refer the matter to a certain designated expert and accept his or her written determination of the issues as final. Brokers are advised not to use this form without prior approval by the attorneys for both parties.

Risk-of-loss problems arise frequently when the buyer takes possession before closing of the transaction. The Model Forms places the burden of loss upon the seller at any time prior to closing. Other forms in common use and the

Uniform Act place the burden upon buyers if they have taken possession. In either event buyers are usually unprotected by insurance if they take possession before close of escrow, since even if they take over the seller's insurance, coverage does not take effect before closing. If buyers move in before title has passed, they should be advised to have their insurance become effective before taking possession (see Form 5:21). If, under these circumstances, a buyer accepts the seller's insurance, the buyer should be named as additional insured.

If the seller is to take back a purchase-money mortgage, a "mortgagee" clause in favor of the seller as lender should be obtained and attached to the policy. The amount should be sufficient to cover the mortgage and to be paid to the seller-lender to the extent of his or her interest. Such protection is especially necessary in California, where the value of the property is a purchase money lender's sole security and source of recovery upon default.

For a clause specifying insurance provisions of the buyer in possession, see Form 5:21.

FORM 5:21   INSURANCE PROVISIONS OF BUYER IN POSSESSION

The buyer agrees, until _____
close of escrow/full payment of purchase price
to procure and maintain in force at buyer's expense to the _____
full insurable value of the
_____ fire and extended coverage insurance in a company
premises/amount of $_____
acceptable to the seller and for the seller's benefit as seller's interest may appear, and to pay all premiums therefor and to deliver all policies and renewals thereof to the seller.

(Optional, continue):

The buyer agrees until _____ to
close of escrow/full payment of purchase price
procure and maintain in force at buyer's expense a public liability insurance policy in a minimum amount of $_____ for each person injured and $_____ for property damage, issued by a company acceptable to seller and for the seller's benefit a seller's interest may appear, and to pay all premiums therefor and to deliver all policies and renewals to the seller.

COMMENT ON FORM 5:21: Under an executory contract for the sale of real property, both the seller and the buyer have an insurable interest. The duty of obtaining insurance coverage should be assigned by the contract to one of the parties. If the seller allows the buyer to take possession while awaiting close of escrow, the buyer should procure insurance protecting the seller. This clause expresses such agreement. (See also discussion of risk of loss above.)

The Liquidated Damage "Clause"

The Liquidated Damage Clause of Model Form II reads:

If Buyer fails to complete said purchase as herein provided by reason of any default of Buyer, Seller shall be released from his obligation to
sell the property to Buyer and may proceed against Buyer upon any claim
or remedy which he may have in law or equity; provided, however, that
by placing their initials here Buyer: (_____) Seller: (_____) agrees that
Seller shall retain the deposit as his liquidated damages. If the described
property is a dwelling with no more than four units, one of which the
buyer intends to occupy as his residence, Seller shall retain as liquidated
damages the deposit actually paid, or an amount therefrom, not more than
3% of the purchase price and promptly return any excess to Buyer. Buyer
and Seller agree to execute a similar liquidated damages provision, such
as California Association of Realtors® Receipt for Increased Deposit
(RID-11) for any increased deposits.

If the parties leave the blanks in this clause open, they in fact chose to
abolish any thought of liquidating damages. Should the Buyer default, the Seller has the option to sue for specific performance or to prove actual damages. If
the parties chose to initial the boxes, the provision purports to entitle the Seller
to retain the deposit as liquidated damages if the Buyer defaults. The deposit
(the liquidated damage amount) becomes a substitute for actual damages. A
new Liquidated Damages Law became effective July 1, 1978. CAR's Liquidated Damage Clause follows this law. The law sets up different standards for non
residential and residential property. As defined in Civil Code Section 1675,
Residential Property is a dwelling containing not more than 4 units, and, at the
time of making the contract, the Buyer intends to occupy the dwelling or one of
the units as his residence. In order to establish that the property is to be occupied as the buyer's residence, fill in the correct box in Paragraph 3 of the
Model Form. If increased deposit is required by the contract, and the total
deposit shall constitute contractual liquidated damages, a new liquidated damage provision satisfying the requirements of the law must be separately signed
or initialed by each party to the contract for each subsequent payment. CAR
Form RID-11 is recommended.

The law provides that 3% of purchase price, to the extent that payment is
actually made in cash, check including a post-dated check, is *valid* as liquidated
damages unless Buyer establishes that such an amount is unreasonable. CAR's
Contract limits the Seller's right to retain from the deposit an amount of not
more than 3% of the purchase price in sale of residential property as defined in
the law. By limiting retention of the deposit by the Seller to the 3% of the
purchase price standard regardless of the size of the deposit, the burden of
proving "unreasonableness" is on the Buyer. Had the contract form allowed
retention of more than 3%, the Seller would have had the burden of proving that
the excess actually paid was reasonable.

In nonresidential property situations, the provision to permit retention of the deposit as liquidated damages is valid unless the party seeking to invalidate the provision establishes "that the *provision* was unreasonable under the circumstances existing at the time the contract was made." For residential property, the law provides that the 3%-of-purchase-price standard is valid to the extent that payment is actually made unless Buyer establishes "that such *amount* is unreasonable as liquidated damages." Reasonableness is determined by taking into account the following:

> "All the circumstances existing at the time of the making of the contract are considered, including the relationship that the damages provided in the contract bear to the range of harm that reasonably could be anticipated at the time of the making of the contract. Other relevant considerations in the determination of whether the amount of liquidated damages is so high or so low as to be unreasonable include, but are not limited to, such matters as the relative equality of the bargaining power of the parties, whether the parties were represented by lawyers at the time the contract was made, the anticipation of the parties that proof of actual damages would be costly or inconvenient, the difficulty of proving causation and foreseeability, and whether the liquidated damages provision is included in a form contract."

An additional element in determining the reasonableness of the amount of liquidated damages in *residential* sales is: the price and other terms of any subsequent sale or contract of sale and purchase of the same property if such sale or contract is made within six (6) months of the Buyer's default. The advantage of the model form is that the liquidated damage clause provides the option of not filling in the two (2) boxes with the Buyer's and Seller's initials so the contract will contain no forfeiture clause. If the Buyer defaults, the matter of damages or action by the Seller is then left for the Seller to decide. The Seller can either proceed in specific performance or sue for *actual* damages. By initialing the blanks, however, the parties are *prefixing* the damages as a substitute for actual damages. Should disputes arise concerning the disposition of the Buyer's deposit, an innovation in the Form is that such a dispute, if it is the only controversy or claim between the parties, may be referred to arbitration under the auspices of the American Arbitration Association. Rules of that non-profit educational association are incorporated in the clause as well as provisions of the Code of Civil Procedure permitting discovery, the taking of depositions, and so on. In such a proceeding, the prevailing party is entitled to attorney's fees and costs. It is to be hoped that the use of the liquidated damage clause will encourage completion of contracts, reduce breaches, and discourage litigation.

The modernized liquidated damage law and the setting of the "3%-of-purchase-price standard" for a valid amount of liquidated damages upon a Buyer's default in the purchase of residential housing is a great step forward. The legislature recognized that generally the Buyer of such housing, including the Buyer who does not read the contract or does not understand it, expects that he or she will lose the "earnest money" deposit if he or she does not complete the purchase of the property. By limiting the amount to 3% of the purchase price, the law protects Buyers of residential housing from forfeiting an unreasonably large amount. The new law, however, places heavy burdens on the real estate licensee to explain the contract provisions to both Buyer and Seller, and to handle this sensitive area skillfully and in the best interest of both parties to the contract.

If the contract is uncompleted because of failure of a condition (for example, inability to obtain financing), the buyer is not in default and is entitled to a return of the deposit despite the wording of the liquidated-damage clause.

Liquidated damages clauses have been subject to two appellate court decisions in 1984. In a case[8] involving an $800,000 residence, escrow instructions contained a liquidated damages clause prepared and included at seller's request limiting damages to $25,000. The clause was not separately signed or initialed, but the signatures were in close proximity to the parties' signatures. Seller sold the property for $65,000 less after the buyer defaulted and sued to have the liquidated damage clause declared invalid. The court held that the clause was voidable and not void. The clause is designed solely for protection of the buyer and a seller is precluded from voiding the clause. The court found substantial compliance with the statutory requirements and limited the seller's recovery to the $25,000. In a case[9] where the buyers of a 36 unit apartment house sought to overturn the trial court's finding that the liquidated damages clause was reasonable, the appellate court found the clause met the formal requirements of the statute and that the buyers failed to meet their burden of proving the clause unreasonable. The liquidated damages equaled less than 2 percent of the total sales price of $1,325,000. There was testimony that an amount of approximately 2 percent was standard in commercial real estate transactions. The clause approved by the court read as follows:

Liquidated damages: Buyer recognizes that Seller's property will be removed from the market during the existence of this agreement and that if this transaction is not consummated because of buyer's default, seller should be entitled to compensation for such detriment: However, it is extremely difficult and impractical to ascertain the extent of the detriment and, to avoid this problem, buyer _____ and seller _____ agree that if this transaction is not consummated because of buyer's default, seller shall be entitled to recover from buyer the amount of all deposits, the sum of twenty-five thousand dollars ($25,000.00) if buyer does not elect to extend close of escrow pursuant to item 18 or the sum of thirty-five thousand dollars ($35,000.00) if buyer does elect to extend close of escrow pursuant to item 18, whichever is applicable together with any interest accrued thereon, as liquidated damages. Said amount has been agreed upon, after negotiation, as the parties' best estimate of seller's damages. The parties agree that the sum stated above as liquidated damages shall be in lieu of any other relief to which seller might otherwise be entitled by virtue of this agreement or by operation of law.

Both buyers' and sellers' attorneys often find fault with the liquidated-damage clauses in printed contract forms. Form 5:22 is a typical example. For a liquidated damages clause with deposit disposition directions to Escrow see Form 5:26.

FORM 5:22   **BUYER'S CHANGE OF**
                        "LIQUIDATED DAMAGE" CLAUSE

If for any reason this transaction is not consummated, the deposit shall be returned to the buyer by the seller or broker on demand. If the buyer defaults in the performance hereunder, the buyer shall only be liable to the seller for his actual, out-of-pocket expenses, and the buyer shall have no other liability. In no event shall the buyer be responsible for commissions to the broker. If suit is brought by the buyer to enforce this agreement or to receive the deposit, seller agrees to pay reasonable attorney's fees.

COMMENT ON FORM 5:22: Sophisticated buyers may insist that any printed liquidated-damage clause be deleted. The above clause is a buyer-oriented substitute. It may well lead to litigation.

On the other hand, sellers frequently wish to provide in the damage clause that the buyer pay the commission upon buyer's default and obligation. Some printed Deposit Receipts incorporate this provision. This condition may be desirable from the broker's point of view but if not specifically made clear to an unsuspecting buyer could be considered overreaching. It may well not be held enforceable. (For a form in common use, see Form 5:23.)

FORM 5:23   **BUYER TO PAY BROKER'S**
                        COMMISSION UPON DEFAULT

If the buyer fails to complete said purchase as herein provided by reason of any default of buyer, seller shall not be obligated to pay the commission due hereunder, and buyer agrees to pay said commission to the broker. In the event suit is instigated to enforce this provision, the prevailing party shall be entitled to reasonable attorney's fees and costs as fixed by the court.

COMMENT ON FORM 5:23: This clause is often inserted in the contract at the request of sellers, especially where the seller did not have the property actively on the market and the broker was procured by the buyer. Appropriate changes in the seller's acceptance clause must be made when this clause is inserted in the contract.

Damages upon Seller's Default

Our Model Forms are silent about a possible seller's default in performance, as are most Deposit Receipt contracts. In most cases, the buyer's measure of damages is illusory, and is in effect limited to a return of the deposit, title-examination costs, and escrow expenses. It therefore seems fair that a contract includes a clause liquidating the buyer's damages against a defaulting seller. Such a provision may obviate the buyer's need to prove the seller's bad faith in order to recover more than the deposit. For a buyer's liquidated-damage clause, see Form 5:24.

FORM 5:24   **"LIQUIDATED DAMAGE" CLAUSE**
                         (SELLER'S DEFAULT)

If seller fails to complete said sale as herein provided by reason of any default of seller, buyer may proceed against seller upon any claim or remedy which he may have in law and equity, provided however that buyer and seller hereby agree that buyer, as buyer's sole right to damages, shall be entitled to recover the deposit and any other monies deposited in escrow or paid to or for seller's account and shall also be entitled to recover from seller the sum of $___ _____, which is hereby agreed to be a reasonable estimate of the damages sustained by buyer, it being impractical or extremely difficult to fix actual damages in case of seller's default.

(Optional, continue):

The prevailing party in any action or proceeding between the parties hereto shall be entitled to reasonable attorney's fees and costs in addition to all other relief to which he may be entitled.

COMMENT ON FORM 5:24: This liquidated-damage clause favors the buyer upon the seller's default. The liquidated damage provision can be included where the buyer wishes protection against a possible default by seller for any reason.

Advice of counsel is suggested before use of any liquidated damage clause intended to protect buyer upon seller's default.

Providing for an Increase in Deposit

Quite often, the initial deposit taken by the broker at the time the offer is made is a token deposit in a small amount. The buyer realizes that the seller may not be willing to take the property off the market for the escrow period without a larger "earnest money" deposit.

The seller may feel unprotected by the token deposit and demand, either by counter-offer or by previous instruction, that an adequate deposit in a given amount be obtained. If additional deposit is to be made, the time limitation for making such deposit and the method of handling the funds should be set forth in the contract.

The Model Form provides a paragraph for increased deposit. In order that the increased deposit together with the initial deposit become liquidated damages, a separate liquidated damage provision must be separately signed or initialled by each party to the contract for each such subsequent payment. The simplest way to comply is to use CAR Form RID 11 and add the provisions of Form 5:25.

FORM 5:25   INCREASED DEPOSIT

Deposit will □ will not □ be increased by $_____ to $_____ within _____ days of acceptance of this offer. Buyer and seller agree to sign CAR Form RID-11.

COMMENT ON FORM 5:25: The increased deposit should be collected as soon after the seller's approval as possible. By that time the buyer should be prepared to proceed.

The "Offer" Clause

The "offer clause" of Model Form reads:

This agreement constitutes an offer to purchase the described property. Unless acceptance is signed by Seller and the signed copy delivered to Buyer, in person or by mail to the address below, within _____ days this offer shall be deemed revoked and the deposit shall be returned. Buyer acknowledges receipt of a copy hereof.

An offer is usually deemed accepted when such acceptance is communicated to the buyer. The offer clause in the Model Forms is unique in that it establishes the *mode* of acceptance of the offer. It suggests that the offer is automatically and apparently revoked if the buyer does not receive a copy of the contract signed by the seller accepting the offer within the prescribed time. This clause, of course, is subject to normal legal interpretation. When a proposal prescribes any conditions concerning the communication of its own acceptance, the general rule is that the proposer is not bound unless the conditions are fulfilled. With the use of the Model Form, other reasonable or usual modes of acceptance are specifically excluded. The contract signed by seller *must* be delivered in person or by mail to the address of the buyer as shown in the contract. To make the task of delivering the contract easier and to insure safe delivery, the broker should include the buyer's business and residence addresses on the contract. These addresses should appear in the spaces provided on the Model Form immediately above the seller's acceptance clause.

The wording of the offer clause on the Model Forms is meant to correct some familiar errors in contract drafting. It will encourage the contract writer to produce a contract that is complete, with proper initialing and signatures. It should also minimize disputes as to whether or not an offer was accepted in a timely manner and when communication of such acceptance was received.

Fears that this clause creates an undue burden on the seller's representative are unfounded. All attorneys and brokers know that an offeror is always permitted by law to withdraw an offer at any time until the offeree has accepted it and communicated acceptance to the offeror.

Because the clause requires that the acceptance be delivered by a certain date, the seller's representative may have to do some nimble footwork to comply with the timetable. Where buyer or seller are not in readily accessible areas, the contract should provide sufficient time to comply.

The "Time Is of the Essence" Clause

Model Form states: "Time is of the essence of this contract" thereby the parties specifically make time of the essence for the performance of any act under the contract. The function of this provision is to assure that performance of any condition occurs by the specific time indicated and not at some indefinite later time.

Again, perhaps the contract is weighted in favor of the buyer. To make time of the essence for both parties reflects the "me-too-ism" lawyers commonly display. In fact, a seller's attorney may well have excellent reasons for resisting a mutual "time is of the essence" provision. Should a late objection to title arise, such as a mechanics lien or the filing of an abstract of judgment, the buyer may be excused from performance because the seller is not at the moment able to deliver clear title. In addition, reconveyances or satisfactions of judgments may not have been recorded, and the time for obtaining them may not be sufficient. Title companies will, in some situations where the liens are minor, withhold sufficient funds from seller's account until the matter can be disposed of, but this is not always possible.

On the other hand, the buyer's obligation on the date of performance is usually just the payment of money. Therefore, a great difference exists between the parties in the extent of the obligations to be performed on time.

Some courts have held that even when time is of the essence of the contract, such provision may be waived by the conduct of the parties.[10]

To be safe in enforcing a time-is-of-the-essence provision, the party who seeks enforcement must place the other party in default by tender of performance, unless tender is excused by the other party's prior repudiation of the contract.

One form of the time-is-of-the-essence clause states: "Time is of the essence of this contract, but the time for any act to be done may be extended not longer than 30 days by the undersigned agent." It has been held that this provision does not make time of the essence of the contract.[11]

A prudent seller considering these vagaries in interpretation may wish to amend the time-is-of-the-essence clause to cover the performance of the buyer only. If such an amendment is not obtainable, the seller may prefer that the clause be eliminated altogether. However, the broker should not suggest such deletion without recommending that the parties obtain independent legal advice on the matter.

Usually the offer section of a broker-prepared marketing contract such as the Model Form ends with a space for the broker's name and the signature of the licensee who prepared the contract, and a space for the buyer's name, address, and telephone numbers.

The contract writer should obtain all the phone numbers where the buyer can be reached and insert them in the contract so they will not be lost. The chances that the buyer and seller may get together behind the broker's back are small; but if the buyer's address is not shown on the Deposit Receipt, the contract is incomplete, since the form specifically states that notice of seller's acceptance must be given to buyer at "the address below."

All buyers who have an interest in the purchase of the property ought to sign the contract.

Figuring Time for Performance

Disputes often arise about whether performance is timely. One of the most common disagreements arises from a misunderstanding in counting the days allowed for performance. When a contract provides for performance "within 10 days from Seller's acceptance," the correct way of counting the days is to exclude the first day, but include the last day. This method is codified in California Civil Code, Section 10, which reads: "The time in which any act provided by law is done is computed by excluding the first day and including the last, unless the last day is a holiday, and then it is also excluded."

Two other code sections are applicable in clarifying time for performance:

Whenever an act is to be performed upon a particular day, which day falls upon a holiday, it may be performed upon the next business day with the same effect as if performed upon the day appointed (Civil Code, Section 11).

A holiday is every Sunday and such other days so specified by the Government Code. For any act to be performed by, at, or through any bank doing business in California, Saturday is considered an additional holiday. An act to be performed by, at, or through a bank on an optional bank holiday may be performed on such day if the bank is open, or at the option of the person obligated to perform may be performed on the next succeeding business day, which is not a Saturday (Civil Code, Section 9).

Because of the optional bank holidays it is not advisable to say "within 10 banking days." Neither is it clear what "working days" are since there is no uniform definition. Assuming a five day work week, the phrase "14 working days" does not mean two weeks by the calendar, but one day less than three weeks. "Business days" are defined as all days other than Sundays and such other days as are specified as holidays in the Government Code (Civil Code, Section 8). The use of the "calendar days" is recommended.

FORM 5:26   **LIQUIDATED DAMAGE CLAUSE WITH ESCROW DIRECTIONS**

If Buyer fails to complete the purchase of the property by reason of default of Buyer, Seller shall be relieved from his obligations to sell the property to Buyer, and Seller may pursue any remedy in law or equity that he may have against Buyer on account of the default provided, however, that by placing their initials here Buyer _____ Seller _____ agree that:

(1) An amount not to exceed three percent of the purchase price of the property shall constitute liquidated damages payable to Seller in the event of a default by Buyer; and

(2) The payment of such liquidated damages to Seller shall constitute the exclusive remedy of Seller on account of the default by Buyer; and

(3) Liquidated damages shall be payable to Seller out of Buyer's deposits toward purchase of the property according to the following procedures.

At any time after the date provided herein for the close of escrow, or any extended date for closing, Seller may give written notice to escrow holder and to Buyer by registered or certified mail, of Seller's determination that Buyer is in default under the contract, and that escrow holder shall, after the expiration of 20 days from the date of mailing of the notice, remit the assessed liquidated damages to Seller and the balance of the funds in the escrow to Buyer, unless within said 20 days, Buyer gives written instructions to escrow holder not to remit funds to Seller.

If Buyer gives such written instructions to escrow holder, the controversy and the disposition of the funds deposited into the escrow by Buyer shall be settled by arbitration in accordance with the Commercial Arbitration Rules of the American Arbitrator Association, Judgment upon the award rendered by the arbitratorial may be entered in any court having jurisdiction hereof.

If the controversy is referred to arbitration, any fee to initiate arbitration shall ultimately be borne as determined by the arbitrator.

Buyer and Seller each agree to indemnify and hold escrow holder harmless from any claim by the other arising out of any distributions made by escrow holder in accordance with and pursuant to the provisions of this paragraph.

COMMENT ON FORM 5:26: This is a complete substitute for the liquidated damage clause in the Model Forms. The wording follows requirements of the California Department of Real Estate in Subdivision sales.

Chapter 6
Seller's Acceptance and Counter-Offers

> *A response to an offer which does not conform to the terms of the offer, but instead proposes new conditions, is not an acceptance, but is a 'counter-offer' which in turn must be accepted to become binding upon the parties.*
>
> *Bullock v. McKeon*
> *104 CA 72, 285 P. 392*

An acceptance clause is usually included in Deposit Receipts. Basically, the clause provides for the seller's acceptance of the buyer's offer on the terms and conditions set forth. In addition, the acceptance clause provides for the payment of the broker's commission. Many forms used by brokers contain a provision that the commission is payable upon demand. Invariably, sellers' attorneys change such wording to provide for payment only upon consummation of the transaction. It is no wonder, then, that the acceptance clause in our Model Form makes payment of the commission dependent upon "recordation of the deed or other evidence of title."

Brokers working under an exclusive-listing agreement with sellers should know that under certain circumstances they agree to give up their traditional right to a full commission even if they produce a buyer who is "ready, willing, and able." On the Model Form, in the event that the buyer defaults the broker agrees to accept an amount not less than one half of the damages collected after "title and escrow expenses and the expenses of collection, if any" have been taken off the top. If the deposit is merely nominal, the broker's commission is reduced to an inconsequential amount.[1] Whether brokers should use forms containing such clauses when they are working with an exclusive listing is a policy decision which every broker must make.

This decision may not be a difficult one, since only rarely will a buyer purchase upon the exact terms of the listing agreement. The rights under the listing agreement concerning the commission evaporate if (1) the accepted offer drawn on the Deposit Receipt is materially different from the terms of the

214

listing, (2) the offer contains conditions precedent for performance by either buyer or seller, or (3) payment of the commission is conditioned upon "recordation of deed or other evidence of title."

The full text of the acceptance clause in the Model Form reads as follows:

Acceptance

The undersigned Seller accepts and agrees to sell the property on the above terms and conditions and agrees to the above confirmation of agency relationships. Seller agrees to pay to Broker(s) _____

_____

compensation for services as follows: _____

_____. Payable: (a) On recordation of the deed or other evidence of title, or (b) if completion of sale is prevented by default of Seller, upon Seller's default, or (c) if completion of sale is prevented by default of Buyer, only if and when Seller collects damages from Buyer, by suit or otherwise, and then in an amount not less than one-half of the damages recovered, but not to exceed the above fee, after first deducting title and escrow expenses and the expenses of collection, if any. Seller shall execute and deliver an escrow instruction irrevocably assigning the compensation for service in an amount equal to the compensation agreed to above. In any action or proceeding between Broker(s) and Seller arising out of this agreement, the prevailing party shall be entitled to reasonable attorneys fees and costs. The undersigned has read and acknowledges receipt of a copy of this agreement and authorizes Broker(s) to deliver a signed copy to Buyer.

As the reader can readily see, the seller is not obligated, under this type of acceptance clause, to collect damages. If the parties mutually rescind and the buyer gets the deposit back, the broker gets nothing, since he or she has also agreed that the commission is payable on "recordation of the deed or other evidence of title." Of course, if the parties rescind for the sole purpose of avoiding payment of the commission, the broker would have a case in tort against both seller and buyer.[2]

Brokers who urge the seller to return the deposit may impliedly waive their right to any portion of it.[3]

The provision for payment of commission "on recordation of the deed or other evidence of title" is unfair to the broker, since he or she becomes the victim of a buyer's default. Some sellers recognize this unfairness and provide in the listing agreement that the Deposit Receipt must obligate a buyer who defaults to pay the broker's commission. For a sample of such a clause, see Form 6:01.

FORM 6:00   **COMMISSION AGREEMENT**

COMMISSION AGREEMENT
CALIFORNIA ASSOCIATION OF REALTORS® STANDARD FORM

THIS IS INTENDED TO BE A LEGALLY BINDING CONTRACT. READ IT CAREFULLY.

Supplement to Real Estate Purchase Contract and Receipt for Deposit dated _____ between

_____ as buyer

and _____ as seller

regarding property, situated in _____ County of.

_____ , California, described as follows: _____

_____

Notice: The amount or rate of real estate commissions is not fixed by law. They are set by each broker individually and may be negotiable between the seller and broker.

Seller has employed _____

_____ as broker(s)

and agrees to pay for services rendered the sum of _____

_____ Dollars ($).

payable as follows:

(a) On recordation of the deed or other evidence of title, or (b) if completion of sale is prevented by default of Seller, upon Seller's default or (c) if completion of sale is prevented by default of Buyer, only if and when Seller collects damages from Buyer, by suit or otherwise and then in an amount not less than one-half of the damages recovered, but not to exceed the above fee, after first deducting title and escrow expenses and the expenses of collection, if any. In any action between Broker and Seller arising out of this agreement, the prevailing party shall be entitled to reasonable attorney's fees and costs.

The undersigned acknowledges receipt of a copy of this page, which constitutes Page _____ of _____ Pages.

Dated: _____ Telephone _____ Seller _____

Address _____ Seller _____

Broker(s) agree to the foregoing. Broker _____ Broker _____

Dated: _____ By _____ Dated: _____ By _____

For these forms. address—California Association of Realtors'
505 Shatto Place. Los Angeles. California 90020
Copyright © 1980 California Association of Realtors*

CA-11

COMMENT ON FORM 6:00: In order to use C.A.R.'s commission form the licensee should insert in the acceptance clause a reference to this form by stating: "Commission to be paid in accordance with attached commission agreement dated _____ 19____." Attach the commission agreement to the original Real Estate Purchase Contract and Deposit Receipt. Of course the seller is entitled to a copy of the commission agreement.

Commissions Are Negotiable

Real estate commissions have always been negotiable but in order to make the public fully aware of this fact, the California Business and Professions Code 10147.5 prescribes that any printed or form agreement that *initially establishes,* or is intended to establish, or alters the terms of any agreement which previously established a right to compensation to be paid to a real estate licensee for the sale of residential real property containing not more than four residential units, or for the sale of a mobilehome, shall contain a statement in not less than 10-bold face type immediately preceding any provision of such agreement relating to compensation of the licensee. The statement is prescribed to read as follows:

NOTICE: The amount or rate of real estate commissions is not fixed by law. They are set by each broker individually and may be negotiable between the seller and broker.

The law also prohibits that the amount or rate of compensation be pre-printed in the agreement. The law additionally defines the provision "alters the terms of any agreement which previously established a right to compensation" as meaning an increase in the rate of compensation, or the amount of compensation if initially established as a flat fee, from the agreement which previously established the right to compensation.

Where the express authorization to sell or other listing agreement contains the prescribed notice, the licensee needs to do no more. However, if the licensee is not operating under any prior agreement which establishes the commission, the Real Estate Purchase Contract and Receipt for Deposit would have to contain the above notice or the use of C.A.R.'s commission form containing the proper notice is recommended. Form 6:00 is C.A.R.'s commission form.

FORM 6:01 **BUYER TO PAY COMMISSION**
UPON DEFAULT

In the event _____
completion of sale is prevented/escrow fails to close

due to buyer's default, buyer agrees to pay the broker(s) named herein the full commission stated in the acceptance clause hereof.

(If contract does not contain a clause for
attorney's fees, insert Form 6:02 or 6:03)

COMMENT ON FORM 6:01: This provision can be inserted either in the buyer's original offer, if he or she is willing to agree thus, or by way of counter-offer as a condition for seller's acceptance. It is found in some clearly over-reaching printed forms. The buyer should be specifically alerted to such provision, especially if the liquidated damage clause is also incorporated in the agreement.

A broker may have an exclusive-listing contract which sets up a different method for the payment of commission in the event of default by buyer or seller including, perhaps, arbitration clauses and so forth. In this situation, it is best to insert a reference to the listing agreement in the space for the commission amount and strike out the balance of the acceptance clause. The reference could read: "Commission to be paid as per listing agreement dated _____ 19__ ___." The seller should be asked to initial the deletion. Such a change obviously does not fall within the admonition against substantial changes in the Deposit Receipt, since a broker may negotiate and draw his or her own employment contract on terms acceptable to the employing principal.

No doubt the situations where brokers actually sue for commission are relatively few.

Subject to Acquiring Title

In Chapter 2, we discussed the necessity for determining the capacity of the parties to enter into a contract. The broker would do well to remember this necessity at the time of obtaining the seller's acceptance. Often, between the time of the listing and the actual sale a change in ownership or the relationship of the parties occurs. The seller may not have acquired proper title to the property at the time of the sale. In order to protect the seller in such situations, the condition precedent, which must be satisfied before the acceptance is valid should be set forth in the contract. If the seller is to obtain clear title from a co-owner or separated spouse, the contract could recite: "Seller's acceptance is conditioned upon seller acquiring title to subject property." All owners should sign the contract unless valid powers of attorney are in existence, corporate resolutions should accompany sales by corporations, and so forth.

A seller who signs a contract with an understanding that other persons or entities must also sign should insist that acceptance be "conditioned upon obtaining the acceptance of _____ . Should such

name of person or entity

acceptance be unobtainable for any reason not later than _____,
19_____ , this agreement shall be null and void.'' Of course, any other wording
expressing the contingency clearly would be acceptable.

If the boxes in the liquidated-damages clause of the Model Form are filled
in, the deposit presumably constitutes damages for the buyer's breach. Should
the buyer abandon the deposit, the broker is entitled to his or her share after the
expenses have been deducted.

Some Forms in common use (but not the Model Form) contain no provision for attorneys' fees if the broker prevails. A clause covering such a contingency is found in Form 6:02.

**FORM 6:02   PROVIDING FOR ATTORNEYS' FEES
                   IN CASE OF LITIGATION**

Broker or agent of either principal, if joined in any litigation arising out of this
agreement and if successful in the defense thereof, shall be entitled to reasonable
attorneys' fees and costs as set by the court.

COMMENT ON FORM 6:02: Many brokers feel that attorneys in suits against
the parties include the broker as a party, even when there is no real need for it.
Involvement in such suits causes the broker additional business expenses.
Brokers therefore encourage the use of the above clause in the hope that the
clause will discourage uncalled for lawsuits against them. (See also Form 6:03.)

Some broker forms include provisions for attorneys' fees in the event that
either of the parties to the contract sue to enforce it. Only rarely is the broker's
interest protected. Some forms contain a clause similar to Form 6:02, but have
no provisions for attorneys' fees concerning suits between the parties. Form
6:03 is all-inclusive.

FORM 6:03   ATTORNEYS' FEES

If action or proceeding is brought to enforce any part of this agreement or if
the brokers or agents named herein are joined in any litigation arising out of this
agreement, any prevailing party to such action or proceeding shall be entitled to
reasonable attorneys' fees and costs as set by the court.

COMMENT ON FORM 6:03: Some printed forms contain clauses providing for
attorneys' fees. In most instances, such clauses cover only the situation between
the parties to the contract. Where brokers are included in the lawsuit, they must
often pay their own attorneys' fees, even if they prevail.

When No Deed Is Recorded.

Some readers may be aware that the wording in the Model Form, "recordation of deed or other evidence of title," is a departure from that in prior forms, which included the delivery of an "Agreement of Sale." This change may have resulted from the misunderstandings which prevailed concerning the wording. Buyers and sellers are entitled to receive a copy of the contract when executed.[4] Taken literally, the old clause could mean that the seller, upon the delivery of the buyer's copy of the Deposit Receipt, was liable for the commission. Of course, the intention was a reference to the installment land sales contract, which was published under the title "Agreement of Sale." Under the present form, when a land contract (security device) is to be delivered unrecorded to the buyer, the contract writer must take care to alter the wording in the acceptance clause subparagraph (a) to read, "upon delivery of the final land sales contract between the parties," or words to that effect.

The contract writer should also note that the Model Form contains a clause whereby the broker specifically consents to the conditions of the acceptance clause. This consent must be dated and signed by the broker or an authorized representative. The consent underscores the waiver of any rights that the broker might have contrary to the rights under the acceptance clause.

Counter-Offers

Most printed forms presently in use are not designed to accommodate counter-offers readily. The forms are intended only to constitute deposit receipts containing the buyer's offer. With the seller's acceptance, a bilateral contract is created. In the event that the seller is unwilling to accept the buyer's offer as written, it becomes necessary for the contract writer to make the appropriate corrections in the acceptance clause and draw the counter-offer on an addendum to the contract. The simplest design for a form made to handle counter-offers would be a deposit-receipt form printed on both sides, with the acceptance clause on the reverse side along with a space for adding the conditions required for the seller's acceptance.

Let us examine our Model Form to see what changes would actually be required. The seller's acceptance is covered in one line: "The undersigned Seller accepts and agrees to sell the property on the above terms and conditions."

If this sentence were changed by adding "with the following changes:" and a space for inserting counter-proposals, the usefulness of the form would be increased considerably. The altered acceptance clause, together with a clause for the buyer's acceptance of the seller's counter-proposals, could then be placed on the reverse side of the form, thus allowing more space for writing on the first page and dispensing with the need for the makeshift arrangements now necessary in filling out the form.

The objection most often raised against accommodating counter-offers in the acceptance clause is that to provide such space would be to *invite* changes. This fear is unfounded. Either the offer is acceptable to the seller, or it isn't.

A broker using the Model Form in preparing counter-offers can inadvertently change the terms of the seller's acceptance and eliminate the printed provisions concerning commission upon default. The broker who draws a contract customarily changes the first line of the acceptance clause by adding, after the word "conditions," the words, "continued on the reverse side hereof." The broker may then strike the balance of the acceptance clause on one side whereas the contract continues as follows, on the reverse side:

> Acceptance
> (continued from the reverse side hereof)
> All of the terms and conditions set out on the reverse side hereof are acceptable to the seller in their entirety, with the following corrections or changes:
>
> 1. _____
> 2. _____
> 3. Seller agrees to pay broker as commission, on demand, the sum of $_____.

Effectively, except where the contract may be conditioned upon the performance of certain conditions by either party, the broker has thus avoided the "consummation" clause and the division of the "forfeited deposit" clause. If the buyer defaults, misunderstandings may arise concerning the disposition of a forfeited deposit.

I have examined many Deposit Receipts drawn by brokers attempting to adapt them for counter-offers, and found that the changes in the form often make the intent of the parties unclear. Quite often, the proper reference is made to the reverse side for further terms, but the acceptance clause on the face of the contract is not signed, and the counter-offer is completely silent as to the payment of commission.

Using Proper Counter-Offer Techniques

Using the proper counter-offer technique is a must. Making deletions or additions of terms on the face of the contract after the buyer has signed it as an offer is not good practice.

Acceptance of an offer must be unqualified; a qualified acceptance is a new offer. When interlineations or additions are made by the party receiving an offer, these interlineations and additions constitute a new offer, or a counter-offer.

Multiple Offer Problems

Whenever very desirable properties appear on the market, the problem of multiple offers occur. One way of handling more than one offer to which a counteroffer is desired is described on page 229.

This method, also called the "race to the seller," is criticized because it invites fence jumping by aggressive salespersons, who try to reach the seller directly and get approval of a counteroffer, which on its surface appears to be satisfactory, but may contain flaws. There is also the possibility that two accepted counteroffers are received at the exact same time, with the result that the seller has "sold" the property to two different buyers. Some brokers have tried to solve this sticky problem by setting a time and place for delivery to the seller of all accepted or improved counteroffers. This creates a kind of auction setting without the safeguards of the established rules of genuine auctions.

Two solutions described as "practical" have seriously been proposed in a leading real estate magazine. It is suggested that the seller prepare, but *not sign,* new deposit receipts for each buyer. The idea is that "these multiple offers" or proposals can then be given to competing buyers along with the invitation to "make an offer" on the specified terms. Assuming that the interested buyers submit new offers with their signatures, "the seller can then pick and choose among all outstanding offers and accept, reject, or further counter any and all."

The other suggestion involves the seller again preparing, but not signing, two or more counteroffer forms. Even after they are signed by the buyer, no binding contract is created until one counteroffer form is also signed by the seller.

The two schemes can best be characterized as "teaser" offer methods without more (see Form 6:04). The seller has no control over what different sales associates represent or what these unsigned "invitations to bid" mean in the negotiating process. A buyer may sign the "invitation" on the exact terms and still not get the property. Use of these methods may lead to disputes and tension between buyers, sellers and their agents.

There are, of course, other and safer alternatives. Without preparing unsigned deposit receipts or counteroffer forms, a seller can make a request for submission of new offers. Some minimum requirements can be transmitted to all buyers. The seller can inform the buyers that a certain minimum price is desired and the type and length for release of contingencies. Because no unsigned form is presented, the possibility of misunderstandings is minimized.

Sealed bids are sometimes used in probate sales. A similar method can be adopted for multiple offers. The seller can agree to accept the best offer at the seller's sole discretion. Any auction setting of this nature often offends some buyers and their agents, but it does work for the benefit of the seller. Since not all offers deserve a counteroffer, a seller can reject such offers out of hand. It may be possible to narrow down the most attractive offer to counter by requesting additional information regarding the buyer, such as a fuller filled-in loan application signed by the buyer. The latter will assist the seller in determining whether the buyer will qualify for the proposed financing. If seller is to carry financing, the same information can be requested. Only serious buyers will reply to such requests. Avoiding multiple counteroffers is, of course, the safest. The listing broker often has a conflict of interest in the preference for an offer obtained by the listing licensee or an associate in the listing firm. The desire to keep the whole commission "in house" is a powerful motivation for influencing the seller to accept the "house" offer. But keep in mind that implied in the employment agreement with the seller is a covenant of good faith and honest dealing. The Agency Relationship Disclosure Statement sets forth the duties owed the seller as well as the buyer. If those duties and responsibilities are kept well in mind, temptations as discussed above should be easy to resist.

FORM 6:04   MULTIPLE "INVITATIONS FOR BID"

_____ have received multiple offers for _____
  I/We   my/our property

None of these were acceptable. Instead of making multiple counteroffers, our broker has prepared several identical fully filled in Real Estate Contracts and Receipts for Deposit. They are not signed by _____ and are not to be considered counteroffers. They are invita-
  me/us

tions to bid on the minimum terms of the forms. Should you sign one of these proposed contracts, you should know that _____ reserve
                                                       I/we

the sole right to accept, reject, counter or choose the offer which in _____ sole opinion, judgment and discretion best expresses
  my/our

_____ needs.
  my/our

You can facilitate the selection process by submitting a completely filled in Loan application form. Thereby we can better evaluate your offer.

Thank you for your interest.

Dated _____   Seller _____

                                                 Seller _____

The simplest and safest method of incorporating a counter-offer short of rewriting the whole contract, which often is psychologically inadvisable, is to use the original form with a counter-offer addendum. The suggested change in the printed acceptance clause should be initialed by the seller, who should also sign the printed acceptance clause as well as the counter-offer.

Some salespersons hastily shortchange themselves by forgetting to change the commission dollar amount when the seller increases the selling price. Because counter-offers are sometimes passed back and forth, many brokers insist that their salespersons always state the commission as a percentage of the sales price rather than as a dollar amount.

When the seller's counter-offer has been signed by the seller it should be immediately presented to buyer. If the buyer accepts, he or she should execute the acceptance and receive a copy of the completed contract. CAR's printed Counter Offer form provides space for the buyer's counter-offer to the seller's counter-offer.

However, any changes by the buyer constitute a new proposal and prevent the formation of a contract. Such changes reject the seller's counter-offer and bar its subsequent acceptance. To form a contract, the new proposal must in turn be accepted by the seller. To facilitate this process the contract should state the changes clearly.

In multiple-listing situations, the listing broker often encounters offers from cooperating brokers written so poorly that they are unacceptable. Rather than drawing a new Deposit Receipt, the experienced broker uses the counter-offer technique of acceptance. If there are no substantial changes in the terms, the broker may limit the changes to a rewording of the clauses as he or she sets up the contract point by point in the counter-offer. Substantial changes may call for extensive rewriting and redrafting of most of the blank spaces. In preparing such a counter-proposal, reference can be made, with advantage, to the various paragraphs.

A change in the purchase price can be made simply by stating, "(1) Purchase price to be increased to $_____."

If the terms-of-payment clause must also be changed, it is safer to rewrite the whole clause rather than making reference to the original. At the time the clause is revised, the seller can insert any desired conditions for carrying financing that are now shown on the face of the contract.

The following is a list of the most common conditions desired by sellers in counter-offers:

1. Increase in purchase price or cash deposit.
2. Change of amount and terms in loans to be carried.
3. Change in date of possession and demand for free occupancy.
4. Limitations upon liability for termite work, repairs, and the like.
5. Limitations on time allowed for the buyer to obtain needed financing, and the right of the seller to assist in finding a lender.

6. Protective provisions for the seller where the buyer's offer is conditioned upon sale of other property.

7. The seller's right to accept other offers until counter-offer is accepted.

8. Simultaneous execution of more than one counter-offer.

9. Limitations on the seller's warranties, or demands that the buyer accept property as is.

10. Demand that the buyer be responsible for the broker's commission on buyer's default.

Most of these subjects and the relevant clauses are covered in Chapters 3 and 5, and it would be repetitious to reiterate the provisions here. Suffice it to say that all the clauses in this book can be adapted easily to counter-offer requirements. For examples see Forms 6:05 and 6:06. CAR has a universal counter offer form to be used in sales of Real Estate, Mobilehomes and Business Opportunities.

FORM 6:05   **INCREASE IN PURCHASE PRICE BY INCREASING SECOND LOAN**

1) Purchase price to be increased to $_____.
2) The note to seller to be increased to $_____, by buyer executing a note and _____ in that amount in favor of
deed of trust

seller secured by the property, payable in _____
monthly/quarterly/

_____ installments of $_____,
semi-annual/annual

_____, _____ interest at the rate of ___% per annum,
or more   plus/including

(Optional, continue):

due in full _____
months/years/from close of escrow _____, 19___
_____ .

in the event of sale or transfer of title to subject property

COMMENT ON FORM 6:05: Normally it is not good practice to take short-cuts by adjusting the purchase-price increase in the form of a statement, such as "price to be increased to $____, by increasing the second loan to $____." Even though it may take longer, rewriting the terms-of-payment clause entirely is the safest procedure. Rewriting also makes it possible to insert any restrictions the seller may wish on the second loan. (See Form 3:26).

Unrecorded Easements and Licenses

In Chapter 5 we discussed the necessity for inserting a clause in the contract pertaining to covenants, conditions, restrictions, and easements. It was pointed out that the Model Form places the burden upon sellers to disclose any such items known to them which may not be part of the official records. Assume for a moment that the broker has drawn the offer including any clause in Forms 5:01, 5:02, or 5:03. Upon presentation of the offer, the seller should be asked whether or not to his or her knowledge there exist any agreements, easements, or licenses by which anyone has obtained some "right," in the widest understanding of this word, in the seller's property. Such inquiry may disclose an encroachment agreement; or, for example, permission for a neighbor to use a part of the land. This permission may not be found in a recorded document. The seller's acceptance of the buyer's offer should be made contingent upon the buyer's approval of any such agreements. The clause describing this condition becomes part of a counter-offer, and until the buyer has specifically approved it, no binding contract exists (see Form 6:06).

FORM 6:06   COVENANT OR EASEMENT NOT MENTIONED IN OFFER (Precede with Form 6:04)

_____ . The title to be delivered to buyer shall, in addition
(number)
to the liens, encumbrances, easements, restrictions, rights and conditions of record set forth in paragraph _____ hereof, be subject to the following:

_____
(describe)
_____ a copy of which has been exhibited
created by a document in writing dated
to and approved by buyer.

COMMENT ON FORM 6:06: The most practical way of alerting the buyer to an agreement affecting the property which was not previously revealed is to make it part of the counter-offer. A copy of the document, if any, should be exhibited to the buyer; and if acceptable, it should be initialed. The counter-offer as a whole must be ratified by the buyer.

When the Seller Reserves Right to Accept Other Offers

As discussed earlier, transactions are made daily where the buyer, for example, makes the offer conditioned upon prior sale of his or her property. Sellers faced with such an offer have two choices: They may accept the offer outright and give the buyer a time limitation by which he or she must either perform or waive the condition. Or sellers may accept the offer but keep showing the property to other prospective buyers, giving the first buyer the right to first refusal. If the buyer after notice does not waive the prior-sale condition, the seller is free to accept the next buyer's offer. These conditional sales call for very careful handling by the broker, and often cause controversy.

Another common practice, especially in multiple-listing situations, is the conditional acceptance of a buyer's offer in form of a counter-offer which reserves to the seller the right to accept any offer from other buyers at any time prior to receipt of the first offeror's written acceptance.

In all fairness to the buyer who makes an offer which the seller is willing to counter, a firm time limitation of not more than twenty-four hours for acceptance of a counter-offer should be allowed.

Clauses often used in the counter-offer situations discussed in this section are found in Forms 6:07 and 6:08. Clauses relating to the acceptance of counter-offers are found in Forms 6:09 and 6:10.

FORM 6:07   **SELLER RESERVES RIGHT TO**
                  ACCEPT OTHER OFFERS
                  (Precede with Form 6:04)

(Where buyer's offer is subject to sale of buyer's property)

_____ Seller reserves the right to continue to offer the herein
(number)
described property for sale. Should seller receive another offer in writing, acceptable to him, buyer shall have _____ hours from receipt of written notice to
48/72
waive the condition of sale of buyer's other property.

Failure to waive such contingency in writing to the seller within the time stated in seller's notice to buyer, shall terminate this agreement. The deposit and other sums paid hereunder shall then be returned to buyer and seller shall have no further liability hereunder.

COMMENT ON FORM 6:07: It is never a good idea to make delivery of such notice to ''seller's agent.'' Because cooperating brokers may also be considered ''seller's agents,'' it is better practice to prescribe that notice in writing is to be delivered by mail or in person to the seller. See also Standard Contingency Form 4:50 and CAR's Contingency Release form series.

FORM 6:08   **BUYER'S WAIVER OF CONDITION FOR**
                  SALE OF OTHER PROPERTY

To (Name of Seller);
The undersigned, designated the buyer in the Real Estate Purchase Contract and Receipt for Deposit dated _____, 19_____, naming

_____
(name of seller)
as seller pertaining to the property described as _____ ,
(description)
hereby waive the condition for _____
the sale of my property at _____/close of escrow, etc.

(Form continues on next page)

and agree to purchase the property described in said contract in accordance with all of the other terms and conditions set forth therein.

_____, 19_____.

_____
(signature of buyer(s)

I hereby acknowledge
receipt of a copy of
the above waiver.

_____, 19_____.

_____
(signature of seller(s)

COMMENT ON FORM 6:08: This waiver can be adapted for use in connection with the waiver of any condition precedent to buyer's duty of performance. It is always good practice to have the seller acknowledge receipt of a copy of such waiver to assure that seller will perform his or her end of the bargain.

FORM 6:09   **OPEN-END ACCEPTANCE**
                    (Precede with Form 6:04)

_____ Seller reserves the right to continue to offer the herein de-
    (number)
scribed property for sale and to accept any offer acceptable to him at any time prior to delivery to seller in person of a copy of the counter-offer contained herein, duly accepted and signed by buyer. Unless this counter-offer is accepted in this manner, _____
          within _____ days hereof/on or before _____, 19_____ at _____ a.m./p.m.
it shall be deemed revoked and the deposit shall be returned to buyer.

COMMENT ON FORM 6:09: The interesting thing about this commonly used clause is that it is most often employed where the listing broker or salesperson has not obtained the offer to which the seller is making a counter-offer. The justification is that the listing broker in a multiple-listing situation should not be obligated to take the listing off the market while another broker's buyer deliberates. CAR's counter-offer form (Form 6:04) contains a similar clause and sets forth the mode of acceptance of the counter offer in the same manner as the Model Form. Brokers using this must be careful that the seller does not inadvertently accept two offers. Such an accident can happen easily where acceptance of the counter-offer is to be delivered to the seller's agent, and the document is delivered to an empty office. To avoid this possibility it is better to provide for the exact manner of notice of buyer number one's acceptance as above. The seller should indicate receipt of the accepted counter-offer and agree to perform (see Form 6:10).

**FORM 6:10   RECEIPT FOR COPY OF ACCEPTANCE
OF A COUNTER OFFER**

The undersigned _____ hereby acknowledges receipt of a copy
                    seller/buyer

of his counter-offer dated _____, 19_____, which copy is signed and

accepted by _____. I/we hereby agree to _____ the
              buyer/seller   sell/buy

property described therein on the terms and conditions set forth in the agreement

accepted and signed by both parties.

_____, 19_____.

                                    _____
                                          Signature Seller/Buyer

COMMENT ON FORM 6:10: This clause can be used as an acknowledgment of
the receipt by either party of the other party's acceptance of a counter-offer.

When More Than One Counter-Offer Is
Proposed

Naturally, a seller is entitled to see all offers, regardless of the source, and
to decide which offer to accept. Sometimes, when two offers are received, the
seller wishes to reject both but also wants to give both parties a chance to accept
a counter-proposition. Though this procedure may lead to a resolution, it does
open the door to controversies. In such situations, brokers must take care to
insert identical provisions in the counter-offers (see Form 6:11).

Even after an offer is finally accepted by the seller and an actual sale
made, the California Real Estate Commissioner insists that licensees *must*
present all new offers to the seller. The only exceptions are where the seller has
authorized the licensee *not* to bring in any further offers or where an offer is
deemed to be frivolous. The concept of course is that the decision with regards
to considering any offer, other than the previously accepted one, is the principals and not the licensees. Licensees should be careful not to encourage the
seller to breach any agreement, since such encouragement may constitute tor-
tious conduct for which the licensee could be held legally liable.

**FORM 6:11   IDENTICAL COUNTER-OFFERS
(Precede with Form 6:04)**

_____ Buyer is hereby informed and understands that seller has
   (number)

made _____ written, identical counter-offers including this.
        amount

(Form continues on next page)

The seller will perform under the contract containing the buyer's written acceptance of the seller's counter-offer which is first delivered to _____

name

_____ as seller's agent or to seller personally.
of broker

In any event, if buyer does not accept seller's counter-offer _____

within

_____
days hereof/on or before _____ 19_____, a.m./p.m.

this counter-offer shall be deemed revoked and the deposit shall be returned to buyer.

COMMENT ON FORM 6:11: Where the seller's listing broker is competing with other brokers' offers, it may be advisable for other brokers to insist upon delivery of acceptance only to the owner personally. Even this precaution may be defeated by telephone acceptance and collusion.

Where this type of form is used, careful sellers often insist that an additional protective clause be inserted: "The seller's determination of which acceptance was first delivered to him or her shall be conclusively binding upon all parties and brokers involved."

To protect the buyer, the broker who delivers acceptance first should obtain a notation on the contract showing the seller's acknowledgment that this counter-offer acceptance was first in time and that the seller will perform this contract. (See Form 6:10).

When the Deposit Is Increased

Form 6:12 contains a clause to be used when the buyer agrees to an increase in the deposit demanded in a counter-offer.

FORM 6:12   **BUYER'S CONDITION FOR**
                       INCREASE OF DEPOSIT
                       (Precede with Form 6:04)

_____ Buyer agrees to increase deposit to $_____ not later than
(number)
_____ days after all of the conditions contained in paragraph(s) _____
_____ have been satisfied.

COMMENT ON FORM 6:12: In most printed forms where there is a provision for increased deposit, such an increase must be made "upon seller's approval" of buyer's offer. If certain financing, clear title, satisfactory leases, and termite certification are conditions of the agreement for buyer's benefit, the buyer need only increase the deposit when all of these conditions are satisfied. This takes the "sting" out of the increase, because it is unlikely that buyer will willfully default if the transaction satisfies the conditions he or she demanded.

This clause can be used as a counter-offer by the buyer if the seller insists on increased deposit. It should be used only if the conditions inserted for buyer's benefit contain certain time limitations for performance. Otherwise, as a practical matter, there may be no increase in the deposit before time for closing.

Back-Up Deals

Some sellers are persuaded to enter into so-called back-up deals, which are contingent upon the failure to perform by a buyer whose previous offer has been accepted by the seller. The first accepted deal may be subject to financing which the seller and the seller's advisors actually consider impossible to obtain. Such a contract will usually contain a time limitation within which the first buyer must perform. The back-up deal is specifically made contingent upon the first buyer's failure to perform within the specified time. When buyer number 1 defaults, the seller attempts to perform with buyer number 2. However, the seller may find that he or she has not effectively terminated buyer number 1's rights either by failing to fulfill all the conditions to be performed by seller under the first contract or by failing to make a full and adequate tender of performance. A subsequent tender of performance by buyer number 1 may place the seller in the entangled situation of being obligated to perform with both purchasers.

Whenever a seller wants to accept a back-up deal, he or she should make performance under contract number 2 contingent not just upon failure of performance by buyer number 1, but also upon the obtaining of a complete release from buyer number 1 of all claims he or she might otherwise have against sellers and the property.

Form 6:13 is an example of a clause to be inserted in a back-up contract.

**FORM 6:13   BACK-UP DEAL CONTINGENT UPON
                   RELEASE OF PRIOR DEAL**

Seller's acceptance hereof and obligation to perform hereunder is specifically conditioned upon the failure of the buyer under a _____ ,
                                                                  (title of contract)
dated _____, 19____, to perform on or before _____,
19____ and the obtaining by seller of a written release from the buyer under said contract of all claims against the seller and to any rights, title or interest that the buyer might otherwise have to the property described herein.

COMMENT ON FORM 6:13: Back-up deals are common in situations where the first deal approved by the seller appears to be shaky and another prospect is willing to make an offer conditioned upon the failure of the first offeror to perform. In order to protect the seller, back-up deals should always be made conditioned upon the seller's receiving a complete release from the first offeror. Sometimes buyers will not execute a release because of disappointment in not getting the deal. The seller must then protect himself by making proper tender of performance to effectively cut off any rights that the non-releasing "buyer" may have.

While the use of counter-offers is a genuine sales technique, it should be applied with caution. The legitimate use is, of course, in situations where the buyer's initial offer is unacceptable to the seller either in price or terms. The practical use of counter-offers in tidying up a defectively drawn contract is acceptable, but only when such use does not result in loss of the sale. Changes are not always for the better. If an impasse arises because of language, the broker or lawyer drawing the contract should be firm, but not intransigent. Any overzealousness or insistence on a particular term on the broker's part may not be appreciated by the client if it causes the loss of the deal.

In using counter-offers, be positive but do not write up counter-offers that are clearly "bait" offers, intended only to encourage the seller to lower the price. The broker's job is to obtain the best possible price for the seller, not to undermine the seller's resolve. The broker should, of course, present all offers and leave the decision of acceptance to the seller. But the broker is the negotiator, and should be a master salesperson. He or she is clearly in the position to advise the seller, particularly where a choice of actions is involved. For example, encouraging a seller to refuse a very low offer outright may be better than allowing the offer to be recognized with a counter-offer. Only when the parties are reasonably close to agreement will a counter-offer bridge the gap. However, sometimes a transaction requires more than one round of offers and counter-offers for completion. And often the rejection of a counter-offer results in the seller's adopting a more realistic viewpoint. Only skillful negotiation will lead to successful transactions.

Checklist for Counter-Offers

1. Begin by amending the acceptance clause to incorporate reference to the counter-offer.

2. If a separate acceptance clause is not inserted in the provisions of the counter-offer, have the seller sign the printed acceptance clause as amended.

3. Always date the addendum and make proper reference to the contract of which it is a part.

4. Set the counter-offer up in numbered "points." Refer to the contract paragraphs where possible, and rewrite whole paragraphs where necessary.

5. Do not make "piecemeal" changes in important terms. Rewrite the whole paragraph in which the terms occur for better clarity.

6. Do not make changes in the contract simply for the sake of change.

7. Don't be a "me-too-er," if the other party wishes to have some particular right or remedy inserted.

8. Don't let disagreement about language "kill" a deal.

9. Be sure that all changes are properly initialed, and that all parties receive copies of the final contract executed by both sides.

10. Use a simple checklist for all points to be included in the counter-offer when drafting it.

Chapter 7
Mobilehome Sales

"Mobilehome" is a structure transportable in one or more sections designed and equipped to contain not more than two dwelling units to be used with or without a foundation system.

Section 18008, Cal. Health and Safety code

California's real estate brokers and their licensed sales associates, under amended provisions of the Business and Professions Code commencing with Section 10131.6, "... may sell or offer to sell, buy or offer to buy, solicit prospective purchasers of, solicit or obtain listings of, or negotiate the purchase, sale, or exchange of any mobilehome if the mobilehome has been registered under the provisions of part 2 (commencing with Section 18000) of Division 13 of Health and Safety Code for at least one year ..."

This development does not mean that real estate licensees automatically have become "vehicle dealers," licensed to sell new and used mobilehomes. The real estate licensees' right to sell used mobilehomes is specifically restricted as follows:

1. A real estate broker may advertise and offer for sale only used mobilehomes and only when they are located on certain kinds of real property. The mobilehome must be in place (a) on a lot rented or leased for human habitation within an established mobilehome park as defined by Section 18214 of the Health and Safety Code (and the broker's advertising or offering for sale in this case may not be contrary to any terms of a contract between the seller of the mobilehome and the park owner); or (b) otherwise located, pursuant to a local zoning ordinance or permit, on a lot where its presence has been authorized or its continued presence and such use would be authorized for a total and uninterrupted period of at least one year.

2. A mobilehome is defined as "a structure transportable in one or more sections, designed and equipped to contain not more than two dwelling units to be used with or without a foundation system." Mobilehome does not include a recreational vehicle, a commercial coach, or factory-built housing.

3. A real estate broker may not maintain his or her place of business

where two or more mobilehomes are displayed and offered for sale by such person unless the real estate broker is also licensed as a mobilehome dealer. This provision would prohibit a real estate broker solely licensed as such from having a place of business within a mobilehome park, or upon a lot where the presence of mobilehomes is authorized by local zoning ordinance or permit if two or more of the mobilehomes are offered for sale by the real estate licensee.

4. A real estate broker who accepts funds from others in connection with a mobilehome transaction is not subject to the escrow regulations pertaining to licensed mobilehome dealers. However, under similar provisions of the Real Estate Act (Business and Professions Code, Section 10145) the broker must place such funds immediately into a neutral escrow depository. The funds may be disbursed only in accordance with instructions by the principals. Proper records must be maintained as prescribed by the Department of Real Estate

Differences Between Mobilehome Sales and Real Estate Sales

The used mobilehome business is complicated. The listing procedure as well as the sales transaction differs from that in the home sales with which the real estate licensee is usually most familiar. The mobilehome is personal property and was prior to July 1, 1980 subject to registration under the Vehicle Code [635.5350 *et seq.*] and after that date under the Health and Safety Code. Mobilehomes manufactured after July 1, 1980 or such previous registered homes upon request by owner, legal owner and junior lien holder, will be placed on the county assessors personal property assessment roll and taxed accordingly. Certain equipment is required under the Health and Safety Code, Section 18025, and under regulations in twenty five California Administrative Code sections beginning with section 5500. Accessories and appliances are personal property or chattel, and unlike similar items in a real estate home transaction, they are considered part of the unit. In order to function in this area, the real estate licensee must therefore be familiar with the many laws which apply to mobilehomes. These laws can of course be mastered, but the list itself may seem intimidating. It includes the Real Estate Act, Health and Safety Code, Commercial Code, Revenue and Taxation Code, Business and Professions Code and the Civil Code, together with all regulations as found in the Administrative Code. In addition certain HUD regulations and the federal Truth-in-Lending Act apply, as do local zoning ordinances.

It is particularly important that the agent examine all ownership papers carefully and become convinced that the purported owner is in fact the owner. Disciplinary as well as criminal action can be imposed upon any agent who knowingly participates in the purchase, sale, or other acquisition of or disposal of a stolen mobilehome.

A mobilehome must conform with the requirements of the Health and Safety Code, Section 18000 *et seq*. These requirements pertain to occupancy, attachments to mobilehomes, accessories, waste discharge, plumbing, heating, electricity, alterations or conversions, insignia, fire prevention, enforcement and other matters. The seller should be queried about any modifications that have been made. Certain modifications, particularly those involving utility hook-ups, windows, venting, and so on, may only be made by a contractor with a specialty contractor's license who is approved by the Department of Housing and under local permits. If the seller discloses such modifications or the licensee discovers them, full disclosure must be made to the buyer. Inspection by the Department of Housing (HCD) and full correctional modifications are necessary, because it is unlawful for anyone, including a broker, to sell, offer for sale, rent, or lease a mobilehome which has been altered or converted without the department's approval.

Under Section 10131.7(g) of the Business and Professions Code it is unlawful for a real estate licensee

> to fail or neglect properly to cause the endorsement, dating and delivery (or fail to endorse, date and deliver) of the certificate of ownership of the mobilehome, and, when having possession, to fail to deliver the registration card to a transferee who is lawfully entitled to a transfer of registration. . . .

If escrow is "properly" instructed and the instruments are adequately delivered to the escrow holder, the broker should be able to rely upon escrow to carry out the task of giving timely notice of the transfer to the Department of Housing.

The Use Tax

The purchase of a mobilehome which is not on the county assessors personal property secured tax roll is subject to a use tax. The rate of tax which is figured on the vehicle price only is presently 6½% in the counties of Alameda, Contra Costa, San Francisco and Santa Clara and 6% in all other counties. The Department of Housing and Community Development (HCD) acts as an agent for the Board in collecting the use tax at the time of registration.

In sales of mobilehomes located in mobilehome parks, the overall purchase price includes a consideration for the value of in-place location separately identified, but not subject to use tax. Other items that are not included in the purchase price for computation of use tax are awnings, skirting, carport, patio, landscaping and shrubs, all unattached furnishings and separately stated escrow fees. The application for transfer of registration must be accompanied by a certification of the "sales price" on a HCD form signed under penalty of perjury by the buyer. The certificate is reviewed by the Board of Equalization and the facts stated therein are subject to the Board's verification. No broker should be party to giving false or inaccurate information about the sales price. A broker doing so is not only subject to disciplinary action by the Real Estate Commissioner but may also face both civil and criminal prosecution. "Sales price" shall be based upon the current value of the used mobilehome as specified by a recognized value guide approved by the State Board of Equalization. If the guide does not specify age, model and manufacturer or the actual sales price of the used mobilehome is less than the guide's current value, the actual sales price as evidenced by the sales agreement prevails as base. (Rev. & Tax. Code Section 6276.1.)

All new mobilehomes constructed before July 1, 1980 and any older mobilehome, which have by request by the owners and lenders been transferred to HCD registration, are assessed on the County Tax Assessors secured property roll at full cash value. The mobilehome may be reassessed after sale. The tax is prorated at close of escrow. Mobilehomes affixed to a permanent foundation are real estate and taxed as such.

In trades of mobilehomes when no actual selling price is understood by the parties, a buyer must declare a value using the HCD Certificational Purchase Price Form. There is, of course, no use tax applied to the price of land, where a legal lot is involved in the sale. It is good practice to include in the "Terms of Sale" clause a statement as: "Buyer shall pay Use Tax of $_____ and HCD transfer fees of $_____." To be safe escrow should be instructed to obtain a county tax collector's tax clearance certificate that no local property tax is due, or that such taxes have been paid not requiring transfer of registration.

The Real Estate Settlement Procedures Act applies to any federally related mortgage loan on a parcel of land on which a loan is to be secured, and on which a mobilehome is located if owned or to be owned by the borrower, and covered or to be covered by the mortgage, or purchased using part or all of the proceeds of the loan. No charge may be made for preparing a truth-in-lending statement on a mobilehome loan covered by the settlement act. The Real Estate Settlement Procedures Act does not apply to a transaction involving a mobilehome where the loan is not secured by an interest in real property, but the security interest is in the mobilehome itself.

When Land Is Involved

The real estate broker must be particularly careful if the mobilehome is located on a lot not in an established mobilehome park. In such situations, a greater burden may rest upon the broker, since a real estate licensee is expected to be very familiar with zoning laws and regulations. The seller should be able to exhibit a permit. The broker should inquire in the local county or city department about the legality of the lot, and obtain assurance that the continued presence and use of the lot as a mobilehome site will be authorized for "a total and uninterrupted period of at least one year."

CAR's mobilehome Purchase Contract form (see pp. 242, 243) is not designed to be used where a parcel of real estate is involved in a transaction concerning the sale of a mobilehome. A combination form designed for this situation would be too cumbersome and contain too much "boiler plate." If a mobilehome sale also includes land or improved real property, the use of two interlocking contracts is recommended—ideally, CAR's Mobilehome Purchase Contract for the mobilehome, and CAR's Real Estate Purchase Contract and Receipt for Deposit for the real estate. The contracts can be linked together with the use of the wording in Form 7:01. See page 253 for how to handle sales of mobilehomes placed upon a permanent foundation system.

FORM 7:01   SALE OF MOBILEHOME ON LEGAL LOT
AFTER LEGAL DESCRIPTION OF LOT
INSERT IN TERMS-OF-PAYMENT CLAUSE:

For purposes of this sale the sales price is allocated as follows:
$_____ for the real property $_____ for the mobilehome sold simultaneously herewith under that certain Mobilehome Purchase Contract and Receipt for Deposit executed by the parties hereto. Performance of the two contracts is concurrent and not severable.

COMMENT ON FORM 7:01: In most sales of legal lots and a mobilehome situated thereon, the purchase price may have to be allocated. This is particularly necessary if one part of the sales price is to be secured by the real property and another part to be secured by a loan on the mobilehome.

This clause is designed to be inserted in the Real Estate Purchase Contract and Receipt for Deposit. A similar nonseverable clause should be inserted in the Mobilehome Purchase Contract and Receipt for Deposit. The following wording can be used: "This contract is entered into simultaneously with that certain Real Estate Purchase Contract and Receipt for Deposit between the parties dated _____, 19_____. Performance of the two contracts is concurrent and not severable."

A real estate licensee is not permitted to sell a used mobilehome situated on a lot where its continued presence and use for human habitation would not be authorized for a total and uninterrupted period of at least one year. Many mobilehomes are presently situated illegally. Several counties have adopted very stringent regulations concerning mobilehome location outside of mobilehome parks.[1]

The Mobilehome Purchase Contract and Receipt for Deposit

CAR's Mobilehome Purchase Contract Receipt for Deposit looks familiar (see pp. 242, 243). Its style and most of its contents are similar to those of the real estate contract. However, the two contracts do differ significantly in the way they are to be prepared.

Initially, the contract is a unilateral offer from the buyer to purchase the described mobilehome on certain specific terms. With the seller's acceptance, a bilateral contract is created. When properly filled out, the form serves also as the final employment contract between the seller and the broker, fixing the exact amount due for the broker's service payable upon close of escrow.

The contract uses "the close of escrow" as definition of consummation rather than the recording of title or any other definition because of the closing procedures in mobilehome sales. For one thing, there is no recordation of a deed in the sale of a mobilehome. The security agreement need not be either recorded locally or filed with the Secretary of State. A seller who carries the loan or an institutional lender obtains "legal owner" status by an endorsement of the Certification of Ownership. Also, it is often difficult to determine the exact day of the transfer. Some transactions are considered "closed" when the lender obtains special power of attorney from both parties to sign the HCD papers. These documents include an authorization prepared by the seller to pay off the existing loan, if any. If the transaction is handled in escrow, the method is similar.

Under the terms of the CAR mobilehome contract, the sale is consummated at close of escrow when the funds, including the commission to the broker, can be disbursed.

The Real Estate Commissioner has adopted regulations which spell out the real estate broker's duty to deliver the necessary documentation and fees to the Department of Housing Development.[2]

Filling in the Form

One of the advantages of the CAR form is that it provides an excellent checklist to keep the salesperson from overlooking important items. The 1978 version has minor changes but important practical improvements. Let's examine the contract point by point (refer to form on pp. 242, 243):

(A) Insert the name of the city where the buyer actually signs the offer to purchase. In inserting the date, do not abbreviate.

(B) The full name (a) of the person(s) receiving the receipt for deposit, which is incorporated in the offer to purchase, should be spelled correctly. Designations such as "husband and wife," "unmarried woman," and so forth may be valuable for identification.

(C) The amount of the deposit should be written in both words and figures in the appropriate space.

If the deposit is a postdated check, the seller should be alerted to this fact. Authorization to hold it until the date indicated should be written into the contract. A broker who fails to fill in this section carefully or to handle the deposit in accordance with the Real Estate Commissioner's regulations may be subject to disciplinary action.

The purchase price offered should be written in both words and figures in the spaces provided. If a different price is later negotiated, changes should never be made on the face of the contract, but should be handled as indicated in the discussion of counter-offers in Chapter 6.

(D) There is sufficient space to insert a street address when a mobilehome is located on a lot which is not in a park. In that event, strike the words "Mobilehome Park, Space No. _____." If a legal description is necessary, attach a separate piece of paper and incorporate the description thereon in the contract by inserting after the printed words "situated at . . ." the phrase "as shown in Exhibit 'A' attached hereto and incorporated herein by reference."

The mobilehome should be described with sufficient particularity so that it can be readily identified. The form gives adequate space for inserting most of the characteristics of the mobilehome. The real estate licensee should be particularly careful to insert all the information suggested by the form.

Serial numbers for each utility and crossover side (X and XX) side should be located and listed. Beware if you cannot find the HCD tab, a requirement on all units for human habitation since 1958. Check with the HCD which will make an inspection for a fee.

Mobilehomes come with certain required equipment: furnace, water heater, gas and electric equipment, range and oven. A Department of Housing insignia is required and no alterations that do not comply with HDC regulations are permitted. The form includes the above-named appliances as standard equipment but calls for the enumeration of other appliances which may be present and part of the sale. The licensee should be careful to list these items since the seller may exclude an unlisted item from the sale. Some of the more common improvement accessories, such as carport awning, patio awning, porch, and screen room, should be shown with sizes. If additional personal property is included in the purchase price, attach an initialed inventory thereof and incorporate in the supplement paragraphs and have buyer initial its inclusion.

Terms of Sale

1. Paragraph 1 is the nearly all-inclusive basic terms-of-sale clause. As with the sale of real estate, most of the broker's problems arise here. This is the place for setting forth any terms and conditions of a factual nature applicable to this sale, such as financing, prior sale of other property, and the repairs and personal property to be included in the sale.

This statement on the form will serve as a practical checklist of the items mentioned. If the space is insufficient for listing all factual terms of the sale, add an addendum, attach it firmly to the contract, and incorporate it in the contract by a reference such as, "See attached addendum Exhibit 'A,' which is part of this contract." The rider should be initialed by both parties to insure its authenticity. As with real estate contracts, extensive riders should be avoided.

CALIFORNIA ASSOCIATION OF REALTORS® STANDARD FORM

MOBILEHOME PURCHASE CONTRACT AND
RECEIPT FOR DEPOSIT

(Mobilehome Registered at Least One Year Under Vehicle Code Div. 3
or Part 2 of Division 13 of Health & Safety Code)
THIS IS MORE THAN A RECEIPT FOR MONEY. IT IS INTENDED TO BE A LEGALLY BINDING CONTRACT. READ IT CAREFULLY.

_____ , California _____ , 19 _____

Received from _____

herein called Buyer, the sum of _____ Dollars $ _____

evidenced by cash ☐, cashier's check ☐, or _____ ☐ personal check ☐ payable to _____

_____ , to be held uncashed until acceptance of this offer, as deposit on account of purchase price of

_____ Dollars $ _____

for the purchase of mobilehome situated at _____

County of _____ , California in _____

Mobilehome Park, Space # _____ , described as follows: Make _____

Model _____ Year _____ Net Length _____ Expando _____ Width _____

Serial #'s:		CAL. HCD #'s:	HUD #'s:	19	License #'s:
_____	U (A)	_____	_____		_____
_____	X (B)	_____	_____		_____
_____	XX (C)	_____	_____		_____
_____	XXX (D)	_____	_____		_____

together with all built-in appliances, heating units and water heater and the following additional equipment:

_____

_____

_____

_____

1.   Buyer will deposit in escrow with _____ the balance of purchase price as follows:

_____

_____

_____

_____

_____

_____

_____

(Set forth above any terms and conditions of this sale, such as financing, repairs and personal property to be included in the sale.)

2.   Deposit will ☐ will not ☐ be increased by $_____ to $_____ within _____ days of acceptance of this offer.

3.   The supplements initialed below are incorporated as part of this agreement.   Other

_____ HCD certification of purchase price   _____ Occupancy Agreement   _____   _____

_____ Structural Pest Control Certification Agreement   _____ VA Amendment   _____   _____

_____ Special Studies Zone Disclosure   _____ FHA Amendment   _____   _____

4.   Buyer and Seller acknowledge receipt of a copy of this page, Page 1 of   Pages.

X _____   X _____
   BUYER   SELLER

X _____   X _____
   BUYER   SELLER

THIS STANDARDIZED DOCUMENT FOR USE IN SIMPLE TRANSACTIONS HAS BEEN APPROVED BY THE CALIFORNIA ASSOCIATION OF REALTORS® IN FORM ONLY. NO REPRESENTATION IS MADE AS TO THE APPROVAL OF THE FORM OF SUPPLEMENTS, THE LEGAL VALIDITY OF ANY PROVISION OR THE ADEQUACY OF ANY PROVISION IN ANY SPECIFIC TRANSACTION. IT SHOULD NOT BE USED IN COMPLEX TRANSACTIONS OR WITH EXTENSIVE RIDERS OR ADDITIONS.

For these forms, address California Association of Realtors
525 So. Virgil Avenue, Los Angeles, California 90020
(Revised 1982)   FORM.MHD-11-1

MOBILEHOME PURCHASE CONTRACT AND RECEIPT FOR DEPOSIT
The following terms and conditions are hereby incorporated in and made a part of Buyer's Offer

5.   Title is to be free of liens, encumbrances, recorded, filed or registered, or known to seller except as set forth above.

6.   Unless otherwise designated in the escrow instructions of Buyer, title shall vest as follows: _____

(The manner of taking title may have significant consequences. Therefore, give this matter serious consideration.)

7.   Evidence of title shall be in form of a duly endorsed, dated and delivered Certificate of Ownership and delivery of current Registration Certificate, as required by the law. If seller fails to deliver title as herein provided, Buyer may terminate this agreement and the deposit shall thereupon be returned to Buyer.

8.   Buyer acknowledges that present or any future movement of the mobilehome may be limited by law and is subject to the regulations current at that time by the Department of Transportation.

9.   Buyer acknowledges that Seller hereby is not assigning or subletting the space the mobilehome occupies in its present location unless such letting is specifically made part of this agreement. If the described mobilehome is located in a mobilehome park in which it is to remain, the buyer by his signature below represents that he has agreed to the terms of a rental agreement for the space involved.

10.   Possession shall be delivered to Buyer (a) on close of escrow, or (b) not later than _____ days after closing escrow, or (c) _____

11.   Escrow instructions signed by Buyer and Seller shall be delivered to the escrow holder within _____ days from the Seller's acceptance hereof and shall provide for closing within _____ days from the Seller's acceptance hereof, subject to written extensions signed by Buyer and Seller.

12.   If the mobilehome is destroyed or materially damaged prior to close of escrow, then, on demand by Buyer, any deposit made by Buyer shall be returned to Buyer and this contract thereupon shall terminate.

13.   If Broker is a participant of a Board multiple listing service ("MLS"), the Broker is authorized to report the sale, its price, terms and financing for the information, publication, dissemination, and use of the authorized Board members.

14.   **If Buyer fails to complete said purchase as herein provided by reason of any default of Buyer, Seller shall be released from the obligation to sell the mobilehome to Buyer and may proceed against Buyer upon any claim or remedy which Seller may have in law or equity provided, however, that by placing their initials here Buyer: ( ) Seller: ( ) agree that Seller shall retain the deposit as Seller's liquidated damages, and that it would be impractical or extremely difficult to fix the actual damages suffered because of such default; that the amount paid by Buyer as deposit constitutes a reasonable estimate and agreed stipulation of such damages.**

15.   If the only controversy or claim between the parties arises out of or relates to the disposition of the Buyer's deposit, such controversy or claim shall, at the election of the parties, be decided by arbitration in accordance with the Rules of the American Arbitration Association, and judgment upon the award rendered by the Arbitrator(s) may be entered in any court having jurisdiction thereof. The provisions of Code of Civil Procedure Section 1283.05 shall be applicable to such arbit

16.   In any action or proceeding arising out of this agreement, the prevailing party shall be entitled to reasonable attorney's fees and costs.

17.   Time is of the essence. All modifications or extensions shall be in writing signed by the parties.

18.   This constitutes an offer to purchase the described mobilehome. Unless acceptance is signed by Seller and the signed copy delivered to Buyer, in person or by mail to the address below, within _____ days, this offer shall be deemed revoked and the deposit shall be returned. Buyer acknowledges receipt of a copy hereof.

Real Estate Broker _____   Buyer _____

By _____   _____

Address _____   Address _____

Telephone _____   Telephone _____

ACCEPTANCE

The undersigned Seller accepts and agrees to sell the mobilehome on the above terms and conditions. Seller has employed _____

_____ as Broker(s) and agrees to pay for services the sum of

_____ Dollars ($ _____), payable as follows:

(a) On close of escrow, or (b) if completion of sale is prevented by default of Seller, upon Seller's default or (c) if completion of sale is prevented by default of Buyer, only if and when Seller collects damages from Buyer, by suit or otherwise and then in an amount of one-half of the damages recovered, but not to exceed the above fee after first deducting escrow expenses and the expenses of collection, if any. In any action between Broker and Seller arising out of this agreement, the prevailing party shall be entitled to reasonable attorney's fees and costs. The undersigned acknowledges receipt of a copy and authorizes Broker(s) to deliver a signed copy to Buyer. Page 2 of _____ Pages.

Dated: _____ Telephone _____   Seller _____

Address _____   Seller _____

Broker (s) agree to the foregoing. Broker _____   Broker _____

Dated: _____ By _____   Dated: _____ By _____

For these forms, address California Association of Realtors®
525 So. Virgil Avenue, Los Angeles, California 90020
(Revised 1982)   **FORM MHD-11-2**

Again, the word "financing" in the contract stands for "terms of payment." Here the broker must be extremely careful to set forth the terms with certainty. If material elements are left to verbal agreement or future negotiations, no enforceable contract is created.

Financing

The financing of mobilehomes is different from the financing of real estate. New mobilehomes are often sold on conditional sales contracts. Most used mobilehomes, however, are sold with direct loans. At present, most lenders require a minimum down payment of 15 percent and a security agreement and promissory note executed by the buyer. The lender is then known as the "legal owner" and buyer is designated as the "registered owner" on the certificate of ownership. A junior loan can also be recorded on the certificate of ownership as a security interest after filing a statement of lien with HCD.

Some lenders, particularly credit unions, make nonvariable-interest mobilehome loans at simple interest. In such a situation, the drafter should fill in the terms-of-payment clause of the purchase contract in the usual way. See Form 7:02.

FORM 7:02   NEW LOAN ON MOBILEHOME
(Simple interest)

$_____ cash including above deposit.

$_____ as loan proceeds conditioned upon buyer's ability to obtain a loan in that amount secured by a security agreement on the subject mobilehome, payable in monthly installments of $_____ including interest at _____% per annum. Prepayment penalty not to exceed six months interest."

COMMENT ON FORM 7:02: The loan described here is not the most common type of loan on mobilehomes, but it is, of course, the most advantageous type. Private lenders including sellers sometimes make this type of loan.

As more lenders get into the act of financing mobilehomes, we can expect that the use of simple interest loans will prevail, probably with a variable-interest-rate feature. In such cases, the terms-of-payment clause can be written as in Form 7:03:

FORM 7:03   VARIABLE INTEREST LOAN

$_____ cash including above deposit.

$_____ as loan proceeds conditioned upon buyer's ability to obtain a variable interest loan in that amount secured by a security agreement on subject mobilehome, payable in monthly installments of $_____ including interest at close of escrow of _____% per annum."

COMMENT ON FORM 7:03: As variable interest loans become more common in real estate transactions, we can expect that they will also be in the mobile-home field.

**FORM 7:04   LOAN ON REAL ESTATE INCLUDED
IN SALE OF MOBILEHOME**

$_____ as loan proceeds conditioned upon buyer's ability to obtain a new first _____ loan in that amount secured by the above-described real

type

property, payable at $_____ _____

monthly/quarterly

_____ including interest at ____% per annum

semi-annually/annually

_____.

at close of escrow

COMMENT ON FORM 7:04: Many of the clauses shown in Chapter 3 can be adapted to use in a sale of a legal lot on which a mobilehome is situated.

New Forms and Laws

Revised versions of CAR's Mobilehome forms will be published in 1989. The contract will contain preprinted finance clauses and a general arbitration clause.

In 1988, several mobilehome bills became law. A Park management is now restricted from:

1. requiring a buyer to provide copies of personal income tax returns to obtain approval for residency;

2. charging a transfer, selling fee, or residence fee as a condition of sale of a mobilehome or for approval of residency;

3. demanding more than 2 months rent as deposit for initial occupancy. At the end of 12 consecutive months of prompt payment the deposit must be refunded;

4. prohibiting a mobilehome owner from listing the home with an agent other than management or require the homeowner list with management as a condition for approval of the buyer or for residency in the park.

FORM 7:05   **ADD-ON INTEREST LOAN**

_____ cash including above deposit.

$_____ as loan proceeds conditioned upon buyer's ability to obtain a loan providing such proceeds secured by a security agreement on the subject home, payable in _____ monthly installments including a Finance Charge at the Annual Percentage Rate of _____%. Precomputed interest refunded if loan is prepaid in full based upon the rule of 78's.

Buyer shall pay Use Tax of $_____ and HCD transfer fees of $_____ _____.

COMMENT ON FORM 7:05: Add-on interest loans are not very common in the sale of mobilehomes. VA loans for mobilehomes are authorized to veterans who have not used any of their available loan guaranty entitlement. The interest rate on such financing is different from that on conventional home loans. Specific information and required clauses can be obtained from lenders.

Junior Loans

With the change from DMV to HCD mobilehome owners also were afforded the opportunity to create secondary financing on their homes. Previously no method existed whereby a junior encumbrance could be recorded secured by a mobilehome.

Where a buyer is to take title subject to or assume an existing loan and seller is to take back a second loan the contract clause can read as in Form 7:06.

FORM 7:06   **ASSUMPTION OF LOAN AND**
                        JUNIOR LIEN TO SELLER

$_____, conditioned upon buyer's ability to
         balance of loan

_____ the existing first loan with an unpaid
       take title subject to/assume

balance in that approximate amount payable over a remaining term of approximately _____ at _____
          _____ months/years   amount of periodic payment

_____ including interest at _____%.
     monthly/quarterly

$_____ by buyer executing a note and a security agree-
     amount seller to carry

ment in that amount in favor of seller secured by the mobilehome and registered as a lien junior only to the legal owner of record with HCD on the Certificate of

Ownership, payable in equal _____ installments of $_____,
monthly/quarterly
or more, including interest at _____% per annum.

(Optional)

due in full _____ .
_____ months/_____ years from close of escrow.

COMMENT ON FORM 7:06: In the sale of mobilehomes the security agreement is not "recorded" by filing an UCC-Financing Statement with the Secretary of State. The first lender is always the "legal owner", the buyer the "registered owner", a holder of a second or third interest in the mobilehome is a "junior lienholder." By filing with HCD on a prescribed form called "Statement of Lien" a junior lien holder and the registered owner request that the Department "record and rank, in priority of receipt" the lien as a security interest following the legal owner of record. The Statement of Lien form is forwarded to HCD together with the registered owner's copy of the last issued registration card and the appropriate fee.

A seller of a mobilehome will, unless owning it free and clear, not be in possession of the "pink slip." The seller's copy of the Certificate of Ownership, also called the "Registration Card" may not carry the latest information of existing liens. A careful broker should therefore insist that escrow obtain an "Information/Title Search." Most title companies and escrow companies have an information account with HCD and can get the relevant information by telecopier.

Approval of Buyer as Tenant

If the seller is to make any repairs of the mobilehome before transfer of title, such repairs should be noted in the contract. If the home is located in a mobilehome park, Form 7:07 is recommended.

FORM 7:07   APPROVAL OF BUYER AS TENANT

This offer is subject to buyer's approval of the rental agreement for the space involved within _____ days of seller's acceptance. If not disapproved in writing within such time this condition shall be deemed waived and Buyer shall deliver to escrow an executed rental agreement.

Buyer acknowledges that Park Management has a right to prior approval of Buyer as tenant. Disapproval shall terminate this agreement and cause return of the deposit.

COMMENT ON FORM 7:07: The sale of a mobilehome does not automatically transfer to the buyer the right to become a tenant in the mobilehome park where it is located. However, many protective laws are now on the books. The broker should arrange for the park management to meet the prospective buyer and approve the buyer as a potential tenant in the park.

Taking Title

The seller must deliver clear title. At the time of the making of the offer and when it is presented to the owner, there may be some outstanding liens. The original dealer may have a conditional sales contract, which may have been assigned to a financial institution. An escrow company will be able to ascertain the liens and any delinquent fees.

Under Section 18080 of the Health & Safety Code, co-ownership title to a mobilehome may be taken as follows:

18080.   Ownership registration and title to a manufactured home, mobilehome, or commercial coach subject to registration may be held by two or more coowners as follows:

(a) A manufactured home, mobilehome, or commercial coach may be registered in the names of two or more persons as joint tenants. Upon the death of a joint tenant the interest of the decedent shall pass to the survivor or survivors. The signature of each joint tenant or survivor or survivors, as the case may be, shall be required to tranfer or encumber the title to the manufactured home, mobilehome, or commercial coach.

(b) A manufactured home, mobilehome, or commercial coach may be registered in the names of two or more persons as tenants in common. If the names of the tenants in common are separated by the word "and", each tenant in common may transfer his or her individual interest in the manufactured home, mobilehome, commercial coach, or truck camper without signature of the other tenant or tenants in common. However, the signature of each tenant in common shall be required to transfer full interest in the title to a new registered owner. If the names of the tenants in common are separated by the word "or", any one of the tenants in common may transfer full interest in the title to the manufactured home, mobilehome, commercial coach, or truck camper to a new registered owner without the signature of the other tenant or tenants in common. The signature of each tenant in common is required in all case to encumber the title to the manufactured home, mobilehome, or commercial coach.

(c) A manufactured home, mobilehome, commercial coach, or truck camper may be registered as community property in the names of a husband and wife. The signature of each spouse shall be required to transfer or encumber the title to the manufactured home, mobilehome, commercial coach, or truck camper.

(d) All manufactured homes, mobilehomes, commercial coaches, or truck campers registered, on or before January 1, 1985, in the names of two or more persons as tenants in common, as provided in subdivion (b) shall be considered to be the same as if the names of the tenants in common were separated by the word "or", as provided in subdivision (b).

The broker should insert the exact manner in which buyer wishes to take title.

Moving a Mobilehome

The buyer acknowledges that any future moving of the mobilehome is subject to regulations of the Department of Transportation. The local California Highway Patrol office can give current information. The broker should be particularly careful about making any representations concerning this matter. If the mobilehome is later to be moved, the buyer should have an opportunity to have a licensed transporter or specialty contractor familiar with such matters examine the unit before close of escrow. Form 7:08 contains a proposed clause for specifying such a condition.

FORM 7:08   MOVING A MOBILEHOME

This offer is subject to inspection by buyer's authorized agents of the mobilehome to determine the feasibility of its towing to a new location. Buyer may terminate this agreement if the inspection discloses conditions unsatisfactory to the buyer. If notice of such disapproval has not been delivered in person or in writing to the seller within _____ days of date of seller's acceptance, this condition shall be deemed waived. Any removal of the mobilehome shall be at buyer's expense and risk.

COMMENT ON FORM 7:08: This clause permits the buyer to have the mobilehome inspected to ascertain if it can be moved. Real Estate licensee's should recognize their limitations on sale of mobilehomes which will affect a sale of a mobilehome to be moved.

Where the buyer has had the mobilehome inspected and is satisfied that he or she wants to purchase it, the waiver in Form 7:08 should be incorporated in the contract.

Renting Space

Buyer acknowledges in the contract that the seller is not assigning any interest in the rental agreement with the park where the unit is situated. The buyer should, with the broker's help, make a separate arrangement with the park management. Such an arrangement should be made in writing, especially when an over-age unit (20 years old or 25 years old if manufactured after September 15, 1971) is involved.

The latest rules and regulations of the park should be delivered to the buyer and a receipt for them should be obtained. Mobilehome tenants are protected by specific park-tenant legislation.

Terms of Possession

When the terms of possession are left to future negotiations, trouble may arise. Terms should be specified in the contract. Possession on date of closing of escrow can be inconvenient for the owner. But if the seller is to remain in possession after closing, the broker should take care to use an "occupancy agreement after sale." The payment for the stipulated hold-over period can be adjusted in the sales price or the proration arrangement, or by fixing a per diem rate sufficient to encourage performance.

The Cut-off Date

The cut-off date called for in the contract is the date of seller's acceptance, so remember to date the acceptance clause on the line next to the seller's signature. This cut-off date also covers both the delivery date for escrow instructions and the closing date.

Risk of Loss

Under the provision of the form, destruction of the property at any time before close of escrow is the seller's risk.

Lenders require special types of insurance for their mobilehome loans. The broker should inquire into requirements of the particular lender and assist the buyer in obtaining the desired insurance. The licensee should also provide for cancellation of the owner's insurance in the escrow instructions. Mobilehome dealers usually do not prorate taxes or registration fees, and space rental is the practice when real estate licensees are involved in the sales.

Liquidation of Damages

The text of the liquidated-damage clause in the CAR mobilehome form is different from the real property sales form because the 3% of purchase price liquidated damages presumption does not apply to mobilehome sales.

As with the clause on the real property-sales form, the advantage of the CAR clause is that it gives the parties an option. Leaving the boxes in the clause empty abolishes the idea of liquidation of damages. The buyer, however, is warned by the terms of the contract that if he or she defaults, the seller is released from the obligation to sell the mobilehome to the buyer, and "may proceed against buyer upon any claim or remedy which he may have in law or equity." This warning by itself may be a deterrent against a reneging buyer.

The clause also aids the broker in explaining to a disappointed seller the rights of a buyer whose contract cannot be performed because of failure of a condition. The failure to perform must be "by reason of any default of buyer." Inability to obtain financing, if a condition of the contract, is not a "default," and the buyer is entitled to a return of his deposit.

The "Mode of Acceptance" Clause

The "mode of acceptance" clause declares that the offer is deemed "revoked" if the buyer does not receive a copy of the contract containing the signed acceptance of the offer by the seller within the prescribed time. This copy must be delivered in person or by mail.

This clause is an obvious protection for all parties. If, for example, a seller's absence from the place of negotiation will make strict compliance with the provisions of this clause impossible, the form should be adapted to the prevailing situation. Where acceptance may of necessity be by telegram, the following amendment of the clause can be made and initialed by the buyer: "Unless acceptance hereof (insert: 'by telegraph addressed to buyer and broker') signed by seller. . . ." At the end of the clause insert: "A copy of an acceptance hereof signed by seller shall be delivered to buyer in person or by mail within _____ days of the date of telegram."

Attorneys' Fees

In the event of dispute the contract provides that the prevailing party is entitled to reasonable attorneys' fees and costs.

"Time Is of the Essence" Clause

The form contains a time-is-of-the-essence clause. As in the property sales contract, the reason for this clause is to be certain the performance of any condition occurs on the time indicated, and not at some indefinite later date. All parties should agree on the contract to any necessary extensions of time.

Broker Information

(E) Insert the broker's name and the salesperson's signature, the office address, and telephone number. It may be practical to include a residence telephone number for the broker here.

The Buyer's Signature

(F) This is the space for the buyer's final offer and signature. The contract should be signed by all buyers unless one signer has a valid power of attorney. The buyer's home and business addresses and telephone numbers should appear on the contract to make it easier to deliver the copy of the signed acceptance.

The Seller's Acceptance

(G) The balance of the contract contains the acceptance provisions. This section contains blanks for inserting the names of cooperating brokers as well as the amount of brokers' commissions which are negotiable. See page 222.

If the listing agreement provides for specific terms for payment of the commission or for a different division of any retained deposit, this part of the acceptance clause should be deleted and the following phrase substituted: "and for the Broker(s) services agree to pay Broker(s) a commission [insert: in accordance with the Exclusive Listing Agreement dated _____, 19_____.].

Seller's and Buyer's Disclaimer

It is unlawful under the Health and Safety Code for an owner to modify the original equipment or the electrical and plumbing system of a mobilehome without using a licensed contractor authorized to perform such work. It is often impossible for a layperson to discover such modifications with the naked eye. Since it is illegal for a broker as well as a seller to sell such unlawfully modified units, some licensees attempt to limit their exposure to future liability by requiring seller and buyer to sign a separate document ascertaining that the seller has not violated the code and that the buyer releases the broker from liability. For such a disclaimer see Form 7:08.

FORM 7:09   SELLER'S WARRANTY, BUYER'S DISCLAIMER

This statement is part of the Mobilehome Purchase Contract and Receipt for Deposit between the parties hereto dated _____, 19_____ and incorporated therein for all purposes by this reference.

Seller warrants to buyer 1) that the mobilehome described in said Purchase Contract complies with the Health and Safety Code and has not been modified or changed in violation thereof; 2) that the mobilehome is either: a) located within an established mobilehome park as defined in Section 18214 of the Health and Safety Code and the sale is not contrary to any terms between seller and the mobilehome park owners, or (b) located pursuant to a local zoning ordinance or permit on a lot where its presence has been authorized or its continued presence and such use would be authorized for a total and uninterrupted period of at least one year; 3) that the mechanical equipment, electrical, gas and heating systems, and water and plumbing systems and all built-in appliances are and will at close of escrow be in good operating condition and that the roof is watertight.

Buyer acknowledges that:

In purchasing this property, buyer has made an independent inspection of the mobilehome and the park or lot on which it is located and is satisfied with regards thereto.

Buyer has not relied upon any representations of seller's agent and hereby releases the agent _____ Realty Company from any claim or demand including attorneys' fees which may arise from the subject transaction.

Seller _____   Buyer _____

Seller _____   Buyer _____

Dated _____ , 19_____   Dated _____ , 19_____

COMMENT ON FORM 7:09: The protection of such a waiver and warranty depends on the circumstances in each situation. The best protection for all parties is of course full disclosure and the absence of unsupported statements by seller or broker.

Mobilehomes on Foundations Are Real Property

As part of the reorganization package Section 18551 of the Health and Safety Code was amended and the new rules became operative July 1, 1980. This section provides for the placement of mobilehomes on foundation systems and requires specific fees, forms, documents and items to be used, transmitted and recorded in conjunction with the installation of mobilehomes on foundation systems. The Department of Health and Community Development's regulations supersede any ordinance enacted by any city or county applicable to mobilehome foundation systems. No local agency can require that any mobilehome currently on private property be placed on a permanent foundation system.

Unless a real estate licensee is also licensed as a mobilehome dealer it's unlikely that the licensee will be involved in the sale of a new or used mobilehome which is to be moved and placed on a foundation system. The licensee obviously can negotiate the sale of the lot or parcel, whereon the foundation is to be erected. Once placed upon a permanent foundation a mobilehome is real property and the real estate licensee can sell or finance it. The sale should be handled as all other real estate transactions except that it may be prudent to include in the Real Estate Purchase Contract and Receipt for Deposit the statement in Form 7:10.

FORM 7:10   MOBILHOME ON PERMANENT FOUNDATION WARRANTY

Seller warrants that the mobilehome has been installed on a foundation system in accordance with Health and Safety Code Section 18551 and regulations promulgated thereunder and that a Certificate of Occupancy has been duly issued and recorded.

COMMENT ON FORM 7:10: A title search will disclose the recording of the Certificate of Occupancy which is proof certain that the local enforcement agency has approved the installation. Once installed on a foundation system, a mobilehome is subject to state enforced Health and Safety standards for mobilehomes pursuant to Section 18040 of the Health and Safety Code.

More Affordable Housing

Two new additions to the Government Code should do much to create affordable housing through mobilehomes on foundation systems. Section 65852.3 reads:

A city, including a charter city, county, or city and county shall not prohibit the installation of mobilehomes certified under the National Mobile Home Construction and Safety Standards Act of 1974 (42 U.S.C. Section 5401, et seq.) on a foundation system, pursuant to Section 18551 of the Health and Safety Code, on lots zoned for single-family dwellings. However, a city, including a charter city, county, or city and county may designate lots zoned for single-family dwellings for mobilehomes as described in this section, which lots are determine to be compatible for such mobilehome use. A city, including a charter city, county, or city and county may subject any such mobilehome and the lot on which it placed to any or all of the same development standards to which a conventional single-family residential dwelling on the same lot would be subject, including, but not limited to, building setback standards, side and rear year requirements, standards for enclosures, access, and vehicle parking and architectural, aesthetic requirements, and minimum square footage requirements. However, any architectural requirements imposed on the mobilehome structure itself, exclusive of any requirement for any and all additional enclosures, shall be limited to its roof overhang, roofing material, and siding material. In no case may a city, including a charter city, county, or city and county apply any development standards which will have the effect of totally precluding mobilehomes from being installed as permanent residences.

Section 65852.7 follows up by declaring that a mobilehome park as defined, with certain limitations and subject to the requirements of a use permit is permitted use, on land planned and zoned for residential use. The law also permits any mobilehome park completed on or after January 1, 1982 to be constructed in a manner to allow mobilehomes sited in the park to be placed on foundation systems and would allow mobilehomes in such parks to be placed upon foundation systems. It also prohibits a city or county to require that the average density be less than that permitted by the zoning ordinance for other affordable housing or that a clubhouse or other recreational facilities be built in a mobilehome park if not required in developments containing a like number of dwelling units.

Seismic Safety of Mobilehomes

In the 1982 session of the California Legislature, Section 18613.5 was added to the Health and Safety Code which provides that purchasers of mobilehomes for human occupancy be offered earthquake-resistant bracing systems which meet generally accepted seismic safety standards. Form 7:11 is designed for use in a resale of a mobilehome fitted with such a bracing system.

FORM 7:11   MOBILEHOME BRACING SYSTEM WARRANTY

Seller represents that the subject mobilehome has been installed with an earthquake-resistant bracing system which has met the certification standards of the Department of Health and Community Development.

COMMENT ON FORM 7:11: Where a mobilehome is located in a Special Studies Zone area, earthquake-resistant bracing system is a precaution. If such system is not installed the real estate licensee should inform a buyer that such protection is available.

Check List for Mobilehome Sales

1. New mobilehomes sold by mobilehome dealers only.

2. Mobilehomes registered more than one (1) year under Vehicle Code or Health & Safety Code and located in a mobilehome park or lot where its continued presence and use is authorized for an uninterrupted one (1) year may also be sold by real estate licensees.

3. Use tax to be collected on all mobilehomes registered under Health & Safety Code.

4. "Gross Receipts" and "Sales Price" of a used mobilehome sold in California is based on the current value as set forth in an approved value guide. If the guide does not specify age, model and manufacturer, the actual sales price shall be used for use tax purposes.

5. Junior loan is secured by mobilehome through listing on Owner's Registration Certificate issued by Department of Housing and Community Development (HDC).

6. Mobilehomes affixed to permanent foundation is real estate and a real estate license is required to sell such mobilehomes as agent.

7. Mobilehomes subject to certain restrictions can be installed on permanent foundations on lots zoned for single resident occupancy.

8. Use Mobilehome Contracts for mobilehomes located in parks or on approved lots.

9. Use Real Estate Contracts when land is involved or mobilehome is affixed on permanent foundation.

The whole area of mobilehome law is subject to change as the attractions of mobilehome living continue to grow. A real estate licensee who wishes to engage in the business of selling used mobilehomes should obtain copies of all laws and regulations which have an impact on mobilehome sales. Mastery of the intricacies of the mobilehome business and a thorough knowledge of the laws which govern it are preconditions to success.

Chapter 8
Exchange Agreements

> ... *The advice I give you is not to convert the lands you now hold into cash faster than a certain prospect of vesting it in other lands more convenient requires of you. This will, in effect, exchange land for land, it being of no concern to you how much the money depreciates if you can get land of equal value to that you sell* ...
>
> George Washington in a
> letter to his Stepson
> J. P. Curtis[1]

A certain aura or mystique has always shrouded the concept of exchanging real property. While bartering and trading of commodities and services have been known and practiced for ages, the tax-free real estate exchange is a direct result of the capital gains tax laws. Washington and his stepson did not have to worry about such taxes. Nevertheless, the recommendation to exchange given by George Washington is as good today as it was when he told his stepson to take that route. Real property nowadays is exchanged rather than sold in order to avoid recognition of gain on the disposition of the property. If an owner sells property, a capital gain tax must be paid on the sale. This will result in having less funds with which to purchase other property. Should the owner decide to exchange the property, however, the entire value of the property can be reinvested in the new property.

Real estate exchanges are complex. Even the so called "simple" exchange improperly handled and documented can have disastrous tax results. The importance of having competent advice and counseling throughout the process from a knowledgeable real estate licensee, a real estate attorney and a tax accountant cannot be overestimated.

In this chapter, we will discuss the factual contractual aspects of exchanging. In most communities real estate exchange counselors can be found who often juggle multi-cornered exchanges involving properties in several states at once. Some professional exchangors have developed uncanny instincts for

matching properties and people. They are also very familiar with tax consequences of exchanges and are adept in negotiating with accountants and attorneys.

Exchanging is not for amateurs but it is one of the tools of the trade which
is available to all real estate licensees and they should all be thoroughly familiar
with it. The clauses collected in this chapter are designed to be used in connection with the CAR Exchange Agreement. Most of the clauses can be incorporated in other existing exchange forms, provided that they are properly adapted
and that conflicting printed clauses in the form are deleted.

In exchanging, the use of exact contracts, correct tax strategy and adequate escrow instructions are vitally important. Although a taxpayer's intent, in
terms of tax motive, is generally rejected by the Courts, the taxpayer's intent to
exchange has, in several cases, been determinative of the character of the transaction. Intent to exchange has also sometimes been found in the original agreement. Therefore, the mechanics of an exchange are as important as intent to
convince the tax authorities that a ''tax-free'' exchange was desired and not a
sale resulting in capital gains treatment. Exchange agreements and escrow instructions must stand the scrutiny of the parties' tax advisors as well as eagle-
eyed IRS auditors and perhaps the Courts. The agreements should be prepared
with the utmost care, and the procedure in closing the transaction should follow
the guidelines which have developed over the years from the various court
decisions. Real estate licensees should not be dispensing specific tax advice.
Generally speaking, property owners do not disclose to the exchangor every
aspect of the financial situation which may effect the tax outcome. In every
specific transaction it is important to interview skillfully and to obtain information and assistance from knowledgeable sources who are also advising the
parties.

This chapter should not be considered an isolated affair. The general text
treatments in the preceeding chapters apply to exchange contracts. Most of the
previously discussed clauses can be appropriately adapted to exchange agreements. They are therefore not repeated here. Instead, we will concentrate on the
aspects of contract writing which are peculiar to exchanges. See also Chapter 9.

Requirements of a "Tax-Free" Exchange

The ''Tax-Free'' Exchange is really not tax free. Rather it defers recognition of any gain to the time when the taxpayer sells the property acquired in the
exchange. In order to qualify as a ''tax-free'' exchange under IRC Section
1031, certain requirements must be satisfied. The property must have been held
for productive use in a trade or business, or for investment, and must be traded
solely for property of ''like kind'' to be held for either productive use in a
business or for investment. It cannot be property held primarily for sale, such as
real property held for sale by a real estate dealer. Real property, whether improved or unimproved, qualify as ''like kind.'' Any personal property involved
in a transaction must be isolated from the real property, or the personal property

will be treated as having been sold by the taxpayer rather than exchanged. A farm can be traded for a city apartment house, but if the farm contains the taxpayer's residence, that portion of the property constituting the residence will not qualify as a "tax-free" exchange. However, the residence may be exempt from taxation under another provision of the Internal Revenue Code, Section 1034, if the property the farm is exchanged for contains a new residence, or if the taxpayer acquires another residence either 24 months before or after the exchange.

If an exchange of property for other property of "like kind" is within the rule set forth above, and other "unlike" property or money is also received in the exchange, the gain, if any, is recognized but not in excess of the sum of the money and the fair market value of the other property received. Thus, the taxpayer in a "tax-free" exchange can have the gain recognized to the extent that "boot" is received. Where a taxpayer exchanges mortgaged real estate for other real estate in an otherwise "tax-free" exchange, the amount of the mortgage of which the taxpayer is relieved is treated as "boot." On the other hand, no gain would be recognized by the taxpayer if the mortgage on the property acquired in the exchange is either equal to or exceeds the mortgage on the property that the taxpayer is exchanging. Unless an exchange is structured properly, the taxpayer may be subjected to a recognized gain which could have been avoided had the transaction been cast in a different manner.

A serious tax consequence can occur when the taxpayer has taken substantial depreciation on the property that is being traded in and the property that is acquired is not depreciable, such as unimproved farm property. Here the taxpayer will recognize ordinary income to the extent that "depreciation recapture" exceeds the fair market value of the depreciable property received in the exchange. If the taxpayer has a loss, the transaction should be planned as a sale rather than an exchange. Under certain circumstances an owner of property may wish to avoid the tax-deferred status of an exchange. Therefore, transactions should be analyzed and a comparison made of the actual net tax savings which would be achieved by a "tax-free" exchange against the savings which would be realized by a taxable sale and a reinvesting in depreciable property.

Because of the rule of tax deferment upon the sale of a residence and the purchase or building of a new residence within 24 months, many people believe that a sale with immediate reinvestment in similar property will also qualify for tax deferment treatment. Even a sale of property held for investment or for productive use in the taxpayer's trade or business and a reinvestment of the proceeds in "like kind" property will *not* qualify as a "tax free" exchange. An exchange will qualify for no gains recognition only if the exchange is a reciprocal transfer of such properties, if it is documented correctly, and if it involves no "boot."

For more complex tax information concerning exchanges and the tax consequences thereof, the reader is referred to the many tax services or professionals available to investors.

Basic Exchanges

Once it has been determined that the tax advantages of the exchange route exceeds the sale and reinvestment method, the different ways of arranging an exchange can be explored.

The simplest type of exchange is a two-party or two-way exchange. Multiple exchanges are actually series of two-way exchanges. To find two property owners who wish just to "swap" is a rare event. Usually one of the parties does not want to keep the other's property but desires to either exchange it or "cash-it-out" and a three-party exchange is born.

From the tax point of view, exchanges break down into four basic types. They are:

1. The straight across two-party exchange of "like-kind" properties;
2. The simple three-way exchange (a two-way exchange with a cash-out);
3. A three-way exchange in which a purchase and sale occurs first before the two-way exchange;
4. The exchange of three or more properties.

Of course there are refinements and variations, but these usually are the four basic components. The real estate licensee's efforts are concentrated upon structuring the exchange so that the parties obtain the properties which they desire. The tax attorney or accountant follows the established tax guidelines for the basic types so that the transaction or the part or parts of the transaction which one or more of the parties intend to be a "tax-free" exchange, will, in fact, be so treated by the IRS "when the dust has settled."

Each party to an exchange may have different goals and tax problems. What may be a taxable sale to one party in a transaction may be a "tax-free" exchange to another. A real estate dealer may be excluded from "tax-free" benefits because the property is held for sale to customers, while an ordinary investor may be able to arrange a "tax-free" exchange with the dealer's property as a component to the transaction.

A simple three-way exchange consisting of a two-way exchange with a cash-out can be drawn on CAR's exchange agreement form. If more properties are involved, additional exchange agreements must be prepared separately and escrow instructions for the individual escrows prepared separately.

A simple three-way exchange with a cash-out has two components: (1) a straight forward two-way exchange which, if handled properly, qualifies for "tax-free" treatment under Section 1031 of the Internal Revenue Code; and (2) a taxable purchase and sale which must be kept completely separate in a different escrow, and for which a Real Estate Purchase Contract and Receipt For Deposit can be used and signed by the second party to the exchange as Seller, subject to acquiring it in the exchange.

The Goal Is Enforceable Exchange Agreements

The suggested methodology in the following clauses may momentarily confuse experienced exchangors because it is different from what has been taught in exchange courses in the past. Since a CAR's comprehensive form is available, the time has come to make the exchange contract process easier and more understandable to the participants in the transaction be it broker, owner or advisors. The goal is enforceable contracts of exchange which are not too dissimilar in their general terms to purchase contracts. Some of the clauses which follow could of course be preprinted in the form and their inclusion or exclusion be decided by marking of appropriate boxes. However, there are sound legal reasons why printed contractual forms should not be designed in this manner. As a general rule, the more any real estate agreement reflects the parties' *actual careful consideration* of a given problem, the greater will be the protection for the broker and the principal against a subsequent claim of misrepresentation or concealment. Excessive "boiler plate" clauses lead to litigation and create misunderstandings. The extra work of *writing* the contract is worth the effort. In order to dissect the exchange agreement into its separate parts, we will start with the beginning of first party's offer in an exchange, where the first party proposes to make a straight two-way exchange. All of the clauses up to and including Form 8:09 are part of the original offer and included in the exchange agreement. Some of the clauses are often found in a printed form but are included here in order to show the place where the suggested clauses fit into the form. CAR's form substitutes the principals names for the designations as first, second party.

FORM 8:01   THE BASIC TWO-WAY EXCHANGE (Parcel A)

First Party hereby offers to exchange the following described property, also designated as Parcel _____ situated in _____ County of _____ .

A
City

California:
DESCRIPTION:
(When Property A is exchanged free of loans, continue):
Subject to: Free and clear of encumbrances.

    (Where existing conventional loan is "assumed," continue):

Subject to:
    (1) Second party's ability to _____

take title subject to/assume the existing

_____ loan of record with an unpaid balance of approximately $_____

VIR

payable over a remaining term of approximately _____ at

years/months

(Form continues on next page)

$_____, _____, _____
amount of periodic payment   or more   monthly/quarterly/semiannually/annually

including interest at _____ ____%
                              (correct new interest rate)/not to exceed

per annum, _____.
              at close of escrow

(If Second Party is to assume, continue):

Second party agrees to execute lender's assumption agreement, if any, and pay an assumption fee not to exceed _____ .
                              $____/____ points

(Where second loan is involved, continue):

(2) Second party's ability to _____
                                    take title subject to/assume

the existing second loan of record with an unpaid balance of $_____, pay-able over a remaining term of approximately _____, _____ ,
                                                              years/months

at $_____ _____', ____
      amount of periodic payment   monthly/quarterly/semiannually/annually   or more

including interest at ____% per annum,

(If note contains "balloon" clause, continue):

due in full _____, 19_____. _____
                month   with a remaining balance payable of

_____.
   approximately $_____

(Optional continue):

Any adjustment in existing balances by obligatory payment will be made in escrow.

COMMENT ON FORM 8:01: This form contains three different situations common to most exchanges. If the property of the exchanging taxpayer (First Party) is not mortgaged, the first clause should be used. If the offer proposes that the second party is either to take title subject to or assume an existing loan, the second clause should be used. The "correct new interest rate" is the rate at which the exchangor knows that the lending institution will allow the loan to be assumed. When an additional existing second loan is to be assumed, the last clauses can be included.

When the existing mortgages are not to be assumed or taken subject to, but are to be paid off by the taxpayer before exchanging, they *need not be listed.* In such a situation, the first party is not offering the property subject to a loan. Its appearance in the contract is surplus and confusing. The existing encumbrance will, of course, show up on the preliminary title report if not reconveyed before the report is obtained. However, the First Party, by stating that the property is to be delivered "free and clear of encumbrances," is in fact agreeing to pay off the existing loan. By paying it off prior to the exchange a possible "boot" situation is also avoided.

The second half of the exchange concerns Parcel B Form: 8:02.

FORM 8:02   THE BASIC TWO-WAY EXCHANGE (Parcel B)

First party to assume existing loans for the following described property of _____ .
Second party, also designated as Parcel _____ situated in _____ ,
                                        B   City

County of _____ , California.
DESCRIPTION:

(When Parcel A is exchanged free of Loans, continue):

Free and Clear of Encumbrances.

(Where existing conventional loan is assumed, continue):

SUBJECT TO:
    (1) First Party's ability to _____
                                      take title subject to/assume

the existing first _____ loan of record with a balance in the approximate
                        VIR

amount of $ _____ payable over a remaining term of approximately
_____ at $ _____ , _____
        years/months   amount of periodic payment   or more
_____ including interest at
      monthly/quarterly/semiannually/annually
_____ per annum _____ at close of escrow.
  (correct new interest rate) not to exceed

(If First Party is to assume, continue):

First Party agrees to execute lender's assumption agreement, if any, and pay an assumption fee not to exceed _____ .
                                    $____/____ points

(Where second loan is involved, continue):

    (2) First Party's ability to _____ the
                                take title subject to/assume

existing second loan of record with an unpaid balance in approximate amount of
$____ , payable over a remaining term of approximately _____ , _____
                                              years/months

at $ _____ , _____ , _____
      amount of periodic payment   or more   monthly/
_____ including interest at _____% per annum,
  quarterly/semiannually/annually,

(Form continues on next page)

(If note contains "balloon" clause, continue):

due in full _____, 19_____, _____
                                                    with a remaining balance payable

_____.
        of approximately $_____

(Optional, continue):

A copy of the _____ and _____ have been exhibited
                    note/notes   first/second deed of trust
to and approved by the First Party.

(Optional, continue):
(Select one of the following clauses):

Any adjustment in existing balances by obligatory payment will be made in escrow.

Any adjustment in existing balances including reduction of principal through obligatory payments is to be made in the principal amount of the second loan to second party.

COMMENT ON FORM 8:02: The above clauses are identical to the clauses in Form 8:01 except that they are designed to cover the loan or loans, if any, the First Party proposes to assume or take title "subject to." See the comments on Form 8:01.

Forms 8:01 and 8:02 cover most situations, except where the second loan to be placed upon Second Party's property to assist in equalizing equities may be a new loan to be taken back by the Second Party. Form 8:03 is a second loan in favor of the Second Party. This clause can be used in connection with Form 8:02 where the first loan is being "assumed."

FORM 8:03   SECOND LOAN ON PARCEL B TO BE CARRIED BY SECOND PARTY

Subject to:

First party executing a note and _____
                                                    mortgage/Deed of Trust
in the amount of $_____ in favor of Second Party secured by Parcel B
payable in equal _____ installments of $_____
                      monthly/quarterly/semiannually/annual
_____, _____ interest at the rate of _____% per annum from
    or more   plus/including
date of closing.

(Limited installments and payoff within specified time continue):

due in full _____ from date of closing):
_____ months/_____ years

(If "acceleration" clause upon sale at holder's option, continue):

   and at holder's option in the event of sale or transfer of title to subject property.

(Optional):

Said note and _____ shall be drawn on
purchase money mortgage/deed of trust

the standard form _____ of _____ .
form no.   name of title company

COMMENT ON FORM 8:03: In California, a mortgage or deed of trust taken back by the Seller is by definition always a "purchase money" mortgage or deed of trust and subject to the antideficiency statutes. It is possible for the Second Party to finance Parcel B by a tax-deferring installment loan while the taxpayer makes a "tax-free" exchange of the equity in Parcel A for the equity above the loan taken back by the Second Party secured by Parcel B. Form 8:04 is an installment tax clause.

FORM 8:04 INSTALLMENT SALE TYPE LOAN ON PARCEL B

Subject to:
   First Party executing a note and Deed of Trust in the amount of $_____
___ in favor of Second Party secured by Parcel B, payable in equal _____
monthly/
_____ installments of $_____ _____
quarterly/semiannually/annual   plus/including
interest at the rate of _____% per annum from date of closing

(Where limited installments and payoff within specified time, continue):

due in full _____ from date of closing
_____ months/_____ years

(If "balloon" payment, continue):

with a final installment of approximately $_____ .

(Continue):

   Said note shall provide for interest payments only in the calendar year of the exchange and provide for statutory clauses for prepayment and late payments.

COMMENT ON FORM 8:04: See sections on tax installment sales prepayment and late charges in Chapter 3.

If the First Party is to qualify for new first loan to be obtained from lending institution and secured by Parcel B, Form 8:05 can be used.

FORM 8:05   NEW FIRST LOAN ON PARCEL B

Subject to Second Party's ability to obtain from _____
an institutional lender/

_____ or other source acceptable to Second Party a first _____ loan in
name of lender   type

the amount of $_____ secured by the Parcel _____ payable at $_____
                                                          B

_____ , including interest at the rate of ____%
monthly/quarterly/semiannually/annual

per annum _____ with a prepayment
              at close of escrow/and taxes and fire insurance

penalty not to exceed _____
                          _____% of original principal/_____ months unearned interest

Second Party to pay set-up charges not to exceed _____ .
                                                        $_____/_____ points

COMMENT ON FORM 8:05: The clause above can be used where the exact terms of the new loan are known based upon a prior commitment. "Institutional" or "conventional" lender may not include a pension fund or a Small Business Corporation, Credit Union, etc.

Forms 8:01 and 8:05 inclusive are the clauses which can be used in all two-way exchanges, which means that they are usable in all situations since multi-cornered exchanges are a series of two-way exchanges. However, in all exchanges beginning with the simplest three-way exchanges, some property has to be cashed out. In such situations Form 8:06 can be used.

FORM 8:06   CASH OUT

(When inserted in First Party's original offer, continue):

This exchange is conditioned upon

(When inserted in the acceptance counter proposal of Second Party of First Party's offer, continue):

The Second Party's acceptance hereof is conditioned upon

(continue in either situation):

(1) The sale by Second Party of _____
First Party's property/Parcel A

during the escrow period for not less than $_____ with a cash down
payment of not less than $_____ and subject to Buyer's ability to
year   VIR

obtain a new first _____ _____ loan of not less than $_____
type   year

secured by the property payable at no more than $_____, in _____
monthly/

_____ installments, including interest not to exceed
quarterly/semiannually/annually

_____% per annum _____
at close of escrow

(Optional)

and _____ to be amortized over not less than _____ years.
taxes and insurance

(Optional)

$_____ by Buyer executing a note and Deed of Trust in that amount
in favor of _____ secured by the property payable in
second party/private lender

in _____ installments of $_____, _____,
monthly/quarterly/semiannually/annual
or more

_____ at the rate of ____% per annum from date of closing.
including/plus interest

(Continue in all situations)

(2) That Second Party not be liable for any expense, prepayment penalties,
loan charges or commissions of any kind whatsoever in the resale of Parcel
_____, the property of First Party, who shall pay such expenses in cash in es-
A
crow.

COMMENT ON FORM 8:06: Where the exchangor knows that the owner of
Parcel B will not accept Parcel A, but will wish to cash out immediately, the
first optional clause is used. If the Second Party, when the offer is presented,
counters with a cash out the alternative wording is inserted in the counter offer.
Often the Second Party is willing to assist in financing of the cash out. The
clause provides for such possibility. Of course if the Second Party is to carry the
first loan, an appropriate provision from Chapter 3 can be adapted.

Usually the Second Party, who only takes title to Parcel A for minutes,
does not want to take any responsibility for such resale. A hold harmless clause
may already be in the printed form, if not, Form 8:07 can be inserted.

FORM 8:07   **HOLD HARMLESS PROVISION**

First Party agrees to hold Second Party harmless from, and on account of, any loss or damage sustained by Second Party as a result of any warranty and representation made by him to the purchaser of First Party's property in reliance upon First Party's representations and warranties to Second Party either by this agreement or in any statement made or document delivered to escrow holder or purchaser.

COMMENT ON FORM 8:07: In the resale of Parcel A it is important that no other representations be made than those which the taxpayer owning Parcel A made to induce the owner of Parcel B to make the exchange. The ultimate buyer of Parcel A should be treated as any other buyer and the contract for purchase contain such protective clauses as is appropriate. If the resale is handled with integrity and all appropriate disclosures are made, the hold harmless clause may never have to be invoked. CAR's form contains an extensive hold harmless clause.

FORM 8:08   **REAL ESTATE LICENSEE BUYING
                      "CASH OUT" PROPERTY**

In order to facilitate the exchange between First Party and Second Party, both parties hereby agree that _____ may
                                           name of real estate licensee or company
acquire Parcel _____ from Second Party as a principal buying the property
                   A
for _____ own account for occupancy, investment or possible resale. Such
      his/her
purchase shall not change the relationship between the parties and the agent nor
affect _____ rights to commissions in the
            name of real estate licensee or company
exchange.

COMMENT ON FORM 8:08: Sometimes the only way a three-way exchange or a multiple-property exchange can be closed is for the real estate licensee involved to purchase one of the properties. In such case, the above agreement should be dated and signed by all parties to the exchange. Such an agreement will not protect the licensee who obtains a ''secret profit'' by an immediate resale to a purchaser with whom the licensee negotiated during the exchange period.

Exchange for "Suitable Property"

When the exchange property has not been located, many property owners are locked into their property because they have exhausted their depreciation and cannot afford to make an outright sale. Such property owners are often resigned to keep the property while secretly harboring a desire for acquiring another type of property. Owners of unimproved land have similar tax problems. Such owners are reluctant to make offers for exchange in order not to "cheapen" the value of their holdings. Whether or not there is validity to this judgment, this attitude makes a satisfactory transaction more difficult. Often, however, such taxpayers' dilemma comes to light when a very advantageous offer to purchase is presented, which the taxpayer would like to accept but, cannot because of the tax consequences. The situation can be analyzed as follows:

Taxpayer owns Parcel A;

B wants to purchase Parcel A for cash or acceptable terms;

Taxpayer is unwilling and unable to sell Parcel A outright, but desires to acquire other property in lieu of Parcel A.

The following solutions can be suggested:

1. B can make a firm offer to buy Parcel A, allowing the taxpayer time (3 to 6 months) to locate suitable property and the transaction can close by (a) owner of suitable property to accept Parcel A in trade and "cash out" Parcel A to B, or (b) B can purchase the suitable property and take Parcel A in trade.

Usually B will insist that if the taxpayer has not located suitable property within the time limit agreed upon, the taxpayer will be obligated to sell Parcel A outright to B.

2. Taxpayer can give B an option to exchange Parcel A. Upon the exercise of the option, the taxpayer has an agreed upon time to locate suitable property, and the transaction can close in the manner set forth in 1(a) or (b) above. The option for exchange may provide that if suitable property is not found within the agreed time limit, it becomes an option to purchase.

In either of the above situations the transactions must be carefully structured and documented. No shortcuts or improper sequence of depositing of funds or closing of escrows are advisable. The IRS will attempt to sever the transaction into its components to find a sale rather than an exchange. If the exchange agreement provides for an alternative outright sale of Parcel A to B, and the exchange escrow closed later than the cut off date for the alternative sale, the transaction may be deemed a sale. This contention would arise from the fact that once the cut off date has passed, the taxpayer is obligated to make an outright sale of Parcel A to B and accept cash from B rather than suitable property. Therefore the exchange escrow *must* be closed before the cut-off day. If not, the contract must be modified prior to the time the taxpayer, under the original agreement, is obligated to sell Parcel A for cash.

Another trap for the unwary can occur if taxpayer receives, either directly or constructively, any cash or the right to receive cash other than what is expected as cash "boot." Separate escrows should be maintained and transfers of funds from escrow to escrow made only on written letter of demand.

The taxpayer himself may locate the parcel of "suitable property" for which he is willing to exchange Parcel A. He should not, however, enter into negotiations between B and and the owner of the "suitable property" or sign any agreements which obligate him to purchase the property. The taxpayer must avoid being characterized as "agent" for B. In the "cash out" situation in a three-way exchange, the taxpayer should also not enter into any formal or informal agreements with the ultimate buyer of Parcel A, but strictly limit his negotiations to the owner of Parcel B, the property he wishes to acquire in the exchange. The taxpayers counsel and tax advisor should examine the exchange agreements, deposit receipts, and so on, eliminate any language which is incorrect, or cancel such agreements and prepare new exchange agreements which clearly will support the intent to create a "tax-free" exchange.

Form 8:09 is an agreement by which the taxpayer agrees to exchange Parcel A for "suitable property" to be acquired by B, providing alternatively that if such property is not found within the agreed upon time, Parcel A will be sold to B outright.

FORM 8:09   EXCHANGE OR SALE AGREEMENT
(Preceed with Form 8:01 continue):

For the following described property of _____ Second Party, also
insert name
designated as Parcel ____ situated in _____ County of _____
_____, California.

It is First Party's intent and preference to exchange rather than sell Parcel A for other property of a similar kind. Therefore, Second Party agrees that First Party shall have until _____ to locate and notify Second
day before escrow to close
Party in writing of such other suitable property which will be acceptable to First Party in exchange for Parcel A. In the event of such notification Second Party shall enter into a separate Purchase Agreement and Escrow with the owner of such Parcel, designated as Parcel B, for the purchase of Parcel B. Second party shall close the escrow with Owner of Parcel B, only if all of the following conditions have been met:

1. The Purchase price for Parcel B is acceptable to First Party.

2. The purchase price of Parcel B is payable in the following manner: (designate).

3. The total transaction-expenses, escrow, title and recording fees to Second Party do not exceed $_____.

4. The owner of Parcel B executes a CAR Real Estate Purchase Contract and Receipt for Deposit which incorporates the provisions hereof.

5. The closing of the escrow with the owner of Parcel B is made contingent upon the concurrent closing of the escrow provided for by this agreement.

(When unequal exchange value, continue):

For purposes of the exchange the value of Parcel A is as follows:
Agreed value $ _____
Encumbrance $ _____
Equity $ _____
First Party shall pay Second Party through the escrow provided for herein, at close of escrow in cash an amount equal to the difference, if any, between the exchange value of Parcel A and the cost of Parcel B to Second Party together with all transaction-costs such as escrow fees, title insurance premiums and recording fees.

(Alternative Sales Provision, continue):

If this transaction is not concluded as an exchange on or before the date provided for herein, First Party shall promptly convey Parcel A to Second Party on the following terms and conditions: (insert Sales terms and type of loan, etc.).

COMMENT ON FORM 8:09: This is an agreement for a tentative exchange for property to be located, and contains alternative sales agreement in the event the exchange fails. The alternative sale can be evidenced by a fully filled in Real Estate Purchase Contract and Receipt for Deposit attached to the Exchange Agreement by inserting the following: "As set forth in the attached Real Estate Purchase Contract and Receipt for Deposit which shall be deemed executed upon the date following the day First Party's right to locate property for exchange expired."

It is important that the parties agree that they will cancel or modify any previous agreements which may jeopardize a "tax-free" exchange. See form 8:12

Some exchangors include a "value clause" in all exchanges to show how equities are balanced.

Other Terms and Conditions of Exchanges

Usually in broker forms provisions, in the printed part includes escrow, prorations, title and title insurance clauses. Of course, the contract should, in appropriate situations, contain protective clauses with regard to inspection of books, units and warranties of no notice of violations, or of no offsets available to the tenants. Such clauses are found in Chapter 4 and are therefore not repeated here.

Since it will be cumbersome to amend the Structural Pest Control Certification agreement for exchange use, the following clause can be used either in the contract or as a separate supplement incorporated in the contract by reference Form 8:10.

FORM 8:10   STRUCTURAL PEST CONTROL CERTIFICATION
AGREEMENT FOR EXCHANGES

This Agreement is part of and is hereby incorporated in the Exchange Agreement between the parties hereof dated _____, 19_____, pertaining to the property described as follows:

PARCEL A:

Description

PARCEL B:

Description

A. _____ shall at _____ expense provide
      First Party/Second Party/Each Party   his/her
_____ within _____ days from date of Second
      First Party/Second Party/the other
Party's approval hereof with a current written inspection report from a licensed structural pest control operator of the main building and all attached structures.

B. All work recommended in the report to:
  1. Repair damage caused by infestation or infection of wood-destroying pests or organisms found; and
  2. To correct infestation or conditions that caused such infestation or infection; and
  3. To repair plumbing leaks affecting wood members, shall be done at the expense of the party conveying the property.

C. Any work recommended to correct conditions usually deemed likely to lead to infestation or infection of wood-destroying pests or organisms, but where no evidence of existing infestation or infection is found with respect to such conditions, is *not* the responsibility of the party conveying property, but shall, if required by lender be at the expense of the party acquiring it.

D. If it is recommended in the report that inaccessible areas be inspected, such inspection and repair to entry of the inaccessible area, if no damage is found, shall be at the acquiring party's expense. Otherwise responsibility for repair of damage or correction of conditions found shall be subject to the provisions of B and C above.

The structural pest control operator shall deliver to the party entitled thereto a certification that the property acquired in the exchange is at the day of the report or of the Notice of Work Completed free of active infestation or infection of wood-destroying pests or organisms.

_____ , California   _____ , California
_____ , 19____   _____ , 19____

First Party: Second Party:

_____   _____

_____   _____

COMMENT ON FORM 8:10: The regular Structural Pest Control Certification Agreement may need so many changes in an exchange situation that the above simplified form is suggested. It can be used whether only one or both of the parcels is to be inspected by inserting the appropriate wording as indicated. For additional information or for clauses limiting responsibilities to specific dollar amounts, see Chapter 4.

The form should be attached to the offer and indicated in the supplement clause of the exchange agreement. It should be signed by the first party at the time of the offer. The second party, if approving the terms of the agreement, will sign when the exchange offer is approved.

FORM 8:11 INTENT TO EXCHANGE

It is the intention of the parties hereto that the mutual conveyances agreed to herein shall qualify as an "exchange" within the meaning of Section 1031 of the Internal Revenue Code of 1954 and _____
                                                    Section 18081 of the California Revenue and Taxation
_____. Failure to so qualify however shall not affect the
Code/correct local/state code
validity of this agreement.

COMMENT ON FORM 8:11: While intent is not tantamount to proof of an exchange, it can be important that the contract indicates the taxpayer's intent to exchange rather than to sell. CAR's form contains an intent to exchange clause.

FORM 8:12 FACILITATING THE EXCHANGE

Each party agrees to cancel, supersede or modify this agreement and execute and deliver to escrow any instrument or to perform any act reasonably necessary to carry out the provisions of this agreement.

COMMENT ON FORM 8:12: It may be important to cancel preliminary agreements or change contracts to comply with the advice of the parties' counsel. The above clause is designed to indicate that the parties are to cooperate in facilitating the exchange by executing such instruments as are necessary.

FORM 8:13 NO TAX ADVICE

A real estate broker is qualified to give advice about real estate. For tax and legal advice each party acknowledges being advised to seek advice in such matters from competent professionals.

COMMENT ON FORM 8:14: A real estate licensee should not give tax advice even if no one can be a competent exchangor without having practical tax knowledge. In substantial transactions both a knowledgeable tax attorney and an accountant are helpful professionals.

Objections to Title

Many forms in present use contain provisions which allow the parties to file objections to the preliminary title report. This is of course only reasonable. Such clauses can also permit the conveying party to choose to correct any objections to title, or decline and cancel the agreement. The type of clause, which the real estate licensee should look out for, extends the time for the conveying party to cure the defaults in title to some time up to ninety (90) days. The danger in such a "boilerplate" clause is that it tries to be everything to everybody. Exchanges are, however, sensitive endeavors. An unanticipated delay can destroy important tax advantages and play havoc with timetables. The title reports should be examined immediately upon approval of the transaction to avoid later delays. It is good practice to obtain written approval of preliminary title reports or set forth only the acceptable exceptions of the report. Clauses in Chapter 5 can be adapted to these purposes.

Non Simultaneous Exchanges

"Starker II", a case decided by the Ninth Circuit Court of Appeals, considered the question of the availability of tax-deferred exchange treatment where the taxpayer does *not* receive title to the exchange property at the time the taxpayer transfers title to the property to be relinquished. The court held that a non-simultaneous exchange can qualify for tax-deferred exchange treatment.

With the time constraint removed taxpayers were able to market their properties with far greater assurance of finding satisfactory exchange properties.

The IRS never accepted Starker II as the last word, and Congress in the Tax Reform Act of 1984 has seriously limited the effect of Starker II.

In Starker II the court approved the exchange despite the fact that approximately two years elapsed between the transfer by T. J. Starker of his timberland and his receipt of the last exchange of property.

The Act generally imposes a 180-day time limit on the completion of like-kind exchanges and also requires that property to be received in the exchange be identified within 45 days after the date of the original property transfer. The identification requirement may be met by designating the property to be received in the contract between the parties. A limited number of properties may be identified and the particular property to be transferred must be determined by contingencies beyond the control of both parties.

The Senate Committee found that the Starker situation resembled less a like-kind exchange and more a sale of one property followed, at some future point, by a purchase of a second property or properties. The unlimited time permitted by Starker, the Committee found, could result in that the consequences of deferred exchanges might not be determined for many years after the transaction was initiated.

These considerations led to the 180-day limit in the Act. Specifically, the Act provides that any property received by the taxpayer more than 180 days (but not later than the due date, including extensions, for the transferor's return for the tax year in which the transfer of the relinquished property occurred) after the date on which the taxpayer transferred property relinquished in the exchange, will not be treated as like-kind property exchange.

The 180-day deadline is the *maximum* deferral period. For corporations it can be as little as 74 days; for individuals 105 days. The reason for this is that the deadline expires on the *earlier* of the 180th day following the transfer of the relinquished property *or* the due date of the tax return for the year of the exchange. Extensions for filing returns will also extend the deferral period (up to 180 days) to find suitable exchange property.

The change in the law is contained in IRC 1031(a)3, which reads as follows:

(3) Requirement that property be identified and that exchange be completed not more than 180 days after transfer of exchanged property.
—For purposes of this subsection, any property received by the taxpayer shall be treated as property which is not like-kind property if—

(A) such property is not identified as property to be received in the exchange before the day which is 45 days after the date on which the taxpayer transfers the property relinquished in the exchange, or

(B) such property is received after the earlier of—
(i) the day which is 180 days after the date on which the taxpayer transfers the property relinquished in the exchange, or
(ii) the due date (determined with regard to extension) for the transferor's return of the tax imposed by this chapter for the taxable year in which the transfer of the relinquished property occurs.

An example of identification is given in the Conference Committee report: If "A" transferred real estate in exchange for a promise by "B" to transfer property "1" to A if zoning changes are approved and property "2" if they are not, the exchange would quality for like-kind treatment. As under present law, the new rules would not permit a taxpayer who received cash and later purchases the designated property to claim like-kind exchange treatment.

A Corporate "Strawman" Program for Exchanges

In *Starker,* the proceeds for T.J. Starker's timberland was held on the books of the second party, Crown Zellerbach. This would not work today. Various ingenious methods for "parking" the proceeds from taxpayers property have been proposed. All have included the risk that the IRS might claim that the taxpayer had "constructive" receipt of the funds.

Wells Fargo Escrow Services, in cooperation with Equity Exchange Corporation, have devised an exchange structuring, which should be useful in delayed exchanges and in multi-sided exchanges, land consolidations, or where the transaction involves uncooperative or unsophisticated parties. The key in the program is the formation of a single purpose intermediate corporation, a "strawman." It's the strawman who enters into the exchange agreement with the taxpayer. The corporation life ends when the exchange is fully consummated at which time it is dissolved. The proceeds from the taxpayer's parcel(s) is held in escrow and subject to investment directives from the strawman corporation. When the target property transaction is to be closed, the escrow provides the funds to the intermediary corporation to purchase the property and concurrently the corporation deeds the target property to the taxpayer in consummation of the exchange. No legal or tax advice is provided by the two services. The parties rely on their regular advisers, brokers, attorneys and accountants, who review all documentation. For additional information contact a local Wells Fargo Escrow office or Equity Exchange Corporation: (800) 255-3636. The above is offered only as information. No endorsement is intended. Other similar services may be available in your community.

Real estate licensees should tread carefully in this area. Competent tax advice by the taxpayer's own advisors is a must. Adequate documentation with a properly drawn exchange agreement and escrow instructions is essential.

Problems of the Non-Simultaneous Exchange

Normally if a taxpayer is relieved of mortgage liability on property exchange, the amount of the mortgage is deemed "boot," and to that amount the taxpayer must recognize any gain on the exchange. In a simultaneous exchange, the taxpayer may avoid this problem by receiving property subject to an equivalent mortgage and by assuming liability under that mortgage.

In a non-simultaneous exchange the taxpayer may be relieved of mortgage liability when his property is transferred to the ultimate transferee but not assume an equivalent liability until much later when he receives exchange property from the trustee. The government may claim that the mortgage-boot determination should be made as of the time the taxpayer's property is transferred to the ultimate transferee since at that time the taxpayer will stop making mortgage payments and be relieved of mortgage liability. The taxpayer will not have received exchange property yet nor assumed an equivalent mortgage on it. Therefore, it could be claimed the taxpayer has received "mortgage boot" and his gain should be recognized to that extent.

Sample Exchange No. 1

Form 8:14 is a fully filled in Exchange Agreement covering a three-way exchange (a two-way exchange with a cash out provided for in the original proposal). This type exchange is known as the "Missouri Waltz: One, Two and Cash-Out." Let's take a look at this typical exchange transaction and examine the anatomy of the C.A.R. Exchange Agreement using the form as set forth on page 280.

Anatomy of the C.A.R. Exchange Agreement

Let's turn first to the introductory part of the Exchange Agreement. On the first line we insert the names of the offeror—the person who initiates the exchange and usually the taxpayer with the eminent tax-problem. The form makes it possible to avoid the legalese "first party-second party" syndrome by simply using a last name designation. The properties involved can also be described by numbers thereby eliminating the necessity for repetitive property descriptions.

Next comes the description of Property No. 1 and the encumbrance on the property, which is held by a state chartered Savings and Loan Association. Thereafter it is Property No. 2's turn, which is also described and its encumbrance (a private loan) set forth.

Then follows the Terms and Conditions clause, which we have divided into alphabetically designated subsections. Here exchangors often disagree about to setting forth the exchange values. Some believe that it is not helpful, while others feel it is a selling point. Sub-sections 'B, C and D" indicate how the equities are balanced by cash and notes. Sub-section "E" is a "cash out" condition inserted here, because the broker knew that "Have-It" would not consider the trade unless it was conditioned upon his ability to resell Property One to a "take out" buyer. In this case we of course had the "take out" buyer who had made an offer to purchase on the exact terms as found in Sub-section "E." As it can be seen, this sale is based upon an all-inclusive deed of trust sale incorporating the underlying loan held by the Savings and Loan. The all-inclusive note contains a due-on-sale clause. See Discussion about Due on Sale Clause in Chapter 3, and Chapter 9 Creative Financing, which also includes clauses which may be inserted to strengthen the take back note holder's position.

Sub-section "F" simply spells out how adjustments in loan balances are to be handled in escrow. The supplements clause is self-explanatory. The supplements can be counted into the total pages of the contract or can be treated as exhibits and numbered accordingly.

The caveat at the bottom of page 1 may be self-serving, but it is also a warning to the real estate licensee not to give tax advice, and is designed to alert the parties to obtain competent advice from other professionals in areas outside the expertise of the broker.

How to Use the Printed Clauses

The numbered terms and conditions of the contract are all contained on page 2 of the form. They are all important to the transaction. As a user of the form, you should become thoroughly familiar with these printed provisions. In some situations one or more of the printed clauses may have to be alerted or deleted. If there is an inconsistency between a specific provision inserted in the contract and a general provision, the specific provision ordinarily qualifies the meaning of the general provision. Thus the written parts control the printed parts.

Let's take the printed clauses in the order they appear.

1. *Escrow clause*. Usually a longer escrow period is desirable in exchange situations. In our example it is not necessary because we have the take out buyer and the financing all worked out. In certain parts of the state preliminary escrow instructions are delivered to the escrow company when the escrow is opened with complete instructions to follow just before closing. Where this practice is followed, a short period of a few days is usually inserted in the space for the delivery of instructions. In other parts of the state the time limit for both the delivery of instructions and the period providing for closure "within _____ days from acceptance" is the same. We have used the first option in the example.

Problems can arise with this arrangement in that sometimes escrow instructions without the principals proper understanding and intent may supersede the original contract between the parties and perhaps authorize closing beyond the day set for performance in the contract. The real estate licensee should recognize that to abbrogate the responsibility for the completion of the transaction to an escrow holder without maintaining supervision of the escrow and providing continuing advice to the principals may not be in their best interest or the licensee's. The "boiler-plate" printed clauses in escrow instructions should be examined very carefully by the exchangor, since some obscure clause may be detrimental to the transaction. A good, responsible and cooperative working relationship with a qualified escrow officer can greatly assist in making the paperwork involved become the adequate documentation so necessary to convince tax authorities.

In this clause it is also determined how the escrow fee (not including the premium for title insurance) is to be paid.

2. *Title clause.* It says, that "title is to be free of liens, encumbrances, easements, restrictions, rights and conditions of record or known to the conveying party, other than the following . . ."

An initial similar wording is found in the C.A.R. Deposit Receipt. Suggestions have been made that it would serve the purpose to insert the word "None." A little reflection will make it clear that the opposite result of what was contemplated would result, since no property is "free" of the enumerated exceptions to a "clear" title. To insert: "Covenants, Conditions, Restrictions and easements of record" also defeats the purpose of the clause. This would be tantamount to giving a "blank check" to every potential objection to the title. Where there is no question of intended future use of the property the following compromise may be inserted, (1) current property taxes; (2) covenants, conditions, restrictions and public utility easements of record, if any, provided the same do not adversely affect the continued use of the property for the purpose for which it is presently being used, unless reasonably disapproved by acquiring party in writing within _____ days of receipt of a current preliminary title report furnished at _____ expense; and (3) _____ .

The better solution however is to obtain a preliminary title report on the properties in question and fill in the space as in the example. If this is not possible, the following wording may be used: "Such exceptions as shown on a current preliminary title report to be furnished at _____ expense and which are not unreasonable disapproved in writing by _____ within _____ days of receipt."

Obviously the acquiring party is entitled to examine the preliminary title report.

The form gives the acquiring party the right to terminate the agreement if title is not delivered as represented and releases that party of any responsibility for a broker's commission in such an event. The clause makes it possible to add additional title insurance coverage other than the Standard California Land Title Association policy.

3. *Vesting title clause.* The wording of this clause should be noticed: "Unless otherwise designated in escrow instructions, title to the property acquired shall vest as follows . . ." Thus even if the party at the time the offer is made has certain ideas of the manner in which title is to be vested, corrections or changes can be made in the escrow instructions. The conveying party may not be willing to accept change in the manner in which title is to be vested, if it means substitution of another acquiring party through the emergence of a "nominee" or "assignee."

Where a contract is not to be assigned, the following wording can be inserted in the "Terms and Conditions" clause: "In the event this contract is assigned without the written consent of the conveying party, it shall become null and void.'' It has been held that a contract may be declared "void" if assigned without consent. If the acquiring party has not at the time of entering into the exchange decided upon how to take title, insert: "Instructions to follow in escrow.'' Real Estate Licensees should not give title advice because it involves both giving legal and tax advice.

4. *Proration clause.* This clause is self-explanatory, but a problem may arise with regard to bonds, which are a lien. Either they may be part of the purchase price, be assumed by the acquiring party or be paid by the conveying party. The appropriate language should be inserted to cover the various situations. Many properties involved in an exchange may have no bond problem, in which case the paragraph should be deleted and the deletions initialed.

5. *Possession clause.* It is divided into two parts so that the different properties can have their own individual provision including possible payment for rent for a party remaining in physical possession of all or a part of the premises.

6. *Hold harmless clause.* This clause is designed to cover the "cash out" situation so common to exchanges. The party who is going only to be a "conduit" in transferring the property to the ultimate "take out" buyer should be held harmless from any representations made by the conveying party to him about the property and "passed on" to the buyer, provided these representations are identical.

The agents are not specifically named in the clause. Each principal is responsible for the acts of his agents. A broker may of course be personally liable for his own representation. The broker has recourse against false information elicited from the principal by the terms of the listing agreement and as determined by law based upon the brokers reasonable reliance upon information received.

7. *Code violations clause.* The parties warrant that they have no notices of violations filed or issued by any governmental agency against the property. If there are specific illegalities involved or other reservations from this statement, the specifics of these should be set forth in the "Terms and conditions" clause.

8. *Lease conditions.* This clause covers two items. First: that there are no side-agreements not disclosed in rental or lease agreements. Second: that the rental and lease agreements are to be delivered to the acquiring party within a specified time and, if not, disproved in writing that this condition is waived.

9. *Mode of acceptance.* This is similar to the Mode of Acceptance clause in the C.A.R.'s Deposit Receipt. If it is not possible to comply with its provisions because the parties are at great distances, it may be necessary to provide for acceptance by "mailgram" or telegram. In such a case the mode of acceptance should be incorporated in the "Terms and Conditions" clause or a supplement thereto.

10. *Broker clause.* The name of the broker should be inserted. The clause authorizes the broker to represent both sides to the exchange and to receive compensation from both. Some experienced exchangors prefer to only represent

one party to an exchange and invite cooperation with another broker to avoid the dual agency. However, if full disclosure is made and the broker acts in proper fiduciary manner, this clause constitutes the authorization for cooperating with other brokers and to divide the compensation as they agree between themselves.

11. *Exchange intent.* Although a taxpayer's intent, in terms of tax motive, is generally rejected by the Courts, the taxpayer's intent to exchange has, in several cases, been determinative of the character of the transaction. The agreement indicates this intent, but it also states that should the transaction "fail" to qualify as a tax deferred exchange under both federal and state law, that this will not affect the validity of the contract to exchange.

12. *Additional instrument clause.* This provision expresses the parties agreement to cooperate in expediting the transaction by doing such acts and execute such documents which are "reasonably necessary" to carry out the agreement.

13. *Attorneys fees.* Should action be taken to enforce the agreement, this clause provides that the prevailing party may recover reasonable attorneys fees and costs.

14. *Time of essence clause.* Provides that the times set forth in the contract are essential for performance, and that any changes must be made in writing only.

Both parties are to sign page 2 of the agreement.

Finally, on page 3 is the agreement to pay the broker a fee for services rendered, if the broker obtains the signature of the other party. The fee is to be paid when the deed is recorded or a Real Property Contract (Land Sales Contract) is delivered, or in the event of a default if the completion of the exchange is prevented by the offering party. Again if an action or proceeding is instituted to enforce the fee agreement, the prevailing party is entitled to reasonable attorneys fees and costs.

This offer is to be signed by the offeror and the broker to consent to the fee arrangement.

Most exchangors use separate fee agreements. They do not insert the actual dollar amount of the fee in the exchange agreement itself.

Moving along to the "Acceptance Clause," we have completed the Missouri waltz. Again, the broker's name and the fee arrangement is inserted as well as the acquiring party's instructions about how title is to be vested. There is also an attorneys fee provision in this section. The signatures and dates should be added and the broker should sign the consent to the fee arrangement. Note that each party should have a copy of each signed page at the time they sign the agreement. When both have signed, each party is entitled to the immediate receipt of a fully signed copy of the final document.

FORM 8:14   EXCHANGE AGREEMENT

EXCHANGE AGREEMENT

THIS IS INTENDED TO BE A LEGALLY BINDING CONTRACT. READ IT CAREFULLY.

William Got-It and Mary Got It, his wife

herein called   Got-It   , offers to exchange

the following described property, designated as Property No. ONE   situated in   Euphoria

County of Dreams   State of California

Lot and improvements known as 14 Grey Cross Drive, consisting of a four unit apartment house, together with 4 stoves and 4 refrigerators located on the property and used it its operation.
Subject to a first loan in favor of BIGGIE State Savings and Loan with an approximate balance of $30,000.00 payable at $352.63 per month including interest at 7%.

for the following described property of Gertrude Have-It

herein called Have-It   , designated as Property No. TWO

situated in Moss End

County of Buts   , State of California

Lot and improvements known as 456 Gothen Ave, consisting of a 16 unit unfurnished apartment house together with 14 stoves and It refrigerators located on the property and used in its operation. Subject to a first loan in favor of Elsie Goldenrock with an approximate balance of $130,000.00 payable at $1,250.00 per month including interest at 8 ½% due in full in 19xx.

Terms and Conditions of Exchange:

A. For purposes of this exchange the following values are agreed upon:

Property No ONE	$70,000	Property No TWO	$200,000
Existing loan	30,000	Existing loan	130,000
Equity	40,000	Equity	70,000

B. $20,000 in cash to be paid by Got-It to Haveit;
C. Haveit to take title to property No ONE subject to the existing loan
D. $10,000 by Got-It executing a Note and Deed of Trust in that amount in favor of Have-It secured by Property No TWO payable at $212.48 monthly including an annual interest of 10% due in full in five years and in the event of sale or transfer of the property.
E. This exhange is conditioned upon the sale by Have-It of property No. ONE during the excrow period for not less than $70,000 with a Cash down payment of not less than $14,000; buyer to execute an All-inclusive Note and an All-inclusive Deed of Trust for the balance of the purchase price in favor of Have-It payable at $747.87 monthly including annual interest at 10% from the date of closing. The principal amount of the All-inclusive Note shall include the unpaid principal balance of the underlying obligation to Biggie State Savings and Loan. The Note shall be payable in full on the day on which the final installment on the underlying note becomes due and payable and in the event of sale or transfer of the property.
F. Any differences in unpaid balances shall be adjusted in cash in escrow.

The supplements initialled below are incorporated as part of this agreement.

Other

____ Structural Pest Control Certification Agreement   Inventory of personal property for ____
____ Special Studies Zone Disclosure   Property No. TWO
____ Flood Insurance Disclosure

Both parties acknowledge receipt of a copy of this page. Page 1 of 3 Pages.

x _William Got-it_   x _Gertrude Have-it_

x _Mary Got-It_   x _____

A REAL ESTATE BROKER IS THE PERSON QUALIFIED TO ADVISE ON REAL ESTATE. IF YOU DESIRE LEGAL OR TAX ADVICE, CONSULT A COMPETENT PROFESSIONAL.

For these forms, address California Association of Realtors®
505 Shatto Place, Los Angeles, California 90020
Copyright 1978, California Association of Realtors®   FORM E-11-1

EXCHANGE AGREEMENT

The following terms and conditions are hereby incorporated in and made a part of the offer.

1. The parties hereto shall deliver signed escrow instructions to **All Powerful Title Company**
, escrow holder, within _____ days from acceptance,
which shall provide for closing within **30** days from acceptance. Escrow fees shall be paid as follows:
Each party to pay the escrow fee for the property conveyed

2. Title is to be free of liens, encumbrances, easements, restrictions, rights and conditions of record or known to the conveying party, other than the following: **exceptions No. 1, 2 and 4 as shown in preliminary title report No. 73265 for property No ONE and exceptions 1 and 2 in preliminary title report No. 2376 pertaining to property No TWO**
Each party shall provide the other with (a) a standard California Land Title Association policy, or (b) _____, issued by **All Powerful Title Company**
to be paid for as follows: **Property No ONE: Have-It Property No. TWO: by Got-It**
showing title vested in the acquiring party subject only to the above and to any liens or encumbrances to be recorded in accordance with this agreement. If the conveying party fails to deliver title as above, the acquiring party may terminate this agreement and shall be released from payment of any compensation to broker(s) for services rendered.

3. Unless otherwise designated in escrow instructions, title to the property acquired shall vest as follows
William Got-It and Mary Got-It his wife, as their community property
(The manner of taking title may have significant legal and tax consequences. Therefore, give this matter serious consideration.)

4. Property taxes, premiums on insurance acceptable to the party acquiring the property insured, rents, interest and
existing service contracts shall be prorated as of (a) the date of recordation of deed,
or (b) **N/A**
Any bond or assessment which is a lien on a party's property shall be paid or assumed as follows: **N/A**

5(A). Possession of Property No **ONE** shall be delivered (a) on close of escrow, ~~or (b)~~

5(B). Possession of Property No **TWO** shall be delivered (a) on close of escrow, ~~or (b)~~ except **Apt. 101, to be vacated by Have-It not later than 30 days from date of closing.**

6. If, as a part of this exchange, any property is to be sold to a third party, the original transferor shall indemnify and hold harmless the party conveying the property to the third party from all claims, liability, loss, damage and expenses including reasonable attorneys' fees and costs incurred by reason of any warranties or representations made by conveying party to the purchaser provided they conform to the warranties and representations made by the original transferor either by this agreement or in any statement made or document delivered to the conveying party or to the designated escrow holder.

7. Each party warrants that he has no knowledge of the existence of any notices of violations of city, county or state building, zoning, fire and health codes, ordinances, or other governmental regulations filed or issued against his property.

8. Each party represents to the other that no tenant, if any, is entitled to any rebate, concession or other benefit except as set forth in rental agreements and leases, copies of which are to be exchanged or delivered within **Five** days of acceptance. If such rental agreements or leases are not disapproved in writing within **Five** days of receipt thereof, this condition shall be deemed waived.

9. Unless acceptance of this offer is signed by the other party hereto and the signed copy delivered to the undersigned, in person or by mail to the address below, within **Three** days, this offer shall be deemed revoked.

10. Each party agrees that **Old Broker's Company** broker
address **P. O. Box 555, Euphoria, California** California
telephone **202-5454** can act as agent for, and may accept compensation for services from, each party herein. Broker is authorized to cooperate with other brokers and to divide such compensation as agreed by them.

11. It is the intention of the parties to the extent permitted by law, that the mutual conveyances agreed to herein will qualify as an "exchange" within the meaning of Section 1031 of the Internal Revenue Code of 1954 and Section 18081 of the California Revenue and Taxation Code. Failure to so qualify however, shall not affect the validity of this agreement.

12. Each party agrees to execute and deliver to escrow any instrument or to perform any act reasonably necessary to carry out the provisions of this agreement.

13. In any action or proceeding arising out of this agreement, the prevailing party shall be entitled to reasonable attorneys' fees and costs.

14. Time is of the essence of this agreement. All modifications or extensions shall be in writing signed by the parties.

Both parties acknowledge receipt of a copy of this page. Page 2 of **3** Pages.

x _William Got-It_ .... x _Gertrude Have-It_
x _Mary Got-It_ x

For these forms, address California Association of Realtors®
505 Shatto Place, Los Angeles, California 90020 (Revised 1978)
Copyright ©1978, California Association of Realtors®   FORM E-11-2

EXCHANGE AGREEMENT

The following terms and conditions are hereby incorporated in and made a part of the offer.

If the other party hereto accepts the foregoing offer, I agree to pay to   Old Broker's Company
as broker for services rendered as follows: in accordance with fee agreement dated November 19xx

payable (a) on recordation of deed or on delivery of a Real Property Contract as defined by Civil Code Section 2985; or (b) upon default if completion of the exchange is prevented by me; or (c)

In any action or proceeding arising out of this agreement, the prevailing party shall be entitled to reasonable attorney's fees and costs.

Receipt of a copy hereof is hereby acknowledged. Page 3 of   3 Pages.

Euphoria _____, State ____ California _____, Dated: ___ January 10 _____, 19 xx

Address: ___ 1203 Park Lane _____   x _William Got-it_

___ Euphoria, California _____   x _Mary Got-it_

Telephone: ___ 202-4971 _____   x _____

Broker(s) agree to the foregoing.

Dated: ___ January 10 _____, 19 XX   Dated: _____, 19 ___

Broker   Old Broker's Company _____   Broker _____

By _Young Newman_   By _____

ACCEPTANCE

The foregoing offer and agreement to exchange the properties upon the terms and conditions stated is hereby accepted and I agree
to pay   Old Broker's Company, P. O. Box 555, Euphoria

California, telephone 202-5454   as broker(s) for services rendered as follows:
   in accordance with fee agreement dated January 12, 19xx

payable as follows: (a) on recordation of Deed or delivery of Real Property Sales Contract as defined by Civil Code Section 2985; (b) upon default if completion is prevented by me; or (c) Old Broker's Company

Unless otherwise designated in the escrow instructions, title to the property acquired shall vest as follows:
   Gertrude Have-It, a single woman

(The manner of taking title may have significant legal and tax consequences. Therefore, give this matter serious consideration.)

In any action or proceeding arising out of this agreement, the prevailing party shall be entitled to reasonable attorneys' fees and costs.

Receipt of a copy hereof is acknowledged and broker is authorized to deliver a signed copy to the other party named above. Page 3 of   Pages.

Euphoria _____, State ____ California _____, Dated: ___ January 12 ____ 19 xx

Address: _456 Gothen Ave._ _____   x _Gertrude Have-it_
   Moss End, California _____   x _____

Telephone: 308-6275 _____   x _____

Broker(s) agree to the foregoing:

Dated: ___ January 12 _____, 19 XX   Dated: _____, 19 ___

Broker   Old Broker's Company _____   Broker _____

By _Young Newman_   By _____

For these forms, address California Association of Realtors®
505 Shatto Place, Los Angeles, California 90020
Copyright © 1978, California Association of Realtors®   FORM E-11-3

065

BROKER'S COPY
CALIFORNIA ASSOCIATION OF REALTORS® STANDARD FORM

1st Page of Take-out Buyer's offer

REAL ESTATE PURCHASE CONTRACT
AND RECEIPT FOR DEPOSIT

THIS IS MORE THAN A RECEIPT FOR MONEY. IT IS INTENDED TO BE A LEGALLY BINDING CONTRACT. READ IT CAREFULLY.

Euphoria , California, January 10 , 19 XX

Received from Novice Vendee
herein called Buyer, the sum of Five Hundred and no/100 Dollars $500.00
evidenced by cash ☐, cashier's check ☐, or ☐, personal check ☒ payable to All Powerful
Title Company , to be held uncashed until acceptance of this offer, as deposit on account of purchase price of
Seventy Thousand and no/100 Dollars $70,000.00
for the purchase of property, situated in Euphoria , County of Dreams , California,
described as follows: 14 Grey Cross Drive, a four unit apartment house

1. Buyer will deposit in escrow with All Powerful Title Company the balance of purchase price as follows:
$14,000 in cash including above deposit
$56,000 by Buyer executing an All-inclusive Note and Deed of Trust in favor
of seller secured by the property payable at $747.87 monthly including
annual interest at 10% from date of closing. The principal amount of
the All-inclusive Note shall include the unpaid principal balance of
the underlying obligation to Biggie Savings and Loan. The Note shall
be payable in full on the day on which the final installment on the
underlying Note became due and payable, and in the event of sale or
transfer of the property. Any differences in unpaid balances shall be
adjusted in Cash in escrow.
It is the sellers intent and preference to exchange the above-described
property for other property of a similar kind rather than selling it.
1. seller shall have 120 days from the date of acceptance hereof to locate such
suitable property for exchange; Buyer further agrees:
2. to accept title to property described herein directly from the owner(s) of
the exchange property
3. that the closing of the escrow contemplated herein shall be concurrent with
with the closing of the exchange transaction.
4. that each party agree to cancel, supersede or modify this agreement to
execute and deliver to escrow any instrument or to perform any act provided
such actions are necessary to carry out the provisions of this agreement
with the intent to qualify the seller's transaction as an IRC § 1031
exchange. - If this transaction is not concluded as an exchange on or
before the date provided for above, seller shall promptly convey the property
described herein upon the terms and conditions set forth in this agreement.

Set forth above any terms and conditions of a factual nature applicable to this sale, such as financing, prior sale of other property, the matter of structural pest control inspection, repairs and personal property to be included in the sale.

2. Deposit will ☒ will not ☐ be increased by $1,600.00 to $2,100.00 within 3 days of acceptance of this offer. Buyer and Seller to execute CAR Form RID 11

3. Buyer does ☐ does not ☐ intend to occupy subject property as his residence.

4. The supplements initialed below are incorporated as part of this agreement

___ Structural Pest Control Certification Agreement   ___ Occupancy Agreement
___ Special Studies Zone Disclosure   ___ VA Amendment
___ Flood Insurance Disclosure   ___ FHA Amendment

Other Inventory of personal
property included in purchase
price

5. Buyer and Seller acknowledge receipt of a copy of this page, which constitutes Page 1 of 2 Pages.

X _Novee Vendee_
BUYER

X _____
BUYER

X _William St...._
SELLER

X _____ _Jct-15_
SELLER

A REAL ESTATE BROKER IS THE PERSON QUALIFIED TO ADVISE ON REAL ESTATE. IF YOU DESIRE LEGAL ADVICE CONSULT YOUR ATTORNEY.

THIS STANDARIZED DOCUMENT FOR USE IN SIMPLE TRANSACTIONS HAS BEEN APPROVED BY THE CALIFORNIA ASSOCIATION OF REALTORS® AND THE STATE BAR OF CALIFORNIA IN FORM ONLY. NO REPRESENTATION IS MADE AS TO THE APPROVAL OF THE FORM OF SUPPLEMENTS. THE LEGAL VALIDITY OF ANY PROVISION. OR THE ADEQUACY OF ANY PROVISION IN ANY SPECIFIC TRANSACTION IT SHOULD NOT BE USED IN COMPLEX TRANSACTIONS OR WITH EXTENSIVE RIDERS OR ADDITIONS

066

For these forms, address California Association of Realtors®
505 Shatto Place, Los Angeles, California 90020
(Revised 1978)

D-11-1 NCR SETS

COMMENT ON FORM NO. 8:14: Some experienced exchangors do not subscribe to having the exchange values set forth in the contract. Of course, the actual exchange value will essentially be "revealed" to the parties. Under Section 10141 of the California Business and Professional Code the price, the added considerations and a description of the property in an exchange shall be given to the parties within one month after closing of the transaction by the licensee or through an escrow holder's closing statement containing such information.

Sample Exchange No. 2

Form 8:15 also involves a three-way exchange. However in this exchange transaction, the taxpayer offer to exchange but is met with a counter offer making the exchange conditioned upon a cash-out of the taxpayer's property. Part of the consideration and equalizing of equities consists of an assignment of a Deed of Trust on unrelated property.

FORM 8:15

EXCHANGE AGREEMENT

THIS IS INTENDED TO BE A LEGALLY BINDING CONTRACT. READ IT CAREFULLY.

Richard Roeone and Elsie Roeone, husband and wife

ein called_____ Roeone _____, offers to exchange
.ie following described property, designated as Property No. __One__ situated in __San Fantasia__,
County of_____ Dreams _____, State of_____ Euphoria _____:

Lot and improvements commonly known as 209 Old Mill Road, a duplex
containing two 2-bedroom units, being free and clear of encumbrances.

for the following described property of___ Madeline Gotit and Josephine Gotit

herein called_____ Gotit _____, designated as Property No. __Two__,
ituated in _____ Grapefruit Town
County of_____ Nectarine _____, State of_____ Euphoria _____:

Lot and improvements known as 400 Deer Road, a 16 unit apartment house
subject to a first loan with Biggie Savings and Loan with an approximate
balance of $170,000 payable at $1,817.50 monthly including interest at
8% per annum.

Terms and Conditions of Exchange:

A1. For purposes of this excahnge, the following values are agreed upon:
   Property No. 1: $106,000   Property No. 2: $350,000
                                     Existing loan   170,000
   Equity $106,000   Equity   180,000
A2. $50,000 cash to be paid by Roeone to Gotit
A3. $20,000 by Roeone executing a Note and Deed of Trust in that amount in
    favor of Gotit secured by Property No. 2 payable at $424.95
    monthly including interest at 10%, due in full in 5 years and
    in the event of sale or transfer of the property.
A4. $ 4,000 by Roeone assigning without recourse to Gotit a note dated May 6,19XX
    with an unpaid balance in that approximate amount payable $60.00
    monthly including interest at 9% due in full 19XW secured by
    Deed of Trust on 99 Overpriced Alley, Grapefruit, Euphoria.

A5. $170,000 by Roeone taking title subject to existing loan in that approximate
    amount.

Any adjustment in existing balances shall be made in cash. Only obligatory
payments shall be made during escrow.

The supplements initialled below are incorporated as part of this agreement.
                                          Other 9/19-19XX
___Structural Pest Control Certification Agreement   Inventory of personal property (Property No. 2)
___Special Studies Zone Disclosure   Income and expense statement (Property No. 1)
___Flood Insurance Disclosure   Income and expense statement (Property No. 2)
Both parties acknowledge receipt of a copy of this page. Page 1 of 3 Pages.

X _Richard Roeone_   X _Madeline Gotit_

v _Elsie Roeone_   X _Josephine Gotit_

                                                      069
For these forms, address California Association of Realtors®

EXCHANGE AGREEMENT

The following terms and conditions are hereby incorporated in and made a part of the offer.

1.   The parties hereto shall deliver signed escrow instructions to Gold Edge Escrow Co.

_____, escrow holder, within 10 days from acceptance,

.ch shall provide for closing within 60 days from acceptance. Escrow fees shall be paid as follows: Roeone to pay escrow charge on Property No. 1; Gotit to pay escrow charge on Property No. 2.

-.   Title is to be free of liens, encumbrances, easements, restrictions, rights and conditions of record or known to the conveying party, other than the following: Property No. 2: adjoining building shares rear entrance for garbage collection by agreement in writing. Subject to each party examining preliminary title report on property to be acquired. If no objection in writing within 5 days of receipt, this condition is deemed waived Each party shall provide the other with (a) a standard California Land Title Association policy, or (b)

_____, issued by T.I.T. Insurance Co.

to be paid for as follows: by each acquiring party for the property acquired

showing title vested in the acquiring party subject only to the above and to any liens or encumbrances to be recorded in accordance with this agreement. If the conveying party fails to deliver title as above, the acquiring party may terminate this agreement and shall be released from payment of any compensation to broker(s) for services rendered.

3.   Unless otherwise designated in escrow instructions, title to the property acquired shall vest as follows:

Richard Roeone and Elsie Roeone, his wife, as community property

(The manner of taking title may have significant legal and tax consequences. Therefore, give this matter serious consideration.)

4.   Property taxes, premiums on insurance acceptable to the party acquiring the property insured, rents, interest and

shall be prorated as of (a) the date of recordation of deed,

aXXX security deposits to paid in escrow

Any bond or assessment which is a lien on a party's property shall be paid or assumed as follows: Not applicable

5 (A). Possession of Property No. 1   shall be delivered (a) on close of escrow, aX(b)XXX XaXZ XtaX Z XZ XZ XdaysXatterXataseXofz 2atZOXZ X(Z)X)

5 (B). Possession of Property No. 2   shall be delivered (a) on close of escrow, aX(b)XXX XaXX XtaX XZ XZ XZ XdayXatterXZXXaseXofX WX(XaXZ)X except Apt. No. 2, which Gotit shall vacate not later than 30 days from .lose of escrow. $450.00 shall be withheld in escrow as rent for said period.

6   If, as a part of this exchange, any property is to be sold to a third party, the original transferor shall indemnify and hold harmless .arty conveying the property to the third party from all claims, liability, loss, damage and expenses including reasonable attorneys' fees and costs incurred by reason of any warranties or representations made by conveying party to the purchaser provided they conform to the warranties and representations made by the original transferor either by this agreement or in any statement made or document delivered to the conveying party or to the designated escrow holder.

7.   Each party warrants that he has no knowledge of the existence of any notices of violations of city, county or state building, zoning, fire and health codes, ordinances, or other governmental regulations filed or issued against his property.

8.   Each party represents to the other that no tenant, if any, is entitled to any rebate, concession or other benefit except as set forth in rental agreements and leases, copies of which are to be exchanged or delivered within five days of acceptance. If such rental agreements or leases are not disapproved in writing within five days of receipt thereof, this condition shall be deemed waived.

9.   Unless acceptance of this offer is signed by the other party hereto and the signed copy delivered to the undersigned, in person or by mail to the address below, within three days, this offer shall be deemed revoked.

10.   Each party agrees that Old Broker's Co.   broker

address Old Broker Building, 50 Gray Cross Lane, San Mathew   , California

telephone 348-8292   can act as agent for, and may accept compensation for

services from, each party herein. Broker is authorized to cooperate with other brokers and to divide such compensation as agreed by them.

11.   It is the intention of the parties to the extent permitted by law, that the mutual conveyances agreed to herein will qualify as an "exchange" within the meaning of Section 1031 of the Internal Revenue Code of 1954 and Section 18081 of the California Revenue and Taxation Code. Failure to so qualify however, shall not affect the validity of this agreement.

12.   Each party agrees to execute and deliver to escrow any instrument or to perform any act reasonably necessary to carry out the provisions of this agreement.

13.   In any action or proceeding arising out of this agreement, the prevailing party shall be entitled to reasonable attorneys' fees and costs.

14.   Time is of the essence of this agreement. All modifications or extensions shall be in writing signed by the parties.

Both parties acknowledge receipt of a copy of this page. Page 2 of 3 Pages.

x _Richard Roeone_   x _Jacqueline Gotit_

x _Elsie Roeone_   x _Jacqueline Gotit_

FORM E-11-2 NCR

COUNTER-OFFER

This is a counter-offer to the Exchange Agreement dated September 19, 19XX between ROEONE and GOTIT.

Gotit accepts all of the terms and conditions set forth in the above designated agreement with the following changes or amendments subject to the following conditions:

(1)   The sale by Gotit of Property No. 1 during the escrow period for not less than $68,000 and subject to Buyer's ability to obtain a new first loan of not less than 80% of sales price secured by the property.

(2)   That Gotit not be liable for any expense, prepayment penalties, loan charges or commissions of any kind whatsoever in the resale of the Property No. 1. Roeone shall pay such expenses in cash in escrow.

(3)   That the exchange and sale escrows be closed concurrently.

(4)   Unless a copy of this Counter-Offer, duly accepted by Roeone, is personally delivered to Gotit on or before September 20, 19XX at 5:00 P.M., this offer shall be deemed revoked.

Receipt of a copy hereof is hereby acknowledged.

DATED: September 20, 19XX

TIME: 5:30 pm   X _Madeline Gotit_

                                         X _Josephine Gotit_

The undersigned accepts and agrees to the above, Receipt of a copy hereof is hereby acknowledged.

DATED: September 20, 19XX

TIME: 7:00 pm   X _Richard Roeone_

                                         X _Elsie Roeone_

Receipt of Roeone's acceptance is hereby acknowledged.

DATE: September 20, 19XX   _Madeline Gotit_

                                         Josephine Gotit

A Checklist for Exchanges

In order to prepare an adequate Exchange Agreement, the following facts should be ascertained:

1. The names and capacities of all parties (owners) or the properties involved.

2. The method of taking title to property received in the exchange.

3. Legal descriptions of Parcels A and B.

4. The exceptions to title for each parcel.

5. An agreed upon exchange value for each of the parcels.

6. The loans on each parcel, balance due, payments, interest rate, delinquency, if any, and date to which interest is paid.

7. The necessity, if any, for equalization of equities, and the method: cash or loan.

8. If alternative sale, if exchange does not materialize, the price and terms.

9. The price and terms in a cash out of Parcel A.

10. Personal property included in the sale and any encumbrances thereon.

11. Determination of "boot" if any.

12. Prorations.

13. Escrow holder, escrow fees and closing date.

14. Commission agreements for real estate brokers.

15. Escrow instructions.

16. Inspections, termite reports, disclosures required by law.

17. The tax consequences for each party by having the transaction reviewed by their respective tax advisors before execution of the exchange agreement.

18. Contract for Starker II type delayed exchanges should be drafted by the parties legal advisors in cooperation with broker(s) and the parties tax advisers.

Chapter 9
Creative Financing

*No matter how much the world changes, Buyers and Sellers will always need each other.**

©*Ashleigh Brilliant 1981*
"Pot-Shots" No. 2239

Creative financing—or more correctly—seller-assisted financing has always been with us. The new "creative financing" has turned sellers into lenders and created a fertile field for abuse, fraud, and illegal transactions. The creativity encompasses the no down-payment promotion, the more than 100% financing of "buyer walk-aways" and inadequate financing documents such as wrap-arounds uncoordinated to the underlying obligations. When all this is combined with short terms and huge balloon payments, the stage is set for creative litigation, bankruptcy and foreclosure.

True and sound creative financing include proper disclosure to both buyer and seller of the inherent risks and a frank explanation of alternatives. The structuring of creative financing depends upon the buyer's planning horizon. Properties with "assumable" mortgages at the original lower than market rate of interest sell at premium prices. Creative financing can distort values. Sales at inflated premium prices play havoc with the comparable price appraisal system. Payment of such premium may be a rational decision if recoverable in three to four years, but may be an unwise investment if the period is much longer since most American families move every seven years. The buyer's tax rate may be of importance in the strategy decision since not all taxpayers will be able to use the total interest deductions. For sellers the participation in financing, whether first loans, wrap-arounds, or large seconds, may give the illusions of big profits. Most often first loans, unless written on standardized federal mortgage documents, will not qualify for sale in the national secondary market. If sold on the private "secondary" market, a healthy discount will illustrate to the seller

---

*Since I first met Ashleigh Brilliant several books ago, I have enjoyed his *"Pot-Shots"* and books. This one is from the delightful collection, *Appreciate Me Now and Avoid the Rush*, Woodbridge Press, available from Brilliant Enterprises, 177 W. Valerio St., Santa Barbara, CA 93101.

that the creative financing in fact meant selling the property at a discounted price. A cash sale at a realistic price could have netted the seller the same amount in immediate cash but might have hurt the seller's pride. The short-term financing, or similarly short buy downs with 3 to 4 year due dates, can lead to increased buyer frustration and later foreclosures, when the illusion of refinancing turns out to be just an illusion. If the real estate licensees and the escrow holders are not extremely careful in their disclosures and in preparing adequate loan documents the commission and fees earned could be wasted in future litigation. So creative financing is not a panacea.

Real estate investors and their brokers as well as sophisticated home buyers will undoubtedly have to use computer-assisted calculations to weigh the advantages and disadvantages of creative financing. Each situation will be different. The form of disclosures will undergo changes. In California, a statute, Civil Code Section 2956 et seq, effective July 1983 requires in-depth disclosures of seller-arranger financing. Use CAR form SFD 11. Inevitably an array of disclosure statements will have to be attached to the real estate contract and delivered prior to closing. Nevertheless the basic "disclosure" of financing terms starts with the contract. The clauses found in this chapter address themselves to how to handle this problem. We will begin with reminding our readers of the existence of the many clauses suited for "creative financing" found in chapter 3 of this book and therefore not repeated in this chapter.

Where to Find Other Creative Financing Clauses

The following forms are basic in creative owner-assisted financing:

	Form No.:
Buyer to Assume or Take Subject to Existing Loan or Loans	3.05/3.06
Seller to Carry Purchase Money Deed of Trust	3.17/3.19
Seller to Carry Loan with Balloon Payment	3.18
Seller to Carry Tax Installment Note and Deed of Trust	3.24
Seller to Carry Second Deed of Trust	3.26
Seller to Carry Blanket Loan	3.29
Seller to Take Deed of Trust on Other Property as Part Payment	3.32
Seller to Take Boat, Car, etc., as Down Payment	3.33
Seller to Carry Contract of Sale	3.40
Lease with Option to Buy	3.42/3.43

Planning Ahead

More than half of the homes sold in the U.S. in the last several years have included some seller-assisted financing. Owners commonly have provided first loans, secured by deeds of trust or mortgages, second loans similarly secured, or custom tailored as "wrap-arounds" and installment sales land contracts. Very little of this financing has been originated on documents acceptable in the national "secondary market." Most have been documented on local title company forms which have prevented the loans from being readily sold to investors other than private investors at substantial discounts. Proper planning however, can place many owner take-back loans in a more advantageous position.

Through the use of Fannie Mae (Federal National Mortgage Association) approved forms a private lender can obtain mortgage insurance against default and the loan can be sold to Fannie Mae. Such loan can carry almost any interest imaginable with adjustable rate terms built in or include a graduated payment schedule. Private mortgage insurance issued by recognized private mortgage underwriter is required where the home owner's equity is less than 20%. The maximum loan amount acceptable to Fannie Mae for one to four-family property is regularly adjusted.[1] The necessary forms and current maximum loan amount can be obtained through a lender qualified to deal with Fannie Mae. The program is called the "vendor program" and information is available from Fannie Mae, 3900 Wisconsin Avenue, Washington, D.C. 20016. Other home-seller programs with mortgage insurance are also available.

Even if a seller doesn't want to cash in the take-back loan immediately there are obvious benefits in originating the loan on the national standard forms so at a later time the loan can be converted to cash. Obtaining this type of loan documentation can be a condition of furnishing of financing by a seller. See Form 9:01.

FORM 9:01   **FANNIE MAE FORMS**

(Precede with any form for seller financing from this book and Continue):

Said note and _____ shall be drawn on forms
              mortgage/deed of trust
acceptable to the Federal National Mortgage Association (Fannie Mae).

(Optional):

Seller's obligation to provide the above-described financing is conditioned upon seller's ability to obtain private mortgage insurance issued by a Fannie Mae approved underwriter. Cost of such insurance estimated at $_____ shall be paid by _____.
         buyer/seller

COMMENT ON FORM 9:01: Where the forms are available at the time the offer is drafted they can either in blank or fully filled in with the financing terms be attached to the agreement as exhibits and incorporated therein by reference. The clause can read:

"Said note and _____ shall be drawn as shown
                               mortgage/deed of trust

in Exhibits A and B attached hereto and incorporated by reference." The secret in obtaining Fannie Mae acceptance is to use an approved lender as the conduit to Fannie Mae as early in the transaction as possible.

Alternative Financing

Creative financing also includes the use of any one of the new alternative financing instruments available from conventional lenders. Form 9:02 is compatible with the loan plans offered as VRM, ROM, FPM, RRM, ARM, AML, GPM, GPAML, PSAM, NIRP, etc. (See explanation of these loans page 60). The form can be used alone when such loan is available and acceptable to the buyer without any "creative" addition. If "buy down plan" is to be added, include Form 9:03.

FORM 9:02   ALTERNATIVE INSTRUMENT FINANCING

$_____ as loan proceeds conditioned upon buyer's ability to
_____ from _____
   obtain/assume   an institutional lender/name
a first _____
                        type/adjustable interest loan
for a minimum of _____ years term _____ payable
                                              with _____ year amortization
initially at $_____, _____
                              monthly, quarterly, semi-annually/annually
including interest at an initial interest rate not to exceed _____% per annum for
_____ years, adjustable thereafter every _____ months, to the rate determined by
the lender, subject to any one or more of the following limitations:

_____ %   per annum maximum interest adjustment in any period
_____ %   per annum maximum interest increase during loan term
_____ %   maximum interest increase during loan term
_____ %   maximum change in _____
                                                      installment
payment of principal and interest at each adjustment period.

_____ % maximum monthly payment of principal and interest. If the interest rate changes so that this maximum will not amortize the loan over its remaining term, the loan term will be recast, when negative amortization reaches ____% of contract rate. Loan to be assumable for _____ times prepayment penalty _____.

COMMENT ON FORM 9:02: This form can be adapted to an addendum for use with the contract whenever any of the alternative financing instruments are used. If used in an individual transaction only the limitation which applies can be copied into the terms of payment clause. Minor changes may be necessary to accurately describe the loan. If a lender provides printed material describing in detail the type of loan to be obtained by the buyer the following language can be included: ''Buyer acknowledges receipt of a brochure entitled _____
name

issued by _____ which explains the loan terms in more
name of lender

detail and buyer agrees that in entering into the loan transaction that _____
he/she/they

have not relied upon any representation made by seller or seller's agent regarding such loan.

In the fifth alternative maximum in the form, the maximum amount of actual dollar payment can be used by deleting the percentage sign and substituting it with a dollar sign.

FORM 9:03   **BUY DOWN**

(Precede with Form 3:14, 3:15 or 9:02 and Continue):

Seller shall pay the loan buy down fee charged by lender for reducing the interest rate during the first _____ years of the loan whereby the interest for the first _____ will be ____% per annum.
year/years

(If different rate for period of years add):

for the second year _____% per annum and for the third year _____% per annum.

(Continue in all cases):

and _____% per annum thereafter _____
subject to any variable/adjustable interest feature

(Optional continue):

Seller's obligation to pay such discount points shall be limited to a total amount of $_____.

COMMENT ON FORM 9:03: Buy down fee is not truly discount points because a lender may receive both discount points and buy down fees. In some contracts these charges are lumped together as "discount points." Where a principal is also to pay true discount points the above terms of payment clause should be so amended. The disclaimer in comment to Form 9:02 may be added to explain variable or adjustable interest provisions, if any.

Potpourri of Acquisition Techniques Applying Creative Financing

Creative acquisition techniques go hand in hand with creative financing. It's often hard to recognize what is what, since the structuring of financing is the very heart of a real estate transaction. The purpose of this book is not to encourage any particular acquisition technique. Here we are concerned with how to best memorialize in the agreement the terms and conditions of the transaction. A sale can be structured in a multitude of ways.

The following clauses are intended to provide some choices in structuring creative financing.

Modification of Loan Terms

A common technique in recent years of high interest rates has been to create short term seller take-back loans. It may be impossible to refinance these short terms loans. To avoid losses, foreclosures, bankruptcy and litigation involving brokers, mortgage loan brokers and the principals, negotiations for extensions of the seller take back loan will become a temporary solution. Form 9:04 is an example of an extension or modification agreement of an existing note secured by a mortgage or deed of trust.

FORM 9:04   MODIFICATION AGREEMENT

This Agreement, made and entered into, this _____ day of _____ _____ 19_____ by and between _____, herein called Borrower, and _____, herein called Lender.

Lender is the holder of a certain promissory note dated _____ in the amount of $_____, executed by _____, herein called Borrower, which note is secured by a deed of trust dated _____ and recorded _____ in Book _____ Official Records, Page _____, COUNTY OF _____ STATE OF CALIFORNIA; and
The parties hereto desire to modify the terms of said note:

In consideration of valuable considerations paid by Borrower to Lender, the parties agree:

1. That the principal balance outstanding on said Note as of _____
___ is $_____ with interest at _____ paid to _____.

2. The parties hereby modify the terms of said Note as follows:

    (a) The total indebtedness as shown in paragraph (1) shall be paid in monthly installments of $_____ each, or more, including interest at _____ percent per annum, payable on the _____ day of each and every month beginning and continuing until _____ , on which date the balance of principal then remaining unpaid, together with interest thereon, shall be due and payable.

    (b) Said promissory note and deed of trust, is hereby extended to _____ _____.

    (c) (Optional continue with late charge Form 9:17).

    (d) Borrower agrees to pay the indebtedness evidenced by said note as so modified and perform each and every obligation contained therein, or in any instrument at any time given to evidence or secure said indebtedness, or any part thereof, and also to comply with any covenant, condition or obligation in said deed of trust.

3. Borrower agrees to pay Lender on or before _____, 19_____, the additional sum of $_____ as compensation for Lender's costs and legal expenses incurred in connection with this modification agreement.

4. Borrower acknowledges that the funds represented by said note and this modification agreement were not primarily intended or used for personal, family or household purposes.

IT IS UNDERSTOOD AND AGREED that all terms and conditions of the above mentioned promissory note and deed of trust, including prior obligations thereof, if any, shall remain in full force and effect without change, except as hereinabove otherwise specifically provided.

_____   _____
Lender   Borrower

COMMENT ON FORM 9:04: The modification can also include a principal balance reduction or increase.

Anticipation of Refinancing Problems

In short term take-back loans or in hard-money loans where the lender is cooperative a safety valve permitting extension on certain conditions is an anticipatory precaution. To give the buyer such a protection the clause in Form 4:05 in the real estate contract and a corresponding clause in the note should be included.

FORM 9:05   **EXTENSION OPTION**

(Precede with Forms for seller take-back loans and Continue):

   In the event buyer is unable to obtain a new first loan at an initial interest rate not to exceed _____% for a term of not less than _____ years at the time when above described loan matures, the holder thereof shall permit a one time extension of the maturity date for a period of _____ months.

(Continue):

on the same terms and conditions as the original loan

(or):
(Continue):

provided buyer reduces the unpaid balance then due by the sum of _____
                                                                    $_____/

_____on the date of original maturity.
_____%

(or):
(Continue):

the terms of the loan to be modified as follows _____
                                                   set forth modification of payments,

_____
interest rate, added security, etc.

COMMENT ON FORM 9:05: An escape hatch in the form of a potential extension is favorable to a buyer under volatile interest conditions when new financing is hard to come by. It is particularly important in a balloon payment situation. It is always easier to negotiate such protection for the borrower at the time of sale, than when the balloon is ready to pop.

Subordination

   Refinancing can be structured into the original transaction in many ways depending upon the type of property and the seller's genuine desire to assist the buyer in financing. A typical situation is where a buyer buys subject to a first loan which has a short remaining time before it matures and seller is taking back a purchase money second. When the first is paid off the seller's loan moves up in first place. Buyer cannot refinance with a new first loan without paying off the seller's second loan. When anticipation of refinancing is structured into the original deal it's easier to obtain the seller's cooperation. The seller can agree to subordinate to a new first loan but limit the new one to an amount not larger than the loan being paid off. Seller can also subordinate to a larger loan upon participating partially or totally in any excess over the amount of payoff. See Form 9:06. See also Page 97. Revenue Bill of 1987 restricts interest deductibility on refinancing.[2]

FORM 9:06   SUBORDINATION TO REFINANCED LOAN

The _____ in favor of seller shall contain a
<small>mortgage/deed of trust</small>

subordination clause providing that said _____ may
<small>mortgage/deed of trust</small>

at any time and provided that _____
<small>the payments under said mortgage/deed of trust and taxes are</small>

_____ ,
<small>not then in default/no unrescinded notice of default under its terms then appears of record</small>

be made subject to and subordinated to a new _____
<small>mortgage/deed of trust</small>

to be executed by buyer in favor of any banking, federal or state savings and loan
association, insurance company, or pension fund _____
<small>in an amount not in excess</small>

_____
<small>of the amount necessary to pay off the existing first loan including prepayment penalties,</small>

_____ said new loan shall be payable at not more than
<small>reconveyance fees and recording fees;</small>

$_____ , _____
<small>monthly/quarterly/semi-annually/annually</small>

including interest not to exceed _____% per annum or if variable or adjustable
with a maximum increase over the life of the loan not to exceed _____%.

(Optional, Continue):

In the event buyer is able to obtain a new loan in an amount in excess of the amount necessary to pay off the existing first loan as set forth above, such excess amount after first deducting all loan originations fees, points, and recording fees shall be shared _____% to buyer and _____% to seller who shall reduce the unpaid principal balance of the subordinated loan with the cash received. Each party shall execute such instruments, documents, or agreements reasonably necessary to carry out this agreement.

COMMENT ON FORM 9:06: The clause in the mortgage or deed of trust should be drafted by counsel and approved by counsel for the title company acting as trustee under the deed of trust insuring the title.

Call Option for Vendor-Lender

Sellers often are forced to sell their property with a fixed rate interest loan amortized over 30 years but with an earlier 10–15 year due date. This may constitute a discount of the price and stops the seller effectively from reinvesting the proceeds in higher interest-bearing investments. Sellers can bail themselves out if there is a sharp interest rate increase by using another tactic. Into the loan can be written an option to demand payment in full after a period of years. A seven-year call option in a 15-year loan is not an unreasonable provision. See Form 9:07.

FORM 9:07   CALL OPTION IN PURCHASE MONEY LOANS

(precede with Forms for Seller take-back loans and Continue):

Seller shall have the option to require payment in full of the unpaid balance and accrued interest on the _____ anniversary of the date of the note or within thirty (30) days thereafter. If Lender exercises such option to accelerate, Lender shall mail Borrower notice of acceleration. Such notice shall provide a period of not less than thirty (30) days from the date the notice is mailed or delivered within which Borrower may pay the sums declared due. If Borrower fails to pay such sums prior to the expiration of such period, Lender may, without further notice or demand on Borrower, invoke any remedies permitted by applicable law.

COMMENT ON FORM 9:07: A corresponding clause should be inserted in the promissory note. Such provision may enhance the value of the note should seller need to raise cash selling the note and the mortgage.

Postponed Payback Provisions

Most of the clauses describing take-back loans in this chapter and in the Terms of Payment chapter can be adjusted so that payments can be postponed to a specific date or partial payments of interest be allowed together with a "catch-up" provision. The following clause is an example of how to structure such deferred payback.

FORM 9:08   NO PAYMENT FOR SPECIFIED PERIOD

(Precede with Forms 3:14, 3:26 or 9:02, Continue):

Payments to begin _____ from date of closing of escrow.
                      months/years

(Where payments are to be increased at specified time):

and continuing for _____ , when installments shall
                      _____ months/_____ years

be $_____.

(Where payments are less than the full interest on the loan and payor is to "catch up" at specified time):

Any accrued interest shall be paid in full on the _____

date/_____th anniversary

_____
date of note.

(With balloon payment):

_____ one final installment of approximately $_____ on the

and together with

_____th anniversary of the note.

COMMENT ON FORM 9:08: The above clause should be used with caution because such postponement of payments may be utilized by an unscrupulous buyer to "milk" the property.

Built-in Discount of Seller's Mortgage

Where a seller is carrying back a loan regardless of its pecking order of recording, a buyer can negotiate an automatic benefit. The seller may have indicated that he eventually is going to cash in the mortgage. The buyer can obtain the right to purchase the mortgage at a discount on a sliding scale as the loan ages. Form 9:09 shows how.

FORM 9:09   **SLIDING SCALE DISCOUNT OF**
PURCHASE LOAN

(Precede with any purchase money loan form):

Buyer shall have the option to pay off

_____ at a discount of

said loan/loan in favor of seller

_____ %   in the first year, _____% in the second year and

_____ %   in the third year and no discount thereafter.

Provided however that this option is only available to buyer if at the time of exercising the option, _____

the payments due under said mortgage/deed of trust and taxes are not then in

_____
default/no rescinded notice of default under its terms then appears of record

Buyer shall exercise the option by giving seller 30 days notice prior to date of payoff.

COMMENT ON FORM 9:09: Such discount is not unusual. It is important that the option is spelled out carefully in the note so that it will also be binding upon any holder other than the seller.

Interesting Ways with Interest

The following clauses illustrate individual methods of delaying payment of interest.

FORM 9:10   **INTEREST POSTPONED**

$_____ by buyer executing a note and _____
     amount seller to carry
_____ in that amount in favor of seller secured by the property pay-
mortgage deed of trust
able as follows:

Interest at the rate of _____% per annum from date of close of escrow and annually on the _____ .
                    anniversary thereof/on _____
                                                date
(Continue):

Principal payable on a date _____ from date of close
                                    days/months
of escrow, _____ thereafter until_____ years from date
        monthly/quarterly/semiannually/annually
of close of escrow, when the balance of _____ $ _____ shall become
                                        approximately
due and payable.

(Optional if no "prepayment penalty"):

The entire balance of principal may be prepaid at any time prior to maturity, on _____ days prior written notice, with interest to the date of such payment only.

(Optional if "prepayment penalty" clause):

The entire balance of principal may be prepaid at any time prior to maturity on _____ days prior written notice and upon payment of _____ months unearned interest in addition to interest to date of such payment.

COMMENT ON 9:10: Where a buyer contemplates selling the property in a few years and the cash flow is insufficient, payment of interest at the end of each year may be just the way to go. If the buyer contemplates selling the property in three years, only two payments of interest will be paid out of earnings, while the last payment can come from the proceeds of the sale. The pre-payment clause in Form 9:10 cannot be used in sales in California for dwellings with not more than four units.

FORM 9:11   SALE ON ALL-INCLUSIVE DEED OF TRUST

$_____, cash down payment including deposit

$_____, by buyer executing an All-Inclusive note and an All-Inclusive deed of trust in favor of seller secured by the property.

(If interest rate on total amount of All-Inclusive note is fixed, continue):

payable in _____ equal _____
monthly/quarterly/semi-annual/annual

installments of $_____, _____ interest at the rate of
or more/plus/including

_____% per annum from date of closing.

(If interest rate is to be less on the amount of principal consisting of existing loan, continue):

payable in _____ equal _____
monthly/quarterly/semi-annual/annual

installments of $_____, with interest from date of closing as hereinafter provided:

(Optional):
(Installment Tax Sale, California, continue):

payable interest only in installments of $_____ from date of closing and continuing until _____ ;
end of calendar year/date

thereafter, principal and interest payments to be paid as provided herein.

(Continue):

Interest on the note shall be payable at the following rates:

(1) _____% per annum on the unpaid principal balance of the underlying _____
_____; and
note/notes

(2) _____% per annum on that portion of the unpaid principal balance on the All-Inclusive note which represents the excess over the unpaid principal balance of the underlying note.

(In all cases, continue):

The principal amount of the All-Inclusive note shall include the unpaid principal balance(s) of the following described underlying obligation(s):

(Form continues on next page)

The unpaid balance of $_____ as of _____
the date of execution hereof/_____
date
of the promissory note dated _____ 19____ in the original amount of
$_____ with interest of ____% per annum, executed by _____
_____, in favor of _____, as beneficiary
lender
recorded _____ 19____ Document No.: ____ Book ____ page
____ official records of _____ County, California.

and later assigned to _____ as beneficiary.

COMMENT ON 9:11: The above wording can be simplified if the all-inclusive or the "wrap-around" instruments are prepared in advance and can be attached as exhibits to the contract. Otherwise it is best to include the key provisions of the all inclusive financing in the contract. The wrap-around note and deed of trust must be carefully drawn and should not be left to drafting by an escrow holder without legal supervision. While standard deed of trusts can be modified, the safer way is to use the special wrap-around notes and deeds of trust, the institutional trustee, the title company which is to insure title may provide. The wrap-around deed of trust and note must conform to the terms and conditions of the underlying loan's similar instruments.

Any event which triggers or permits acceleration of the underlying note and deed of trust must also permit acceleration under the wrap-around instruments. The late charge prepayment and provisions should be compatible. If prepayment is permitted, the note must show who is to pay prepayment charges on the underlying obligation. If prepayment is restricted on the underlying note, the all-inclusive note should either prohibit prepayment or limit the prepayment to any amount in excess of the unpaid balance of the underlying debt. Sellers and buyers should anticipate the situation where the balance of the underlying note equals the balance on the wrap-around note. Is the buyer then entitled to reconveyance of the wrap-around deed of trust or is seller still entitled to continue receipt of the interest differential, even if his principal interest in the wrap-around has been reduced to zero? What ever the decision is it must be spelled out in the wrap-around note.

Special consideration of the loan amortization is also necessary. Preferably the amortization should be set up so that the balance of the wrap-around note during its term exceeds the balance of the underlying note. Some buyers have reservations about the seller maintaining control over the security by remaining liable for making the payments on the underlying deed of trust. The buyer may want a third party collection agent. This may cause the seller to realize a taxable gain where the encumbrances exceed the seller's adjusted basis in the property, because this structuring of the transaction may be treated by the IRS as an assumption of the underlying loan by the buyer. To assure the buyer protection the seller can provide the buyer, within a certain time frame, with proof of payment. The buyer can also file a Request for Notice of Default or Sale or have such request incorporated in the wrap-around deed of trust.

Usually the title company which may have to insure title after default will spell out the rights of the parties in case of default and foreclosure. Knowledgeable handling of foreclosure proceedings is a must in wrap-around situations.

Lease Options

The use of options as an acquisition technique is covered elsewhere in this book. Leases with a long term option to purchase has become a financing tool where an enforceable "due on sale" clause is found in an existing encumbrance. Short term leases with options to purchase have different purposes such as 1) a "soft sell" buying technique, 2) making difficult to sell property easier to market, 3) obtaining increased "cash flow" by higher rent because of the option to purchase feature of the lease, 4) tying up a new home during the rental term and using that period to dispose of present residence and 5) it can mean for brokers earning both leasing and selling commissions on the same property.

Leases with option to purchase can trigger "due on sale clauses." See page 60. Form 3:41 can be adopted as a disclosure form. If an offer to lease is considered necessary such form should be utilized, preferably with a copy of the proposed lease and the option attached as exhibits. A residential lease form can be used and the option can be written either as in Form 3:42 or as in Form 9:12.

FORM 9:12   LEASE WITH OPTION TO PURCHASE

The lessee shall have the option to purchase the property at any time during the term of the lease, provided that the lessee has complied with all of the terms of the lease and the rent is current for a purchase price of $_____ and on the following terms and conditions:

(Insert all terms of payment, personal property included in sale, etc.)

The option shall be exercised by mailing or delivering written notice _____ days to the lessor prior to the expiration of the lease. If mailed notice shall be effected by registered or certified mail, postage prepaid, return receipt requested, and shall be deemed communicated as of _____
                                        mailing/actual receipt/_____ from date of mailing
Notices hereunder shall be addressed as follows:

Lessee _____

Lessor _____

Optionee _____ this option.
                        may/may not assign

(Optional continue):

If optionee fails to exercise this option in accordance with its terms and within the option period, then this option and the rights of optionee shall automatically and immediately terminate without notice.

(Form continues on next page)

Any extension of this lease or holding over by the lessee upon expiration of the original lease term shall not extend the time for exercise of this option unless the option itself is extended by an instrument in writing executed by both lessor and lessee.

If the option is not exercised, optionee hereby agree to properly execute, acknowledge and deliver to optionor within _____ days of request therefor a quit claim deed, release or other document required by optionor or a title insurance company to verify the termination of the option agreement. If any action or proceeding to enforce this agreement the prevailing party shall be entitled to reasonable attorney's fees and costs.

COMMENT ON FORM 9:12: All of the terms of the option should be spelled out. Some printed forms have inadequate information regarding title, proration, insurance, risk of loss, etc. See recommendations contained in Comments on Form 3:43.

Right of First Refusal

Some sellers are reluctant to grant a tenant an option to purchase especially if the price is fixed at the outset and is not to be determined at the time the option is exercised. Tenants are also not too eager to sign a lease where the option to purchase is based upon a future price. An often employed compromise is the "Right of First Refusal", as set forth in Form 9:13.

FORM 9:13   RIGHT OF FIRST REFUSAL

If during the term of this lease or any extension thereof, not including a holding over after the expiration of the original term or extension thereof, the lessor shall receive an offer to purchase _____
the leased premises/or the property of which they

_____ or if lessor intends to enter into an agreement for the sale of said
are a part

_____lessor shall first give lessee written notice setting forth the
premises/property

name and address of the prospective buyer, the purchase price, and all the terms and conditions of the proposed sale. After delivery or mailing of such notice in accordance with the conditions for delivery of notice under this lease, lessee shall have the right to purchase the _____
premises/property

upon the same terms and conditions. This right of first refusal shall be exercised by delivery or mailing such election to lessor prior to the expiration of said fifteen (15) days. Should tenant elect not to purchase on such terms and within said fifteen (15) days, the right of first refusal shall be deemed expired and lessor may proceed to sell the _____
premises/property

upon the terms and conditions set forth in the notice to lessee.

COMMENT ON FORM 9:13: Right to First Refusal is enforceable. It gives the tenant less protection than an option to purchase, but is more flexible for the lessor. See Form 4:41 for clause, when the owner has given tenant Right of First Refusal, but wants to sell.

A private lender may be willing to limit the right to exercise a due-on-sale clause to the *Wellenkamp* concepts: impaired security or increased risk of default. An appropriate provision can be inserted in the Real Estate Purchase Contract and Receipt for Deposit. See Form 9:14.

**FORM 9:14   LIMITED "DUE-ON-SALE" CLAUSE
SUBJECT TO CREDIT WORTHINESS**

(Precede with forms for seller take-back loans and continue):

The _____ in favor of _____
       mortgage/deed of trust   lender (name/seller)

shall contain the following:

If trustor sells or transfers all or any part of the property or an interest therein excluding (a) the creation of a lien or encumbrance subordinate to this

_____
mortgage/deed of trust

(b) transfers set forth in California Civil Code Section 2924.6, trustor shall not later than ten (10) days before completion of such sale or transfer cause to be submitted information required by beneficiary to evaluate the transferee as if a new loan were being made to the transferee. Trustor will continue to be obligated under the note and this _____ unless
                  mortgage/deed of trust

beneficiary releases borrower in writing.

If beneficiary, on the basis of any information obtained regarding the transferee, reasonably determines that the lender's security may be impaired, or that there is an unacceptable likelihood of a breach of any covenants or agreement in this deed of trust, or if the required information is not submitted, beneficiary may declare all of the sums secured by this _____ to be immediately
                  mortgage/deed of trust

due and payable

(Optional, continue):

If lender exercises such option to accelerate, lender shall mail borrower notice of acceleration. Such notice shall provide a period of not less than thirty (30) from the date the notice is mailed or delivered within which borrower may pay the sums declared due. If borrower fails to pay such sums prior to the expiration of such period, lender may, without further notice or demand on borrower, invoke any remedies permitted by applicable law.

COMMENT ON FORM 9:14: The clauses modified by changing "trustor" to "maker" and "beneficiary" to "payee" should also be part of the promissory note. CC 2924.6 prohibits lenders from acceleration if the transfer is a) a result of death of obligor and an obligor spouse is the transferred, b) to a wife of obligor, c) transfer into an intervivos trust, d) a result of divorce or property settlement wherein the obligor continues to be obligated to make the loan payments and a spouse, also an obligor, becomes the sole owner. These rules are similar to the regulations under the Garn Act. See page 60.

Some lenders may be able to prove the buyer's lack of credit worthiness or an increased risk of default due to the buyer's management ability. One expert has observed that short of finding that the buyer is an insolvent arsonist, such proof may be difficult.

Creative acquisition of real property includes some bartering or the use of personal property as down payment. See Form 3:33. However, the title may be clouded. To discover any encumbrances a Uniform Commercial Code Title Search should be undertaken as envisioned in Form 9:15.

FORM 9:15   UCC FINANCING SEARCH BY ESCROW

The escrow holder shall be instructed to order a Uniform Commercial Code Financing Statement search covering the personal property described _____

_____.
above/in exhibit _____.

(Where existing loans are to be paid off, continue):

Any encumbrances disclosed by the UCC search and approved by seller shall be paid from funds due seller in escrow, making the transfer of the personal property free and clear of any encumbrances.

(Continue in all cases):

Seller shall deliver to escrow a bill of sale for the personal property together with an assignment of all warranties or guarantees of any kind seller may have concerning the personal property.

COMMENT ON FORM 9:15: Whenever substantial personal property is included in a sale, the UCC search is an excellent precaution. If the personal property constitutes the majority of assets such as inventory, the bulk transfer requirements of Commercial Code Sections 6101–6111 may also have to be complied with. See also discussion after Form 4:41 and Forms 4:42–4:45.

Letters of Intent

Particularly in larger transactions investors often start negotiations with a letter of intent. If approved by the seller a binding contract will have been created. The letter of intent sets the negotiations going and a more final contract normally is executed by the parties. The following form is a draft copy of a letter used by a large California investment company in acquiring (many) of the extensive residential investments the company owns and manages.

FORM 9:16   LETTER OF INTENT TO PURCHASE PROPERTY

This is a firm offer by _____ or its nominee, to purchase the _____-unit apartment complex including land and improvements known as _____ in _____ upon the following terms and conditions.

1. Purchase Price: $_____ (price to vary according to the outstanding principal balance of mortgages at time of closing).
2. Cash to Seller: $_____ (Firm)
3. A nonrecourse Second Note and Deed of Trust to Seller: $_____ at _____% payable $_____ monthly. Buyer to receive a 15% discount if paid off during the first five (5) years.
4. Buyer to take subject to a First Note and Deed of Trust in the approximate amount of $_____ at _____% interest, payable $_____ monthly.
5. Buyer to pay a real estate commission to _____ in the amount of $_____. No real estate commission to be paid by Seller.
6. Seller to provide and pay for the cost of title insurance, loan transfer fees, transfer taxes and recording costs.
7. Standard prorations to be performed at close of escrow in cash.
8. Buyer to have twenty (20) days from the date of execution of this agreement to examine and approve, in its sole discretion, the property, and its books and records.
9. Seller has represented that for the past twelve (12) months the Real and Personal Property taxes are approximately $_____ for the project. If the actual taxes are greater than $_____, then the Buyer may capitalize the difference at 8% and deduct said amount from the purchase price and cash.
10. Seller has represented that for the past twelve (12) months the gas, electric, water, sewer, and trash costs were approximately $_____ for the project. If the actual utilities are greater than $_____, then the Buyer may capitalize the difference at 8% and deduct said amount from the purchase price and cash.

(Form continues on next page)

11. Seller has represented that the annualized rent roll is $_____ from apartments only. If at closing the actual annualized rent roll is less than $_____, then the Buyer may capitalize the difference at 8% and deduct the amount from the purchase price and cash. Vacancies shall be treated as rented at street rents.

12. This agreement to be superseded by formal documentation between Buyer and Seller within ten (10) days of Buyer's approval, as referred to in Paragraph 7, above. Upon execution of said formal documentation, Buyer to deposit $50,000 in escrow as a good-faith deposit. Said sum to be liquidated damages in the event of default by Buyer.

13. Close of escrow to be on or before _____ at Buyer's election.

COMMENT ON FORM 9:16: Letters of Intent can also be used in exchange and lease proposals. Such letters should be prepared with care to cover all relevant items. The legal effectiveness of a letter of intent should be determined by counsel.

Late Charges

While late charges are prescribed by statute in California for single family, owner-occupied homes, there is no statutory limitations on other property loans. However, late charges are in the nature of liquidated damages. Form 9:17 is designed to comply with the liquidated damages law in California CC 1671(b) for owner take-back credit sales.

FORM 9:17   LATE CHARGES IN INCOME PROPERTY LOANS

The note in favor of seller shall contain the following:

The maker(s) acknowledge(s) that if payment is made late that the payee will incur additional costs such as, but not limited to, processing and accounting charges. In the event that any installment is not received by payee when due, maker(s) shall pay to payee a late charge payment of ____% of the past due amount. The parties agree that proof of actual damages would be costly or impractical and that the late charge represents a reasonable sum considering all of the circumstances existing on the date of this note and is a fair and reasonable estimate of the cost that payee will incur as a result of late payment. Acceptance of any late charge payment shall not be deemed a waiver of the default caused by the past due amount and shall not constitute a waiver of any other rights and remedies available to payee.

COMMENT ON FORM 9:17: See Form 3:22.

Letter of Credit

Many investors wish to maintain full use of their cash until payment is required under the terms of the Contract to Purchase Real Estate. The use of a letter of credit helps the investors in obtaining high return on the cash which would ordinarily be paid over as "earnest money." Letters of credit may be the next best thing to cash and protects the seller almost as well against default.

A letter of credit should be issued by an institutional lender and obligate the issuer to honor drafts or demands of the beneficiary of the credit up to a given amount. For the seller's (beneficiary's) protection it should be irrevocable and the issuer primarily liable.

Letters of credit are most often used as deposits on purchases or as security "deposits" on long term leases. The letter of credit is an instrument which is also useful in syndication, where partnership contributions are held in escrow during the formation. A standby letter of credit may also assist a seller in tax planning conforming to Treasury Regulation Section 15A.453-1(b)(3)(iii).

FORM 9:18   LETTER OF CREDIT AS DEPOSIT

(Insert in deposit section of C.A.R. form the deposit as "by letter of credit" and in terms of payment the following):

The letter of credit to be provided as deposit hereunder shall be issued by

_____
name of financial institution/a commercial bank

in the amount of $_____, be irrevocable, and payable on demand to escrow holder, but no demand shall be effective before _____. The letter of
                                                          date/occurrence

credit shall be delivered to _____ not later than
                                        seller/escrow holder

_____, if not, this agreement shall be deemed terminated and of no further
  date

effect.

COMMENT ON FORM 9:18: The contract and letter of credit should spell out the condition, event or occurrence if other than a date, when payment may be demanded. Appropriate instructions should be delivered to escrow of such condition and give authorization for demand for payment by escrow holder.

Tax Service

Whenever a seller furnishes substantial financing assistance to a buyer it is good practice to protect the continued investment in the property by watching that the property taxes are paid promptly. Institutional lenders require that the borrower pay for a tax service, which twice a year check that the property tax installments have been paid. A private lender should insist on such protection as well. See Form 9:19.

FORM 9:19   REQUEST FOR TAX SERVICE

Escrow shall be instructed to obtain tax services at _____
buyer's/seller's
expense on the seller take-back loan. The service shall be retained during the term of the loan.

COMMENT ON FORM 9:19: Most title companies have subsidiaries which for a minimal fee provide property tax service which notifies the holder of any tax delinquencies.

Home Equity Sale Contracts on Residences in Foreclosure in California

A chapter of the Civil Code entitled "Home Equity Sales Contracts" requires the execution of a written contract between an "equity seller" and "equity purchaser" on the sale or conveyance of "a residence in foreclosure." A "residence in foreclosure" is defined as residential property consisting of four or fewer units, one of which is occupied as the principal residence of the owner, against which there is an outstanding, recorded Notice of Default.

The law specifies certain requirements for a Home Equity Sales Contract, and requires that the contract contain a right of cancellation permitting the seller to cancel the contract until midnight of the fifth business day following its execution or until 8:00 A.M. on the day scheduled for the trustees' sale, whichever occurs first.

An equity contract shall be written in letters of a size equal to 10-point bold type, in the same language principally used by the equity purchaser and equity seller to negotiate the sale of the residence in foreclosure and shall be fully completed and signed and dated by the equity seller and equity purchaser prior to the execution of any instrument of conveyance of the residence in foreclosure.

The contract shall contain the entire agreement of the parties and shall include the following terms:

(a) The name, business address, and the telephone number of the equity purchaser.

(b) The address of the residence in foreclosure.

(c) The total consideration to be given by the equity purchaser in connection with or incident to the sale.

(d) A complete description of the terms of payment or other consideration including, but not limited to, any services of any nature which the equity purchaser represents he will perform for the equity seller before or after the sale.

(e) The time at which possession is to be transferred to the equity purchaser.

(f) The terms of any rental agreement.

(g) A notice of cancellation as provided in subdivision (b) of Section 1695.5.

(h) The following notice in at least 14-point boldface type, if the contract is printed or in capital letters if the contract is typed, and completed with the name of the equity purchaser, immediately above the statement required by Section 1695.5(a):

NOTICE REQUIRED BY CALIFORNIA LAW
Until your right to cancel this contract has ended, _____ (Name) or anyone working for _____ (Name) CANNOT ask you to sign or have you sign any deed or any other document.

The contract shall contain in immediate proximity to the space reserved for the equity seller's signature a conspicuous statement in a size equal to at least 12-point bold type, if the contract is printed or in capital letters if the contract is typed, as provided by Section 1695.5, as follows:

You may cancel this contract for the sale of your house without any penalty or obligation at any time before _____ (Date and time of day). See the attached notice of cancellation form for an explanation of this right.

The equity purchaser shall accurately enter the date and time of day on which the rescission right ends.

The contract shall be accompanied by a completed form in duplicate, captioned "notice of cancellation" in a size equal to 12-point bold type, if the contract is printed or in capital letters if the contract is typed, followed by a space in which the equity purchaser shall enter the date on which the equity seller executes any contract. This form shall be attached to the contract, shall be easily detachable, and shall contain in type of at least 10-point, if the contract is printed or in capital letters if the contract is typed, the following statement written in the same language as used in the contract:

NOTICE OF CANCELLATION
_____
(Enter date contract signed)

You may cancel this contract for the sale of your house, without any penalty or obligation, at any time before _____ ___ (Enter date and time of day).

To cancel this transaction, personally deliver a signed and dated copy of this cancellation notice, or send a telegram to _____ _____ (Name of purchaser), at _____ (Street address of purchaser's place of business) NOT LATER THAN _____ _____ (Enter date and time of day). I hereby cancel this transaction _____ _____ (Date).

_____
(Seller's signature)

The equity purchaser shall provide the equity seller with a copy of the contract and the attached notice of cancellation.

The legislation prohibits certain actions by equity purchasers during the cancellation period (e.g., paying equity seller any consideration, recording any document signed by the equity seller, etc.).

An "equity purchase" takes place where the property is 1) acquired by persons unrelated to the equity seller by blood or marriage, 2) acquired directly from the equity seller and the property is *not* to be occupied as the purchaser's residence and 3) not acquired in satisfaction of voluntary indebtedness (deed in lieu of foreclosure), or pursuant to statute or judgment of Court.

The legislation makes it unlawful for any person to initiate, enter into, negotiate, or consummate any transaction involving residential property in foreclosure whereby the transaction, by its terms, takes *unconscionable advantage* of the property owner in foreclosure. Where any of these acts occurs, the transaction is voidable and may be rescinded within two years of the date of the recordation of the conveyance of the residential real property in foreclosure.

A subsequent resale of residence to a *bona fide purchaser* cuts off the equity seller's right to rescind, unless the equity seller has recorded a Notice of Rescission of the sale. But this does not prevent the equity seller from filing a civil action seeking actual and exemplary damages.

Where the purchaser does not fall within the definition of an "equity purchaser", but is a bona fide purchaser for value who buys the property directly from the seller to use as a personal residence, a regular Real Estate Purchase Contract and Receipt of Deposit can be used. It should specifically state that the buyer is purchasing the property for use as a personal residence to fall within the exemption of the Home Equity Sales Contracts Act. Form 9:20.

FORM 9:20   PURCHASE OF RESIDENCE IN FORECLOSURE

Buyer acknowledges that the property is in foreclosure and that a sale may be subject to the provision of Civil Code Sections 1695–1695.14 "Home Equity Sales Contracts" and that title insurance may be difficult to obtain.

Buyer is allowed _____ days from date of seller's acceptance hereof, for inquiries concerning obtaining title insurance insuring buyer's title. If such inquiry discloses conditions or information unsatisfactory to the buyer, _____ may
he/she
cancel this agreement. If notice in writing thereof has not been delivered to seller within such time, this condition shall be deemed waived.

COMMENT ON FORM 9:20: Real Estate licensees should be cautious in representing principals in transactions where foreclosure has been started and should disclose potential problems and advise their principals to consult with an attorney or a title company before proceeding.

Private lenders may again enforce the due-on-sale clause in new loans upon resale. Sophisticated buyers may wish to negotiate limitations on such exercise. Contractual limitations are enforceable. See form 9:21.

FORM 9:21   **ONE-TIME TRANSFER**

(Precede with Form 3:17, or 3:18, 3:19, 3:26, 3:27, 3:28)

The note and deed of trust in favor of seller shall contain the following:
Notwithstanding anything to the contrary contained herein, the payor-trustor may transfer title to or an interest in the subject property *once* during the terms of the loan,

(Optional continue):

provided that the unpaid principal balance at the time of the transfer be reduced by _____
$ _____/_____%.

(Optional continue):

and provided that the terms of the loan be modified as follows:
The _____ installments _____
    monthly/quarterly/semiannually/annually   including/plus
interest at _____% per annum, or more _____
                                       and become due in full
_____ from date of close of resale escrow.
_____ months/ _____ years

(Optional continue):

Transferee to execute such written assumption agreement as beneficiary may require _____
        and original payee/trustor to execute such written guarantee of payment as beneficiary
_____ Assumption fee to be _____
may require. $ _____/ _____ points.

(Optional continue):

Transferee shall not later than ten (10) days before completion of such sale or transfer cause to submit to beneficiary customary credit information. Beneficiary's waiver of acceleration shall be conditioned upon transferee meeting credit standards customarily applied by other similarly situated lenders or sellers in the geographical market within which the transaction is occuring for similar loans and property.

(Continue in all cases):

The one time waiver of the beneficiary's option to accelerate shall not be construed as a waiver of such right upon future transfers of title or interests in the subject property.

Chapter 10
Options

To buy or not to buy: that is the option . . .

Anon.

An option to purchase real property is distinguishable from a Real Estate Purchase Contract and Receipt for Deposit. An option is a contract by which the owner (optionor) of the property gives a potential buyer (optionee) the exclusive right to purchase the property within a limited time without imposing a duty to purchase. A Real Estate Contract and Receipt for Deposit *obligates* the buyer to purchase on the terms and conditions of the contract. The right to purchase under an option for which a consideration has been given is irrevocable.

An option has many advantages to a buyer. Some of these are: a) no one else can buy the property during the option period, b) the option period can be used to investigate the property, c) negotiation for adjoining properties can be made in secret, d) financing can be arranged, e) speculation in increase in value is possible with small outlay.

Should an optionor refuse to convey the property after a valid exercise of the option, the optionee is entitled to specific performance. Once the option is exercised a bilateral contract is created. A court will determine whether the price for the purchase is just and reasonable as of the time the option was entered into and not on the date of its exercise.

When an option is exercised it creates a real property contract for the sale of the property which relates back to the date of the option agreement. Normally the contract binds the optionor to the terms on that date. The priority rights of the optionee takes precedence over any party who had knowledge, actual or constructive, of the existence of the option and failed to record first. Death of the optionor does not cancel the option. The optionee can enforce the contract with the assistance of the probate court unless there are conflicting claims necessitating litigation. An option can be assigned if assignment is not restricted.

C.A.R.'s option form combines the option grant with space for specific terms and "boiler-plate" for the sales and title provisions.

To avoid future misunderstandings it is paramount to establish the option period. It can of course begin upon the date of its execution or at a future date.

It can also be conditioned upon the happening of a specific event. The option period can be extended as agreed to between the parties.

The benefits to the seller are also substantial. The seller avoids executing a purchase agreement riddled with contingencies and with conditions precedent to the buyers' performance. Such conditions often give rise to questions of whether or not they have been satisfied. Tax advantages can also accrue from the proper timing of options, postponing the optionee's right to exercise it to a time most advantageous to the optionor.

Options are often used in complex transactions and nearly always in land development. The technique of executing successive options in sales of lots to be developed may be more desirable than transfer of title and holding a purchase money mortgage with releases. Basically options are subject to fewer restrictions than real estate contracts in general. Retention of forfeited deposits under real estate contracts are not automatic. On failure of the optionee to exercise the option the consideration paid for the option may be retained by the optionor without the pitfalls inherent in real estate sales contracts.

An option can take several forms. It can be a separate option agreement with a Real Estate Purchase Contract attached, a method often used in options contained in leases. In such situations the option agreement contains only the grant of the option and the manner in which it is to be exercised. All the other terms and conditions are found in the Real Estate Sales Contract attached to the document incorporating the option. See Forms 3:42, 3:43 and 9:12.

FORM 10:01   EXTENSION OF OPTION PERIOD

Optionor further grant to optionee the right to extend the original option period until noon on _____ 19____, provided optionee is not in breach of this agreement and give notice and tender additional consideration in the sum of _____ dollars $_____ before the expiration of the original option period.

COMMENT ON FORM 10:01: A right to extend the option period is valuable to the optionee who may have to make extensive investigations of the property to overcome problems about zoning and permits. A prepermitted extension even for an additional consideration may give the optionee sufficient time and avoid the loss of the original consideration paid for the option.

Consideration for Option to be Applied to Purchase Price

Where there is no consideration for an option the optionor can revoke the unilateral offer to sell the property at any time prior to acceptance by the optionee. Any consideration is deemed sufficient to create a binding option. The consideration paid for an option, such as a lump sum or rent payments or part thereof are often applied to the purchase price. The option itself or the attached Real Estate Purchase Agreement and Receipt for Deposit should set forth in detail how the consideration will be applied. See Form 10:02.

FORM 10:02 CREDIT FOR OPTION CONSIDERATION

If this option ______________ thereof is exercised in accor-
(or any extension)
dance with its terms, ________ the consideration paid Optionor by Optionee
(____% of)
______________________ apply to the purchase price.
(shall/shall not)

(If limited to the consideration for orginal term, continue):

Any consideration paid for any extension of the original term ________
(shall not/shall)
______________________ apply to the purchase price.
(only to the extent of ______%.)

COMMENTS ON FORM 10:02: Extension consideration may be treated differently from the original consideration for the first term of the option.

Recording of the Option

In many situations neither party to an option desire any public notices of the option. However, the buyer is exposed to risk of prior liens or encumbrances being recorded and taking priority over the option. To protect against such eventualities a memorandum of the option can be recorded to give constructive notice of the existance of the option. Such memorandum should be prepared by the optionee's attorney because it should contain only such provisions of the option agreement necessary to protect the interest of the parties. The option agreement itself should protect the optionee from any changes in the status of the title or use of the property during the option period. See Form 10:03.

FORM 10:03 WARRANTY AGAINST ENCUMBRANCES ON OPTIONED PROPERTY

Optionor agrees during the term of the option or any extension thereof not to encumber the property in any manner nor grant any contractual or property right in the subject property without the prior written consent of optionee.

COMMENTS ON FORM 10:03: If the property contains units to be rented during the option period Form 4:37 can be inserted.

Entry upon Option Property

Where property is to be investigated, surveys obtained and test borings made, the option should provide for permission to enter the land for these purposes as set forth in Form 10:04.

FORM 10:04   RIGHT OF ENTRY ON OPTION PROPERTY

During the term of the option or any extension thereof, optionee shall have the right to enter upon subject property for the purpose of making a survey and conducting test borings, soil tests and engineer's studies at optionee's expense. Optionee shall at all times keep the property free and clear of mechanic's liens and shall indemnify and hold the optionor harmless from any liability for loss or damage to the property and for any injuries to or death of persons as a result of any acts of optionee, optionee's agents and independent contractors by reason of the right granted herein.

COMMENT ON FORM 10:04: This form should be adapted to the circumstances of the transaction.

FORM 10:05   OPTIONOR'S COOPERATION IN OBTAINING PERMITS

Should optionee desire to make application for rezoning of the property or any part thereof, or seek approval of plans or permits required by any governmental agency in order to develop the property in a manner satisfactory to optionee, optionor shall upon request execute any and all instruments and documents or to join in any applications which may be required. Optionee agrees to hold optionor harmless from any cost and expenses incurred in obtaining such approvals or permits.

COMMENT ON FORM 10:05: In most situations the municipal or county or state agency require that the owner of the property join in the type of application contemplated under this clause.

Risk of Loss

C.A.R.'s Real Estate Purchase Option form does not contain a risk of loss clause just as the C.A.R. Real Estate Purchase Contract and Receipt for Deposit. Both forms are designed to rely on the Uniform Vendor and Purchaser Risk Act which is deemed incorporated in any contract for sale of real property in states where this law has been adopted. See Chapter 5 and Forms 5:17, 5:18 and 5:19, which can be incorporated in the option form as described. California law is unclear, but may follow other jurisdictions, which hold that the optionee can enforce the option and purchase the property at the option price less the value of the damaged or destroyed improvements. The optionor appears not to be obligated to repair the damage and, unless there is a total destruction, no refund of the option consideration to the optionee will be allowed. The provisions for risk of loss should be inserted in the option itself particularly if the option is contained in a lease.

Under the Uniform Act the risk of loss is borne by the optionor if the optionee does not exercise the option. Of course clauses can be drafted which favor either party. Form 10:06 suggests some alternatives.

FORM 10:06   **RISK OF LOSS**

If the improvements on the property are destroyed or materially damaged prior to the exercise of the option, optionee shall be entitled:

(First alternative):

to within _____ days of notice thereof the right to terminate this agreement and obtain a refund of the consideration paid optionor prorated according to the duration of the option period from date of option to the date of the material loss or damage.

(Second alternative):

upon exercise of the option to offset the insurance proceeds collected for said material loss or damage against the purchase price.

COMMENT ON FORM 10:06: Material loss is defined in Form 5:18 which may also be included in the option. Where substantial improvements are included in the purchase price, the issues of risk of loss and condemnation should be referred to counsel for the parties.

Condemnation

California law has evolved to a point where an optionee, instead of having just a contract right, may be considered to have a compensable property right in the event of condemnation proceedings. If there is no specific statement in the option agreement, California case law appears to be that the optionee in a condemnation situation would receive the excess, if any, of the amount of the award above the option price.

Where the consideration for the option is only nominal it seems unfair that the optionee is to share in a condemnation award. The option can then simply provide: "The optionee shall have no compensable interest and right to share in any condemnation award if all or part of the property is taken under eminent domain."

If the consideration for the option is considerable, an election to proceed or to share in the award may be more protective to the prospective buyer.

FORM 10:07   **CONDEMNATION**

If during the option period and before close of escrow any condemnation or eminent domain proceeding or any proceeding in lieu of condemnation be instigated against the subject property or any part thereof, the party receiving notice of such proceeding shall promptly notify the other party thereof.

Optionee shall be entitled to _____ days of receipt of notice of such proceeding to terminate this agreement and optionor shall upon notice of such termination refund to optionee all consideration paid for the option.

Should optionee elect to proceed with the purchase in accordance with the terms of the option, optionee shall have a compensable interest and right to share in the condemnation award to the extent of the excess, if any, of the total award above the purchase price designated in the option.

COMMENTS ON FORM 10:07: Condemnation clauses should be carefully studied by counsel for the parties and the tailor made to fit the particular transaction.

Exercise of Option

When the optionee desires to exercise the option notice to the optionor must be given *exactly* as prescribed in the option agreement and within the expiration date of the option or any extension thereof. See Form 10:08.

FORM 10:08   NOTICE OF EXERCISE OF OPTION

Notice is hereby given that the undersigned optionee exercises the right to purchase the property described in the Real Estate Purchase Option dated _____ 19_____, between _____ as optionor and _____
            name of optionor   name of optionee
as optionee, in accordance with all of the terms and conditions of the option.
Dated _____ 19_____

COMMENT ON FORM 10:08: This notice should be signed by the optionee in the same manner as appearing on the original agreement unless signed by an assignee, which should be identified as such. Delivery of the notice should strictly follow the provisions for notice in the agreement.

FORM 10:09   CAR'S REAL ESTATE PURCHASE OPTION

California Association of Realtors® Standard Form

REAL ESTATE PURCHASE OPTION

THIS IS INTENDED TO BE A LEGALLY BINDING CONTRACT. READ IT CAREFULLY.

_____ , California. _____ , 19 ____

Received from _____ ,

herein called Optionee, the sum of _____ Dollars $ _____

evidenced by cash ☐, cashier's check ☐, or _____ ☐, personal check ☐ payable to _____

_____ ,

receipt of which is hereby acknowledged. In consideration of this payment, _____ ,

herein called Optionor, grants to Optionee the option for the period beginning _____ 19 ____

and terminating at noon on _____ 19 ____ to purchase the real property situated in

_____ County of _____ , California,

described as follows: _____

_____

for the purchase price of _____ Dollars $ _____

upon the following terms and conditions:

1. _____

Set forth above any terms and conditions of a factual nature applicable to this transaction, such as financing, the matter of structural pest control inspection, repairs and personal property to be included in the purchase price.

2.   This option is ☐ is not ☐ assignable by Optionee.

3.   The supplements initialed below are incorporated as part of this agreement.

Other

____ Structural Pest Control Certification Agreement   ____ Occupancy Agreement   ____ _____

____ Special Studies Zone Disclosure   ____ VA Amendment   ____ _____

____ Flood Insurance Disclosure   ____ FHA Amendment   ____ _____

4.   Optionor and Optionee acknowledge receipt of a copy of this page, which constitutes Page 1 of _____ Pages.

X _____   X _____
OPTIONEE   OPTIONOR

X _____   X _____
OPTIONEE   OPTIONOR

A REAL ESTATE BROKER IS THE PERSON QUALIFIED TO ADVISE ON REAL ESTATE. IF YOU DESIRE LEGAL ADVICE CONSULT YOUR ATTORNEY.

To order, contact California Association of Realtors®
525 So. Virgil Avenue, Los Angeles, California 90020
Copyright © (1982) California Association of Realtors®

REAL ESTATE PURCHASE OPTION

The following terms and conditions are hereby incorporated in and made a part of the Option.

5. Optionee may exercise this option by execution and tender to Optionor of a notice thereof which shall be delivered not less than _____ days prior to the expiration date of this option.

6. Unless otherwise provided herein, any notice, tender or delivery to be given hereunder by either party to the other may be effected by personal delivery in writing or by registered or certified mail, postage prepaid, return receipt requested, and shall be deemed communicated as of mailing. Mailed notices shall be addressed as set forth below, but each party may change his or her address by written notice to the other.

7. If Optionee fails to exercise this option in accordance with its terms and within the option period or any extension thereof, then this option and the rights of Optionee shall automatically and immediately terminate without notice. Thereafter, Optionee shall properly execute, acknowledge, and deliver to Optionor within ten (10) days of request therefor, a release, quitclaim deed, or any other document required by Optionor or a title insurance company to verify the termination of this Agreement.

8. In the event this option or any extension thereof is not exercised, all sums paid and services rendered to Optionor by Optionee shall be retained by Optionor in consideration of the granting of this option.

9. Optionor and Optionee shall deliver signed instructions to the escrow holder, _____ , within _____ days from exercise of this option which shall provide for closing within _____ days from Optionor's acceptance. Escrow fees to be paid as follows: _____

10. Title is to be free of liens, easements, restrictions, rights and conditions of record or known to Optionor, other than the following: (1) Current property taxes, (2) covenants, conditions, restrictions, and public utility easements of record, if any, provided the same do not adversely affect the continued use of the property for the purposes for which it is presently being used, unless reasonably disapproved by Optionee in writing within _____ days of receipt of a current preliminary title report furnished at _____ expense, and (3) _____ .
Optionor shall furnish Optionee at _____ expense a standard California Land Title Association policy issued by _____ Company, showing title vested in Optionee subject only to the above. If Optionor (1) is unwilling or unable to eliminate any title matter disapproved by Optionee as above, Optionor may terminate this agreement, or (2) fails to deliver title as above, Optionee may terminate this agreement; in either case, the option payment shall be returned to Optionee.

11. Property taxes, premiums on insurance acceptable to Optionee, rents, interest and _____ shall be prorated as of (a) the date of recordation of deed; or (b) _____ . Any bond or assessment which is a lien shall be _____ by _____ .

paid/assumed
_____ shall pay cost of transfer taxes, if any.

12. Possession shall be delivered to Optionee (a) on close of escrow, or (b) not later than _____ days after close of escrow or (c) _____

13. Unless otherwise designated in the escrow instructions of Optionee, title shall vest as follows: _____

14. In any action or proceeding arising out of this agreement, the prevailing party shall be entitled to reasonable attorney's fees and costs.

15. Time is of the essence. All modifications or extensions shall be in writing signed by the parties.

X _____   X _____
OPTIONEE   OPTIONOR
X _____   X _____
OPTIONEE   OPTIONOR

Address: _____   Address: _____

_____   _____

Telephone: _____   Telephone: _____

NOTICE: The amount or rate of real estate commissions is not fixed by law. They are set by each Broker individually and may be negotiable between the Optionor and Broker.

Upon execution of this option, the Optionor agrees to pay to _____ , the Broker in this transaction, the sum of $ _____ (Dollars) and in the event the option or any modification thereof is exercised, Optionor agrees to pay Broker the additional sum of $ _____ (Dollars).

In any action between Broker and Optionor arising out of this agreement, the prevailing party shall be entitled to reasonable attorney's fees and costs. The undersigned acknowledges receipt of a copy and authorizes Broker(s) to deliver a signed copy to Optionee.

Dated: _____ Telephone: _____   X _____
                                               OPTIONOR
                                               X _____
                                               OPTIONOR
Address: _____   _____

Broker(s) agree to the foregoing. Broker: _____   Broker: _____

Dated: _____ by _____   Dated: _____ by _____

0-11-2

Page _____ of _____ Pages

11
Disclosures: Right and Wrong

Realtors spell 100% relief: D-I-S-C-L-O-S-U-R-E, but is anyone *relieved?*

Are you now or have you ever been a dual agent?

In the sale of real property "disclosure" has become the buzzword. In the past it was caveat emptor: let the buyer beware. That was followed by caveat venditor: let the seller beware. Now it's the broker's turn with Caveat Realtor: let the Realtor beware.

Disclosures come in many disguises. They can be true revelations. Some of the disclosures in Chapter 4 may fall in that category. Others belong in the mundane area of making known certain facts which rarely can remain hidden. In consumer law *full disclosure* is the legal obligation to reveal *all* details of a transaction—an obligation more honored in the breach than the observance.

Most disclosures are not voluntary but mandated by statute or case law. They are often originated by a special interest group to avoid a worse fate.

Take the "Defect Disclosure Statement", sometimes called "Listing Information Disclosure Statement", which has been used by listing brokers in many states for decades. Presumably, such statements induce a seller to carefully review the information set forth in the listing agreement. In requiring the seller to disclose defects in the property the seller may be protected from wittingly or unwittingly failing to disclose material facts about the listed property.

A defect disclosure statement may also provide the broker with some protection from any claim from the buyer that the broker in cahoots with the seller did not disclose known defects. There are however some drawbacks with defect statements. They are not harmless to the seller's pecuniary interest and they could be a trap for the unwary seller. The representation of a list of stated defects may raise the presumption that otherwise the property is free of defects. Even with the use of a defect statement a broker may not be "safe" by taking the seller at his or her word. Courts have viewed the listing brokers liability differently. If a broker in a multiple listing information sheet uses words like "IN TOP SHAPE" and the house in fact is not, the broker may be held liable, because the broker should recognize that even if the broker had no direct contact with the buyer a third party within the class the broker wanted to reach has a right to rely that the listing broker's representation is correct.[1] Another court has ruled that an erroneous description in a listing agreement was not actionable because it is merely a statement of opinion rather than a material fact.[2] Failure by brokers to disclose material facts have also created a split in court decisions. Several courts in the Southern states have refused to hold brokers liable for non-disclosure of known facts. California, however, meted out both compensatory damages and punitive damages, including damages for intentional infliction of emotional harm to a broker who failed to disclose the existence of a more complete termite report than the one the broker showed the buyer.[3] In an Illinois case the broker however was not held liable for concealing information on flood damage where the broker made no statements regarding such damage and took no active steps to conceal the situation.[4] Where brokers were not aware of defects several courts have found no liability on the broker's part, especially where defects were not readily visible. Where a buyer has been represented by an agent the listing broker has been found not to have a fiduciary duty to the prospective buyer.[5] A California buyer was held to have stated a cause of action for rescission and damages for the seller's and broker's failure to disclose the "ill-repute" of the property in not telling the buyer that a murder had occurred in the house ten years prior to the sale. The court noted that physical usefulness is not, and never has been, the sole criterion of evaluation.[6] See page 344.

Two cases decided in 1984 involved the issue of whether to extend the broker's duty to require that the broker discover defects and alert the buyer of them. In a Vermont case[7] the court declined to impose such a duty on the broker, while the court in the California case *Easton v. Strassburger*[8], established such a duty.

The Vermont court went as far as saying: "Real Estate Brokers and agents are marketing agents, not structural engineers or contractors. They have no duty to verify independently representations made by a seller unless they are aware of facts that 'tend to indicate that such representations are false' ". The seller in an Alaska case informed the broker that a water well on the property was adequate to service the property. The broker passed on the information. After the sale the buyer discovered the well to be inadequate. The Alaska Supreme Court rejected the broker's contention that he was merely acting as a conduit for the seller's original misrepresentation. The court said: "There is a duty on the part of real estate brokers to be accurate and knowledgeable concerning the products they are in the business of selling." Thus, under this case a broker is under an obligation to verify information before repeating it.[9]

The *Easton* case pushed the broker's duty beyond those situations in which the broker has some reason to suspect the accuracy of information received from the seller or a third party. The court created a duty of brokers to disclose defects of property offered for sale which a reasonably competent and diligent inspection would reveal.

California's law prior to *Easton* required that the broker disclose all material facts known or accessible only to the broker or the broker's principal. Under *Easton,* a broker is responsible not only for what is known or accessible

only to the broker or the broker's principal but also for what the broker "should
have known," following a reasonably competent and diligent inspection. In
other words, the court imposed an affirmative duty on the broker and held that
the duty of a real estate broker representing the seller to disclose facts:

". . . includes the affirmative duty to conduct a reasonably competent and
diligent inspection of the residential property listed for sale and to disclose
to prospective purchasers all facts materially affecting the value or desirability of the property that such an investigation would reveal."

In effect, the court has eliminated a broker's ability to rely on the fact that the
broker did not know of a problem. The standard now created requires the broker
to investigate and to ascertain whether problem conditions exist as evidenced by
"red flag" indicators of problems.

Easton—The Facts

The *Easton* case involved the sale of a home built on fill that had not been
properly engineered and compacted. The owners did not disclose to the agents
or buyers past slide activity and the corrective action they had taken. The buyers
purchased unaware of any soils problems or the past history of slides and subsequently suffered excessive damages.

The court pointed out that the listing agents, although aware of problems
they admittedly referred to as "red flags," chose to ignore those obvious indicators and did not disclose or make recommendations concerning those "red
flags."

The evidence before the court indicated that:

At least one of the listing agents knew the property was built on fill ("red
flag");

The listing agents had seen netting ("red flag") which had been placed on
a slope to repair the slide that had occurred most recently prior to the sale;

One of the listing agents testified that he had observed that the floor of the
guest house was not level ("red flag"), while the other agent testified that
uneven floors were "red flag" indicators of soils problems.

Throughout the course of the trial, fraud and negligent misrepresentation
theories were advanced. It became evident during the course of those proceedings that the plaintiffs (buyers) were not able legally or factually to establish
fraud or negligent misrepresentation. The plaintiffs subsequently changed their
legal theory and pursued a "simple negligence" theory seeking to impose liability on the brokers.

The court in stretching to achieve equity expanded the law of broker
liability into the "simple negligence" area and found the broker responsible not
because they failed to disclose facts that they knew, not because they made

affirmative representations without sufficient factual basis, but because the brokers did not disclose what they *should* have known. The brokers admittedly were aware of the "red flags" that indicated underlying serious problems. Therefore, the court established a duty which must be complied with or the broker runs the risk of being found negligent as were the agents in *Easton*.

Easton raises the question as to what constitutes a "reasonably competent and diligent inspection" sufficient to satisfy the *Easton* duty. The court gives minimal assistance by merely saying that such an inspection must be something ". . . more than a casual visual inspection and a general inquiry of the owners." The court also does not answer the question: How *red* must the flags be?

In *Easton* the brokers used a "defect statement", but the seller was less than candid in answering the questions which also were not specific enough.

Realtors (Members of the National Association of Realtors) have little grounds for reacting with dismay over the *Easton* ruling. In some sense the Realtors brought the *Easton* duty upon themselves in the old-fashioned way— they earned it. The court took judicial notice of Article 9 of the Realtors code of ethics which states:

> "The Realtor shall avoid exaggeration, misrepresentation, or concealment of pertinent facts. He has an affirmative obligation to discover adverse factors that a reasonably competent and diligent investigation would disclose."

It can of course be argued that this was a professional creed to be aspired to which now has risen to broker liability under the law. That may be the reason for the National Association of Realtors eliminating "diligent investigation" in a revision of its Code.

To minimize the impact of *Easton* and to tighten the standard of care and standarize the required disclosures by sellers, the matter was referred to the State Legislature. Two bills were introduced and passed. Unfortunately, this legislation raises new questions and problems for both sellers and brokers. The least controversial bill more clearly defines the broker's duty without reversing *Easton*. That bill, which was amended in the 1986 Session, adds Section 2079, et al., to the Civil Code and basically provides:

(1) That an insurer who provides professional liability insurance for real estate licensees shall not exclude coverage for liability arising from the breach of duty established in *Easton*.
(2) Statutorily enunciates the *Easton* duty (by paraphrasing the court) of a broker "to conduct a reasonably competent and diligent visual inspection of the property offered for sale and to disclose to a prospective purchaser all facts materially affecting the value or desirability of the property that such an investigation would reveal."
   (a) Limits this liability to sales, option to purchase, exchanges and stock cooperatives of residential property of 1 to 4 units.
   (b) Extends the duty to both the listing broker and the cooperating broker, if

any. Although the jury in *Easton* gave judgment against both brokers, the court's finding is limited to the listing broker because the cooperating broker was not a defendant in the action.

(c) Defines a sale as including a lease with an option, a ground lease coupled with improvements, or an installment land sale contract.

(3) Provides that the standard of care is the degree of care which a reasonably prudent real estate licensee would exercise and is measured by the degree of knowledge through education, experience and examination, required to obtain a real estate license. The *Easton* court did not deal with the standard of care, although it discussed the fact that the broker held himself or herself out as having greater knowledge than the public.

(4) Specifies that the inspection does not involve an area which is normally inaccessible to such an inspection, nor include the common areas in a condominium type situation if the broker has furnished to the prospective buyer, copies of the reports of the owner's association respecting the conditions of the property and the reserves established for replacement or repair.

(5) Establishes a statute of limitation of two years from date of recordation, close of escrow or the date of occupancy, whichever occurs first.

(6) Provides that the bill does not relieve a buyer of the duty to exercise reasonable care to protect himself or herself including noting those facts which are known to the buyer or within the diligent attention and observation of the buyer. The *Easton* court did not specifically make a finding on this point, but indicated that the broker would have a defense for the defects in the property which would be apparent to the buyer.

A Real Estate Transfer Statement

The second bill subtly shifts part of the burden created by *Easton* from the broker to the seller. It adds a new article to the Civil Code beginning with Section 1102. Instead of the voluntary listing Information Disclosure Statement the code itself prescribes a Real Estate Transfer Statement which a transferor (seller) must deliver to a prospective transferee, as soon as practicable before transfer of title. The broker who obtains the buyer's offer has the duty to deliver the statement and if such statement is not available the broker must notify the transferee of the rights under the law to obtain the statement. The law limits the disclosure to transactions involving property improved with not less than one or more than four dwelling units.

Certain transfers are exempted from compliance with the required disclosures.

The Statute uses very innovative and ingenious language which is an open invitation to tests in court of its precise meaning. The disclosures shall be made on a "Real Estate Transfer Disclosure Statement," which is set forth in full in the Statute. Absolute match is apparently not necessary since the use of reports by various experts such as contractors and engineers fulfills the requirements of the disclosure statement or parts thereof.

Other provisions of the statute are:

(1) Any person or entity, other than a real estate licensee, acting in the capacity of an escrow agent having actual knowledge that the transfer is subject to the provisions of the Statute shall advise the transferor and transferee of the existence of the law and the necessity for disclosure as soon as practicable after such knowledge is received.

(2) The specification of items for disclosure in the disclosure form does not limit or abridge any obligation for disclosure created by any other provision of law or which may exist in order to avoid fraud, misrepresentation or deceit. And,

(3) The disclosure law became operative January 1, 1987.

CAR's Model form 11 and the Investment Property contract both contain references to the delivery of the Real Estate Transfer Statement required by law. Brokers representing buyers should incorporate the Real Estate Transfer Statement in the contract by reference and a provision that the Seller *warrants,* that the information is true and correct. The necessity for this cautionary approach will become clear from perusing the following comments.

Disturbingly, the scope and purpose of the statutory statement is pronounced with startling confusion. The "caveats" in the preamble contradict the specifics of the text. The buyer is warned that the "disclosure" is not a "warranty of any kind" and not a substitute for "inspections" or "warranties" the principal(s) may wish to obtain. In the text the seller is admonished that the seller "is giving the information with the knowledge that even though this is not a warranty" that "prospective buyers may rely on such information" in deciding to buy the property. The form further emphasizes that it is *"not* intended to be part of any contract between buyer and seller." Whose "intent" one might ask.

All is not lost, however, even if the statement is left to stand alone, for just above the seller's signature is a difinitive declaration: "Seller *certifies* that the information herein is true and correct to the best of the seller's knowledge. . . ." So why all the doubletalk? Of course by adding the seductive "best knowledge" modification the "certification" may have been made meaningless. A seller's degree of knowledge is hard to prove short of the appearance of a "smoking gun." The courts, however, may make short shift of the multiple disclaimers.

Form 11:01 is the statutory language contained in the California *Easton* legislation.

FORM: 11:01   REAL ESTATE TRANSFER DISCLOSURE STATEMENT

REAL ESTATE TRANSFER DISCLOSURE STATEMENT
(CALIFORNIA CIVIL CODE 1102, ET SEQ.)
CALIFORNIA ASSOCIATION OF REALTORS® (CAR) STANDARD FORM

THIS DISCLOSURE STATEMENT CONCERNS THE REAL PROPERTY SITUATED IN THE CITY OF _____
_____ , COUNTY OF _____ , STATE OF CALIFORNIA,
DESCRIBED AS _____ .

THIS STATEMENT IS A DISCLOSURE OF THE CONDITION OF THE ABOVE DESCRIBED PROPERTY IN COMPLIANCE WITH SECTION 1102 OF THE CIVIL CODE AS OF _____ , 19____ . IT IS NOT A WARRANTY OF ANY KIND BY THE SELLER(S) OR ANY AGENT(S) REPRESENTING ANY PRINCIPAL(S) IN THIS TRANSACTION, AND IS NOT A SUBSTITUTE FOR ANY INSPECTIONS OR WARRANTIES THE PRINCIPAL(S) MAY WISH TO OBTAIN.

I
COORDINATION WITH OTHER DISCLOSURE FORMS

This Real Estate Transfer Disclosure Statement is made pursuant to Section 1102 of the Civil Code. Other statutes require disclosures, depending upon the details of the particular real estate transaction (for example: special study zone and purchase—money liens on residential property).

Substituted Disclosures: The following disclosures have or will be made in connection with this real estate transfer, and are intended to satisfy the disclosure obligations on this form, where the subject matter is the same: _____
_____
_____

_____
(list all substituted disclosure forms to be used in connection with this transaction)
II
SELLER'S INFORMATION

The Seller discloses the following information with the knowledge that even though this is not a warranty, prospective Buyers may rely on this information in deciding whether and on what terms to purchase the subject property. Seller hereby authorizes any agent(s) representing any principal(s) in this transaction to provide a copy of this statement to any person or entity in connection with any actual or anticipated sale of the property.

THE FOLLOWING ARE REPRESENTATIONS MADE BY THE SELLER(S) AND ARE NOT THE REPRESENTATIONS OF THE AGENT(S), IF ANY. THIS INFORMATION IS A DISCLOSURE AND IS NOT INTENDED TO BE PART OF ANY CONTRACT BETWEEN THE BUYER AND SELLER.

Seller ☐ is ☐ is not occupying the property.

A. The subject property has the items checked below (read across):

☐ Range	☐ Oven	☐ Microwave
☐ Dishwasher	☐ Trash Compactor	☐ Garbage Disposal
☐ Washer/Dryer Hookups	☐ Window Screens	☐ Rain Gutters
☐ Burglar Alarms	☐ Smoke Detector(s)	☐ Fire Alarm
☐ T.V. Antenna	☐ Satellite Dish	☐ Intercom
☐ Central Heating	☐ Central Air Conditioning	☐ Evaporator Cooler(s)
☐ Wall/Window Air Conditioning	☐ Sprinklers	☐ Public Sewer System
☐ Septic Tank	☐ Sump Pump	☐ Water Softener
☐ Patio/Decking	☐ Built-in Barbeque	☐ Gazebo
☐ Sauna	☐ Pool	☐ Spa ☐ Hot Tub
☐ Security Gate(s)	☐ Garage Door Opener(s)	☐ Number of Remote Controls _____
Garage: ☐ Attached	☐ Not Attached	☐ Carport
Pool/Spa Heater: ☐ Gas	☐ Solar	☐ Electric
Water Heater: ☐ Gas	☐ Solar	☐ Electric
Water Supply: ☐ City	☐ Well	☐ Private Utility ☐ Other _____
Gas Supply: ☐ Utility	☐ Bottled	

Exhaust Fan(s) in _____ 220 Volt Wiring in _____
Fireplace(s) in _____ ☐ Gas Starter

(Form continues on next page)

☐ Roof(s): Type: _____ Age: _____ (approx.)
☐ Other: _____
Are there, to the best of your (Seller's) knowledge, any of the above that are not in operating condition? ☐ Yes ☐ No If yes, then describe. (Attach additional sheets if necessary.): _____

B. Are you (Seller) aware of any significant defects/malfunctions in any of the following? ☐ Yes ☐ No If yes, check appropriate space(s) below.
☐ Interior Walls ☐ Ceilings ☐ Floors ☐ Exterior Walls ☐ Insulation ☐ Roof(s) ☐ Windows ☐ Doors ☐ Foundation ☐ Slab(s) ☐ Driveways ☐ Sidewalks ☐ Walls/Fences ☐ Electrical Systems ☐ Plumbing/Sewers/Septics ☐ Other Structural Components
(Describe: _____)

If any of the above is checked, explain. (Attach additional sheets if necessary.): _____

Subject Property Address _____

C. Are you (Seller) aware of any of the following:

1. Features of the property shared in common with adjoining landowners, such as walls, fences, and driveways, whose use or responsibility for maintenance may have an effect on the subject property. ☐ Yes ☐ No
2. Any encroachments, easements or similar matters that may affect your interest in the subject property. ☐ Yes ☐ No
3. Room additions, structural modifications, or other alterations or repairs made without necessary permits. ☐ Yes ☐ No
4. Room additions, structural modifications, or other alterations or repairs not in compliance with building codes. ☐ Yes ☐ No
5. Landfill (compacted or otherwise) on the property or any portion thereof. ☐ Yes ☐ No
6. Any settling from any cause, or slippage, sliding, or other soil problems. ☐ Yes ☐ No
7. Flooding, drainage or grading problems. ☐ Yes ☐ No
8. Major damage to the property or any of the structures from fire, earthquake, floods, or landslides. ☐ Yes ☐ No
9. Any zoning violations, non-conforming uses, violations of "setback" requirements. ☐ Yes ☐ No
10. Neighborhood noise problems or other nuisances. ☐ Yes ☐ No
11. CC&R's or other deed restrictions or obligations. ☐ Yes ☐ No
12. Homeowners' Association which has any authority over the subject property. ☐ Yes ☐ No
13. Any "common area" (facilities such as pools, tennis courts, walkways, or other areas co-owned in undivided interest with others). ☐ Yes ☐ No
14. Any notices of abatement or citations against the property. ☐ Yes ☐ No
15. Any lawsuits against the seller threatening to or affecting this real property. ☐ Yes ☐ No

If the answer to any of these is yes, explain. (Attach additional sheets if necessary.): _____

Seller certifies that the information herein is true and correct to the best of the Seller's knowledge as of the date signed by the Seller.

Seller _____ Date _____

Seller _____ Date _____

(Form continues on next page)

III
AGENT'S INSPECTION DISCLOSURE
(To be completed only if the seller is represented by an agent in this transaction.)
THE UNDERSIGNED, BASED ON THE ABOVE INQUIRY OF THE SELLER(S) AS TO THE CONDITION OF THE PROPERTY AND BASED ON A REASONABLY COMPETENT AND DILIGENT VISUAL INSPECTION OF THE ACCESSIBLE AREAS OF THE PROPERTY IN CONJUNCTION WITH THAT INQUIRY, STATES THE FOLLOWING:

_____
_____
_____

Agent (Broker
Representing Seller) _____ By _____ Date _____
                        (Please Print)   (Associate Licensee or Broker-Signature)

IV
AGENT'S INSPECTION DISCLOSURE
(To be completed only if the agent who has obtained the offer is other than the agent above.)
THE UNDERSIGNED, BASED ON A REASONABLY COMPETENT AND DILIGENT VISUAL INSPECTION OF THE ACCESSIBLE AREAS OF THE PROPERTY, STATES THE FOLLOWING:

_____
_____

Agent (Broker
obtaining the Offer) _____ By _____ Date _____
                        (Please Print)   (Associate Licensee or Broker-Signature)

V
BUYER(S) AND SELLER(S) MAY WISH TO OBTAIN PROFESSIONAL ADVICE AND/OR INSPECTIONS OF THE PROPERTY AND TO PROVIDE FOR APPROPRIATE PROVISIONS IN A CONTRACT BETWEEN BUYER AND SELLER(S) WITH RESPECT TO ANY ADVICE/INSPECTIONS/DEFECTS.

I/WE ACKNOWLEDGE RECEIPT OF A COPY OF THIS STATEMENT.

Seller_____ Date _____   Buyer_____ Date _____

Seller_____ Date _____   Buyer_____ Date _____

Agent (Broker
Representing Seller) _____ By _____ Date _____
                        (Please Print)   (Associate Licensee or Broker-Signature)

Agent (Broker
obtaining the Offer) _____ By _____ Date _____
                        (Please Print)   (Associate Licensee or Broker-Signature)

A REAL ESTATE BROKER IS QUALIFIED TO ADVISE ON REAL ESTATE. IF YOU DESIRE LEGAL ADVICE, CONSULT YOUR ATTORNEY.

To order, contact—California Association of Realtors®
525 S. Virgil Avenue, Los Angeles, California 90020
Copyright© 1986, California Association of Realtors®

┌─── OFFICE USE ONLY ───┐
│ Reviewed by Broker or Designee _____
│
│ Date _____
└──────────────────────┘

COMMENT ON FORM 11:01: The statutory form as amended in 1986 is still inadequate for the intended purpose. The questionnaire itself does not trigger a reluctant seller's memory. Asking a seller if there are ''any defects/ malfunctions'' in the ''septic tank'' is only rarely going to give answers to the more relevant questions: a) where is the septic system, b) are there any abandoned septic tanks on the property, c) has the property been expanded beyond the system's capacity, d) have leach lines caused water to surface, e) when was soil percolation last tested and what was the result? Other pertinent questions can be asked about most of the items in the disclosure statement. Will sellers volunteer information beyond the minimum asked for? Even a seller who answers all questions truthfully may be found to have failed to disclose material facts that a more comprehensive and better-drafted disclosure statement would have unearthed.

The risk of producing so-called "experts" reports could give sellers nightmares. If more than one report exists all, even a vindictive one, must be produced. It's a Pandora's Box.

Recognizing the shortcomings of the statutory form several larger real estate firms insist on having sellers respond to supplementary disclosure forms. The supplements contain direct and specific questions elaborating on the limited disclosures of the statutory version. A requirement for such additional disclosures should be part of every contract prepared by a buyers broker.

The *Easton* case and the legislation codifying it places burdens on a broker to assess the seller's credibility. The broker must construct an impression of the seller and compare the seller's representations with the broker's own observations of the property. The broker is in a dilemma. Is the seller a reliable source of information? Is the seller knowingly withholding facts about the property which may be adverse to the interests of the buyer or broker? Because real estate brokers have different educational and social backgrounds, they have different perceptions of dimensions for assessing credibility. The brokers may be attracted to sellers they perceive as similar to themselves and therefore assess credibility to the sellers who appear to be of "like kind." The more inquisitive and specific the information questionnaire, the better is the chance for digging out the correct disclosures. The California statutory statement fails miserably in that respect. In order to obtain the necessary and correct answers the broker must learn to rephrase the questions and elaborate upon too generalized inquiries provided for in the terse language. If this is not done, the whole interview process will be an exercise in futility and the answers given may be as unresponsive as the answers the seller in *Easton* gave the agent and lead to similar consequences.

The 1986 "clean up" legislation made a major change in the Disclosure Statement. It added an inspection disclosure space to be used by the agent who has "obtained the offer" if other than the agent representing the seller. Nowhere in the act or the statement, however, is there any reference to the exact extent of the broker's duties to disclose by any reference to Civil Code Section 2079.

The legislative history would indicate that a *transferor's* duty to execute a Real Estate Transfer Statement can not be waived by the transferee. Civil Code Section 2079 does not prescribe any particular manner in which the broker's inspection is to be disclosed, or whether it can be waived. Brokers ought, however, not attempt to obtain waivers since the courts are likely to decide that a waiver may be "against public policy". CAR's version of the Disclosure Statement, TDS-14, contains on the reverse side a copy of the relevant provisions of the *Easton* legislation.

The 1986 legislation also repealed, effective January 1, 1987, Civil Code Section 1134.5, the "structural addition" disclosure law. It is substituted by two questions in the Real Estate Transfer Statement.

The following transfers listed in Section 1102.1 are exempt from the disclosure requirements:

(a) Transfers which are required to be preceded by the furnishing to a prospective transferee of a copy of a public report, pursuant to Section 11018.1 of the Business and Professions Code, and transfers which can be made without a public report pursuant to Section 11010.4 of the Business and Professions Code.

(b) Transfers pursuant to court order, including, but not limited to, transfers ordered by a probate court in administration of an estate, transfers pursuant to a writ of execution, transfers by any foreclosure sale, transfers by a trustee in bankruptcy, transfers by eminent domain, and transfers resulting from a decree for specific performance.

(c) Transfers to a mortgagee by a mortgagor or successor in interest who is in default, transfers to a beneficiary of a deed of trust by a trustor or successor in interest who is in default, transfers by any foreclosure sale after default, transfers by any foreclosure sale after default in an obligation insured by a mortgage, transfers by a sale under a power of sale or any foreclosure sale under a decree of foreclosure after default in an obligation secured by a deed of trust or secured by any other instrument containing a power of sale, or transfers by a mortgagee or a beneficiary under a deed of trust who has acquired the real property at a sale conducted pursuant to a power of sale under a mortgage or deed of trust or a sale pursuant to a decree of foreclosure or has acquired the real property by a deed in lieu of foreclosure.

(d) Transfers by a fiduciary in the course of the administration of a decedent's estate, guardianship, conservatorship, or trust.

(e) Transfers from one co-owner to one or more other co-owners.

(f) Transfers made to a spouse, or to a person or persons in the lineal line of consanguinity of one or more of the transferors.

(g) Transfers between spouses resulting from a decree of dissolution of marriage or a decree of legal separation or from a property settlement agreement incidental to such a decree.

(h) Transfers by the Controller in the course of administering Chapter 7 (commencing with Section 1500) of Title 10 of Part 3 of the Code of Civil Procedure.

(i) Transfers under Chapter 7 (commencing with Section 3691) or Chapter 8 (commencing with Section 3771) of Part 6 of Division 1 of the Revenue and Taxation Code.

(j) Transfers or exchanges to or from any government entity.

Right to Cancellation

The disclosure must be delivered as soon as practicable before transfer of title or before execution of a "Real Property Sales Contract" (installment land contract defined in Civil Code §2985). If the disclosure or material amendment to a previous disclosure is delivered after execution of an offer to purchase, the transferee (buyer) has three days after delivery in person or five days after delivery by deposit in the mail in which to terminate his or her offer by delivery of a written notice of termination to the transferor, or his or her agent. Form 11:02 can be attached to the disclosure form giving notice of the buyer's right to terminate the contract.

FORM 11:02   NOTICE OF RIGHT TO TERMINATE OFFER

To_____
       Buyer

Regarding property described as: _____

_____

Date of Delivery of this Notice ☐ In person to Transferee

on _____, 19____

☐ By deposit in mail on

_____, 19____

Attached hereto is:

☐ Real Estate Transfer Disclosure Statement

You have three days after delivery to you in person or five days after delivery by deposit in the mail, to terminate your offer to purchase the above-described property.

To cancel this transaction mail or deliver a signed and dated copy of this cancellation notice, or any other written notice, or send a telegram sent not later than midnight of _____, 19____ to either of the following named

(date)

persons:

Seller_____   _____
         Name   City   Address   Zip

Broker_____   _____
         Name   City   Address   Zip

Buyer's Record of Cancellation

I hereby cancel this transaction on this _____ day of _____, 19____. Written cancellation notice was ☐ delivered in person, ☐ mailed or ☐ telegram sent on this _____ day of _____, 19____. I hereby demand return of my deposit of $_____.

Buyer:_____

Buyer:_____

COMMENT ON FORM 11:02: This notice is only necessary if the disclosures are given *after* buyer signs an offer to purchase. If the disclosures are given before the offer is signed by buyer, seller or broker should obtain a signed receipt from buyer or have buyer acknowledge receipt of the disclosures by inserting a statement to that effect in the Real Estate Purchase Agreement Receipt for Deposit.

When Disclosure Is Not Forthcoming

In hopefully rare circumstances the broker who has the duty to deliver the transferor's disclosure may not be able to obtain a signed disclosure statement. The broker must then advise the transferee of the transferee's rights.

FORM 11:03   NOTICE OF RIGHT TO RECEIVE DISCLOSURE

To _____
    Buyer-Transferee
Regarding property described as _____
_____

Date of delivery of this notice:
☐ personally to Transferee on _____, 19____
☐ by deposit in mail on _____, 19____
☐ Attached hereto is a copy of Real Estate Transfer Disclosure Statement
_____
    CAR Form TDS-14
☐ Copy of _____
          letters to transferor/and the agent representing transferor
          dated _____, 19____

You are advised that under California Civil Code Section 1102 you have the right to receive from the transferor (seller) disclosures of the condition of the property.

We have been unable to obtain a Real Estate Transfer Disclosure Statement from the Transferor or the transferor's real estate agent.

It is recommended that you obtain legal advice about your rights and the manner in which the rights may be enforced.
_____, 19____
Broker _____ by _____

COMMENT ON FORM 11:03: Where more than one real estate broker is acting as agent in a transaction the broker who obtained the offer has the duty to deliver the disclosure unless the transferor is writing has given other instructions for delivery. If the broker who is responsible for delivering the disclosure can not obtain the document required, the broker must in writing advise the transferee of the failure to obtain the information. The broker must maintain a record of the action the broker has taken to effect compliance with the law.

Agency Relationship Disclosures

In most real property sale transactions some form of agency relationship is established between one or more real estate brokers and one or more of the principals to those transactions. There are no specific statutory provisions defining or guiding real property agency relationships. They are subject to the general law of agency as established in the Civil Code, the common law, and the growing body of judicial opinions.

A variety of agency relationships (including subagency relationships) exist in common real estate practice. These include situations in which only one agent functions in a transaction and that agent represents only one of the parties to the transaction, and in still other circumstances "represents" both parties. Other situations involve two or more agents in the transaction including cases in which both agents represent one party and the other party is not represented by an agent or in which one agent represents each of the principals or in which one or more of the agents "represents" both of the principals.

In a growing body of law the duties of a real estate agent to the party which he or she does *not* represent in the transaction are evolving rapidly and approach to a significant degree the fiduciary duty which the agent owes to his or her principal.

The declaration of the parties in an agreement respecting the nature of the relationship are not controlling, the courts have repeatedly intoned. Whether an agent is the agent for the seller or the buyer is a question of fact. "Not all professional contact between a real estate broker and a person desiring to buy or lease real estate need lead to a relation of agency between them, as the broker can act solely on behalf of the adverse party . . . *or sometimes only as a middleman.*"[11]

Unfortunately, in dealing with the broker's relationship with buyers and sellers, the courts have gotten entangled in legalistic principles of agency. These ancient principles do not offer guidelines for realistic solutions. Rather than to apply agency rules, Licensee "Standard of Conduct" in dealings with parties of limited experience, as opposed to commercial dealings, should be the criterion. However, it would take such bold action to change this of which the real estate industry probably is not capable.

All the talk of the "professional" agent cannot hide the fact that when all is said and done, the broker represents not the seller or the buyer, but only himself. He is in the marketing business acting as a negotiating middleman to bring two opposite parties together. But for the courts' insistence upon finding "agency", when things turn sour, the broker may be stricken by the gruesome disease of dual agency with the sequella of conflict of interest or schizophrenia. People diagnosed as schizophrenic usually have aspects of themselves which are disassociated but simultaneous. The broker does not know he is schizophrenic. He lives in a reality which acknowledges that he is the seller's agent, but that will not stop him from embracing the faith of believing and acting as the buyer's agent too and see no conflict at all. It's the kind of faith *Mark Twain's* schoolboy nailed when he said: "Faith is believing what you know ain't so." Likewise, a broker presumed through the transaction to be acting for the seller and not for the buyer may innocently induce faith in him by the buyer, but such faith does not shift the agency. If nothing goes wrong, adherence to the principle of indifference by the buyer may save all.

Not all states are opposed to dual agency. Louisiana has a fundamental law that the broker is the agent of both parties:

"The broker or intermediary is he who is employed to negotiate a matter between two parties and who, for that reason, is considered the mandatory of both." CC 3016. "The obligations of a broker are similar to those of an ordinary mandatory, with this difference, that his engagement is double, and requires that he should observe the same fidelity towards all parties, and not favor one more than another." CC 3017

"Brokers are . . . as other agents, answerable for fraud and faults."
CC 3018

Most courts have not condemned dual representation, but demanded faithful fiduciary duty to both principals.

To be or not to be an agent of buyer, seller or dual is a complex issue. It cannot be wrapped up in a hasty bundle labeled "all or nothing", "good or bad". Such simplification is not warranted. It was Justice Frankfurter who called it this "great either or".

Some simplistic attempts to disclosure have been instigated by real estate firms by inserting in the Real Estate Purchase Contract and Receipt for Deposit a reference to agency relations including dual agency. Here is an example:

"DUAL REPRESENTATION. The parties acknowledge that Realty Company represents both Buyer and Seller in this transaction and each hereby consents to such dual representation and waives any conflict of interest arising out of such dual representation."

This approach is insufficient and the unapproved disclosure is aborted by typographical concealment in an excessive mass of boilerplate. It also seems to be more designed to protect the broker than the public. The disclosure is not *timely* made, not particularly *meaningful,* and what is worse, there is no *informed* consent.

Different Approaches

In several states legislation has been introduced in the area of agency relationship in real estate transactions.

Pennsylvania in 1984, provided by law that in "any sales agreement or sales contract, a broker shall make the following disclosures to any prospective buyer of real property: . . . a statement that the broker is the agent of the seller, not the buyer."

The Hawaii Legislature has enacted a measure in 1985 effective January 1, 1988, providing that it has a basis for licensee discipline "when the licensee fails to obtain on the contract between the parties to the real estate transaction confirmation of who the broker represents."

In Maine, legislation was introduced making it a basis for discipline upon "failure of the licensee to make written disclosure to the seller at or before the time a listing agreement is signed, that the licensee is the agent of the seller; or failure of a licensee to make written disclosure to a potential buyer at or before the time the buyer makes an offer to purchase real estate that the licensee is the agent of the seller, not the buyer. This obligation does not apply when a prospective buyer retains a broker as his own agent. The bill has been withdrawn for future action.

In Minnesota a 1985 law provides:

"(a) no person licensed . . . or who otherwise acts as a real estate broker or sales person shall represent any party or parties to a real estate transaction . . . unless he or she makes an affirmative written disclosure to all parties to the transaction as to which party he or she represents in the transaction. The disclosure shall be . . . acknowledged by signatures of the buyer and seller.

"(b) the disclosure . . . must be made by the licensee prior to an offer being made or accepted by the buyer. A change in licensee's representation that makes the initial disclosure incomplete, misleading or inaccurate requires that the new disclosures be made at once.

"(c) the seller may, in the listing agreement, authorize the seller's broker to disburse part of the broker's compensation to other brokers, including the buyer's brokers solely representing the buyer. A broker representing a buyer shall make known to the seller or the seller's agent the fact of agency before showing or negotiations are initiated."

Consumer protection laws have been enacted in a number of states. These laws include real estate transactions. Real estate licensees who misrepresent are subject to deceptive trade practices actions in addition to suits for rescision, return of commissions and money damages. In Texas, the Deceptive Trade Practices Act gives buyers and sellers of real estate a statutory remedy against false and unconscionable conduct. Texas license law provides for suspension or revocation of license if a licensee fails to "make clear to all parties to a transaction which party he is acting for."

None of the mentioned states have attempted to clarify by definition or otherwise what the agency relationship or relationships may be. Nor does the legislation specifically attempt to help broker, salespersons, buyers or sellers or the general public to understand what the obligations are of an agent to his or her principal and the obligations to other parties.

The California Approach

In California, the California Association of Realtors' bill on agency relationship was passed in the 1986 session of the Legislature. Basically, the law contains the following features:

(1) A series of legislative findings about present agency practices, judicial interpretations and the lack of uniformity in the manner in which common law rules are applied; plus a statement of legislative intent.

(2) Defines the terms relating to real estate sales and agency relationships in nontechnical terms, and provides for furnishing these definitions to buyers and sellers. For example: (a) By defining a buyer as one who seeks the services of any agent in more than a casual, transitory or preliminary manner with the object of buying, the law clarifies that the broker's duties encompass this relationship even though a sale is never consummated and the broker receives no compensation. (b) Sets forth the existing rule relating to subagency, which again is frequently misunderstood in a real estate sale transaction.

(3) Requires a listing agent and selling agent to furnish to both buyer and seller a disclosure statement outlining the agency relationship options available under existing law and in the market place and the duties of each agent to each of the principals in the transaction. This written disclosure form, contained in the statute must be furnished as soon as practicable, and be receipted for by buyer and seller.

(4) Reiterates case law that the agency relationship is not necessarily determined by whether either the buyer or seller pay compensation to the agent.

(5) Provides that when a broker acts as a dual agent that he or she may not disclose to the buyer, without the express permission of the seller, that the seller is willing to sell the property at a price that is less than the listing price; and will not disclose to the seller, without the express permission of the buyer, that the buyer will pay a price that is greater than the offering price.

(6) The effective date of the bill was January 1, 1988.

The disclosure form is of special interest to this book's author because of his involvement in its drafting. It remains to be seen if the pioneering by California Realtors will be followed by other states. Here is the main text of the disclosure form:

FORM 11:04   **DISCLOSURE REGARDING**

REAL ESTATE AGENCY RELATIONSHIP
(As required by the Civil Code)

When you enter into a discussion with a real estate agent regarding a real estate transaction, you should from the outset understand what type of agency relationship or representation you wish to have with the agent in the transaction.

SELLER'S AGENT

A Seller's agent under a listing agreement with the Seller acts as the agent for the Seller only. A Seller's agent or a subagent of that agent has the following affirmative obligations:

To the Seller:

(a) A fiduciary duty of utmost care, integrity, honesty, and loyalty in dealings with the Seller.

To the Buyer and the Seller:

(a) Diligent exercise of reasonable skill and care in performance of the agent's duties.

(b) A duty of honest and fair dealing and good faith.

(c) A duty of disclose all facts known to the agent materially affecting the value or desirability of the property that are not known to, or within the diligent attention and observation of, the parties.

An agent is not obligated to reveal to either party any confidential information obtained from the other party which does not involve the affirmative duties set forth above.

BUYER'S AGENT

A selling agent can, with a Buyer's consent, agree to act as agent for the Buyer only. In these situations, the agent is not the Seller's agent, even if by agreement the agent may receive compensation for services rendered, either in full or in part from the Seller. An agent acting only for a buyer has the following affirmative obligations:

To the Buyer:

(a) A fiduciary duty of utmost care, integrity, honesty, and loyalty in dealings with the Buyer.

To the Buyer and the Seller:

(a) Diligent exercise of reasonable skill and care in performance of the agent's duties.

(b) A duty of honest and fair dealing and good faith.

(c) A duty to disclose all facts known to the agent materially affecting the value or desirability of the property that are not known to, or within the diligent attention and observation of, the parties. An agent is not obligated to reveal to either party any confidential information obtained from the other party which does not involve the affirmative duties set forth above.

AGENT REPRESENTING BOTH SELLER AND BUYER

A real estate agent, either acting directly or through one or more associate licensees, can legally be the agent of both the Seller and the Buyer in a transaction, but only with the knowledge and consent of both the Seller and the Buyer.

In a dual agency situation, the agent has the following affirmative obligations to both the Seller and the Buyer:

(a) A fiduciary duty of utmost care, integrity, honesty and loyalty in the dealings with either Seller or the Buyer.

(b) Other duties to the Seller and the Buyer as stated above in their respective sections.

In representing both Seller and Buyer, the agent may not, without the express permission of the respective party, disclose to the other party that the Seller will accept a price less than the listing price or that the Buyer will pay a price greater than the price offered.

The above duties of the agent in a real estate transaction do not relieve a Seller or Buyer from the responsibility to protect their own interests. You should carefully read all agreements to assure that they adequately express your understanding of the transaction. A real estate agent is a person qualified to advise about real estate. If legal or tax advice is desired, consult a competent professional.

Throughout your real property transaction you may receive more than one disclosure form, depending upon the number of agents assisting in the transaction. The law requires each agent with whom you have more than a casual relationship to present you with this disclosure form. You should read its contents each time it is presented to you, considering the relationship between you and the real estate agent in your specific transaction.

This disclosure form includes the provisions of Article 2.5 (commencing with

Section 2373) of Chapter 2 of Title 9 of Part 4 of Division 3 of Civil Code set forth on the reverse hereof. Read it càrefully.

_____	_____
Agent	Buyer/Seller (date)
	(Signature)
_____	_____
Associate Licensee (date)	Buyer/Seller (date)
(Signature)	(Signature)

The confirmation of the agency relationship can be inserted in the sales contract or incorporated in a separate writing, but must be in the following form:

FORM 11:05   CONFIRMATION OF AGENCY RELATIONSHIP

_____ is the agent of (check one):
(Name of Listing Agent)

☐ the seller exclusively; or

☐ both the buyer and seller.

_____ is the agent of (check one):
(Name of Selling Agent if not the same
as Listing Agent)

☐ the buyer exclusively; or

☐ the seller exclusively; or

☐ both the buyer and seller.

COMMENT ON FORM 11:05: It is unfortunate that the "confirmation of the chosen agency relationship is so incomplete. It contains no acknowledgment by the parties of the timely receipt of the "Disclosure", nor does it specifically indicate "informed consent" in the election of "dual agency", if that is the parties' decision. It is not made clear that the parties are waiving potential conflicts of interest. Nowhere in the Statute itself, which is to be reproduced on the reverse side of the Disclosure statement, are the implications of possible disadvantages or risks of common representation explained in plain English. Since one out of every five Americans is functionally illiterate it becomes important that the information given to the public be in "plain English". Several times in the "Disclosure" the phrase "fiduciary relationship" appears, yet there is no definition in the Statute of these words. Future revisions should remedy this oversight. Leaving explanations to licensees may be courting disaster. This legislation is a lawyer's dream of a lucrative retirement plan come true.

Brokers and their associates should therefore not engage in the illusion that getting the parties' signatures to "a confirmation", buried in the Real Estate Contract And Receipt for Deposit, will get them home scott-free. As the Statute states in its archaic style: "Nothing in this article shall be construed to either diminish the duty of disclosure owed buyers and seller by agents and their associate licensees, subagents, and employees or agents and their associate licensees, subagents, and employees, from liability for their conduct in connection with acts governed by this article or for any breach of fiduciary duty or a duty of disclosure." In other words: "Don't do nothing illegal, - or else."

It may become good practice, and adding a small measure of protection for brokers, to use Form 11:06 as a "separate writing executed or acknowledged" by the agent(s) and the buyer and seller, respectively, "prior to or coincident with the execution" of the contract to "purchase and sell real property".

FORM 11:06   CONFIRMATION OF AGENCY RELATIONSHIP

_____ is the agent of (check one):
(Name of Listing Agent)

☐ the seller exclusively; or

☐ both the buyer and seller.

_____ is the agent of (check one):
(Name of Selling Agent if not the
same as the Listing Agent)

☐ the buyer exclusively; or

☐ the seller exclusively; or

☐ both the buyer and seller

Seller and Buyer acknowledge receipt of a copy hereof.

_____, CA. DATED:_____   _____, CA. DATED:____

Listing Agent _____   Seller_____

by_____   Seller_____

_____, CA. DATED:_____   _____, CA. DATED:____

Selling Agent _____   Buyer_____

by_____   Buyer_____

_____, CA. DATED:_____   _____, CA. DATED:____

The above "Confirmation of Agency Relationship" concerns the Real Estate Purchase Contract and Receipt for Deposit dated _____, 19____, for the purchase and sale of the property situated in _____, County of _____, California, described as follows: _____

_____ .

Seller and Buyer acknowledge that they have timely received copies of the statutory "Disclosure regarding Real Estate Agency Relationship", and have read the information contained therein. In establishing the agency relationship confirmed above, Seller and Buyer represent, that they have made the decision based upon the information in the Disclosure statement only and not relied upon any representations made by the Broker(s), associate licensees, subagents or employees.

If Seller and Buyer elected dual representation by the agent(s), they understand that an agent representing both parties must be impartial between the principals. Seller and Buyer acknowledge receipt of a copy hereof.

_____, CA. DATED: _____   _____, CA. DATED:____

Seller_____   Buyer_____

Seller_____   Buyer_____

A Real Estate Broker is the person qualified to advise on Real Estate Transactions. If you desire legal or tax advice, contact an appropriate Professional.

COMMENT ON FORM 11:06: The Agency Relationship law in California mandates disclosure for one-to-four residential units only. The Real Estate Commissioner has already indicated that the Department of Real Estate will enforce existing law regarding undisclosed dual agency in "mixed use" and commercial and industrial real estate transactions. A majority of brokerage firms is expected to use the Disclosure Statement in all their transactions.

It has taken many years before the National Association of Realtors acknowledged that the public perception of agency status in the ordinary real estate transaction was in a state of confusion. But in 1986, a task force finally admitted that a clarification of the agency status of the real estate broker/salesperson vis-a-vis real estate seller and real estate buyer was an "immediate and pressing need". The task force drew some guidelines for states that choose to implement an agency disclosure program.

Because the sale of real estate often crosses state boundaries it remains to be seen if the scattered state approach to the problem will work. The enactment of different disclosure statements to be used in each state undoubtedly will create problems where brokers from more than one state are involved in transactions crossing state lines. The Commissioners on Uniform State Laws may have to gear up. If the confusion spreads Congress might opt to develop a national "Truth in Real Estate Agency" law.

The agency disclosure laws will call for a massive educational effort for both the public and the industry. In California, beginning July 1, 1987, real estate licensees will have to take a 3-hour continuing education course in agency relationship.

The real test will, of course, be in the market place. Will it change the real estate business? If members of the public, "voluntarily" or somehow "persuaded" by an agent, choose "dual agency", will this work to the advantage of all?

The time tested representation of the seller only has been difficult enough. Taking on "legitimized" dual agency with its equal fiduciary obligations towards both parties may make some astute brokers true believers of the Biblical reminder: "No man can serve two masters" (Matthew VI, 24). At least the Agency Disclosure laws now on the books in several states bring the issue of whom the broker represents out in the open. Thereafter, as it was said in "Punch" magazine more than a hundred years ago: "You pays your money and you takes your choice".

Because as shown above state laws differ, you should not rely solely on the material in this chapter. You are warned to make yourself aware of particular problems and their legal interpretation in your state. Brokers and sellers in states where they are subject to extended liability in sales or real property may take some solace in the fact that they are not alone. Real Estate law leads all other legal fields in legal malpractice claims against attorneys.

Disclosure of Death on the Premises

As mentioned on page 323, a California court held that a buyer had a valid cause of action against a broker and seller for failure to disclose that several murders had occurred on the property some ten years before the sale. Because of the uncertainty of the parameters of this case, legislation was introduced to limit the exposure of sellers and their agents. It's doubtful if the legislation solved the dilemma. The statute relieves sellers and brokers of any obligation to disclose the occurrence of death on real property beyond three years from the date of the incident. But the statute is silent about whether an affirmative duty to disclose exist during the first three years. Obviously if the facts are identical or substantially similar to the court case, liability may attach for the first three years after the incident. Still unclarified are issues such as suicide, accidental death, single murder, etc.

The safest procedure for the broker is to ask the seller and then disclose if the facts so demand. Another California statute provides that disclosure of the *cause* of death arising from acquired immune deficiency syndrome (AIDS) need not be made.

Illustration of Some Other Specific Disclosure Rules Created by California Statutory Law

1. Disclosure of Special Studies (geologic) Zones (Public Resources Code §2621.9)
2. Reporting Sales Price (B & P Code §10141)
3. Recording Deeds of Trust (B & P Code §10141.15)
4. Delivery of Copies of Contract to Principal (B & P Code §10142)
5. Creative Financing Disclosure (C.C. §2956)
6. Pest Control Disclosure (C.C. §1099)
7. Mortgage Loan Disclosure Statement (B & P Code §10240)
8. Delivery of Condominium Documents (C.C. §1360)
9. Delivery of Subdivision Final Public report before obtaining offer (Subdivided Lands Law, B & P Code §11018.1)
10. Delivery of Blanket Encumbrance Disclosure Caveat (C.C. §1133)
11. Delivery of Statement of all substantial defects, or a disclaimer in condominium conversion projects of 5 or more units (C.C. §1134.5)

The above list is not presented as being complete.

Chapter 12
New Types of Form Contracts

*Simplicity, Simplicity, Simplicity! I say,
let your affairs be as two or three, and
not a hundred or a thousand . . . Simplify. Simplify.*

Thoreau, Walden

With the advent of conglomerates in the real estate brokerage business the format of printed real estate contracts have dramatically changed in many states. All-inclusive type forms is the new mode. They cover anything from pre-print-ed terms of payment clauses to multiple disclosures accompanied by numerous disclaimers that the sales agent made no representations on which either the seller or the buyer may rely. Gone is the single page real estate contract which was usually neutral as between seller and buyer. Now the emphasis seems to be on convenience to the marketing salesperson.

The printed agreement with their expandable "additional terms" pages are extremely difficult to compare. Boilerplate clauses which look familiar even to a trained legal eye may include words which totally change the meaning of the familiar text. Such forms place burdens of interpretation, that few salesper-sons and fewer buyers and sellers are capable of overcoming. In multiple offer situations confusion over which offer is the best is a common occurrence. New-er versions of these multi-paged "monster" contracts are constantly introduced. This adds to the confusion and leads to sellers and buyers finding to their chagrin that they have agreed to provisons in the contract which were concealed in the massive boilerplate. A Real Estate Agent in California is by both statute and case law under a duty to disclose to his or her principal the contents of the deposit receipt.[1] But how is the agent to perform that duty when the deposit receipt is so complex and contains clauses which may be detrimental to the interests of one or the other of the principals of the transaction?

Since the larger chain brokerage firms pioneered the "Chinese menu" forms they soon had imitators from print shops, smaller real estate firms, as well as from some local Boards of Realtors.

Anatomy of CAR's Long Form (Model Form II)

Even the California Association of Realtors joined in, but in a more considered and careful manner. CAR's approach was to incorporate Model Form I's text in the new "Long Form", which comes in two versions: with or without the financing terms identical to the Financing Supplement. Many required disclosures which are available separately as addenda to the modular letter size form are included in the "Long Form". So there is much familiar text.

Model Form II acts as a checklist for a contract that is complete in all salient respects. Of course printed paragraphs that are not applicable should be deleted and any changes should be dated and initialled by the principals to the transaction. Let's examine the contract point by point (refer to the printed form on page 348.

First, insert the name of the place where the Buyer actually signs the offer to purchase. In inserting the date, avoid abbreviations. The full name of the person(s) to whom the receipt for deposit is given should be stated here. Write the deposit and purchase price both in letters and figures in the spaces provided. If the listing agreement prescribes a minimum deposit, the licensee should, of course, obtain such amount. The amount of deposit assumes added significance in a contract which includes a completed liquidated damage clause (paragraph 10) herein if initialled by buyer and seller).

In the appropriate box, identify the type of deposit receipt. If the check is postdated, obtain the seller's authorization in writing to hold the check until the date indicated. Describe the property in sufficient detail. Whether the description is long or short, it calls for accuracy.

1. Financing

Obviously, only the most common forms of financing can be covered in preprinted text. If creative financing utilizing special conditions of the Seller's take-back loan is involved, the additional financing terms can be included in Paragraph 1:J or incorporated in the contract with a reference such as, "Additional terms of note in favor of Seller are set forth in Exhibit 'A' attached hereto and incorporated herein by reference." Better yet, use the blank first page shown on page 348. The preprinted finance terms version appears on page 18.

Pay attention to paragraph K which obligates the buyer to be diligent in applying for financing. Space is provided for notice of the time period within which financing should be obtained.

2. Occupancy

If the property is a one- to four-unit building, one unit of which is to be occupied by the buyer, and if the liquidated damage clause is to be initialled, mark this paragraph accordingly. It will facilitate proof in a controversy over disposition of a deposit.

3. Supplements

If part of the negotiated agreement between buyer and seller includes the subject matter specified in any one of the three referenced CAR supplements, then the appropriate box(es) should be checked. Other designated supplements can also be attached when the appropriate box is checked.

4. Escrow

Insert the name of the proposed escrow holder. Determine the times for delivery of preliminary and final escrow instructions and which party is to pay the fees. Have both buyer and seller initial this page and next two pages of the contract.

5. Title

This wording constitutes a reasonable compromise between Seller's legitimate concern about adding an additional "out" for a buyer who suffers from "buyer's remorse", and the need to protect the buyer from an unknowing acceptance of unexpected "clouds" and restrictions on the title. The "(c)" exclusion in this paragraph provides space for unrecorded agreements between adjoining property owners, which would not appear on a title report.

6. Prorations

The usual proration items are mentioned here. Other items should be inserted. Notice the possible elections of the payor of transfer taxes and the caveat that the sale will affect the property taxes.

7. Possession

Several options are listed and space is allotted for additional reference to an "occupancy agreement after sale".

8. Vesting

The vesting of title caveat is often ignored. Too often parties are "advised" to take title as "joint tenants," which might not be to their best advantage. If the buyers do not have a clear understanding of the legal or tax consequences of their decision, the broker should abstain from giving legal advice and specify, "Instructions to follow in Escrow".

9. Multiple Listing Service

This paragraph gives authorization to a participant in MLS to report the sale, price, terms and financing for use by authorized Board members.

10. Liquidated Damages

By initialling this clause, the buyers and sellers can limit the amounts of damages for buyer's default. For a "dwelling with no more than four units, one of which the buyer intends to occupy as his residence," the forfeiture is by law limited to 3 percent of the purchase price.

If the blanks are not initialled by both parties, the seller's damages for the buyer's breach of contract to purchase such residential property are not predetermined by the amount of the deposit. The seller, in this situation, has the option to seek actual damages, to return the deposit, or to enforce the contract through specific performance.

This is an area that is often neglected. If the buyer initials the box and the seller does not, no enforceable contract may in fact exist. If the parties nevertheless proceed, a dispute can arise in case of default. In cases where a buyer initials the provision in the offer, but the seller is not willing to liquidate damages, the rejection should be spelled out in a counter offer, which can be presented for the buyer's concurrence or disapproval.

If the original deposit is to be increased under the terms of the contract and the liquidated damages clause is initialled by both parties, the law requires a separately signed statement reaffirming the agreement to liquidate the damages.

11.   Arbitration

Under this paragraph the parties are provided the election of arbitration regarding disputes about disposition of the buyer's deposit in case of default.

12.   Attorneys Fees

The prevailing party in any action or proceeding arising out of the contract is entitled to attorneys fees and costs.

13.   Keys

This new paragraph is included to alert the seller of the obligation to provide the buyer with all available keys.

14.   Personal Property

Any items of personal property which may be included in the purchase price should be listed here. A reference to an inventory can be inserted if the space allotted is insufficient.

15.   Fixtures

The most common fixtures are included. Space for additions or exemptions is available.

16.   Smoke Detectors
Insert who pays for installation which is required by law.

17.   Transfer Disclosure.
See page 326.

18.   Tax Withholding

The Internal Revenue Code Sections 1445 and 897, also called FIRPTA, "The Foreign Investment in Real Property Tax Act," together with the Treasury Department's regulation, are the "inspiration" for this paragraph. The clause spells out the obligations of *every* buyer of U.S. property, unless exemptions apply, to withhold from the seller's proceeds 10 percent of the payment.

This clause serves as reminder to the licensee to supervise escrow for compliance with the new tax rules. In doubtful cases, neither escrow nor the real estate licensee should attempt to determine whether an exemption applies. Affidavits in printed forms are available to carry out the provisions of this new law.

19. Entire Contract
This clause includes the "time is of the essence" provision to indicate that performance of any act under the agreement shall take place on the date stated unless the time is extended in writing.

This clause expressly provides that there are no previous understandings or agreements not contained in the writing and the writing supersedes and nullifies any prior statements, promises, understandings, or agreements. The clause is conclusive on the issue of integration and will result in the exclusion of parol evidence of the matters covered. The clause will not, however, prevent the admission of parol evidence to show fraud in the inception or to clarify an ambiguity. The "entire agreement" clause alerts the parties to the fact that their agreement is being treated as a complete and final statement of their rights and duties and that they may not justifiably rely on other oral or written representations which have not been made a part of the final document.

20. Captions
The captions are not intended to be part of the contract, but are for reference purposes only. The clauses outlined above cover the first two pages of the contract. The clauses in paragraph 20, designated by the letters "A" to "L" on the third and fourth pages of the new CAR Form, are optional in that not all of them will necessarily be included in every agreement. The inclusion, therefore, of any particular clause must be initialled by *all* buyers and sellers. If only initialled by one party no contract may exist.

21. A. Physical Inspection
If a contractor's (or other qualified person's) inspection is desired by buyer, this provision spells out the buyer's rights and obligations. If buyer does not object in writing to any adverse conditions shown in the reports, such failure is considered conclusive approval of the property.

B. Geological Inspection
This clause provides opportunity for the buyer to obtain a geological report on the property with the same rights to cancellation as in 20 A. In both instances, the buyer shall, at no cost, deliver copies of any issued reports to the

seller. A reasonable amount of time for the inspection should be indicated in the spaces provided.

C. Condition of Property
This clause obligates the seller to maintain the property in the same condition as when the contract was signed. This warranty continues until physical possession is made available to buyer. Seller also warrants that the roof is free of all known leaks and that the various utility systems and built-in appliances are operative. Space is provided for additions or exemptions.

D. Seller Representations
The seller should be carefully interviewed at the time of the listing with regards to any official notices received from any government agency regarding the legality of the property. Such interviewing should be repeated just before the close of escrow so the seller can comply with the contractual obligation to disclose any later received notice of irregularities.

E. Pest Control
The wording of this clause is a condensed version of CAR's Structural Pest Control Certification Agreement, "SPC-1." See Chapter 4.

F. Flood Hazard Zone
If the property is located in a "Flood Zone," the parties are alerted to the requirement for flood insurance.

G. Special Studies Zone
This clause and the preceding one supersede CAR's Special Studies Zone and Flood Hazards Disclosure Statement. It contains the same wording and provides for the insertion of the time period allotted for the buyer to make necessary inquiries and to make objections, if any, in writing.

H. Energy Conservation Retrofit
This paragraph refers to local ordinances which demand compliance with minimum energy conservation. If buyer is to receive credit in escrow for the cost, the contract should so provide. Paragraph 20L ("Other Terms and Conditions") can be used for such agreement and other terms. This is also a good place to insert references to any addenda to the contract.

I. Home Protection Plan
Such plans are popular in many areas. The clause provides space for insertion of the designated party who will pay for the plan. If the parties do not want such a plan, the waiver should be filled out and initialled.

J. Condominium/P.U.D.

In this paragraph, the seller's duty to deliver certain information and documents in the sale of condominiums and Planned Unit Developments (P.U.D.) are set forth. The real estate licensee should carefully examine such documents and include the necessary information in the spaces provided. Again, the buyer can be given a reasonable time in which to object in writing.

22.   Other Terms and Conditions

Only six lines are available. An addendum may be necessary. Use space to refer to it and incorporate it in the contract.

23.   Agency Confirmation

The statutory requirement.

24.   Offer

The caveat that amendments, modifications and alterations shall be made in writing executed by the buyer and seller is included in the contract form to guard against verbal agreements. Both parties' written consent to extension of time or other modifications should always be obtained.

Sellers should sign and, if the transaction is a cooperative one, both brokers or their licensed representatives should sign and agree to the commission and its division. Commissions are most conveniently expressed as a percentage of the purchase price. This avoids rewriting if counter offers occur.

Acceptance.

The acceptance clause is similar to the clause in model form I. See page 215. It contains the seller's approval of the agency relationship and an agreement to protect the broker's commission.

REAL ESTATE PURCHASE CONTRACT AND RECEIPT FOR DEPOSIT

(LONG FORM — WITH FINANCING CLAUSES)
THIS IS MORE THAN A RECEIPT FOR MONEY. IT IS INTENDED TO BE A LEGALLY BINDING CONTRACT. READ IT CAREFULLY
CALIFORNIA ASSOCIATION OF REALTORS® (CAR) STANDARD FORM

_____, California, _____, 19___

Received from _____

herein called Buyer, the sum of _____ Dollars $ _____

evidenced by ☐ cash, ☐ cashier's check, ☐ personal check or ☐ _____ payable to

_____, to be held uncashed until acceptance of this offer as deposit on account of purchase price of

_____ Dollars $ _____

for the purchase of property, situated in _____, County of _____, California,

described as follows: _____

1. FINANCING: The obtaining of Buyer's financing is a contingency of this agreement.

A. Deposit upon acceptance, to be deposited into _____ .... $ _____

B. INCREASED DEPOSIT within _____ days of Seller's acceptance to be deposited into _____ .... $ _____

C. BALANCE OF DOWN PAYMENT to be deposited into _____ on or before _____ .... $ _____

D. Buyer to apply, qualify for and obtain a NEW FIRST LOAN in the amount of .... $ _____

including interest at origination not to

payable monthly at approximately $ _____ exceed _____ %, ☐ fixed rate, ☐ other _____ all due _____ years from date of

origination. Loan fee not to exceed _____ Seller agrees to pay a maximum of _____

FHA/VA discount points. Additional terms _____

E. Buyer ☐ to assume, ☐ to take title subject to an EXISTING FIRST LOAN with an approximate balance of ... $ _____

in favor of _____ payable monthly at $ _____ including interest

at _____ % ☐ fixed rate, ☐ other _____

Fees not to exceed _____. Disposition of impound account _____

Additional Terms _____

F. Buyer to execute a NOTE SECURED BY a ☐ first, ☐ second, ☐ third DEED OF TRUST in the amount of $ _____

IN FAVOR OF SELLER payable monthly at $ _____ or more, including interest at _____ % all due

_____ years from date of origination, ☐ or upon sale or transfer of subject property. A late charge of

_____ days of the due date. ☐ Deed of Trust to contain a

shall be due on any installment not paid within _____ request for notice of default or sale for the benefit of Seller. Buyer ☐ will, ☐ will not execute a request for notice of

delinquency. Additional terms _____

G. Buyer☐ to assume, ☐ to take title subject to an EXISTING SECOND LOAN with an approximate balance of ... $ _____

in favor of _____ payable monthly at $ _____ including interest

at _____ % ☐ fixed rate, ☐ other _____ Buyer fees not to exceed _____

Additional terms _____

H. Buyer to apply, qualify for and obtain a NEW SECOND LOAN in the amount of .... $ _____

payable monthly at approximately $ _____ including interest at origination not to exceed

_____ % ☐ fixed rate, ☐ other, _____

_____ all due _____ years from date of origination. Buyer's loan fee not to exceed _____

Additional Terms _____

(Form continues on next page.)

I. In the event Buyer assumes or takes title subject to an existing loan, Seller shall provide Buyer with copies of applicable notes and Deeds of Trust. A loan may contain a number of features which affect the loan, such as interest rate changes, monthly payment changes, balloon payments, etc. Buyer shall be allowed _____ calendar days after receipt of such copies to notify seller in writing of disapproval. FAILURE TO SO NOTIFY SELLER SHALL CONCLUSIVELY BE CONSIDERED APPROVAL. Buyer's approval shall not be unreasonably withheld. Difference in existing loan balances shall be adjusted in ☐ Cash, ☐ Other _____

J. Buyer agrees to act diligently and in good faith to obtain all applicable financing. _____

K. ADDITIONAL FINANCING TERMS: _____

L. TOTAL PURCHASE PRICE .... $ _____

2. OCCUPANCY: Buyer ☐ does, ☐ does not intend to occupy subject property as Buyer's primary residence.

3. SUPPLEMENTS: The ATTACHED supplements are incorporated herein:
☐ Interim Occupancy Agreement (CAR FORM IOA-11)
☐ Residential Lease Agreement after Sale (CAR FORM RLAS-11)
☐ VA and FHA Amendments (CAR FORM VA/FHA-11)

Buyer and Seller acknowledge receipt of copy of this page, which constitutes Page 1 of _____ Pages.
Buyer's Initials (_____)(_____)   Seller's Initials (_____)(_____)

THIS STANDARDIZED DOCUMENT FOR USE IN SIMPLE TRANSACTIONS HAS BEEN APPROVED BY THE CALIFORNIA ASSOCIATION OF REALTORS® IN FORM ONLY. NO REPRESENTATION IS MADE AS TO THE APPROVAL OF THE FORM OF ANY SUPPLEMENTS NOT CURRENTLY PUBLISHED BY THE CALIFORNIA ASSOCIATION OF REALTORS® OR THE LEGAL VALIDITY OR ADEQUACY OF ANY PROVISION IN ANY SPECIFIC TRANSACTION. IT SHOULD NOT BE USED IN COMPLEX TRANSACTIONS OR WITH EXTENSIVE RIDERS OR ADDITIONS.

A REAL ESTATE BROKER IS THE PERSON QUALIFIED TO ADVISE ON REAL ESTATE TRANSACTIONS. IF YOU DESIRE LEGAL OR TAX ADVICE, CONSULT AN APPROPRIATE PROFESSIONAL.

To order, contact — California Association of Realtors®
525 S. Virgil Avenue, Los Angeles, California 90020
Copyright© 1986, California Association of Realtors®
Revised 12/86

OFFICE USE ONLY
Reviewed by Broker or Designee _____
Date _____

BUYER'S COPY

EQUAL HOUSING OPPORTUNITY
SF-L6-SF

REAL ESTATE PURCHASE CONTRACT AND RECEIPT FOR DEPOSIT (DLF-14 PAGE 1 OF 4)

(Form continues on next page)

Subject Property Address _____

☐

4. ESCROW: Buyer and Seller shall deliver signed instructions to _____ the escrow holder, within _____ calendar days from Seller's acceptance which shall provide for closing within _____ calendar days from Seller's acceptance. Escrow fees to be paid as follows: _____

5. TITLE: Title is to be free of liens, encumbrances, easements, restrictions, rights and conditions of record or known to Seller, other than the following: (a) Current property taxes, (b) covenants, conditions, restrictions, and public utility easements of record, if any, provided the same do not adversely affect the continued use of the property for the purposes for which it is presently being used, unless reasonably disapproved by Buyer in writing within _____ calendar days of receipt of a current preliminary report furnished at _____ expense, and (c) _____
Seller shall furnish Buyer at _____ expense a standard California Land Title Association policy issued by _____ Company, showing title vested in Buyer subject only to the above. If Seller is unwilling or unable to eliminate any title matter disapproved by Buyer as above, Buyer may terminate this agreement. If Seller fails to deliver title as above, Buyer may terminate this agreement; in either case, the deposit shall be returned to Buyer.

6. PRORATIONS: Property taxes, payments on bonds and assessments assumed by Buyer, interest, rents, association dues, premiums on insurance acceptable to Buyer, and _____ shall be paid current and prorated as of: ☐ the day of recordation of the deed; or ☐ _____. Bonds or assessments now a lien shall be ☐ paid current by Seller, payments not yet due to be assumed by Buyer; or ☐ paid in full by Seller, including payments not yet due; or ☐ _____. The _____ transfer tax County Transfer tax shall be paid by _____ or transfer fee shall be paid by _____. **PROPERTY WILL BE REASSESSED UPON CHANGE OF OWNERSHIP. THIS WILL AFFECT THE TAXES TO BE PAID.** A Supplemental tax bill will be issued, which shall be paid as follows: (a) for periods after close of escrow, by Buyer (or by final acquiring party if part of an exchange), and (b) for periods prior to close of escrow, by Seller. TAX BILLS ISSUED AFTER CLOSE OF ESCROW SHALL BE HANDLED DIRECTLY BETWEEN BUYER AND SELLER.

7. POSSESSION: Possession and occupancy shall be delivered to Buyer, ☐ on close of escrow, or ☐ not later than _____ days after close of escrow, or ☐ _____

8. VESTING: Unless otherwise designated in the escrow instructions of Buyer, title shall vest as follows: _____

(The manner of taking title may have significant legal and tax consequences. Therefore, give this matter serious consideration.)

9. MULTIPLE LISTING SERVICE: If Broker is a Participant of a Board multiple listing service ("MLS"), the Broker is authorized to report the sale, its price, terms, and financing for the publication, dissemination, information, and use of the authorized Board members, MLS Participants and Subscribers.

10. LIQUIDATED DAMAGES: If Buyer fails to complete said purchase as herein provided by reason of any default of Buyer, Seller shall be released from obligation to sell the property to Buyer and may proceed against Buyer upon any claim or remedy which he/she may have in law or equity; provided, however, that by placing their initials here Buyer: ( ) Seller: ( ) agree that Seller shall retain the deposit as liquidated damages. If the described property is a dwelling with no more than four units, one of which the Buyer intends to occupy as his/her residence, Seller shall retain as liquidated damages the deposit actually paid, or an amount therefrom, not more than 3% of the purchase price and promptly return any excess to Buyer. Buyer and Seller agree to execute a similar liquidated damages provision, such as California Association of Realtors® Receipt for Increased Deposit (RID-11), for any increased deposits. (Funds deposited in trust accounts or in escrow are not released automatically in the event of a dispute. Release of funds requires written agreement of the parties or adjudication.)

(Form continues on next page)

11. **ARBITRATION:** If the only controversy or claim between the parties arises out of or relates to the disposition of the Buyer's deposit, such controversy or claim shall at the election of the parties be decided by arbitration. Such arbitration shall be determined in accordance with the Rules of the American Arbitration Association, and judgment upon the award rendered by the Arbitrator(s) may be entered in any court having jurisdiction thereof. The provisions of Code of Civil Procedure Section 1283.05 shall be applicable to such arbitration.

12. **ATTORNEY'S FEES:** In any action or proceeding arising out of this agreement, the prevailing party shall be entitled to reasonable attorney's fees and costs.

13. **KEYS:** Seller shall, when possession is available to Buyer, provide keys and/or means to operate all property locks, and alarms, if any.

14. **PERSONAL PROPERTY:** The following items of personal property, free of liens and without warranty of condition, are included: _____

_____

15. **FIXTURES:** All permanently installed fixtures and fittings that are attached to the property or for which special openings have been made are included in the purchase price, including electrical, light, plumbing and heating fixtures, built-in appliances, screens, awnings, shutters, all window coverings, attached floor coverings, T.V. antennas, air cooler or conditioner, garage door openers and controls, attached fireplace equipment, mailbox, trees and shrubs, and _____ except _____ at the expense of ☐ Buyer, ☐ Seller.

16. **SMOKE DETECTOR(S):** Approved smoke detector(s) shall be installed as required by law.

17. **TRANSFER DISCLOSURE:** Unless exempt, Transferor (Seller), shall comply with Civil Code Sections 1102 et seq., by providing Transferee (Buyer) with a Real Estate Transfer Disclosure Statement: a) ☐ Buyer has received and read a Real Estate Transfer Disclosure Statement; or b) ☐ Seller shall provide Buyer with a Real Estate Transfer Disclosure Statement within _____ calendar days of Seller's acceptance after which Buyer shall have three (3) days after delivery to Buyer, in person, or five (5) days after delivery by deposit in the mail, to terminate this agreement by delivery of a written notice of termination to Seller or Seller's Agent.

18. **TAX WITHHOLDING:** Under the Foreign Investment in Real Property Tax Act (FIRPTA), IRC 1445, *every* Buyer of U.S. real property *must*, unless an exemption applies, deduct and withhold from Seller's proceeds ten percent (10%) of the gross sales price. The primary exemptions are: No withholding is required if (a) Seller provides Buyer with an affidavit under penalty of perjury, that Seller is not a "foreign person," or (b) Seller provides Buyer with a "qualifying statement" issued by the Internal Revenue Service, or (c) if Buyer purchases real property for use as a residence and the purchase price is $300,000.00 or less and if Buyer or a member of Buyer's family has definite plans to reside at the property for at least 50% of the number of days it is in use during each of the first two twelve-months periods after transfer. Seller and Buyer agree to execute and deliver as directed, any instrument, affidavit and statement, or to perform any act reasonably necessary to carry out the provisions of FIRPTA and regulations promulgated thereunder.

19. **ENTIRE CONTRACT:** Time is of the essence. All prior agreements between the parties are incorporated in this agreement which constitutes the entire contract. Its terms are intended by the parties as a final expression of their agreement with respect to such terms as are included herein and may not be contradicted by evidence of any prior agreement or contemporaneous oral agreement. The parties further intend that this agreement constitutes the complete and exclusive statement of its terms and that no extrinsic evidence whatsoever may be introduced in any judicial or arbitration proceeding, if any, involving this agreement.

Buyer and Seller acknowledge receipt of copy of this page, which constitutes Page 2 of _____ Pages.

Buyer's Initials (_____) (_____)   Seller's Initials (_____) (_____)

OFFICE USE ONLY

Reviewed by Broker or Designee

Date

BROKER'S COPY

REAL ESTATE PURCHASE CONTRACT AND RECEIPT FOR DEPOSIT (DL-14 PAGE 2 OF 4)

(Form continues on next page)

Subject Property Address _____

20. CAPTIONS: The captions in this agreement are for convenience of reference only and are not intended as part of this agreement.

21. ADDITIONAL TERMS AND CONDITIONS:
ONLY THE FOLLOWING PARAGRAPHS A THROUGH J *WHEN INITIALED BY BOTH BUYER AND SELLER* ARE INCORPORATED IN THIS AGREEMENT.

Buyer's Initials _____ / _____ **Seller's Initials**

A. PHYSICAL INSPECTION: Within _____ calendar days after Seller's acceptance Buyer shall have the right, at Buyer's expense, to select a licensed contractor(s) or other qualified professional(s), to inspect and investigate the subject property, including, but not limited to structural, plumbing, heating, electrical, built-in appliances, roof, soils, foundation, mechanical systems, pool, pool heater, pool filter, air conditioner, if any, possible environmental hazards such as asbestos, formaldehyde, radon gas and other substances/products. Buyer shall keep the subject property free and clear of any liens, indemnify and hold Seller harmless from all liability, claims, demands, damages or costs, and repair all damages to the property arising from the inspections. All claimed defects concerning the condition of the property that adversely affect the continued use of the property for the purposes for which it is presently being used shall be in writing, supported by written reports, if any, and delivered to Seller within _____ calendar days after Seller's acceptance. Buyer shall furnish Seller copies, at no cost, of all reports concerning the property obtained by Buyer. When such reports disclose conditions or information unsatisfactory to the Buyer, which the Seller is unwilling or unable to correct. Buyer may cancel this agreement. Seller shall make the premises available for all inspections. BUYER'S FAILURE TO NOTIFY SELLER SHALL CONCLUSIVELY BE CONSIDERED APPROVAL.

Buyer's Initials _____ / _____ **Seller's Initials**

B. GEOLOGICAL INSPECTION: Within _____ calendar days after Seller's acceptance. Buyer shall have the right at Buyer's expense, to select a qualified professional to make tests, surveys, or other studies of the subject property. Buyer shall keep the subject property free and clear of any liens, indemnify and hold Seller harmless from all liability, claims, demands, damages or costs, and repair all damages to the property arising from the tests, surveys, or studies. All claimed defects concerning the condition of the property that adversely affect the continued use of the property for the purposes for which it is presently being used shall be in writing, supported by written reports, if any, and delivered to Seller within _____ calendar days after Seller's acceptance. Buyer shall furnish Seller copies, at no cost, of all reports concerning the property obtained by Buyer. When such reports disclose conditions or information unsatisfactory to the Buyer, which the Seller is unwilling or unable to correct. Buyer may cancel this agreement. Seller shall make the premises available for all inspections. BUYER'S FAILURE TO NOTIFY SELLER SHALL CONCLUSIVELY BE CONSIDERED APPROVAL.

Buyer's Initials _____ / _____ **Seller's Initials**

C. CONDITION OF PROPERTY: Seller warrants, through the date possession is made available to Buyer: (1) property and improvements thereon, including landscaping, grounds and pool spa, if any, shall be maintained in the same condition as upon the date of Seller's acceptance; (2) the roof is free of all known leaks and that water, sewer, plumbing, heating, air conditioning, if any, and electrical systems and all built-in appliances are operative; (3) _____ .

(Form continues on next page)

Buyer's Initials _____   **Seller's Initials** _____

_____ / _____   **D. SELLER REPRESENTATION:** Seller warrants that Seller has no knowledge of any notice of violations of City, County, State, Federal, Building, Zoning, Fire, Health Codes or ordinances, or other governmental regulation filed or issued against the property. This warranty shall be effective until the date of close of escrow.

Buyer's Initials _____   **Seller's Initials** _____

_____ / _____   **E. PEST CONTROL:** Within _____ calendar days from the date of Seller's acceptance Seller shall furnish Buyer, at the expense of ☐ Buyer, ☐ Seller, a current written report of an inspection by _____, a licensed Structural Pest Control Operator, of the main building and all structures on the property, except _____

If no infestation or infection by wood destroying pests or organisms is found, the report shall include a written "Certification" as provided in Business and Professions Code 8519(a) that on the date of inspection "no evidence of active infestation or infection was found."

All work recommended in said report to repair damage caused by infestation or infection by wood-destroying pests or organisms found, including leaking shower stalls and replacing of tiles removed for repairs, and all work to correct conditions that cause such infestation or infection shall be done at the expense of Seller.

Funds for work to be performed shall be held in escrow and disbursed upon receipt of written Certification as provided in Business and Professions Code 8519(b) that the property "is now free of evidence of active infestation or infection".

Buyer agrees that any work to correct conditions usually deemed likely to lead to infestation or infection by wood-destroying pests or organisms, but where no evidence of existing infestation or infection is found with respect to such conditions is NOT the responsibility of Seller, and that such work shall be done only if requested by Buyer and then at the expense of Buyer.

If inspection of inaccessible areas is recommended by the report, Buyer has the option of accepting and approving the report or requesting further inspection be made at the Buyer's expense. If further inspection is made and infestation, infection, or damage is found, repair of such damage and all work to correct conditions that caused such infestation or infection and the cost of entry and closing of the inaccessible areas shall be at the expense of Seller. If no infestation, infection, or damage is found, the cost of entry and closing of the inaccessible areas shall be at the expense of Buyer.

Other _____

Buyer's Initials _____   **Seller's Initials** _____

_____ / _____   **F. FLOOD HAZARD AREA DISCLOSURE:** Buyer is informed that subject property is situated in a "Special Flood Hazard Area" as set forth on a Federal Emergency Management Agency (FEMA) "Flood Insurance Rate Map (FIRM) or "Flood Hazard Boundary Map" (FHBM). The law provides that, as a condition of obtaining financing on most structures located in a "Special Flood Hazard Area," lenders require flood insurance where the property or its attachments are security for a loan.

The extent of coverage and the cost may vary. For further information consult the lender or insurance carrier. No representation or recommendation is made by the Seller and the Brokers in this transaction as to the legal effect or economic consequences of the National Flood Insurance Program and related legislation.

Buyer and Seller acknowledge receipt of copy of this page, which constitutes Page 3 of _____ Pages.

Buyer's Initials (_____) (_____)   Seller's Initials (_____) (_____)

OFFICE USE ONLY

Reviewed by Broker or Designee _____

Date _____

BROKER'S COPY

REAL ESTATE PURCHASE CONTRACT AND RECEIPT FOR DEPOSIT (DL-14 PAGE 3 OF 4)

(Form continues on next page)

EQUAL HOUSING
OPPORTUNITY
SF Aug 87

Subject Property Address _____
Buyer's Initials _____ **Seller's Initials** _____

G. SPECIAL STUDIES ZONE DISCLOSURE: Buyer is informed that subject property is situated in a Special Studies Zone as designated under Sections 2621-2625, inclusive, of the California Public Resources Code; and, as such, the construction or development on this property of any structure for human occupancy may be subject to the findings of a geologic report prepared by a geologist registered in the State of California, unless such a report is waived by the City or County under the terms of that act. Buyer is allowed _____ calendar days from the date of the Seller's acceptance to make further inquiries at appropriate governmental agencies concerning the use of the subject property under the terms of the Special Studies Zone Act and local building, zoning, fire, health and safety codes. When such inquiries disclose conditions or information unsatisfactory to the Buyer, which the Seller is unwilling or unable to correct, Buyer may cancel this agreement. BUYER'S FAILURE TO NOTIFY SELLER SHALL CONCLUSIVELY BE CONSIDERED APPROVAL.
Buyer's Initials _____ **Seller's Initials** _____

H. ENERGY CONSERVATION RETROFIT: If local ordinance requires that the property be brought in compliance with minimum energy Conservation Standards as a condition of sale or transfer, ☐ Buyer, ☐ Seller shall comply with and pay for these requirements. Where permitted by law, Seller may, if obligated hereunder, satisfy the obligation by authorizing escrow to credit Buyer with sufficient funds to cover the cost of such retrofit.
Buyer's Initials _____ **Seller's Initials** _____

I. HOME PROTECTION PLAN: Buyer and Seller have been informed that Home Protection Plans are available. Such plans may provide additional protection and benefit to a Seller or Buyer. California Association of Realtors* and the Broker(s) in this transaction do not endorse or approve any particular company or program:

a) ☐ A Buyer's coverage Home Protection Plan to be issued by _____ , to be paid by ☐ Seller. ☐ Buyer; or Company, at a cost not to exceed $ _____

b) ☐ Buyer and Seller elect not to purchase a Home Protection Plan.
Buyer's Initials _____ **Seller's Initials** _____

J. CONDOMINIUM/P.U.D.: The subject of this transaction is a condominium / planned unit development (P.U.D.) designated as unit _____ and _____ parking space(s) and an undivided _____ interest in all community areas, and _____. The current monthly assessment charge by the homeowner's association or other governing body(s) is $ _____. As soon as practicable, Seller shall provide Buyer with copies of covenants, conditions and restrictions, articles of incorporation, by-laws, current rules and regulations, most current financial statements, and any other documents as required by law. Seller shall disclose in writing any known pending special assessment, claims, or litigation to Buyer. Buyer shall be allowed _____ calendar days from receipt to review these documents. If such documents disclose conditions or information unsatisfactory to Buyer, Buyer may cancel this agreement. BUYER'S FAILURE TO NOTIFY SELLER SHALL CONCLUSIVELY BE CONSIDERED APPROVAL

22. OTHER TERMS AND CONDITIONS: _____

_____

_____

23. AGENCY CONFIRMATION: The following agency relationship(s) are hereby confirmed for this transaction:
LISTING AGENT: _____ is the agent of (check one):
☐ the Seller exclusively; or ☐ both the Buyer and Seller
SELLING AGENT: _____ (If not the same as Listing Agent) is the agent of (check one):
☐ the Buyer exclusively; or ☐ the Seller exclusively; or ☐ both the Buyer and Seller.

24. AMENDMENTS: This agreement may not be amended, modified, altered or changed in any respect whatsoever except by a further agreement in writing executed by Buyer and Seller.

25. OFFER: This constitutes an offer to purchase the described property. Unless acceptance is signed by Seller and the signed copy delivered in person or by mail to Buyer, or to _____ who is authorized to receive it, in person or by mail at the address below, within _____ calendar days of the date hereof, this offer shall be deemed revoked and the deposit shall be returned. Buyer has read and acknowledges receipt of a copy of this offer.

REAL ESTATE BROKER _____ BUYER _____

By _____ BUYER _____

Address _____ Address _____

Telephone _____ Telephone _____

ACCEPTANCE

The undersigned Seller accepts and agrees to sell the property on the above terms and conditions and agrees to the above confirmation of agency relationships. Seller agrees to pay to Broker(s) _____

compensation for services as follows:

Payable: (a) On recordation of the deed or other evidence of title, or (b) if completion of sale is prevented by default of Seller, upon Seller's default, or (c) if completion of sale is prevented by default of Buyer, only if and when Seller collects damages from Buyer, by suit or otherwise, and then in an amount not less than one-half of the damages recovered, but not to exceed the above fee, after first deducting title and escrow expenses and the expenses of collection, if any. Seller shall execute and deliver an escrow instruction irrevocably assigning the compensation for service in an amount equal to the compensation agreed to above, in any action or proceeding between Broker(s) and Seller arising out of this agreement, the prevailing party shall be entitled to reasonable attorneys fees and costs. The undersigned has read and acknowledges receipt of a copy of this agreement and authorizes Broker(s) to deliver a signed copy to Buyer.

Date _____ Telephone _____ SELLER _____

Address _____ SELLER _____

Real Estate Broker(s) agree to the foregoing.

Broker _____ By _____ Date _____

Broker _____ By _____ Date _____

OFFICE USE ONLY

Reviewed by Broker or Designee _____

Date _____

Page 4 of _____ Pages.

BROKER'S COPY

This form is available for use by the entire real estate industry. The use of this form is not intended to identify the user as a REALTOR®. REALTOR® is a registered collective membership mark which may be used only by real estate licensees who are members of the NATIONAL ASSOCIATION OF REALTORS® and who subscribe to its Code of Ethics.

EQUAL HOUSING OPPORTUNITY
SF-Aug-87

REAL ESTATE PURCHASE CONTRACT AND RECEIPT FOR DEPOSIT (DL-14 PAGE 4 OF 4)

(Form continues on next page)

Epilogue
Terminating an Unsuccessful Agreement

This book is designed to help the contract writer to create successful agreements. However, even the most carefully drawn agreement cannot guarantee performance. Therefore, sadly, it must be admitted that some transactions do not close. When the agreement is terminated before closing some kind of "sign off" must be executed by all parties. Deposits in such cases are quite often forfeited, in whole or in part. A release is necessary to wind up the affairs. Form 13.01 is designed to conclude unsuccessful transactions. It is very explicit and can be adjusted to any situation. CAR has a useful form: RPC-11.

FORM 13:01 RELEASE OF PURCHASE CONTRACT

This release is entered into this _____ day of _____, 19____, between the undersigned buyers, the undersigned sellers and the undersigned Realtor(s), who were parties to that certain _____

Real Estate/Mobilehome

Purchase Contract and Receipt for Deposit dated _____, 19____, covering the following described property:

Now therefore, in consideration of the mutual covenants contained herein the parties agree as follows:

1. Except as hereafter specified in paragraph 2, each of the above-mentioned parties on behalf of himself, his heirs, executors, administrators, and assigns and agents, servants, stockholders, employees, representatives, assigns, and successors hereby fully release and discharge the other party and his heirs, executors, administrators, and assigns and agents, servants, stockholders, employees, representatives, assigns and successors from all claims, actions and administrative proceedings which each party and his above-mentioned successors now have against the other party and his above-mentioned successors stemming from their differences arising after the execution of the contract described above or any other matter whatsoever concerning the property described above.

2. Anything contained in this agreement to the contrary notwithstanding, the release by _____ against the other parties to this agreement of its

name of broker

rights to commissions, attorneys' fees and costs pursuant to the provisions of the

360

Deposit Receipt dated _____ 198____ referred to above, shall be null and void if Buyer has any continuing interest either directly or indirectly or gains financially from a subsequent transfer of the property described above other than the return to Buyer of Buyer's deposit, or if Seller receives any consideration not disclosed herein from Buyer for the rescission of the agreement or release of escrowed funds.

This release, notwithstanding Section 1542 of the California Civil Code which provides that "A general release does not extend to claims which the creditor does not know or suspect to exist in his favor at the time of executing the release which if known by him must have materially affected his settlement with the debtor," shall be a full settlement of said dispute, claim or cause of action. This settlement shall act as a release of future claims that may arise from the above-mentioned dispute whether such claims are, unknown, foreseen or unforeseen.

This mutual release is a compromise of the above-mentioned disputed claim and shall never be treated as an admission of liability by any of the parties for any purpose.

The escrow agent _____ holding the deposit under the terms of said

name
contract is hereby directed and instructed forthwith to disburse said deposit held in escrow in the following manner:

$_____ TO _____

$_____ TO _____

$_____ TO _____

_____

_____
BUYERS

_____

_____
SELLERS

_____
REALTOR

By _____

_____
REALTOR

By _____

COMMENT ON FORM 13:01: The advantage of the release in this form is that it can be used as authorization to the escrow holder for release of a deposit held in escrow. Hopefully the readers' contracts will all be successful agreements and not call for the use of this form.

Notes

Chapter 1

1. Lucas v. Ham (1961), 56 Cal.2d 583, 591; 15 Cal. Reptr. 821, 825.
2. Biakanaja v. Irving (1958), 49 Cal.2d 647; 320 P.2d 16.
3. Devereaux v. Harper, 210 C.A.2d 519; 26 Cal. Reptr. 837.
4. Wilson v. Hesey (1957), 147 C.A.2d 433; 305 P.2d 686.
5. 7 Cal. Jur.3rd Atto. § 172.
6. 4 *California State Bar Journal* (July-August 1967), p. 487; *California Real Estate Magazine* (October 1967), p. 14.
7. *California Real Estate Magazine* (August 1975), p. 1.
8. Gardner v. Convay, 234 Minn. 468; 48 N.W.2d 788.
9. Agran v. Shapiro, 127 C.A.2d Supplement 807; 273 P.2d 619.
10. California Civil Code, Section 1624.
11. California Civil Code, Section 1624.
12. State Bar v. Coldwell Banker Co., Superior Court of California, County of Los Angeles, No. 036, 175, 41 California State Bar Journal (1966), p. 856.

Chapter 2

1. Schaeffer v. Moore, 262 S.W.2d 854, 859. See Cook, "Strawmen in Realty Transactions," 25 Wash. Univ. Law Quar. 232 (1940).
2. Ott v. Home Savings & Loan, 265 F.2d 643.
3. Covington v. Clark, 175 C.A.2d 449; 346 P.2d 229.
4. Giustina v. United States, 190 F. Supplement 303.
5. De St. Germain v. Watson, 95 C.A.2d 862, 214 P.2d 99.
6. California Administrative Code, Title 10, Reg. 2832.
7. California Administrative Code, Title 10, Reg. 2830.
8. Ganiats Construction Inc. v Hesse, 180 C.A.2d 337; 4 Cal. Reptr. 706.
9. California Civil Code, Section 2884.
10. Ganiats Construction Inc. v. Hesse, 180 C.A.2d 337; 4 Cal. Reptr. 706.
11. Corona Unified School District v. Vejar, 165 C.A.2d 561; 332 P.2d 294.
12. Tackett v. Croonquist, 244 C.A.2d 572; 53 Cal. Reptr. 388.
13. Jessie F. Ernie v. Trinity Lutheran Church, 336 P.2d 525, 526.

Chapter 3

1. Burgess v. Rodom, 121 C.A.2d 71; 262 P.2d 335.
2. California Civil Code, Section 3390(5).
3. Doryon v. Salant, 75 C.A.3rd 706.
4. Meyer v. Benko, 55 C.A.3rd 937.
5. Devereaux v. Harper, 210 C.A.2d 519; 26 C.R.837.
6. Corn Belt Savings Bank v. Kriz, 207 Iowa 11, 18; 219 N.W.503, 506. See also First v.

Byrnes, 238 Iowa 712; 28 N.W.2d 509; 172 Amer. Law Rev. 1072. For a comprehensive overview of Dragnet Clause law see California State Bar Journal (July-August 1977) Stephen M. Andress: Union Bank v. Wendland.
7. Gates v. Crocker Anglo National Bank, 257 C.A.2d 857, 65 Cal. Reptr. 536.
8. Wong v. Beneficial Sav. & L. 56 C.A.3d. 286, 128 Cal. Reptr. 338.
9. California Civil Code, Section 2884.
10. Rodriguez v. Barnett, 52 Cal.2d 154; 338 P.2d 907.
11. The clause complies with C.C.2954,9(b) regarding loans secured by four-family owner-occupied dwellings.
12. The clause complies with C.C.2954.4, which regulates late charges on loans on single-family owner-occupied dwellings unless made by lenders otherwise regulated.
13. Internal Revenue Code, Section 453(a), 453(b).

Chapter 4

1. Lingsch v. Savage, 213 C.A.2d 729; 29 Cal. Reptr. 201.
2. Orlando v. Berkally, 220 C.A.2d 224; 33 Cal. Reptr. 860.
3. California Civil Code, Section 1668. See also the cases cited in 1 and 2, and Herzog v. Capital Co., 27 Cal.2d 1349; 164 P.2d 8, and Crawford v. Nastos, 182 C.A.2d 659; 6 Cal. Reptr. 425.
4. Farmland Irr. Co. v. Doppelmaier, 48 C.2d 208; 308 P.2d 732.
5. Ford v. Clyde Cournale, 136 C.A.3rd 172. Hearing denied by Supreme Court.
6. Mathews v. Starritt, 252 C.A.2d, 884.
7. *Black's Law Dictionary*, 3rd ed.
8. California Administrative Code, Title 10, Reg. 2905.
9. Curran v. Heslop, 115 C.A.2d 476; 252 P.2d 378, Hartman v. Rizzuto, 123 C.A.2d 186; 266 P.2d 539.

Chapter 5

1. Brady v. Carman, 179 C.A.2d 63, 68; 3 Cal. Reptr. 612.
2. Wilson v. Hisey, 147 C.A.2d 433; 305 P.2d 686.
3. King v. Stanley, 32 C.A.2d 584; 197 P.2d 321.
4. See Bayse, Clearing Land Titles.
5. Wright v. Lowe, 140 C.A.2d 891; 296 P.2d 34.
6. California Code of Civil Procedure, 1161a(4).
7. California Civil Code, Section 1662.
8. Melvin J. Guthman v. Murray Moss, 150 Cal.App.3d 501.
9. Hong v. Somerset Associates, 161 Cal.App.3d 111.
10. Pease v. Brown, 186 Cal.App.2d 425; 8 Cal. Reptr. 917.
11. Katemis v. Westerlund, 120 Cal.App.2d 537; 261 P.2d 553.

Chapter 6

1. Chapman v. Gilmore, 221 C.A.2d 506; 34 Cal. Reptr. 515.
2. California Auto Court Assn. v. Cohn, 98 C.A.2d 145; 219 P.2d 511.
3. Huttlinger v. Far W. Enterprises, Inc., 131 C.A.2d 808; 281 P.2d 554.

Chapter 7

1. See "How to List and Sell Mobilehomes," CAR.
2. California Administrative Code, Title 10, Regulation 2862.

Chapter 8

1. Basic Writings of George Washington, Saxe Cummings, editor.

Chapter 9

1. Effective January 1, 1988 the limit is $168,700 on single family homes; $215,800 for two-family homes; $260,800 for three-family homes, and $324,150 for loans on four-family properties. Maximum loan amounts in Alaska and Hawaii are 50% higher. The loan-to-value ratio is 95% for one and two-family units and 90% for three and four-family units with mortgage insurance coverage.

2. The Tax Reform Act of 1986 permitted deduction of interest on debt secured by a principal residence or a second home (including improvements) plus debts for educational or medical expenses. The Revenue Bill of 1987 made a substantial change. Effective for tax years beginning after December 31, 1987, deduction of interest for income tax purposes is limited to 1) debt to *acquire* or substantially improve a principal or second residence (up to a total debt of $1 million), plus 2) other debt (not in excess of $100,000) secured by a principal or second residence. This change in the law will have a severe effect on refinancing and increase the cost of borrowing. Some homeowners will not be able to take large amounts of their equity of their appreciated property out taxfree. Where a contract to purchase a residence presupposes a future refinancing, a real estate licensee may be obligated to disclose these tax rules or refer the buyer to the buyer's tax advisor.

Chapter 11

1. Gouveia v. Citicorp, 686 P.2d 262 (N.M. App. 1984).
2. Cooper & Co. v. Bryant, 400 So.2d 1016 (Ala. 1983), Harrell V. Dodson, 398 So.2d 272 (Ala. 1981).
3. Godfrey v. Steinpress, 180 Cal. Aptr. 95 (App. 1482).
4. Russow v. Bobola, 277 N.E.2d 769 (Ill. App. 1972).
5. Stevens v. Jayhawk Realty Co., Inc., 1677 P.2d 1019 (Kan. App. 1984).
6. Reed v. King, 145 Cal.App.3d 261. (Cal 1983) Limited by statute. See page 344.
7. Provost v. Miller, 473 A.2d 1162 (Vt. 1984).
8. Easton v. Strassburger. 152 Cal.App3d 90. (Cal. 1984)
9. Bevins v. Ballard, 655 P.2d 757. (Alaska 1982)
10. California Civil Code. § 1134.5.

Chapter 12

1. Civil Code Section 2020. *Galeppi v. Waugh*, 163 Cal.App.2d 508 (1958).

Index

RECYCLE YOUR OLD EDITIONS OF <u>SUCCESSFUL REAL ESTATE</u> <u>SALES AGREEMENTS</u> AND SAVE 33% OFF THE NEW BOOK PRICE!

Using old editions can be hazardous! Not having benefit of current information can result in professional malpractice. To make it easier for you to be knowledgable, AXIOM will take back your old book and give you a 33% discount off the new edition price.

Send us the cover from your 2nd or 3rd Edition. We will send you the 4th Edition for $11.95 -- A Savings of $6.00! (This offer is available for individuals only.)

I would like to trade in the Old for the New! Enclosed is the front cover of an old SUCCESSFUL REAL ESTATE SALES AGREEMENTS. Send me the 4th Edition at 33% Savings. My address is:

_____
Name (print)   Title

_____
Company (print)

_____
Address (print)

_____
City, State   Zip   Phone (Optional)

I enclose $11.95 + $1.25 Postage/Handling (CA Residents add Sales Tax: San Mateo, LA, Santa Clara & BART Counties, 6-1/2%; Santa Rosa, 7%; all others 6%) for each copy.

Mail to: AXIOM PRESS PUBLISHERS, P. O. BOX L
          San Rafael, CA 94913 (415)956-4859

Find out about WHOLESALE DISCOUNTS ...

SUCCESSFUL REAL ESTATE SALES AGREEMENTS has long been a first choice of Brokers, Managers, and Real Estate Boards as a tool to train their real estate professionals in the fine points of contract preparation. AXIOM PRESS, PUBLISHERS offers wholesale discounts to those who buy the book for resale to their members or for distribution as an educational tool. For more information about discounts please call or write:

AXIOM PRESS PUBLISHERS, P. O. BOX L
San Rafael, CA 94913 (415)956-4859

* * * * * * * * * * *

FOR YOUR NOTES

FOR YOUR NOTES

FOR YOUR NOTES

FOR YOUR NOTES

FOR YOUR NOTES

FOR YOUR NOTES